Human
Resource
Management

Human
Resource
Management

A Customer-Oriented Approach

Diann R. Newman
Florida International University

Richard M. Hodgetts
Florida International University

PRENTICE HALL
Upper Saddle River, New Jersey 07458

Library of Congress Cataloging-in-Publication Data

Newman, Diann R.
    Human resource management : a customer-oriented approach / Diann
  R. Newman, Richard M. Hodgetts.
        p.   cm.
    Includes bibliographical references and indexes.
    ISBN 0-13-253675-7
    1. Personnel management.   2. Personnel management--United States-
  -Case studies.   I. Hodgetts, Richard M.   II. Title.
  HF5549.N445   1998
    658.3--dc21   97-9255
                                                                        CIP

Acquisitions Editor: Neil Marquardt
Editorial/Production Supervision: WordCrafters Editorial Services, Inc.
Director of Manufacturing and Production: Bruce Johnson
Managing Editor: Mary Carnis
Cover Designer: Miguel Ortiz
Interior Designer: Linda Zuk, WordCrafters
Cover Illustration: Matt Bronson
Manufacturing Manager: Ed O'Dougherty
Marketing Manager: Danny Hoyt
Formatting/Page Makeup: WordCrafters Editorial Services, Inc.
Printer/Binder: R.R. Donnelley & Sons Co.

This book was set in Palatino by WordCrafters Editorial Services, Inc., and was printed and
bound by R.R. Donnelley & Sons Co. The cover was printed by Phoenix Color Corp.

Printed in the United States of America

10   9   8   7   6   5   4   3   2   1

ISBN 0-13-253675-7

Prentice-Hall International (UK) Limited, *London*
Prentice-Hall of Australia Pty. Limited, *Sydney*
Prentice-Hall Canada Inc., *Toronto*
Prentice-Hall Hispanoamericana, S.A., *Mexico*
Prentice-Hall of India Private Limited, *New Delhi*
Prentice-Hall of Japan Inc., *Tokyo*
Simon & Schuster Asia Pte. Ltd., *Singapore*
Editora Prentice-Hall do Brasil, Ltda., *Rio de Janeiro*

To Irv Zeldman
with love and gratitude

Brief Contents

Part Four   Understanding Customers   281

Part Five   Horizons   397

Contents

Part Three   Understanding Human Resource Management   155

Chapter Six   Recruiting, Selecting, and Orienting Associates   157

Chapter Eleven   Understanding the International Customer   313

Chapter Twelve   Developing Outstanding Service   341

Preface

At the turn of the century, most people in the United States were engaged in goods-producing jobs such as farming and manufacturing. Today most Americans earn their livelihood by providing services—and this trend will continue for the foreseeable future, in the United States as well as in all other countries. One of the characteristics of economically advancing nations is that they are able to devote an increasing portion of their resources to providing services, because their manufacturing needs can be handled by an ever-smaller percentage of the labor force.

The hospitality industry is an excellent example of a service-sector business; and as world economies become more and more developed, there will be a growing need for hotel, restaurant, travel, and related services. However, not everyone will be able to succeed in this business. Those firms that are able to provide the best service at the most acceptable price are the ones that will lead the others in terms of both market share and profitability. This is where human resource management enters the picture. Anyone can open a hotel, motel, restaurant, or hospitality business; but not everyone can provide the desired degree of service. Effective personnel screening, recruiting, hiring, training, development, and appraisal are critical to success because in this business, people are the most important asset. The overriding objective of this book is to introduce you to the field of human resource management in the hospitality industry and to provide you with critical insights regarding how and why this field is proving to be one of the key factors that determines which service organizations do well and which do not.

How This Book Will Help You

The primary objective of this book is to introduce you to the field of human resource management (HRM) in the hospitality industry and to familiarize you with some of the most important developments that are now taking place. In particular, this book will provide four major benefits:

1. Facts—Not Intuition. The information in this book is based on fact. In gathering the material in each chapter, we have drawn data from research studies in the industry and developments in hospitality organizations. As a result, the data are both current and practical in nature.

2. Comprehensiveness. This book covers all major areas of HRM, from recruiting and selecting to training and development. It also focuses on newly emerging of areas of HRM concern, including identifying and addressing customer needs, ways to develop outstanding service, and steps that leading hospitality organizations are now taking to maintain their total quality service focus.

3. Applicability. No study of HRM would be complete without consideration of the latest theories regarding how to manage personnel effectively. In this book we have presented these ideas in a way that can be of practical value. In all cases, the emphasis is on showing how the theory or information is being used by practicing managers and their organizations to improve service, productivity, and/or profit.

4. Personal Insights. In each chapter we have carefully crafted feedback exercises that provide you with information designed to help you better understand yourself and the way that you carry out human resource management activities such as communicating and leading others. There are also specially designed feedback instruments that provide you with a host of insights regarding what is important to you. Examples include insights regarding how you manage time and stress, what motivates you, and the types of career goals that are important to you.

Some of the information presented in this book will be of value to you almost immediately, including material related to your personal goals, the ways in which you prefer to lead others, and the importance of physical and psychological motivators. Some of the material will be of more value to you later in your career, such as material related to performance evaluation and the career objective formulation. Yet, regardless of where your career takes you, the material in this book is specially designed to help you understand the field of human resources in the hospitality industry and to use this information in a practical way.

Organization and Features

Human resources is a broad field comprising many practices and concepts. *Human Resource Management: A Customer-Oriented Approach* focuses on the most important of these. The organization of this book flows from an introduction to the field at large to an examination of you and how you deal with human-resources-related situations, to the current status of HRM, to the nature and understanding of customers, and then concludes with an examination of future challenges and ways that you can develop an effective career plan. In accordance with this flow, the book is divided into five major parts, as follows:

- Part I examines contemporary issues in human resource management, including HRM functions such as employment, training, development, compensation, benefits, and human resources planning; and HRM challenges such as productivity, diversity, retention of personnel, and the changing role of the customer.

- Part II focuses on human relations skills and an understanding of yourself, with particular attention to who you are, how you can communicate more effectively, ways that you can manage change and conflict productively, and how you can further develop your decision-making skills.

- Part III examines the nature of HRM, with specific consideration given to recruiting, selecting, orienting, training, developing, appraising, and motivating personnel, as well as creating effective associate relations. This section addresses the "nuts and bolts" of HRM: it introduces and explains the various activities typically carried out by human resource management departments.

- Part IV is unique to this book. It introduces and examines a key element in the HRM area that has been previously overlooked by competitive texts: understanding customers. There are two types of customers to which associates must respond: internal and external. The internal customer is the person in the organization who receives the output or service that is being provided. For example, when the chef finishes cooking a meal, it is the server who receives the food. The external customer is the individual outside the organization who receives the output or service that is being provided; in this example, it is the diner. The study of HRM requires that students be able to identify and address customer needs, regardless of whether this customer is internal or external. In Part IV of the book, attention is also focused on understanding international customers, developing outstanding service, and maintaining total quality service. These chapters are designed to show you that HRM is more than just a host of personnel-related functions—the customer plays a major role in this process, and consideration of this individual's needs, expectations, and desires is critical to the study of human resource management.

■ Part V looks at new developments in the HRM field. These include the current challenge of dealing with diversity in the form of age, gender, and ethnicity, as well as ethics and discrimination issues and the responsibilities of employers to employees with disabilities. Attention is also directed toward helping you develop an effective career plan.

Self-Feedback Exercises

At the end of each chapter, and within most chapters as well, self-feedback exercises provide insights and information regarding how you view things and the ways in which you carry out activities. For example, the self-feedback exercise in Chapter 1 helps you understand the type of leader you are; the exercise in Chapter 6 helps you identify what you are looking for in a job; the exercise in Chapter 9 helps you identify the type of power you prefer to use; and the exercise in Chapter 15 provides you with insights regarding how you interact with others.

Useful Tips

Many of the chapters also provide useful tips or guidelines regarding things you should do and not do in managing yourself and/or dealing with others. For example, in Chapter 4 you will learn how to deal with tough customers; in Chapter 7 you will find out how to avoid some of the common training mistakes made by HRM organization; in Chapter 11 you will become privy to some useful HRM tips for doing business in Japan; and in Chapter 14 you will learn a dozen useful ways to value diversity.

Chapter Objectives and Cases

At the beginning of each chapter, a host of learning objectives describe what you will learn and be able to apply when you have finished studying the chapter material. At the end of each chapter are two cases that have been specially written to reinforce these objectives. The purpose of these cases is to provide you with the opportunity to apply the ideas and concepts that have been introduced and explained in the chapter.

Acknowledgments

Many individuals have played an important role in helping us write this book. In particular, we would like to thank the excellent students from the Human Relations in the Hospitality Industry classes at Florida International University for their assistance in researching current information in the hospitality industry. We would also like to thank our colleagues, including Dean Anthony G. Marshall of the FIU School of Hospitality Management; Dean Hal Wyman and Dr. Gary Dessler of the FIU College of Business; Dr. Fred Luthans of the University of Nebraska, Lincoln; and Dr. Jane Gibson of Nova Southeastern University.

We would also like to thank those who were involved in reviewing this text, including Andrew R. Schwarz of Sullivan County Community College, Mark McGrath of the University Tennessee, H. A. Divine of the University of Denver, Earle Bowman of the University of New Haven, Howard Reichbart of Northern Virginia Community College, Patricia Bartholomew of New York City Technical College, Jennifer Adams Aldrich of Johnson and Wales University, Martin Goldman of Mercer County Community College, William Loughheed of Ryerson Polytechnic University, René-Luc Blaquiére of the Institute de Tourism et D'Hôtellerie du Québec, Carl Boger of Kansas State University, Rich Doyon of Quincy College, Jim Buergermeister of the University of Wisconsin-Stout, and C. "Gus" Katisgris of El Centro College.

Finally, we would like to thank our families for their support and understanding while we were writing this book: John, Jeffrey, and Nicole Newman; and Sally, Steven, and Jennifer Hodgetts.

Diann R. Newman

Richard M. Hodgetts

PART ONE

Introduction

This part of the book, which consists of only one chapter, is designed to introduce you to the world of human resource management in the hospitality industry. One of the most common clichés in the industry is, "Our people are our most important asset." This is an accurate statement—for the primary way that hospitality organizations differentiate themselves from their competition is by offering services that others either cannot or will not emulate. There are a wide variety of examples, including express check-in and check-out; varied menus that appeal to children, seniors, international guests, and health-conscious guests; and a staff that does not just meet customer expectations, but exceeds them!

All of this is possible primarily because of personnel—or *associates*, as we shall call them throughout this book—who are carefully screened and selected, well trained, and highly motivated. And this is where human resource management enters the picture. Twenty years ago it was possible to hire friendly, well-intentioned associates and be able to provide service that was as good as the competition. Today this is no longer possible. Every hospitality enterprise is getting better and better at meeting guest needs, and these needs are escalating. As a result, only the best will survive the turbulent environment of the 21st century—and this will require a carefully crafted human resource management strategy.

The overriding purpose of Chapter 1 is to introduce you to the field of human resource management (HRM). In addition to comparing and contrasting the differences in the HRM philosophies of the past and the present, we will focus our attention on HRM challenges currently facing the industry and the role of both the customer and you in this picture.

When you have finished reading Part One, you will be familiar with the general nature of HRM, and will have an understanding of why it is so critical to the survival and growth of hospitality organizations. You will also be aware of some of the major changes that are occurring in the industry, and will know the types of strategies that will have to be employed in meeting these challenges.

CHAPTER ONE

Contemporary Issues in Human Resource Management

LEARNING OBJECTIVES

Human resource management is a critical area of concern in the hospitality industry. One reason is that increased competition is making it more difficult to hire and retain highly qualified associates. A second reason is that the profitability and growth of industry firms is strongly influenced by their ability to effectively manage their human resources. A third is that one of the few ways in which companies can differentiate themselves from the competition is through high-quality service, which can only be accomplished with an effective human resource management strategy. The overriding objective of this chapter is to introduce you to the field of human resource management and set the stage for the chapters to follow. When you have finished studying all of the material in this chapter, you will be able to:

1. Define the term *human resource management* (HRM) and discuss some of the primary HRM functions.

2. Compare and contrast the HRM philosophies associated with the traditional model of human resources and the modern model of human resources.

3. Identify and discuss three major HRM challenges facing the hospitality industry.

4. Discuss the role of the customer in the study of human resource management.

5. Describe the importance of your role in the study of human resource management.

The Nature of Human Resource Management

Human resource management (HRM) is the process by which organizations ensure the effective use of their associates in the pursuit of both organizational and individual goals. In this process, hospitality firms focus their attention on three areas: (1) effective recruiting, screening, hiring, selecting, training, and development of associates; (2) genuine concern for the well-being of the associates as reflected through well-developed reward-and-recognition programs, challenging work, and the opportunity to use their potential to the fullest; and (3) careful consideration of the needs and expectations of the organization's customers, as seen through the creation of total quality service programs and the continual evaluation of guest feedback for the purpose of maintaining these service levels.

HRM Functions

If a hospitality organization is sufficiently large, it will have a human resources (HR) department that provides an array of services to the company at large and departments in particular. For example, an HR department will often handle all personnel record keeping, be responsible for the administration of insurance benefits, and conduct orientation programs for new associates. It will also typically place employment ads with the media and may conduct initial screenings of new job applicants. At this point, the department that will be doing the hiring will often take over and make the final selection. Similarly, the HR department will often conduct a wide variety of training programs, but some of these will be conducted at the department level in the form of on-the-job training.

Many small hotels, motels, restaurants, and other hospitality organizations cannot afford a formal HR department. In these cases, typical HR activities such as recruiting, hiring, and training new associates will be done by the manager in whose department the new hire will work. Meanwhile, the payroll person or the accountant will be responsible for seeing that wages, salaries, benefits, and related HR activities are handled in accord with government regulations.

While a host of HR activities are critical to running an effective hospitality organization, it is possible to gain insight into this myriad of activities by examining a handful of the most important. The following sections describe five of these as they are performed in organizations that have an HR department.

Employment. The employment function includes a great many duties: recruiting, screening, selecting, orienting, and associate evaluation. All of these are support services; they assist the operating managers. For example, the restaurant manager will decide whom to hire. However, the HR department will usually take care of placing the employment ads, gathering information on the job applicants, administering selection tests, and eliminating those who do not meet minimal job requirements. From this pool of talent, the restaurant manager will then make a decision. At this point, the HR department will commonly provide other forms of assistance, such as completion of all paperwork for formally adding these people to the workforce. In the case of employment termination, the process works in reverse. The department manager will decide whom to let go; the HR department will ensure that the individual receives termination benefits and will complete all paperwork associated with the decision.

Training and Development. Operating managers provide some on-the-job training: coaching, counseling, performance appraisal, job rotation, special assignments. The HR department will offer many other types of training and development, including workshops designed to help associates master the technical side of their jobs and seminars to assist managers in developing human relations skills. These workshops and seminars will often cover a wide range of areas, from career planning and time and stress management to effective communication skills and ways to better motivate associates.

Compensation and Benefits. Most hospitality organizations pay competitive wages. The HR department typically coordinates the work of ensuring that pay rates remain competitive by maintaining up-to-date information on wages and salaries in the industry. This is an extremely important function, for research shows that money is a very important motivator for hospitality associates. Organizations that pay less than a competitive wage will have great difficulty attracting and retaining qualified associates. The HR department will also ensure that the company's health insurance, life insurance, unemployment compensation, vacations, and pensions are all in order, and will periodically review these plans to ensure that they are competitive.

Human Resources Planning. Human resources planning involves forecasting human resources demands on the organization and implementing the steps necessary for meeting this demand. Large hospitality organizations will have a formalized HR plan that ties directly into the overall strategic plan. If the latter plan requires the hiring and training of additional groundskeepers for the golf course, for example, the human resources plan will address the ways in which the organization will add these people. Conversely, if the organization decides to sell its golf course, the HR plan will address the steps the firm will take in cutting back the workforce.

Equal Employment Opportunity (EEO). This law requires equal employment opportunity, which means that all individuals have a legal right to be considered for a job solely on the basis of their ability, merit, and potential. Legislation such as Title VII of the Civil Rights Act of 1964 as amended, the Equal Pay Act of 1963, and the Age Discrimination in Employment Act of 1967 as amended forbid discrimination on the basis of race, color, sex, national origin, or religion. The HR department will often have at least some responsibility for EEO compliance and affirmative action. Affirmative action consists of efforts by an organization to ensure *employment neutrality* with regard to race, color, religion, sex, and national origin. For example, if a hotel finds that 40 percent of its workforce are women but only 1 percent of the managerial associates are female, the HR department will develop an affirmative action program to ensure that more women are promoted into the ranks of management. This affirmative action will help ensure that the company is not accused of discrimination in management employment.

The preceding activities help illustrate the broad scope of the HRM function. The primary objective of these activities is to ensure that the best associates are hired, trained, and retained. Some of the specific ways in which this is done will be discussed in Part III of this book. For the moment, however, it is important to remember that the hospitality industry has now entered a human resources era; the way that effective organizations manage their associates is sharply different from what it was in the past.

Human Resources Era

In understanding the scope and significance of the human resources era, it is helpful to compare today's HR philosophy with that of previous decades, which used a traditional model of human resources.

The *traditional model of human resources,* often called *Theory X,* holds that people are basically lazy, have to be closely controlled, and work primarily for pay. If the conditions are tolerable, they will stay with the organization. If they can do better, however, or conditions start getting worse, they will look for employment elsewhere. The traditional model stands in sharp contrast to today's *modern model of human resources,* often called *Theory Y,* which views associates as important assets with untapped potential. The modern model also views associates as self-directed, interested in doing a good job, and willing to participate and assume responsibility. The basic assumptions, policies, and expectations of these models are described in Table 1.1.

Why has the traditional model been replaced by the modern model of human resources? The answer is because the environment of the hospitality industry is changing dramatically; organizations that cannot or will not make the transition to the new model are finding themselves unable to compete effectively. This is clearly seen by the challenges that hospitality firms currently face. When reading the following challenges, examine the values of the two models in Table 1.1 and decide which would be of most use in meeting each respective challenge.

Table 1.1   A Comparison of Human Resource Management Models

Traditional Human Resources Model	*Modern Human Resources Model*
Assumptions	
1. Work is inherently distasteful to most people.	1. Work is not inherently distasteful. Associates want to contribute to meaningful goals that they have helped establish.
2. What workers do is less important than what they earn for doing it.	
3. Few workers want or can handle work that requires creativity, self-direction, or self-control.	2. Most associates are able to exercise far more creativity, responsible self-direction, and self-control than their present jobs demand.
Policies	
1. The manager's basic task is to closely supervise and control the workers.	1. The manager's basic job is to make use of "untapped" human resources.
2. The manager must break down tasks into simple, repetitive, easily learned operations.	2. The manager must create an environment in which all associates can contribute to the limits of their ability.
3. The manager must establish detailed work routines and procedures and enforce them firmly but fairly.	3. The manager must encourage full participation on important matters, continually broadening associate self-direction and control.
Expectations	
1. Workers can tolerate work if the pay is decent and the boss is fair.	1. Expanding associate influence, self-direction, and self-control will lead to direct improvements in operating efficiency.
2. If tasks are simple enough and workers are closely controlled, they will produce the desired amount of work.	2. Work satisfaction may improve as a "by-product" of associates making full use of their resources.

Source: Adapted from Raymond E. Miles, *Theories of Management: Implications for Organizational Behavior and Development* (New York: McGraw-Hill, 1975).

HRM Challenges

A number of human resource management challenges are forcing hospitality organizations to change the way they do things. Three of the most important include productivity, diversity, and retention of associates, which are examined in the following sections.

Productivity. *Productivity* is the ratio of output to input. An example is a restaurant server who is being paid $10 an hour and is responsible for providing service to three tables. Assume that if this individual does an average job, his guests on a particular evening will spend a total of $400 a night. Thus productivity is equal to $400/10 = 40. However, if the server is well trained and knows how to sell the menu properly and provide quality service, the guests will spend a total of $500. As a result of the server's performance, productivity will increase to $500/10 = 50. The restaurant will generate greater revenue (output), while its hourly wage for the server (input) will remain at $10 (although the individual might do quite well with tips). This example helps explain how increased productivity can result in higher sales and profit for the organization, greater revenue (tips) for the server, and better-quality service for the guest.

What are some of the most common ways that hospitality organizations use human resource management ideas to increase their productivity?[1] One is by providing increased training to their associates, so that the associates can offer better service to clients. A related way is by carefully studying jobs and determining how performance can be increased. An example is provided in Figure 1.1, which addresses room service. The figure focuses on three main areas: time, performance, and cost. In analyzing these areas, the hotel has focused its attention on (1) identification of quality standards the organization would like to achieve in its room service; (2) a description of how this service is currently being carried out; and (3) the performance gaps that prevent current service from meeting the desired quality standards. These performance gaps cost the hotel money and reduce its productivity. As seen in the figure, labor costs should be 20 percent or less of the overall bill, but they currently are 25 percent; food preparation is inconsistent; and orders should be taken and delivered within 30 minutes, but it currently takes 40 minutes. Applying these facts to the productivity formula, it is easy to see that output (delivery time) is less than it should be, while input (labor costs) is higher than it should be.

By applying HRM concepts to productivity, hospitality organizations can drive up their service levels and drive down their costs. The result is greater profit, increased compensation for associates, and increased customer satisfaction, which in turn results in repeat business for the organization.

Diversity. Over the past two decades the composition of the U.S. workforce has changed sharply. These changes are well reflected in hospitality organiza-

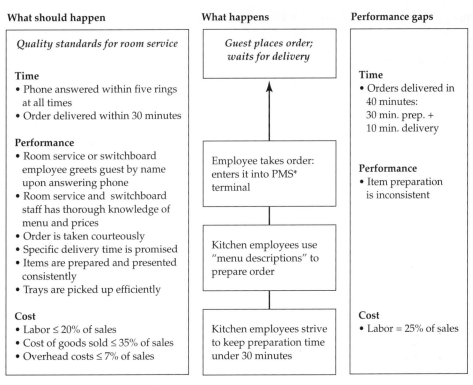

What should happen	What happens	Performance gaps
Quality standards for room service	*Guest places order; waits for delivery*	
Time • Phone answered within five rings at all times • Order delivered within 30 minutes		**Time** • Orders delivered in 40 minutes: 30 min. prep. + 10 min. delivery
Performance • Room service or switchboard employee greets guest by name upon answering phone • Room service and switchboard staff has thorough knowledge of menu and prices • Order is taken courteously • Specific delivery time is promised • Items are prepared and presented consistently • Trays are picked up efficiently	Employee takes order: enters it into PMS* terminal Kitchen employees use "menu descriptions" to prepare order	**Performance** • Item preparation is inconsistent
Cost • Labor ≤ 20% of sales • Cost of goods sold ≤ 35% of sales • Overhead costs ≤ 7% of sales	Kitchen employees strive to keep preparation time under 30 minutes	**Cost** • Labor = 25% of sales

*PMS is Property Management System

Figure 1.1 *Identifying Room Service Performance Gaps*

Source: Jonathan D. Barsky, "Building a Program for World-Class Service," *Cornell Hotel and Restaurant Administration Quarterly*, February 1996, p. 23.

tions, where the numbers of women, minorities, and older associates continue to increase. There are a number of reasons that help account for this changing labor composition. One is that the number of entry-level workers who are American-born White men is rapidly shrinking. In 1985, this group constituted 47 percent of entry-level workers, but by the year 2000 it will account for only 15 percent.[2] The remainder of these workers will be women, African-Americans, Hispanic-Americans, Asian-Americans, Native Americans, and individuals who have immigrated to the United States from other countries. Another reason for the changing labor force composition is legislation that now prohibits discrimination on the basis of race, color, creed, sex, or national origin. In addition, workers with disabilities, pregnant women, and employees over age 40 are provided protection from arbitrary dismissal. As a result, the workforce of the 1990s is quite diverse when compared to that of the 1950s. Moreover, many hospitality jobs do not require much formal education, and because entry-level wages are typically low, those who are willing to do the work for low pay are often hired. As a result, supervisors face the challenge of communicating carefully and completely with associates who are not well trained and, in some cases, do not speak English as a first language.

Additionally, there is growing effort in the upper levels of many organizations to hire and promote women and other minorities, who in the past have been systematically excluded from these positions. HRM programs are now being created to help executive management identify and develop minority talent. In particular, a great deal of attention is being focused on changing top management's stereotypical views.[3] Some of the most common perceptions are that women and other minorities are technically unqualified or do not have the "right" personality for handling senior-level positions. Thanks to HRM efforts, however, many of these perceptions are being altered. Moreover, an increasing number of hospitality organizations are now developing network support systems so that women, African-Americans, and other minorities are formally assigned managers to act as mentors and provide them with advice, guidance, and assistance in overcoming the common barriers that prevent their promotion.[4]

Learning how to manage a diverse workforce can be a major challenge for many hospitality managers. Those who have been in the business for over a decade can see the changes that have occurred, and they are just the tip of the iceberg. The future will see ever greater diversity in the industry. Learning how to manage effectively in this environment will require knowledge and adaptability. Human resource management practices will continue to play a major role in this process.

Retention of Associates. Closely linked to the productivity and diversity challenges is that of retention of associates. Every time an organization has to replace one of its associates, the costs involved include recruiting, selecting, orienting, and training the new associate, to note but four. A satisfied workforce is one of the key elements of a successful hospitality organization. Do you know what creates satisfaction or dissatisfaction among hospitality associates? Take the quiz in Box 1.1 and check your score before continuing to the next paragraph.

What can organizations do to ensure that associate commitment is high and remains that way? One way is to create strategies that help build this devotion. Some of these are provided in Box 1.2. Others are more personal in nature. For example, Marriott International has created a "family hotline" that can be used by associates who need advice and assistance of a personal nature.[5] The company started this service in Florida and has now begun expanding it to sites across the country. The service is aimed at the company's relatively low-wage associates, including part-time and seasonal associates, who can call a toll-free number and receive assistance. Typical inquiries relate to child-care issues, care for the elderly, personal matters, and crisis issues ranging from housing to harassment to domestic abuse. Marriott's feedback on the program has led it to conclude that the service is helping to reduce

Box 1.1
Associate Satisfaction—or Else

How satisfied are hospitality associates with their jobs? Additionally, are there any differences in the needs or desires of specific groups such as teenagers, older associates, African-Americans, Hispanic-Americans, bellhops, servers, and hotel front-desk associates? The following ten questions are drawn from a recent associate satisfaction survey conducted in the industry. Among other areas, the survey measured 79 variables and satisfaction levels with pay and rewards, working conditions, opportunities for promotion, and supervision. In each case, indicate whether you believe the statement is true or false by circling the appropriate response.

T F 1. Of all age groups in the hospitality industry, teenagers have the lowest degree of work satisfaction, while older full-time associates have the highest degree of work satisfaction.

T F 2. Women have higher levels of job satisfaction than do men.

T F 3. African-Americans, Hispanic-Americans, and Asian-Americans have lower levels of job satisfaction than do White Americans.

T F 4. Associates who have received pay raises in the last year of employment report higher levels of satisfaction than those who received no raises.

T F 5. Approximately 75 percent of associates in the hospitality industry intend to make it a career, while the other 25 percent plan on moving to jobs in other industries.

T F 6. Both managers and associates believe that rewards are only weakly tied to performance.

T F 7. Promotion is highly valued by servers and bartenders, but not highly valued by cooks, bellhops, or bussers.

T F 8. Overall satisfaction with supervision in the industry is very low.

T F 9. Most associates believe that management does a very poor job in recruiting, selecting, hiring, and training new associates.

T F 10. By industry segment, hotel workers have the highest levels of satisfaction, while fast-food workers report the lowest levels.

Now check your answers with the scoring key at the end of the chapter and read the explanations of any that you missed.

Source: These data are reported in Pat Raleigh, "Labor Relations Continue to Decline," *Hospitality Human Resources Newsletter,* June 1995, p. 7.

associate absenteeism, tardiness, and turnover, while improving associate commitment and productivity.[6]

Another approach to gaining and maintaining associate commitment is the use of reward-and-recognition programs that identify those who are doing a good job and reinforce these behaviors. Marriott, for example, uses the following strategies:

1. Incentive bonuses that reach all the way down to coffee-shop managers and are based on service quality, cleanliness, and cost effectiveness.

2. A profit-sharing program available to all associates at all levels of the company (associates can invest up to 10 percent of their wages in a profit-sharing trust, thus creating a tangible link between their welfare and the company's success).

3. Use of "phantom shoppers," who are inspectors posing as customers. If the service is very good, the phantom pulls out an ID card and hands the server the card with a $10 bill clipped to the back.

4. Annual performance reviews of all associates, which are used as a basis for both raises and promotions.[7]

In addition, many hospitality organizations use bonuses to supplement the base salaries of their upper-level managers, thus ensuring that they are able to hold on to executive talent. Table 1.2 reports some of the latest data for general managers in four- and five-star hotels. The researchers found that the main reason that general managers move to other organizations is to get better pay and benefits and a chance to hold an equity position in the property. Financial considerations are a key element in ensuring job satisfaction and associate retention.

The Role of the Customer

In the past, the study of human resource management in the hospitality industry had been heavily confined to the ways in which organizations recruited, trained, developed, and motivated their people. Today this restricted view is no longer sufficient to develop the understanding needed for managing human resources in the 21st century. It is now also important to integrate customers into the discussion and analysis of HRM. While it is true that these individuals are external to the enterprise and not under its direct control, it is equally true that hospitality organizations that learn how to address the needs and expectations of guests are better able to survive in this era of high competition. In fact, many firms are finding themselves facing *hypercompetition*, which is characterized by increasing competitive moves that require them to continually adjust. For example, a hotel that lowers its room rates by 10 percent in order to attract more guests will find that within 24 hours all of its com-

Box 1.2

Ways to Build Associate Commitment

Hospitality organizations are now using a host of human resource management strategies to create and sustain associate commitment. Here are six of the most common.

1. *Select associates who have a desire to become "linked" to the organization.* This is done through a careful screening process in which the applicant's values and those of the organization are compared in order to evaluate the "fit" between the two. Does the individual have the same interests as the enterprise? In addition, the person's knowledge, skills, and abilities to perform the job are evaluated in order to determine whether the link between the individual and the firm needs to be further strengthened through training.

2. *Use clear and realistic job interviews.* This is important; most employees who leave a job do so in the first 90 days because the job situation was not clearly explained to them and the work they are doing is not what they expected.

3. *Improve the quality of the early job experience.* Early experiences have a strong impact on how the associate feels about the job. By helping the individual to become integrated into the work group, providing the person with competent and understanding supervision, and clearly spelling out job responsibilities, the early job experience can prove to be a very rewarding one.

4. *Provide jobs that maximize "felt responsibility" for what is happening in and to the organization.* Associates need to be provided with a sense of responsibility for what is happening in their jobs and how this, in turn, has an impact on the organization at large. In this way, they see how they fit into the big picture. For example, many firms have reward systems that are tied to overall organizational profitability; by doing things well, associates know they are helping the company and themselves at the same time.

5. *Integrate associates into the social fabric of the organization.* An individual's attitudes are strongly affected by what fellow associates expect of the person. If these communicated expectations involve messages that say, "We depend on you," linkages are likely to be strengthened. Moreover, if associates have high expectations of everyone in the work group, new associates are likely to set high standards for themselves and work to achieve them.

6. *Demonstrate a genuine concern for associate welfare.* There must be recognition of individual and group accomplishments and contributions on both formal and informal levels. These celebrations help increase linkages within the work group and between the associates and the organization, as well as strengthen associate commitment to the enterprise.

Source: Ken Smith, "Strategies to Build Commitment," *Hospitality Human Resources Newsletter*, July 1995, p. 2.

Table 1.2 Hotel General Manager Compensation

Room Rate	Under $100		$101–$200		Over $200		Overall	
Survey Year	1992	1995	1992	1995	1992	1995	1992	1995
Salary Range (000s)	NA	$55–112	NA	$32–250	NA	$65–185	$45–200	$32–250
Mean Salary (000s)	$75	$88	$114	$111	$132	$122	$107	$111
Mean Annual Bonus	NA	24%	NA	25%	NA	25%	20%	25%
Salary plus Bonus (000s)	NA	$64–130	NA	$35–350	NA	$71–241	NA	$35–350
Housing Provided	0	0	28%	29%	38%	80%	NA	38%
Average Daily Rate	$88	$86	$138	$144	$299	$271	$167	$166
Average Occupancy	71%	75%	66%	71%	75%	72%	71%	72%

Note: All figures rounded to nearest percentage.

NA = Not available.

Source: H. Bruce Dingman and David R. Dingman, "Compensation Survey," *Cornell Hotel and Restaurant Administration Quarterly,* October 1995, p. 28.

petitors have done the same thing. Thus, competition increases and the work-force must continually adjust to these new demanding conditions. In addition, organizations are finding that their customers are becoming more knowl-edgeable and more demanding; they must learn to respond appropriately to this new environment. Fortunately, a well-executed human resource manage-ment program can help the enterprise anticipate and stay abreast of customer demands—although this is no easy task, given the changing nature of the marketplace.

Changing Demands

One expert in hospitality management recently noted: "To survive we have to be quicker, faster, smarter, both internally in how we get things done and externally for the customer."[8] In particular, recent research has found that suc-cessful hospitality organizations need to address two areas: service and price. Guests want to be provided a quality service, in a reasonable amount of time, at a price that is both affordable and competitive. Perhaps even more interest-ing is the fact that many of these customers admit that they would be willing to pay a higher price for quality service delivered in a timely manner. Moreover, quality and time are often related, in that faster service is often regarded as higher-quality as well. For example, one of the most common challenges facing five-star restaurants is that of reducing the time for serving the food. While the chefs typically prepare outstanding cuisine, a typical guest complaint is that it takes too long to be served. When this is accomplished, customer satisfaction increases sharply. So the major question for the restau-rants is: How can food be prepared and served more quickly? The answer is found in total quality management tools and techniques that can be used to reduce time, improve efficiency, and develop teamwork. (Some of the most useful of these approaches are discussed in Chapter 13.) Many of these tools and techniques are a result of effective human resource management prac-tices, and this begins at the point where the organization first brings people into the enterprise.

> The key is finding the right people. It starts in the recruiting process, in the selection process. There are certain people who can intuitively sense what will satisfy each individual customer. They enjoy taking care of a customer's needs—that's not something you can teach a per-son. You can teach procedures, you can teach computer skills, but you can't teach warmth, caring, personality. You've got to set clear, simple goals for your employees and then let them use their own skills in achieving the goals. Simply put, hire for attitude, train for skills.[9]

In particular, associates must be trained to know what guests want—and then go beyond these expectations. A good example is provided by international guests, who are accounting for a growing percentage of hospitality industry revenue in the United States. These individuals often have customs markedly different from those of Americans, and expect to be treated appropriately. For example, many Europeans, especially Germans, are very punctual; when a meeting is scheduled to start at 9 A.M., it begins at 9 A.M. sharp! Associates who are responsible for setting up a meeting room and ensuring that all of the needed equipment is on hand and working properly must have everything in place well before 9 A.M.[10] Europeans also have dining habits that are different from those of Americans. For example, they drink more wine than Americans, eat at a later hour, and view mealtime more as a form of relaxation than do U.S. diners.[11] Hospitality firms are finding that one of the best ways of preparing their associates to deal with international customers is through carefully developed training programs. Another is by ensuring that special facilities and services are available. Some of the most common include multilingual associates who can communicate fluently with foreign guests, acceptance of foreign credit cards, in-house availability of translation services and language interpreters, guest service information in foreign languages, and the availability of foreign-language newspapers.[12]

It's Quality—or Else

There are many reasons why customers must be given quality service. One of the main reasons is that the industry has become so competitive that customers now have a variety of alternatives: once a customer is lost, it can be extremely difficult to win back the individual. A second reason is that most customers do not complain when they have a problem. They simply take their business elsewhere. Researchers have found that over two-thirds of customer dissatisfaction is due to perceived indifference to their problems or concerns on the part of associates. Moreover, dissatisfied guests will typically tell eight to ten people of their dissatisfaction; one out of five will tell 20 people.[13] These statistics help explain why hospitality firms are now developing formal service training programs and are going out of their way to ensure that guests are pleased with their experience, are likely to return, and will tell their friends and acquaintances about their positive encounter. Many companies also include a service component in their employee handbook, so that associates clearly understand the importance assigned to this activity.

Associates are also given training in human relations skill building, thus ensuring that they are better able to interact effectively with customers. At one large regional restaurant chain, for example, the president of the company insists that guest satisfaction be placed ahead of cost. He tells his associates, "If you have to buy someone's complete dinner in order for that person to leave happy, I expect you to buy it. And I mean that. And if a manager ever gets mad at you for doing too much, call me."[14] The chain also teaches its people to follow basic human relations principles. These include:

- Be glad—attitude is everything.
- Use logic and emotion to win customers.
- Make a good impression.
- Never threaten a guest's self-image.
- Develop an interest in the guest, get the person to talk, and then listen.
- Always put guests at ease.
- Always keep eye contact.
- Use humor.
- Be able to laugh at yourself.
- Give guests personal touches.

These guidelines are useful in dealing with most guests, although they do have to be modified for some international clients. For example, Asian customers often do not like to be touched and sometimes regard humor as inappropriate. Additionally, foreign guests sometimes have special requests; one way of improving service quality is to note these requests so that they can be addressed more quickly in the future. For example, many restaurants now compile a card file of ethnic recipes that allow them to better respond to differing culinary needs and preferences. And if the restaurant is frequented by a particular group of visitors, such as Japanese, German, or Brazilian guests, the establishment will add special ethnic dishes to the menu because it knows there will be a demand for these offerings. Many restaurants will also create special multilingual menus that make it easier for their international guests to order, and will typically post these menus outside the restaurant in order to allow their guests a chance to study them before sitting down.[15]

The primary focus of hospitality organizations is the guest. The preceding examples illustrate ways that high-quality service can be provided to these clients. Given that the competition in the industry has increased sharply over the past decade, it is important to be able to provide these services in order to remain viable. An effective human resources strategy is critical to this effort. However, there is another part of the HR equation that has not yet been examined—you, the associate who provides the goods and services.

Your Role

An entire segment of this book is devoted to helping you better understand yourself and how you can improve your own performance. The reason for this emphasis is clearly seen in the very definition of HRM—the process by which organizations ensure the effective use of their associates in the pursuit of both organizational and individual goals. The study of human resource management must focus strongly on the people who are carrying out the work. You are the primary link between the organization and the customer, and throughout this book we are going to present a wealth of ideas that you can use in improving your ability to be an effective associate. In particular, we will address our attention to two key areas: personal insights and confidence building.

Personal Insights

The next part of this book is designed to help you gain personal insights. Who are you? How do you solve problems? How do you manage change and conflict? How do you communicate? Additionally, how can you do a better job of solving problems, managing change and conflict, and communicating? An effective human resources program will help you gain personal insights, teach you how to use your strengths, and point the way for improving your overall performance. One way that we have done this throughout the book is by providing self-feedback exercises that you can use for gaining information and improving performance. These exercises are provided at the end of each chapter as well as within chapters. For example, the exercise at the end of this chapter will give you feedback on how you like to lead people. When you are finished reading this chapter, you can take the quiz and learn whether you are a "take-charge" person or prefer to use negotiation techniques to get things done.

Confidence Building

In addition to providing personal insights, effective human resource management helps build personal confidence and assists people in creating a career plan that is rewarding for them. This is particularly clear in the case of HRM training programs. The Radisson Hotel Corporation of America is a good example. Its customer service training program is called "Yes I Can!" and is designed to provide information that associates require to both anticipate the needs and exceed the expectations of guests. The training has a series of components, each designed to develop human resources. First, general associate training is provided to everyone. Then department-specific training has been designed specifically for each department, with opportunities to practice key service skills for ensuring the maintenance of high standards in difficult service situations. Finally, a follow-up program gets associates involved in setting goals and developing action plans for further improving their department's service. The company explains its overall program philosophy this way:

> Yes I Can! represents the philosophy that our guests and their satisfaction is our No. 1 goal. First, this program helps you see service through the eyes of our guests. Then it helps you build the skills need-

ed to translate this philosophy into providing the most responsive, effective service in the industry—so our guests will want to return again and again.

You'll learn to understand our guests and their service needs. You'll learn how to incorporate the Yes I Can! attitude even when we cannot fulfill a guest's request exactly. Our guests do not want to hear the word "no." Therefore, in these situations, we try to provide an alternative that satisfies our guests.[16]

The purpose of Radisson's training is to help create a positive attitude *and* to show the trainees how the information can be applied in the workplace. This will also be the focus of our attention throughout this book. In accomplishing this objective, we are going to start by helping you gain a better understanding of yourself. We begin this in the next chapter, which is titled, "Who Are You?"

SUMMARY

1. Human resource management (HRM) is the process by which organizations ensure the effective use of their associates in the pursuit of both organizational and individual goals. Some of the major HRM functions include employment, training and development, compensation and benefits, human resources planning, and ensuring equal employment opportunity compliance.

2. The traditional model of human resources is now being replaced by the modern model of human resources. The primary difference is the way in which human resources are viewed. Today managers realize that associates are their most important asset; if these individuals are given the right conditions, they will contribute to the limits of their ability.

3. A number of human resource management challenges are forcing hospitality organizations to change the way they are doing things. One of these challenges is that of improving productivity. A second is learning to manage a diverse workforce. A third is retention of associates through development of programs that create associate satisfaction and result in a stable workforce.

4. Today's hospitality guests are more demanding than ever; if they do not get the service they want, they will go elsewhere. As a result, human resources programs are now being developed that train associates to identify customer needs and provide service that goes beyond each person's expectations. Simply put, it's quality or else!

5. While customer service is critical to the success of every hospitality firm, so too is the associate—you. And no study of human resource manage-

ment would be complete without providing personal and human relations insights into your behavior. In this way, you will be better able to understand yourself—and thus do a better job working with others. This will be the focus of attention in the next part of the book.

KEY TERMS

human resource management
traditional model of human
   resources

modern model of human resources
productivity
hypercompetition

REVIEW AND APPLICATION QUESTIONS

1. Sandra Whitecliff is going to be taking over the human resources (HR) unit for a medium-sized hotel. For the last four years she has been working in the HR area as an assistant manager in a large hotel chain. What are three HR activities on which Sandra is likely to be focusing her attention? Identify and briefly describe each.

2. Many hospitality organizations are strong supporters of the modern human resources model. Why is this? What makes the modern model superior to the traditional model? Cite and explain three reasons.

3. The Shoals, a popular resort restaurant, feels that one of the best ways to improve its profitability and ensure higher incomes for the associates is by improving productivity. How can the restaurant improve productivity in valet parking services, food preparation, and table service? In each case, offer two suggestions for productivity improvement.

4. Why is diversity a current challenge for managers in the hospitality industry? How can a well-designed human resources program help managers meet this challenge? Give two examples.

5. The Garvey Hotel has had high associate turnover in the last two years. How can the hotel reduce this turnover and improve associate commitment to the organization? Offer three practical suggestions.

SELF-FEEDBACK EXERCISE:
WHAT TYPE OF LEADER ARE YOU?

The following statements are designed to provide you with insights regarding how you see yourself as a leader. In the blank space next to each statement, write the number that best describes how frequently you engage (or would engage) in the behavior described when you are in a leadership position. The numbers represent the following:

5 = always

4 = very often

3 = fairly often

2 = occasionally

1 = never

Example:

4	I ask for suggestions from my work group. (This response indicates that the individual feels he or she very often asks for suggestions from the group.)

_____ 1. I delegate decision-making authority to others.

_____ 2. I tell my people what is expected of them.

_____ 3. The decisions I make reflect prior consultations with my people.

_____ 4. I do personal favors for my people.

_____ 5. I make no final decisions until my people are in general agreement with them.

_____ 6. I alone make the final decisions, but I do get my people's opinions before doing so.

_____ 7. I often change my behavior to fit the occasion.

_____ 8. My people and I jointly analyze problems in reaching decisions.

_____ 9. I set deadlines by which my people must finish their work.

_____ 10. I sell my decisions to others through effective persuasion.

_____ 11. I get my people's ideas regarding tentative decisions before making them final.

_____ 12. I show confidence and trust in my people.

_____ 13. I set specific, definite standards of performance that are expected of my people.

_____ 14. I let my people have as much responsibility for final decisions as I do.

_____ **15.** I use rewards and promises of rewards to influence my people.

_____ **16.** I lead with a firm hand.

_____ **17.** My people have as much a voice in decision making as I do.

_____ **18.** I give suggestions, but leave my people free to follow their own course of action.

_____ **19.** Before I make a decision, I look for individual opinions from my people.

_____ **20.** I like to let people make their own decisions.

Scoring: Enter your answers to the statements above in the appropriate spaces below; then compute the average for each group. An interpretation of your responses follows.

Group 1	**Group 2**	**Group 3**	**Group 4**	**Group 5**
2. ___	4. ___	3. ___	5. ___	1. ___
9. ___	7. ___	6. ___	8. ___	12. ___
13. ___	10. ___	11. ___	14. ___	18. ___
16. ___	15. ___	19. ___	17. ___	20. ___
Total ___	___	___	___	___
Average ___	___	___	___	___

Interpretation: This test measures how you see yourself in each of five areas. Fill in your average score for each of the five groups and then read the description that accompanies each.

Average Score	The five areas, represented by Groups 1 to 5 respectively, are these:
_____	**1.** Directive—The higher the score, the more you see yourself as a task-oriented leader.
_____	**2.** Negotiative—The higher the score, the more you see yourself as a leader who gets things done by making deals with group members.
_____	**3.** Consultative—The higher the score, the more you allow your people to have input to the decision you eventually make.
_____	**4.** Participative—The higher the score, the more you share decision-making authority with your people.
_____	**5.** Delegative—The higher the score, the more you let your people obtain results in their own way.

What do your results relate about your leadership style? Was this what you expected? If not, what do you think accounts for this difference in perception?

CASE 1.1: NOT MUCH PROMISE

The Phillipe II hotel is a 700-room establishment located in the middle of a large tourist area. The Phillipe has been in business since 1926 and was once the premier hotel in the area. Over the last two decades, however, the competition has taken market share from the Phillipe; now, the only time the hotel is ever filled to capacity is at the height of the tourist season. This is usually a result of the other hotels in the area recommending the Phillipe because they are unable to accommodate their guests.

The manager of the Phillipe, Bernie Karlow, has been in charge for almost two decades; many people in the area mark the decline of the hotel with his arrival. Bernie has heard this remark on countless occasions and sharply disagrees with it. Last month, he had an opportunity to express his views. A reporter for the local newspaper was doing a story on customer service in the hotel industry and dropped by to talk with Bernie. During the interview, she asked him about his philosophy of managing people. Here is some of what Bernie had to say:

> Most people in this business work for the money. We don't pay very high salaries, but they can make quite a bit in tips. Of course, if they see the opportunity for a better job, they are likely to quickly pursue it. So labor turnover is pretty high. I think this is because most people don't really want to work very hard. They would prefer easier jobs, if they could get them. On the other hand, I think we do a really good job here at the Phillipe in providing customer service. Right now we are at 88 percent of capacity and I expect us to be full by the time we reach the peak of the season in two weeks.

The reporter also talked to some of the hotel's associates and received a different picture. Most of them groused about the poor salaries and heavy work demands. One told the reporter, "Most of us are here to get experience so we can move on to other jobs that offer better opportunities. I don't know anyone who is here at the Phillipe for the long haul. This just isn't the type of hotel that offers much in the way of a promising career."

1. Is Bernie a supporter of the traditional human resources model or the modern human resources model? Explain your answer.

2. What type of a leader do you think Bernie is? Use the self-feedback exercise in this chapter—"What Type of Leader Are You?"—to help you formulate your answer.

3. Based on your responses to the preceding questions, what could Bernie do to improve the situation? Offer three human resource management strategies that could be of value.

CASE 1.2: GETTING THINGS BACK IN SHAPE

The Bayview Resort is a large hotel and golf course complex in the northwestern part of the United States. For many years Bayview was a very popular resort, but beginning in the mid-1980s the resort began to experience strong competition and progressively lost market share. Six months ago the complex was purchased by a group of European investors who are intent on turning things around. They have hired Willa Schurer to manage the operation. Willa was head of a large hotel in the Chicago area; in the three years she was there, she totally turned operations around. The occupancy rate soared from an average of 57 percent up to 89 percent, and associate turnover declined from 97 percent annually to under 15 percent. During this same period, the hotel gained a reputation for outstanding service and was often the first choice for business conventions and large meetings. This success helped increase Willa's visibility in the industry and called her to the attention of the European investors.

In the six months that Willa has been in charge of operations, things have begun to improve sharply. One of her first major decisions was to institute a reward-and-recognition system that allows associates at all levels of the hierarchy to submit ideas for improvement and to share in the financial savings that accrue from the implementation of these suggestions. A second decision was to push authority as far down the line as possible and allow associates to make on-the-spot decisions, resulting in increased customer service. A third decision was to assign associates to groups to study how improvements in operations can be brought about.

Last week Willa received the first biannual report on operations. The data show that revenues are running 19 percent ahead of forecasts, and profits are up 89 percent above initial estimates. Additionally, the number of people applying for jobs at the resort has increased by 47 percent over the previous year. Willa has also been sent a newspaper article which reports that Bayview is now regarded as one of the top ten resorts in the region, a list that it had not made for over fourteen years.

1. Is Willa's management style best described by the traditional or modern model of human relations? Explain.

2. What is Willa doing that might account for the decline in associate turnover? Give two possible explanations.

3. What are two things she is doing to help improve service and productivity? Be specific in your discussion.

ANSWERS AND EXPLANATIONS TO BOX 1.1: "ASSOCIATE SATISFACTION—OR ELSE"

1. True. Satisfaction is partially influenced by the age of the respondent.
2. False. Women have lower levels of job satisfaction than do men.
3. True. The satisfaction levels among White associates, on average, are higher.
4. False. There is no statistical difference between the two groups.
5. False. Approximately 80 percent of associates in the industry do not intend to make it a career.
6. True. Neither group believes that rewards are strongly tied to performance.
7. False. Promotion is highly valued by cooks, bellhops, and bussers, but not by servers and bartenders.
8. True. On this point there is overwhelming agreement.
9. True. They believe management needs to improve sharply in this area.
10. True. Hotel workers are more satisfied than any other group, and fast-food workers are less satisfied than any other group.

How well did you do? Most people get only seven right. Yet regardless of how well you did, the point to remember is that associate satisfaction can be improved if management carries out human resources functions more effectively.

ENDNOTES

1. See John Soeder, Michael Sanson, and Jackie Orihill, "The Profit Motive," *Restaurant Hospitality,* July 1995, pp. 31–36.
2. Catherine Romano, "Managing Change, Diversity, and Emotions," *Management Review,* July 1995, p. 6.
3. Also see Laura M. Graves and Gary N. Powell, "Effects of Sex-Based Preferential Selection and Discrimination on Job Attitudes," *Human Relations,* Vol. 47, No. 2, 1994, pp. 133–155.
4. Judi Brownell, "Women in Hospitality Management: General Managers' Perceptions of Factors Related to Career Development," *International Journal of Hospitality Management,* Vol. 13, No. 2, 1994, pp. 101–117.
5. Susana Barciela, "Don't Ignore Workers' Woes," *Miami Herald,* February 27, 1995, p. 15.
6. For more on this topic, see Shelley Wolson, "Worker Retention," *Restaurant Business,* May 20, 1991, pp. 65–72.

7. Jonathan D. Barsky, "Building a Program for World-Class Service," *Cornell Hotel and Restaurant Administration Quarterly,* February 1996, p. 23.

8. William M. Plamandon, "Who Are the '90s Consumers?" *Lodging,* November 1994, p. 127.

9. Ibid., p. 132.

10. Anthony Hados, "The European Market: A Study in Diversity," *Hospital Marketing Review,* Fall 1995, p. 38.

11. Julie MacDonald, "Gratuity Not Included," *Hotel and Motel Management,* April 25, 1994, p. 35.

12. Jafar Jafari and William Way, "Multicultural Strategies in Tourism," *Cornell Hotel and Restaurant Administration Quarterly,* December 1994, p. 74.

13. Susie Stephenson, "Guest Satisfaction Regardless of Cost," *Restaurants and Institutions,* November 1, 1994, p. 126.

14. Ibid.

15. Reported in "Give Your Food Global Appeal," *Lodging Hospitality,* October 1993, p. 55.

16. Source: Radisson Hotel Corporation, *Employee Handbook.*

PART TWO

Understanding Yourself

This part of the book is designed to provide you with personal insights. The reason that we address this issue before embarking on an examination of human resource management (HRM) topics is that you are a critical part of the HRM equation. As seen in Part I, there are three major areas in the study of HRM: (1) the process itself, such as recruiting, selecting, training, and development; (2) the guest who will be receiving the organization's goods and services; and (3) the associate—you—who will be providing these outputs. Do you have the personality and career interests that are needed to succeed in this industry? One way of answering this question is by gaining some insight into your own behavior. This is the overriding objective of this part of the book.

In Chapter 2, the focus of attention will be on helping you understand yourself. Who are you? What are some of your personal and work-related behaviors and philosophies? How do you see yourself? How do others see you? What are your personal values? These questions will be answered in this chapter; when you are finished reading it, you will have an improved understanding of yourself.

In Chapter 3, you will learn how the communication process works. You will also learn how to identify problem ownership and the most effective approach to use when the person talking to you has a problem, as well as the best approach to employ when you have a problem. In Chapter 3, attention will also be given to the value of assisting skills and the role of active listening. You will also learn to compare and contrast I-messages and you-messages, and will learn how to write an effective confrontive message. Consideration will also be given to the use of face-to-face communication and win-win strategies.

Chapter 4 will provide you with insights regarding how to manage change and conflict effectively. In addition to learning about the nature of change, you will have the chance to examine how you respond to change. You will also learn about conflict and the various approaches that can be used in dealing with it. Attention will also be given to the topic of personal stress; you will learn how to use a stress analysis chart to help you cope. You will also have a chance to identify whether you have a Type A or Type B personality and relate this information to the area of stress. Finally, consideration will be given to time management; you will learn some useful steps to employ in effectively coping with the time management challenges faced by hospitality associates.

Chapter 5 will help you examine your decision-making skills. In particular, attention is directed to the decision-making process and how you carry out these steps. Consideration is also given to the way you perceive things and how you can use creative thinking and brainstorming to improve your problem-solving skills. You will be provided with insight into your decision-making style and learn how you like to process information. You will also find out if you tend to be a logical, systematic thinker; an intuitive, creative thinker; or a combination of both. Additionally, you will have the opportunity to measure your own creative-thinking abilities.

When you have finished this part of the book, you will have obtained a wealth of personal insights. You will have a better idea of what you like and dislike, how you process information and make decisions, how you act (and react) to stressful situations, the ways you currently communicate, and how you can improve your ability to carry out these processes.

CHAPTER TWO

Who Are You?

LEARNING OBJECTIVES

One of the best ways to begin the study of human resources is by gaining some personal insights. By learning more about your personality, values, and behaviors, you also improve your ability to understand and work with others. The overriding objective of this chapter is to help you to understand yourself better. In accomplishing this objective, particular attention will be given to personality and values in both personal and work-related situations. When you have finished studying all of the material in this chapter, you will be able to:

1. Define the term *personality* and examine some of your personal beliefs and biases.
2. Compare and contrast personal and peer-generated feedback of your behaviors.
3. Describe the key factors that influence personality development.
4. Discuss some of your work-related behaviors and philosophies.
5. Identify and profile your personal values.

The Nature of Personality

Why do you act as you do? What explains your behavior? One of the best ways of answering these questions and gaining important personal human relations insights is by examining the topic of personality. *Personality* is an individual's characteristics and behaviors, organized in a way that reflects the unique adjustment the person makes to his or her environment.[1] As a result of personality, an individual will have a stable set of characteristics and tendencies that help describe his or her behavior. And quite often we will draw conclusions about the person based on these behaviors, and then act in accord with our beliefs. For example, suppose that at 6 A.M. a guest approaches the front desk of a San Francisco hotel and nervously asks the registration clerk, "Where can I get a copy of *The Wall Street Journal*?" The associate points to a stack of *Journal*s sitting to her left and says, "Please take one with the compliments of the hotel." The guest takes the one on top and begins rapidly leafing through the pages until he reaches the stock market section. He then slowly and systematically begins running his finger down the page, stopping to circle the latest price of a stock, and then continues. After circling ten closing prices, the guest closes the paper, looks up at the clerk, smiles, and says, "Thank you very much. I hope you have a nice day." The individual then begins walking briskly toward the dining room while humming the opening bars to "Oh, What a Beautiful Morning."

What conclusion can you draw regarding this individual? Does he have a great deal of money invested in the market? Has he invested in high-technology stocks? Did he make a lot of money in the market yesterday? Based on his actions, we can only surmise what is going on. We do not know for sure. Yet, like most people, we often draw conclusions based on how other people act. Simply put, we ask ourselves: If I were in that person's shoes, why would I be acting that way? We assume that the causes of our behavior are universal. In fact, this is incorrect. Moreover, a lot of what we "know" about people is more a reflection of our own experiences, biases, and general personality than it is a reflection of fact.

Personal Beliefs and Biases

Human beings are complex individuals. But in expressing an understanding of them, it is common to find people using reductive clichés. Here are some examples:

- Most hotel guests are extremely pleasant people and seldom get upset about anything.
- Retired people are much better tippers than college students.
- If you treat your guests well, they will respond by coming back again and again.

really don't know what competitive rates are in the city. We heard a lot of good things about your hotel and considered only you. Once our senior-level management gave us the okay, we sent you a fax confirming the arrangement." Henry was delighted with this news, but surprised to learn that it took the company three months to get back to him.

It seems that Henry did not think that the company was going to get back to him. Why not? Because Henry is accustomed to the way Americans do business. They are given a price quote and if they are interested they get back to the person within a week—or they do not get back at all. Henry failed to realize that in Asia, people tend to have a much greater long-term time orientation. Additionally, decision making in Asia is often done in a group. When a hotel provides a price quote, the individual who receives it passes it on to a group of individuals who will collectively make the final decision. This is markedly different from the United States, where managers make quick, final decisions based on the facts that have just been presented to them.

Sociocultural factors also influence the way people behave. The most important of these are imposed during the socialization process, when cultural values and role patterns are transmitted. *Socialization* is the conditioning of an individual's behavior in ways that are customary and acceptable to that person's social environment. This process is a result of the people and groups with whom the person is associated.[3] This social interaction results in the individual acquiring behavioral patterns that help him or her relate to these other people. Socialization begins in early childhood, when a young person learns acceptable behavior for fulfilling physical needs. Later, needs for affection emerge, and behavior oriented toward satisfying this and other learned needs continues to develop. For example, because of socialization, some young women face career conflicts. On one hand, they are encouraged by their family and friends to get a job and begin working their way up the organizational ladder. On the other hand, they are encouraged to have a family and/or spend more time at home with their children. Simply stated: Family, religious affiliation, ethnic background, social class, and one's peer group all play a role in creating personality.

Tony Farino's family opened an Italian restaurant in the Little Italy section of Manhattan in 1917. Tony's Place has long been one of the most popular eating establishments in the area. Two years ago, Tony graduated from New York University and told his father, "I'd like to help you run the restaurant. Perhaps we can expand the facilities and attract even more clientele." Tony's decision means that for the fourth generation, there will be a member of the Farino family running the restaurant. His father was overjoyed with the decision and told Tony, "I thought you might decide to go down to Wall Street to seek your fortune. I'm glad you're going to stay here with the family. We need a person with your ability to ensure that the business reaches its 100th birthday. And, you know, that's not very far away."

Why did Tony decide to stay with the family business? Part of the answer is undoubtedly found in the socialization process. He was born and raised in an environment in which his family ran a restaurant that they had taken over from their own family. The business was part of his lifestyle. So this career choice was not really a difficult one for him. In fact, it was a natural transition.

Situation. Situational factors, often called *life events,* are spontaneous or unpredictable happenings that have a significant influence on future behavior. These events can vary widely and be of a cultural, social, or environmental nature.

> When Jenny McDonald's car broke down, she realized that she would have to get a part-time job in order to pay for the repairs. So while she was carrying a full courseload at the university, she applied for a job at a local hotel, where she was hired as the night clerk every Friday and Saturday. Jenny was the first night clerk the owner had ever hired who kept proper records, accounted for all receipts, and did not sleep through part of her shift. He told her so and encouraged Jenny to think about a career in the hospitality field. "You really do an excellent job, and there are some wonderful careers for people with your personality and drive." The owner also wrote her a letter of recommendation when she graduated, and this helped her land a job as a trainee with a major hotel chain. Today she is vice-president of human resources for a national hotel headquartered in Chicago.

Would Jenny have ended up in the hotel business if her car had not broken down? This is difficult to say, but one thing is certain. The incident proved to be a life event, and the job she took was one that helped start her on a career path.

Your Personality and the Workplace

Remember that in understanding yourself, it is important to examine not just your personality traits or behaviors, but also the environment in which you live and work. For example, you may be a very hard-driving, aggressive person; at home people may be continually telling you to "lighten up." However, if you are the manager of a popular restaurant where there are many activities that need to be coordinated and you need to keep on top of things, your personality may be ideal and may help make you an extremely effective individual. So before concluding our discussion of personality, let's take a look at how you perceive yourself in terms of the workplace. Box 2.4 provides a series of comparative profiles that describe you and your philosophy of how to manage people. As you did in Box 2.2, read the contrasting statements and place an X on the part of the continuum that best describes you. When you are finished, continue on to the next paragraph and read the interpretation of the findings.

The higher your score, the more you see yourself as someone who enjoys working in the hospitality industry. You like people; you like to go out of your way to make them happy; and you believe that most of them complain only when they have a legitimate gripe. Similarly, you enjoy working with your associates; you believe that most of them are giving their best effort and, if left alone, would continue to work hard; and you feel that their creative potential can be tapped even more than it is. Additionally, you have some fixed ideas about yourself, including: you are a flexible person who maintains good self-control; you get a great deal of satisfaction from your work; and you have a positive attitude regarding your associates and customers.

In examining your profile scores, look at each specific response and pick out those that do not fit into the overall pattern. For example, if most of your scores are 6 or higher, but there are four below 6, go back and review these. This analysis provides three important benefits: (1) it helps point out your unique behavioral profile; (2) it illustrates that not everything you do fits into an easily discernible profile; and (3) it provides a basis for evaluating your behavior and deciding whether any changes are warranted. One way of focusing more directly on this last point is to ask your current boss (or someone in the hospitality industry whom you admire or who holds a position to which you aspire) to complete the exercise in Box 2.5. Then compare your profile from Box 2.4 with this one; note any differences between the type of person you see yourself as being and the type of individual who does well in the industry. Then, if there are significant differences between your profile and this person's, there is a basis for evaluation and, possibly, change.

Understanding Your Personal Values

Values are closely linked to personality. If you have the requisite personality to be an effective hotel manager, cruise director, or restaurant manager, there are a number of behaviors that can be used in profiling you. Three of these would be (1) sociability—you like people; (2) helpfulness—you enjoy providing assistance to others; and (3) achievement drive—you like to get things done. Closely linked with these personality traits are your personal values. A *value* is something that is important to you. And like your personality, these values are greatly shaped by those with whom you often interact: parents, friends, acquaintances, teachers, and associates. In fact, learning and experience are the two greatest forces in shaping one's values.[4]

Box 2.4
Your Personality and Philosophy in the Workplace

Read each of the contrasting pairs of statements and decide which one best describes you. Then determine the degree of that statement that comes closest to describing you and place an X over that number.

I like to be in charge of things	8 7 6 5 4 3 2 1		I like events to unfold and I go with the flow
I think people at work are basically lazy and will cut corners whenever they can	1 2 3 4 5 6 7 8		I think people at work try very hard to do a good job, and are basically hardworking and trustworthy
In the workplace, I judge situations on their own merit	8 7 6 5 4 3 2 1		In the workplace, I follow fixed rules of conduct that get me through
I often lose my temper	1 2 3 4 5 6 7 8		I am good at maintaining self-control
I am a fairly self-reliant person	8 7 6 5 4 3 2 1		I depend on others to tell me what to do
I like rules because they help me deal with difficult situations	1 2 3 4 5 6 7 8		When I am faced with a difficult situation, I am good at working out a solution
I am a people-centered manager	8 7 6 5 4 3 2 1		I am a work-centered manager
I think most work problems call for a yes or no answer	1 2 3 4 5 6 7 8		I think most work problems call for a situationally based answer
I think that flexible bosses are the most effective ones	8 7 6 5 4 3 2 1		I think that dogmatic bosses are the most effective ones

Box 2.4   Continued

| I work primarily because of the financial rewards that I receive | 1 | 2 | 3 | 4 | 5 | 6 | 7 | 8 | I work primarily because of the internal satisfaction I get from my job |

| I believe that the creative potential of most people is far greater than that required by their job | 8 | 7 | 6 | 5 | 4 | 3 | 2 | 1 | I believe that the creative potential of most people is much less than that required by their job |

| I am basically controlled by work-related events | 1 | 2 | 3 | 4 | 5 | 6 | 7 | 8 | I am basically in control of work-related events |

| I am a fairly deliberative, computational, and serious individual | 8 | 7 | 6 | 5 | 4 | 3 | 2 | 1 | I am pretty much controlled by my fears, anxieties, and emotions |

| I feel that most people have little control over their actions; it is all genetically determined | 1 | 2 | 3 | 4 | 5 | 6 | 7 | 8 | I feel that most people have a great deal of control over their actions; it is consciously determined |

| I believe that, in order to get people to work, you have to provide them with the opportunity to do things that are personally rewarding | 8 | 7 | 6 | 5 | 4 | 3 | 2 | 1 | I believe that, in order to get people to work, you have to keep them under close watch and threaten them with punishment such as firing |

| I feel that most customers are rude and assertive, but I have learned to put up with their behavior | 1 | 2 | 3 | 4 | 5 | 6 | 7 | 8 | I feel that most customers are good, decent people who are assertive only when they are treated poorly |

Box 2.4   Continued

I believe that a good hospitality manager makes an important contribution to the overall satisfaction and well-being of his or her guests

I believe that a good hospitality manager is a lot like a baby-sitter: firm, tactful, and willing to put up with a lot of ridiculous requests

$$\underline{}\ \underline{}\ \underline{}\ \underline{}\ \underline{}\ \underline{}\ \underline{}\ \underline{}$$
8   7   6   5   4   3   2   1

I feel that most guests are very interested in figuring out how they can take advantage of the services being given to them

I feel that most guests appreciate what is done for them, and very few try to take unfair advantage of the hospitality being shown to them

$$\underline{}\ \underline{}\ \underline{}\ \underline{}\ \underline{}\ \underline{}\ \underline{}\ \underline{}$$
1   2   3   4   5   6   7   8

I truly enjoy working with people

I find most people to be nerve-wracking, but I can put up with them

$$\underline{}\ \underline{}\ \underline{}\ \underline{}\ \underline{}\ \underline{}\ \underline{}\ \underline{}$$
8   7   6   5   4   3   2   1

I enjoy going the extra mile to make a guest pleased with our service

I do the minimum amount of work

$$\underline{}\ \underline{}\ \underline{}\ \underline{}\ \underline{}\ \underline{}\ \underline{}\ \underline{}$$
1   2   3   4   5   6   7   8

Scoring: Add the numbers directly under each X and put the total below.

Total score _____

Before you examine your personal value profile, it is important to realize that there are a number of different types of values. One way of categorizing values is in terms of instrumental and terminal values. An *instrumental value* is the means for achieving a desired goal. A *terminal value* is expressed as a desired goal or end. Here are some examples:

Instrumental Values (Means)	**Terminal Values (Ends)**
honesty	self-respect
independence	a comfortable life
ambition	family security
wisdom	understanding
hard work	a sense of accomplishment

You have been asked to fill out this profile because of your experience and knowledge of the hospitality business. Please read each of the contrasting pairs of statements and decide which one best describes a successful hospitality associate in your career area. Then determine the degree of that statement that comes closest to describing this successful individual and place an X over that number. When you are finished, determine the total score by adding all of the numbers over which you have placed an X and return the form to the individual who gave it to you. Thank you for your assistance.

He or she likes to be in charge of things

$$8 \quad 7 \quad 6 \quad 5 \quad 4 \quad 3 \quad 2 \quad 1$$

He or she likes events to unfold and he or she goes with the flow

He or she thinks people at work are basically lazy and will cut corners whenever they can

$$1 \quad 2 \quad 3 \quad 4 \quad 5 \quad 6 \quad 7 \quad 8$$

He or she thinks people at work try very hard to do a good job, and are basically hard-working and trustworthy

In the workplace, this person judges situations on their own merit

$$8 \quad 7 \quad 6 \quad 5 \quad 4 \quad 3 \quad 2 \quad 1$$

In the workplace, this person follows fixed rules of conduct that get him or her through

This individual often loses his or her temper

$$1 \quad 2 \quad 3 \quad 4 \quad 5 \quad 6 \quad 7 \quad 8$$

This person is good at maintaining self-control

This individual is a fairly self-reliant person

$$8 \quad 7 \quad 6 \quad 5 \quad 4 \quad 3 \quad 2 \quad 1$$

This individual depends on others to tell him or her what to do

This person likes rules because they help him or her deal with difficult situations

$$1 \quad 2 \quad 3 \quad 4 \quad 5 \quad 6 \quad 7 \quad 8$$

When faced with a difficult situation, this person is good at working out a solution

This individual is a people-centered manager

$$8 \quad 7 \quad 6 \quad 5 \quad 4 \quad 3 \quad 2 \quad 1$$

This individual is a work-centered manager

Box 2.5   Continued

This person thinks most work problems call for a yes or no answer

$\overline{}$ $\overline{}$ $\overline{}$ $\overline{}$ $\overline{}$ $\overline{}$ $\overline{}$ $\overline{}$
1   2   3   4   5   6   7   8

This person thinks most work problems call for a situationally-based answer

This individual thinks that flexible bosses are the most effective ones

8   7   6   5   4   3   2   1

This individual thinks that dogmatic bosses are the most effective ones

This person works primarily for the financial rewards that he or she receives

1   2   3   4   5   6   7   8

This person works primarily because of the internal satisfaction he or she gets from the job

This individual believes that the creative potential of most people is far greater than that required by their job

8   7   6   5   4   3   2   1

This individual believes that the creative potential of most people is much less than that required by their job

This person basically is controlled by work-related events

1   2   3   4   5   6   7   8

This person basically is in control of work-related events

This individual is a fairly deliberative, computational, and serious individual

8   7   6   5   4   3   2   1

This person is pretty much controlled by his or her fears, anxieties and emotions

This person feels that most people have little control over their actions; it is all genetically determined

1   2   3   4   5   6   7   8

This individual feels that most people have a great deal of control over their actions; it is consciously determined

Box 2.5   Continued

This individual believes that, in order to get people to work, one must provide them with the opportunity to do things that are personally rewarding

This person believes that, in order to get people to work, one must keep them under close watch and threaten them with punishment such as firing

__8__ __7__ __6__ __5__ __4__ __3__ __2__ __1__

This individual feels that most customers are rude and assertive, but he or she has learned to put up with their behavior

This individual feels that most customers are good, decent people who are assertive only when they are treated poorly

__1__ __2__ __3__ __4__ __5__ __6__ __7__ __8__

This individual believes that a good hospitality manager makes an important contribution to the over-all satisfaction and well-being of his or her guests

This individual believes that a good hospitality manager is a lot like a baby-sitter: firm, tactful, and willing to put up with a lot of ridiculous requests

__8__ __7__ __6__ __5__ __4__ __3__ __2__ __1__

This person feels that most guests are very interested in figuring out how they can take advantage of the services being given to them

This person feels that most guests appreciate what is done for them, and very few try to take unfair advantage of the hospitality being shown to them

__1__ __2__ __3__ __4__ __5__ __6__ __7__ __8__

This person truly enjoys working with people

This person finds most people to be nerve-wracking, but he or she can put up with them

__8__ __7__ __6__ __5__ __4__ __3__ __2__ __1__

Box 2.5 Continued

This person does
the minimum
amount of work

This individual
enjoys going the
extra mile to make
a guest pleased
with the service

$$\underline{\quad} \ \ \underline{\quad} \ \ \underline{\quad} \ \ \underline{\quad} \ \ \underline{\quad} \ \ \underline{\quad} \ \ \underline{\quad} \ \ \underline{\quad}$$
$$\ \ 1 \quad\ 2 \quad\ 3 \quad\ 4 \quad\ 5 \quad\ 6 \quad\ 7 \quad\ 8$$

Scoring: Add the numbers directly under each *X* and put the total below.

Total score _____

So when you answer the question, What is important to me? you may be expressing instrumental and/or terminal values. In either case, your response helps relate some of the things that are important to you.

Another way to examine values is in terms of a predetermined list and the preferences you have for these values. Edward Spraunger has identified six types of values common to everyone: *theoretical, economic, aesthetic, social, political,* and *religious.* (See Box 2.6.) Different occupational groups tend to have different value profiles. For example, professors of biology tend to be highest in theoretical values; businesspeople have very high economic values; artists place great significance on aesthetic values; social workers have high social values; politicians have strong political values; and members of the clergy hold high religious values. However, to some degree, each of these types of values is present within you.

Your Personal Value Profile

The most popular test designed to provide information and insight into personal values is the *Allport-Vernon-Lindzey Study of Values.* This test is designed to measure one's preference for each of Spraunger's value types. From the responses, a value profile can then be constructed for the individual. In fact, the test has been given a sufficient number of times so as to establish value profiles for different groups. Table 2.1 provides such profiles for the average college male, the average college female, a successful male business manager, and a successful female business manager.

Figure 2.2 is a graph of these four profiles. Note that the profile of the successful female manager is similar to that of the successful male manager and distinctly different from that of the average college female. Successful managers seem to have the same basic value profiles regardless of their sex.

Box 2.6
Spraunger's Value Types

Theoretical. The overriding interest of the theoretical person is the discovery of *truth*. This person is interested in facts rather than intuition or hunches. The individual is systematic, logical, and orderly, and approaches problem solving in a rational, scientific way. This individual is extremely successful in handling complex problems, such as how to organize a major party for 1,000 guests who will be flying in from all over the world to attend a wedding reception at the Plaza Hotel.

Economic. The economic person is interested primarily in what is *useful*. This person is concerned with getting things done in the most efficient way possible and often measures success in terms of profit, time saved, and the accumulation of resources. This individual would be extremely effective in managing hotel operations where the profit margin is extremely small and there is a large volume of business.

Aesthetic. The aesthetic person's highest values are *artistic*. This individual enjoys art, music, and literature. He or she also sees high value in form and harmony. This person would be very effective in ensuring that a food presentation is pleasing to the customer, for example, by designing and laying out the offerings in a visually attractive way, thus encouraging the diner to make a selection.

Social. The highest value of the social person is *genuine concern for others*. This individual is kind, sympathetic, unselfish, and enjoys helping people even when there is no monetary reward for doing so. This person does well in most hospitality positions because he or she is primarily interested in pleasing the clientele, and does so not because of a fear of losing the customer's business, but because he or she enjoys being helpful to others.

Political. The political person is interested in *power* or *influence*. This individual likes to be in charge of things and to make decisions. This person does well in managing hospitality organizations because he or she is not afraid to lead. This individual would rather be in charge, and occasionally be wrong, than sit back, assume no responsibility, and let others lead.

Religious. The highest value for the religious person is *unity*. This individual believes that everything in life makes sense, although he or she may not be able to explain the reason for everything. This person typically does not do well in hospitality-related jobs because he or she tends to let things happen rather than making them happen. On the other hand, this value is useful when mistakes happen, despite all efforts to prevent them, and it is necessary to take a philosophical view of the situation and not get upset or angry. The individual often writes off the mistake as "bound to happen from time to time."

Table 2.1   Value Profiles for Various Groups

Spraunger Value	Average College Male[a]	Average College Female[a]	Successful Male Manager[b]	Successful Female Manager[c]
Theoretical	43	36	44	39
Economic	42	37	45	47
Aesthetic	37	44	35	42
Social	37	42	33	31
Political	43	38	44	46
Religious	38	43	39	35

[a]*Study of Values Manual* (Boston: Houghton Mifflin, 1970), p. 11.

[b]William D. Guth and Renato Tagiuri, "Personal Values and Corporate Strategy," *Harvard Business Review,* September–October 1965, p. 126.

[c]Richard M. Hodgetts, Mildred G. Pryor, Harry N. Mills, and Karen Brinkman, "A Profile of the Successful Executive," *Academy of Management Proceedings,* August 1978, p. 378.

What type of value profile do you have? Box 2.7 has been created for the purpose of measuring your profile along the lines of the Spraunger values. Read the instructions and complete your profile before continuing.

As you can see from your profile, there are some values that are very important to you, while others are less important. Of course, if you had a low value for religion, this does not mean that you are not a good person or lack belief in a higher power. However, it does mean that you do not like situations in which you have to accept what happens. If you had a low religious score, you probably had a much higher political and/or economic score, which means that you like to make things happen; you enjoy accounting for your own success rather then relying on some lucky breaks—although you will certainly take them, if they come your way.

Your Work-Related Values

The preceding sections examined your personal values. It is also possible to gain additional insights to your behavior by looking at your work-related values. What things in the workplace are important to you?[5] What do you look for in an organization? For example, would you take a job with the Ritz-Carlton because of its reputation as an outstanding hotel? If so, this tells you something about your values. You prize the quality of an organization's reputation. You would like to be associated with a chain that is considered to be in the top tier. You would like to work for a winner.

Now let's turn the situation around and choose a hotel chain that appeals to a different target market. Would you accept a position with the LaQuinta

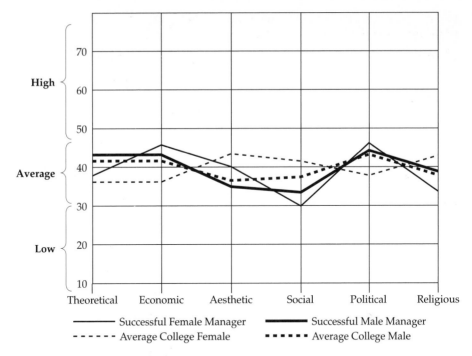

Figure 2.2 *Value Profiles*

hotel chain if you felt that your chances for advancement were better there than anywhere else? If so, this indicates that you value the opportunity for promotion, the chance to move into a higher-management position, and the desire to succeed. You are a high achiever and want the opportunity to reach challenging but attainable goals.[6]

There are a number of ways of gaining insight into your work-related values. Box 2.8 provides an example. Complete the questionnaire and scoring key; then read the interpretation of your scores before continuing.

Box 2.8 is useful in providing you with personal insight into what is important to you at work. In particular (and unlike Box 2.7), you could end up with high scores for all three groups or low scores for all three groups; it could turn out that your work-related values concerning people at large, the organization, and yourself are all very strong values and you believe in them deeply. Or you could find that only one of these groups is extremely important to you. Most hospitality students have high scores in all three, but their highest score is for Group 3. They have strong personal beliefs regarding the need to work hard, do a good job, and be rewarded for their performance. So as you review your scores and interpret the findings, ask yourself how close your scores are to those of others who have taken this test.

Box 2.7
Personal Values and You

The following fifteen statements require you to read and decide how much you agree with the two parts of each statement. Based on your decision, allocate a total of 5 points between the two. For example, if you like baseball a little bit better than football, you would answer the following statement this way:

I like baseball   3
better than football.   2

Of course, if you like baseball a great deal and do not like football, you would give 5 points to baseball and 0 points to football. Remember to give a total of 5 points to each statement, and place your answers in the spaces provided at the right.

1. I would much rather be an outstanding scientist than a successful business person.   a. _____   b. _____

2. I am more interested in dealing with facts than in generating creative, off-the-wall ideas.   c. _____   d. _____

3. I find more enjoyment in solving difficult mathematical problems than in interacting with others at a party.   e. _____   f. _____

4. I would rather win a Nobel Prize for medicine than be elected president of my country.   g. _____   h. _____

5. I believe that religion is a far more important force in helping humankind move forward than is science.   i. _____   j. _____

6. I'd rather be a successful restaurant owner than a successful playwright.   k. _____   l. _____

7. Success is more a matter of hard work than of knowing the right people.   m. _____   n. _____

8. I'd rather be a successful salesperson than a successful hotel manager.   o. _____   p. _____

9. I'd rather be in control of things than have to hope that they will work out well.   q. _____   r. _____

10. I'd rather spend time reading a great novel than attending a wedding reception.   s. _____   t. _____

11. I'd rather be a successful novelist than a two-term U.S. senator.   u. _____   v. _____

12. Who has made a greater contribution to humankind: Leonardo da Vinci or Mother Teresa?   w. _____   x. _____

13. I enjoy interacting with people and creating personal relationships more than I enjoy using these relationships to persuade people to do what I personally want done.   y. _____   z. _____

Box 2.7   Continued

14. I enjoy interacting with people
     more than I enjoy quietly contemplating the meaning of life.

aa. ____
bb. ____

15. If I were a member of the clergy, I would rather be in charge of a
     large urban facility
     than work in a small, rural community.

cc. ____
dd. ____

Scoring: Enter your scores in the scoring key that follows. Be sure to match the letter that accompanied your score in the quiz with that letter in the scoring key. Then total each group of numbers and put the total at the bottom of each column.

Group 1	Group 2	Group 3	Group 4	Group 5	Group 6
a. ___	b. ___	d. ___	f. ___	h. ___	i. ___
c. ___	k. ___	l. ___	n. ___	p. ___	r. ___
e. ___	m. ___	s. ___	t. ___	v. ___	x. ___
g. ___	o. ___	u. ___	y. ___	z. ___	bb. ___
j. ___	q. ___	w. ___	aa. ___	cc. ___	dd. ___
Total ___	___	___	___	___	___

Interpretation: This test measures how important each of the six Spraunger values are to you. Individuals who are effective in the hospitality industry tend to have high scores for at least two of the following:

Theoretical: They like to be technically proficient and know the correct rules, policies, procedures, and techniques needed to carry out their jobs and please their customers.

Economic: They like to get things done quickly and efficiently by looking for short-cuts and eliminating waste.

Aesthetic: They enjoy artistic and eye-appealing layout, design, and presentation, and are particularly effective in food presentation and layout of facilities.

Social: They enjoy working with people and see customer problems as an opportunity to be of assistance.

Political: They like to be in charge and thus ensure that things go well by carefully leading or influencing the outcomes.

Religious: They take things as they happen and do not let mistakes or problems upset them.

Among hospitality students and working associates who have taken this test, the average profile is:

Theoretical   10
Economic   16
Aesthetic   9
Social   16
Political   14
Religious   10

Box 2.8
Your Work-Related Values

Read the following statements and decide how important each is to you by using a scale of 1 to 8. If you totally agree with the statement, enter an 8. If you totally disagree with the statement, enter a 1. Otherwise, choose the appropriate number within this range that most accurately reflects your opinion.

_____ 1. Associate loyalty to the organization is very important.

_____ 2. Organizations should be loyal to their associates, even when economic times are hard.

_____ 3. I like to go the extra mile in getting things done, because that way I know they are done well.

_____ 4. Organizations have a responsibility to help develop the talents of their associates.

_____ 5. It is important to me to have a challenging job.

_____ 6. Associates should be on time for work.

_____ 7. Associates should be honest when dealing with customers.

_____ 8. I want an opportunity for advancement.

_____ 9. It is important for organizations to respect their associates.

_____ 10. It is important to me to work for an organization that is well thought of by its clients.

_____ 11. When an associate has a good idea, the organization should listen to it.

_____ 12. It is important to be respected by one's boss.

_____ 13. The organization should be interested in its associates because they are people, not just because they help the business make money.

_____ 14. At the end of every workday, it is important to me that I feel I have done a good job.

_____ 15. Job competence is extremely important; everyone should strive to be as competent as possible.

_____ 16. It is important for an organization to treat its associates well.

_____ 17. Everyone in the organization should have high performance standards.

_____ 18. I want to work for an organization that promotes associates based on their ability rather than just on longevity.

_____ 19. Associates should be paid an equitable wage regardless of their gender or national origin.

_____ 20. An organization should have a good benefit package.

Box 2.8 Continued

_____ 21. I am willing to work long hours, weekends, and holidays in order to be successful in my career because that is my priority.

Scoring: Match your answers to the preceding statements to the following key. For example, if you put a 7 next to statement 1, place a 7 after the 1 in Group 1 in the key. Similarly, if you put a 6 next to statement 11, place a 6 after the 11 in Group 2 in the key.

Group 1	Group 2	Group 3
1. ____	2. ____	3. ____
6. ____	4. ____	5. ____
7. ____	9. ____	8. ____
12. ____	11. ____	10. ____
15. ____	13. ____	14. ____
17. ____	16. ____	18. ____
19. ____	20. ____	21. ____
Total ____	____	____

Interpretation: Your total in Group 1 measures the importance you assign to work-related values for people in general. Your total in Group 2 measures work-related values in an organizational context. Your total in Group 3 focuses on your own work-related values.

Pulling It All Together

Remember that values are a reflection of your personality. Each, to some degree, reinforces the other and provides an integrated set of beliefs and behaviors that create a lifestyle that works well for you. For example, you may enjoy taking risks and assuming responsibility (personality) and thus feel comfortable managing a restaurant where you are given freedom to do things your own way (values).[7] In drawing all of this together, it is useful to construct a composite of your findings. What type of individual are you? What do you like and dislike? Do you think you have a personality and value system that will allow you to be successful in the hospitality industry? What do you need to do to better prepare yourself for a career in this field? You can obtain answers to these types of questions by asking yourself key insightful queries. Six of these are provided in Box 2.9. After you answer these, compare your responses to those of others in the class and notice how your personality, needs, desires, and aspirations differ from theirs.

Box 2.9
Key Personal Insight Questions

Answer each of the following questions in 25 words or less. Then compare your responses to those of others in the class and note both similarities and differences.

1. Why are you majoring in hospitality management?

2. What do you want to do after you graduate?

3. What are your three most positive traits?

4. Of what are you most proud?

5. What are some of your current life achievements, awards, or victories?

6. Where was your best working experience? Why?

SUMMARY

1. Personality is an individual's characteristics and behaviors, organized in a way that reflects the unique adjustments the person makes to his or her environment. There are a number of factors that influence personality development. These include genetics, environment, cultural and social factors, and socialization. Additionally, life events often play a role.

2. One way to gain insight into your personality is to fill out a self-evaluation profile that describes your behavior, and ask someone who knows you well to use an identical profile evaluation to describe you. Then you can make a comparison of your perceived profile with this individual's view of you. A similar approach can be used in examining your personal philosophy and work-related behaviors.

3. A value is something that is important to you. Values can be expressed in a number of ways, including instrumental values and terminal values. Additionally, Spraunger's value profile can be used. This profile focuses on six types of values: theoretical, economic, aesthetic, social, political, and religious. Most people in the hospitality industry tend to have high theoretical, economic, aesthetic, social, and/or political value scores, depending on the job and hierarchical position.

4. Work-related values identify things that are important on the job. Examples include the organization's reputation, a chance for advancement, and the desire to succeed.

KEY TERMS

personality	theoretical value
socialization	economic value
life events	aesthetic value
value	social value
instrumental value	political value
terminal value	religious value

REVIEW AND APPLICATION QUESTIONS

1. What is meant by the term *personality*? Define it in your own words.

2. Paula Gonzalez is a reservations clerk for a large hotel chain. What type of personality would Paula need in order to be successful in her job? Identify and describe four behaviors that would help make her effective.

3. Harry Baldwin graduated from college last month and has taken a job as a trainee at a five-star restaurant. Harry's current assignment is to become

familiar and comfortable with the clientele by helping to greet them at the entrance, show them to their table, and come around during their meal and ask, "Is everything all right? Is there anything I can do for you?" Harry's boss believes that there are two key factors for success in the restaurant business: great food and great ambiance. Harry is not going to be a chef, but he is being counted on to contribute to the establishment's atmosphere. What type of personality would he need to be successful in this assignment? Identify and describe three observable behaviors.

4. Sally Sondheim is the concierge at a very popular hotel in New York City. The hotel has a very high occupancy rate and is popular with both businesspeople and tourists. What type of behaviors would be important to Sally in carrying out her job? Focus your discussion on these five pairs of contrasting adjectives:

calm—excitable

aloof—sociable

insecure—stable

sophisticated—awkward

loud—soft-spoken

5. What are the four main determinants of personality development? Identify and describe each.

6. In what way do life events significantly influence future behavior? If possible, give an example from your own life.

7. What is meant by the term *value?* How does an instrumental value differ from a terminal value? Explain.

8. What is important to a person with high theoretical values? Economic values? Aesthetic values? Social values? Political values? Religious values?

9. Three individuals have applied for a job as manager of a large hotel. Each was given Spraunger's value profile test (240 points total). Here are the scores for each:

	Applicant 1	Applicant 2	Applicant 3
Theoretical	35	20	40
Economic	45	50	60
Aesthetic	40	50	20
Social	40	55	40
Political	36	30	60
Religious	44	35	20

Based solely on their scores, which one do you think would make the best hotel manager? Defend your answer.

10. Four individuals have applied for the job of customer liaison officer for a major international airline. Each was given Spraunger's value profile test (240 points total). Here are the scores for each:

	Applicant A	Applicant B	Applicant C	Applicant D
Theoretical	26	38	47	40
Economic	38	53	40	32
Aesthetic	36	22	41	40
Social	50	55	40	42
Political	40	47	27	31
Religious	50	25	45	55

Based solely on their scores, which one do you think would make the most effective customer liaison officer? Defend your answer.

SELF-FEEDBACK EXERCISE: INSIGHT INTO YOUR PERSONALITY

The following 20 statements are designed to provide insights regarding how you see yourself. In the blank space next to each of these statements, write the number that best describes how strongly you agree or disagree with the statement, or how true or false the statement is as it applies to you. Use the following key in filling out this exercise:

5 = Strongly agree; definitely true

4 = Generally agree; mostly true

3 = Neither agree nor disagree; neither true nor false

2 = Generally disagree; mostly false

1 = Strongly disagree; definitely false

Example:

_____4_____   I enjoy playing baseball.

The 4 in the space next to the statement indicates that you generally agree that you like to play baseball.

_____ **1.** In some circumstances in the past, I have taken the lead.

_____ **2.** Everyone should place trust in a supernatural force whose decisions he or she always obeys.

_____ **3.** As a rule, I assess my previous actions closely.

_____ **4.** What I earn depends on what I know and how hard I work.

_____ **5.** I often observe those around me to see how my words and actions affect them.

_____ **6.** Generally, those in authority do their share of the unpleasant jobs without passing them on to others.

_____ **7.** I like to perform activities involving selling or salesmanship.

_____ **8.** The remedy for social problems depends on eliminating dishonest, immoral, and mentally inferior people.

_____ **9.** The lowest type of person is the one who does not love and respect his or her parents.

_____ **10.** I would like to take on important responsibilities, such as starting my own restaurant or hotel.

_____ **11.** Most people today earn their pay by their own work.

_____ **12.** I tend to look into and analyze myself.

_____ **13.** My promotions depend more on whom I know than on how well I do my job.

_____ **14.** In a meeting I will speak up when I disagree with someone I am convinced is wrong.

_____ **15.** There are two kinds of people: the weak and the strong.

_____ **16.** I enjoy thinking about complex problems.

_____ **17.** I think it is better to work for a good boss than for myself.

_____ **18.** All children should be taught obedience and respect for authority.

_____ **19.** Those who are in public office usually put their own interests ahead of the public interest.

_____ **20.** Many times I would like to know the real reasons why some people behave as they do.

Scoring: Enter your answers to these questions in the appropriate space in the following scoring key. Where there is an asterisk before the number, use _reverse scoring_ by subtracting your answer from six, _i.e.,_ a 1 becomes a 5, a 4 becomes a 2, and so on.

Group 1	Group 2	Group 3	Group 4
4. ___	1. ___	*2. ___	3. ___
6. ___	7. ___	*8. ___	5. ___
11. ___	10. ___	*9. ___	12. ___
*13. ___	14. ___	*15. ___	16. ___
*19. ___	*17. ___	*18. ___	20. ___
Total ___	___	___	___

Interpretation: Divide each of your totals by five. If there are decimal points, such as in 3.4 or 4.1, keep them in your answers. On a scale of 1 to 5, your answers measure how you see yourself in each of four areas.

Average Score	The four areas represented by Groups 1 to 4, respectively, are these.
_____	1. Fairness—This score measures the extent to which you see the world as treating you fairly.
_____	2. Assertiveness—This score measures the extent to which you see yourself as assertive.
_____	3. Egalitarian—This score measures the extent to which you see yourself as being nonauthoritarian.
_____	4. Introspectiveness—This score measures the extent to which you see yourself as thinking about things that go on around you and trying to determine why they occur.

Assignment: Examine your scores and make a determination regarding how accurately they reflect your personality. Based on your answers, what have you learned about yourself that has been reinforced by this self-feedback exercise? What have you learned that you did not know before?

Now show your scores to someone who knows you and ask this individual to comment on the accuracy of your self-perceptions. Remember that you provided these insights, but those who know you may have other views about you and your personality. Note any differences between what your scores reveal and what this individual shares with you. This will provide you with additional insights that will help you answer the question, Who am I?

CASE 2.1: HE'D LIKE TO GIVE IT A TRY

Chuck Snow is thinking about buying a small 30-unit hotel in Colorado. The location makes it ideal for both winter and summer visitors. During the winter, guests come to ski nearby. During the summer, tourists come to see the sights, hike, and enjoy the mild climate. If Chuck buys the hotel, he will be open approximately 40 weeks a year. The other twelve weeks fall between the end of the ski season and spring, and between the end of the summer tourism and the beginning of the ski season.

For the last six years Chuck has been working as the manager of a much larger hotel in eastern New Jersey, about 35 minutes from downtown Manhattan. He lives approximately eight miles from the hotel and typically puts in a twelve-hour weekday and goes in for a few hours on Saturday and Sunday. If anyone needs to get hold of him, the assistant manager on duty has

Chuck's pager number; it usually takes no more than 30 minutes for Chuck to return the call.

For the last two years Chuck has been looking to buy a hotel and run his own business. "I already work almost 70 hours a week," he told his wife. "What's another five or ten hours? And right now I'm working for a salary. With my own place, I'd be working for me." Four months ago, Chuck learned that the Colorado hotel was for sale. He flew out, talked to the owners, and was given a selling price. Chuck believes that the two owners are somewhat flexible on this price, but there is not a lot of leeway for negotiating. After talking things over with his wife and some personal friends who are interested in making an investment, Chuck believes he can swing the deal. The big question is whether he has the personal skills and abilities to be successful.

Yesterday Chuck sat down and began listing the reasons why he believed he would do well in this new venture. Included on his list were the following personality traits:

hardworking	willing to take risks
persevering	sociable
willing to learn	kind
flexible	calm
confident	adventurous

1. Of the personality traits that Chuck has listed, which five do you believe would be of most value to him? Why?

2. What other traits will Chuck need to possess if he is to be successful? Identify and describe three.

3. In terms of Spraunger's value profile, which two types of values would be of most importance to Chuck? Why?

CASE 2.2: SHE LOVES THE WORK

For the last two years, Barbara Rabinowitz has been the manager of a travel agency. Before Barbara took over, the owner had considered closing the business. He did not want to run it personally, and everyone he hired to manage the agency proved ineffective. The owner decided to give the business one last chance. He heard from a mutual friend that Barbara, who had been working for a travel agency across town, was looking for an opportunity to manage her own agency. The owner interviewed Barbara and decided to give her the job. He has not regretted his decision.

When Barbara took over the reins, the company was losing $5,000 a month. The biggest problem was that expenses were too high. Barbara immediately began cutting overhead and streamlining the operation. She also started calling on potential customers and eventually managed to land seven big corporate accounts. The profit on these accounts is not very great because these companies shop for deals and always manage to get very competitive rates. Additionally, some of the major airlines have announced that they are going to put all travel agents on a fixed fee per ticket, which differs sharply from the percentage arrangement that has been common in the industry for many years. This means that Barbara will have to continue to monitor expenses closely. Nevertheless, she believes the agency will keep showing a healthy profit.

When asked about her successful management of the operation, Barbara offered the following insights. "I got into this business only because I had been laid off and was on my way to a job interview. As I was walking down the street, I bumped into the father of a high-school friend. I hadn't seen him since his son and I graduated. He asked me where I was going and when I told him, he suggested that I consider a job in a travel agency where he was a part-owner. I took the job, and within a couple of days I knew I was going to like this business. And I learned a lot in the three years I was there. I'll bet I eventually did every job in the place. So I knew how to manage an agency. From there I moved on to two other agencies, getting important experience each time, before coming to my present job. And what I like best about this work is that it never stops. There's always another challenge, always another problem. Sometimes I think that day-to-day management in this business means being able to put out one fire after another. However, I love the work. The constant action keeps my adrenalin flowing and my enthusiasm high. I couldn't ask for a better job."

1. In what way did a life event help shape Barbara's career? Explain.

2. In your own words, what type of personality does Barbara have? Describe her in five well-chosen adjectives.

3. What are Barbara's values? From the Spraunger list, choose the three types of values that are most important to her. Defend your choices.

ANSWERS TO BOX 2.1:
"WHAT ARE YOUR PERSONAL BELIEFS?"

1. True		11. False	
2. False		12. False	
3. False		13. False	
4. False		14. False	
5. False		15. True	
6. False		16. False	
7. True		17. True	
8. False		18. False	
9. True		19. True	
10. True		20. False	

ENDNOTES

1. Richard M. Hodgetts, *Organizational Behavior* (New York: Macmillan, 1991), p. 56.
2. Also see Gary Dessler, *Managing Organizations in an Era of Change* (Fort Worth: Dryden Press, 1995), pp. 416–471.
3. Fred Luthans, *Organizational Behavior,* 7th ed. (New York: McGraw-Hill, 1995), pp. 119–121.
4. For more on personal values, see Douglas A. Benton, *Applied Human Relations: An Organizational Approach,* 5th ed. (Upper Saddle River, N.J.: Prentice-Hall, 1995), pp. 42–46.
5. For some insights to this topic, see Franklin Becker and Fritz Steele, *Workplace by Design* (San Francisco: Jossey-Bass, 1995).
6. Richard M. Hodgetts and Donald F. Kuratko, *Effective Small Business Management,* 5th ed. (Fort Worth: Dryden Press, 1995), pp. 34–35.
7. Donald F. Kuratko and Richard M. Hodgetts, *Entrepreneurship: A Contemporary Approach,* 3rd ed. (Fort Worth: Dryden Press, 1995), pp. 95–120.

CHAPTER THREE

Communicating Effectively

LEARNING OBJECTIVES

Communication is critical in helping you get things done. Yet despite its importance, research shows that most people are not very good communicators. One reason is that they fail to understand how the communication process works, where their messages break down, and how to improve their communicative ability. The overriding objective of this chapter is to examine some of the most useful ways of communicating effectively through the use of well-developed strategies. When you have finished studying all of the material in this chapter, you will be able to:

1. Define the term *communication* and explain the communication process.
2. Identify problem ownership and the most effective communication approaches to use both when the other person has the problem and when you have the problem.
3. Discuss the value of assisting skills and understand the benefits of active listening.
4. Compare and contrast I-messages and you-messages and write an effective confrontative message.
5. Describe how face-to-face communication and win-win strategies can be effective strategies.

How Communication Works

Communication is the process of transmitting meanings from sender to receiver. In order to improve your ability to communicate effectively, it is useful to understand how this process works.[1]

In all, there are eight key elements in effective communication. These are diagrammed in Figure 3.1.

First, there must be an idea or message that you want to send to someone. Second, you need to organize or encode this message in some way so that it can be clearly communicated. Third, you must put the idea into a form in which it can be transmitted. Fourth, you need to be aware of noise or other barriers to communication that will prevent the receiver from understanding you. Fifth, those to whom you are communicating must receive the message. Sixth, the receiver must correctly decode or interpret the message. Seventh, you need to ensure that the communication resulted in the desired action. Eighth, if there was a communication breakdown, you need to use feedback to help you make the appropriate correction.[2] The feedback loop is important in helping you communicate more effectively because it allows you to make adjustments whenever there is a problem.[3] The key elements in Figure 3.1 can be used to analyze and evaluate the communication process for every form of communication, regardless of whether you are dealing with an internal customer (an associate or manager) or an external customer (a client or guest).

Problem Ownership

The way that you implement the preceding process will depend on whether or not you are dealing with a problem and, if so, identifying who owns this problem. Once you have done this, you are in a position to take the appropriate action. The following sections examine how this process works, as well as highlight the major roadblocks that can prevent effective communication.

There are three categories of problem ownership: someone else's problem, your problem, or no problem. The first question you need to answer is: Into which of the three categories does the situation fall? Here are six statements made to you by guests and other associates. In each situation, indicate whether there is a problem and, if so, who has it: the other person or you.

Situation 1

Guest: Good morning. How are you?

(Problem? ___ Yes ___ No

If yes, who owns it? ___ the other person ___ you)

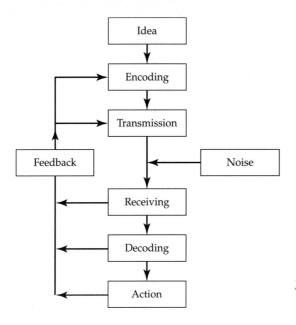

Figure 3.1 *The Communication Process in Action*

Situation 2

Associate: I'm so frustrated because every time I call you I get your silly voice mail.

(Problem? ___ Yes ___ No

If yes, who owns it? ___ the other person ___ you)

Situation 3

Guest: Can you tell me where I can get a newspaper?

(Problem? ___ Yes ___ No

If yes, who owns it? ___ the other person ___ you)

Situation 4

Hotel Manager: I'm concerned that your office is a mess.

(Problem? ___ Yes ___ No

If yes, who owns it? ___ the other person ___ you)

Situation 5

Guest: I've been waiting fifteen minutes for the valet to bring my car. Do you have any idea where he might have gone?

(Problem? ___ Yes ___ No

If yes, who owns it? ___ the other person ___ you)

Situation 6

Associate: You and I have been assigned to prepare the monthly cost control report. You never do your share of the work and I end up doing it. You are not taking this responsibility seriously and I resent it!

(Problem? ___ Yes ___ No

If yes, who owns it? ___ the other person ___ you)

Let us examine each of these six situations. In situation 1, there is no problem. You would simply reply in kind, such as, "I'm fine, thank you. How are you?"

In situation 2, the associate has the problem. After all, it is he or she who is frustrated by the "silly voice mail."

In situation 3, both you and the guest have the problem. This example is particularly important in explaining problem ownership; in the hospitality industry, a guest's problem is often also an associate's problem. This is one of the unique features of a service industry. Additionally, it is not sufficient to simply take steps to solve the problem. You have to ensure that your actions address the matter to the satisfaction of the guest. For example, if a guest wants to buy a newspaper, you may be able to direct the individual to the proper locale by saying, "You can get a paper at the end of this hallway on the right, in the gift shop." In that case, the problem is then resolved. However, if you are working for a hotel or organization where you are trained to walk the guest to the requested location, the problem remains with you. Remember, again, in customer service situations, when a guest has a problem, you also have a problem.

In situation 4, the manager owns the problem. This is because he or she is upset over the condition of your office.

In situation 5, there is a problem and both you and the guest own it. In this situation you would need to convey your concern to the guest and then take action to find out what is going on. For example, you might respond, "Let me check on the status of your car and get right back to you."

In situation 6, there is a problem and the associate owns it. This is because the associate is the one who is upset about the preparation of the report.

It is important to learn to distinguish the source of the problem (*i.e.,* where it is being experienced) and thus its owner. When we determine that the other person owns the problem, we use different communication skills than when we own the problem. Generally speaking, when the other person owns the problem, you are most helpful if you can facilitate his or her own problem solving. In doing so, it is helpful to remember that the person who owns the problem owns the solution. However, this guideline is not applicable if you are in a customer service position in which your job is to take care of your guest's problem. It is also inappropriate when your supervisor has a problem with you and you want to keep your job. Finally, if people other than guests or supervisors have a problem with you, you can listen so that you understand what is upsetting them and then choose whether or not you want to change your behavior to accommodate their needs.

How to Communicate
When Others Own the Problem

When the other person has a problem, you have to be careful regarding how you communicate with the individual. In particular, you need to be familiar with the common types of roadblocks that prevent effective communication, as well as know how to handle the situation constructively.

Typical Roadblocks

There are many types of roadblocks that prevent effective communication when the other person owns the problem. Table 3.1 identifies and describes twelve of the most common as applied to a particular situation. Imagine that another student is telling you about the problems she is having at school. She feels bored and unmotivated and is considering dropping out. The coursework is demanding too much time, considering all her other problems at home. Note how each of the twelve responses in Table 3.1 creates a communication problem. What is the potential negative consequence for each roadblock?

The answer to the preceding question is that the individual is sending a message that may be negatively regarded by the receiver. You may want to "help" by giving advice or asking questions to get at the facts. In spite of good intentions, however, these attempts often create more problems than they solve, and they impede the flow of communication from the other person. Simply put, this is not the way to help a person who owns a problem. There are far more constructive ways, and by using them you can greatly increase your personal communication effectiveness. Before examining these, however, we want to look briefly at other common mistakes that often accompany the roadblocks in Table 3.1.

Common Mistakes

There are two common mistakes that people often make in dealing with someone who has a problem: poor empathy and improper inference.

Poor Empathy. Empathy is the process of putting yourself in another's place and seeing things from that person's point of view.[4] Sometimes this can be

Table 3.1 Typical Communication Roadblocks

Type	Example	Problems
Ordering or commanding	You must study harder. Just toughen up.	Can produce fear or active resistance. May lead to the listener "testing" the statement by deliberately challenging it.
Warning or threatening	If you don't pass your classes, you'll never get a better job.	Can cause resentment, anger, rebellion. Invites the listener to test the consequences.
Moralizing or preaching	You should finish what you start.	Creates guilt feelings. Can cause the listener to "dig in" and offer resistance.
Advising or giving solutions	If I were you, I would stick it out for another semester.	Implies that the listener is not capable of solving the problem. Can cause dependency or resistance.
Persuading with logic or arguing	The facts show that 80 percent of students who leave don't come back.	Provokes counterarguments. Causes the listener to tune out.
Judging, criticizing, or blaming	You're not thinking clearly.	Implies incompetency or poor judgment. Cuts off communication over fear of negative judgment.
Praising or agreeing	I think you're doing a great job. Keep it up.	Can be seen as patronizing or manipulative. Can cause anxiety when the listener's perception does not match the speaker's praise.
Name-calling or ridiculing	Okay, Miss Quitter. You're a loser.	Often provokes verbal retaliation. Can have a negative effect on the self-image of the listener.
Analyzing or diagnosing	You're just tired. You don't really mean that.	Can be frustrating. Can make the listener feel either trapped or not believed.
Reassuring or sympathizing	Don't worry. It's nothing to get upset about.	Can cause the listener to feel misunderstood. Can make the listener believe that it is not all right to feel bad.

Table 3.1 Continued

Type	Example	Problems
Probing or questioning	How long before you graduate?	Since any answer may result in further criticism, the listener may avoid the question or reply with "non-answers." The listener may lose sight of his or her problem while trying to address the speaker's questions.
Diverting, withdrawing, or use of sarcasm	Let's talk about more pleasant things.	Implies that the current conversation is to be avoided. Implies that the listener's problems are unimportant or petty.

Source: Adapted from Dr. Thomas Gordon, *Teacher Effectiveness Training Workbook* (Solana Beach, Calif.: Effectiveness Training, Inc., 1987), pp. 52–54.

extremely difficult because you cannot get sufficient feedback or because you misread the information.

When Clark and Judy Mullen checked into the Fairmore Hotel, they learned that their reservation had been misplaced. They waited 90 minutes in the coffee shop before a room was ready. For the three days they were at the Fairmore, they encountered a number of problems, including a leaky toilet, trouble with the television reception, slow room service, and difficulty getting tee times on the hotel's golf course—even though this was supposed to be part of the guest package. A few hours before Clark checked out, he visited the hotel manager and told him about these problems. The manager listened quietly and promised to adjust the bill accordingly. When Clark checked out, he found that the manager had deducted $50 from the $1,674 bill. A few days later the manager received a call from the chairman of the board of Fairmore, who suggested that Clark be credited for another $500 on his bill. The manager agreed to do so immediately, but defended his actions by telling the chairman, "I had no idea that he felt $50 was not enough. I wish he had told me instead of calling you. I would have been happy to accommodate him."

What went wrong? The hotel manager misread Clark's concern and gave him a small deduction on the bill. Quite obviously Clark felt he was entitled to a great deal more consideration and, since he apparently knew the chairman of the board, he called the individual and asked the person to intercede on his behalf. How could the problem have been avoided? The answer is that the manager should have discussed the situation with Clark and either made a preliminary suggestion ("Let me take $50 off the bill") or tossed the matter back to Clark by saying, "What can I do to correct this situation to your satisfaction?" Perhaps the manager did not realize the size of the final bill. Certainly $50 is not much of a deduction. Or maybe the manager failed to realize how upset Clark was. In either event, it is unlikely that the individual knew of Clark's relationship with the chairman of the board. Simply stated, the manager failed to perceive the significance of the problem and wound up with an upset customer who had other avenues of recourse to resolve the problem. How could all of this have been avoided? By fully understanding the problem, perceiving the problem from Clark's point of view, and getting his input on how the problem could be resolved.

Improper Inferences. An *inference* is an assumption made by the receiver of a message. Whenever vague or incomplete transmissions occur, the person receiving the message has to fill in the hidden meanings by making assumptions about what is being communicated. And each time the person errs when doing this, his or her understanding of the message moves further and further away from the intended meaning. One of the most effective ways of dealing with this problem is to be able to identify when inferences are being used. When you can do this, you are then in a position to deal with them. The story in Box 3.1 reinforces this idea. Read the story and complete the accompanying assignment. Remember that each of the ten statements at the end of the story is true (the story directly states this fact), false (the story says just the opposite), or inferential (the statement may be true or false, but it requires you to make some assumptions). When you are finished, check your answers with the key at the end of the chapter.

How many of the statements did you correctly identify? The average number of right responses is five. Most people miss the inferences because they read facts into the story that were not directly stated. How can you avoid falling into the "inference trap"? The best way is to be sure that you understand what is being communicated and ask questions when you are unsure. In this way, you are able to fill in the inference gaps with facts. Effectively dealing with inferences is an important part of learning how to communicate when you have a problem.

Useful Assisting Techniques

Now that we have discussed common mistakes, we will review effective techniques that can be used when the other person owns the problem. Assisting techniques are methods of helping the person with the problem clarify his or her feelings and in the process often facilitate his or her own problem solving. In employing these techniques, remember that you are *not* responsible for solving the other person's problem. When there is genuine trust, empathy, and

Box 3.1
Mary's Ordeal

Mary Phelps is director of human resources for a major corporation. Last month Mary called a senior executive at the nearby Gallman Estates Hotel, a five-star establishment with a championship golf course. "I have a potential hire coming in next week," Mary explained, "and I want him to have first-class treatment. He is a university professor and Nobel Prize winner and we are interested in talking to him about some important business. I would like to reserve the best suite you have available for the 20th through the 23rd of next month. I would also like to have your limo pick him up at the airport on the 20th and take him back to the airport on the 24th in time for his plane. Finally, on the evening of the 20th I would like to reserve a table for six in your main dining room at 7:30 P.M."

The executive told Mary, "Don't worry about a thing. I'll take care of everything." He then wrote down the professor's name and his time of arrival and departure.

Mary called the hotel at 5 P.M. on the 20th and spoke to the professor. He had arrived only 30 minutes earlier, and he and his wife were in the process of unpacking. "It took us a little longer to get here because there were three other people in the limousine and they were dropped off before us. However, we got here okay and the room is fine. It has a wonderful queen-size bed, and I can see part of the golf course from my balcony."

Mary was puzzled by the size and location of the room. She had felt certain that the professor would be given a pent-house suite with a king-size bed and that the room would overlook the first fairway. She was even more surprised when her party of six was later escorted to a table in the direct flow of traffic, in the middle of the restaurant. There was little opportunity to talk about anything important because so many people were within earshot. This was the first time Mary had ever had a reservation in the club that she was not put in a small, private dining room.

The meetings with the professor went extremely well, and Mary was delighted with the results. However, as she walked him to the limousine that would take him back to the airport, she saw that there were two other couples in the limo. As she reflected on the professor's visit, she wondered whether in the future it would be a good idea to do business with the other five-star hotel in the area.

"I'm rather disappointed in the service I received," she later told the senior executive from Gallman Estates. "I thought your people would do a much better job for us." The executive seemed somewhat surprised and asked if they could meet for lunch and talk about the problem. Mary agreed to do so, but she seems determined to move her future business to the other hotel.

Statements

Indicate whether you believe each of the following statements is true (T), false (F), or an inference (I), based on the information in the story.

Box 3.1　Continued

T　F　I　　**1.** Mary is director of human resources for a major corporation.

T　F　I　　**2.** The professor did not receive a hotel suite, as requested by Mary.

T　F　I　　**3.** Mary asked the hotel executive to send a special limousine for the professor.

T　F　I　　**4.** The hotel did not realize that the professor was going to be accompanied by his wife.

T　F　I　　**5.** The professor's hotel room overlooked part of the golf course.

T　F　I　　**6.** Mary felt that the table reservation in the dining room was not as good as those she had been given on previous occasions.

T　F　I　　**7.** Mary thought that the restaurant was going to give her a private room for the dinner.

T　F　I　　**8.** Mary's reservation at the dining room was for herself, the professor, and four other managers.

T　F　I　　**9.** The limousine taking the professor back to the airport was also dropping off other people at various terminals.

T　F　I　**10.** Mary is going to take her future business to the other five-star hotel in the area.

acceptance, a number of useful assisting techniques help convey these feelings. The following sections examine four of these.

Silence. Silence can be a very constructive way of helping someone else deal with a problem. Quite often, silence encourages the other person to talk, simply because the individual is not being interrupted. By letting the other person tell you what is bothering him or her, you promote communication and provide a basis for problem solving.

Acknowledgments. *Acknowledgments* are nonevaluative responses that indicate you are paying attention. These can be either verbal or nonverbal, just as long as they let the other person know that you are tuned in to what he or she is saying. Examples include saying "Uh-huh," "Oh," "I see," and nodding your head. Here is an example of how they can be used by a manager:

Associate: I'll never get this report finished on time.

Manager: (Silence, nods)

Associate: I have been here since 3 P.M. and everyone else on the committee has dropped their material on my desk and expect me to coordinate it all into a final report.

Manager: Uh-huh.

Associate: George didn't get all of the data we needed on guest registrations, and Margaret failed to provide the information on guaranteed reservations.

Manager: I see.

Associate: Well, I'm not going to fail just because they don't want to contribute their part of the effort.

Manager: Uh-huh.

Associate: I'm going to take what I've got here and pull it together as best I can. Then we can have a meeting in the morning and go over what else we still need.

Manager: (Nods)

Obviously the associate was upset over the failure to get adequate support from the other members of the committee. However, after talking about it for a few minutes, the individual decided to go ahead and make the best of a bad situation. Notice that the manager did not direct or guide the individual except to encourage the person to keep talking.

Door Openers. *Door openers* are statements that encourage an individual to say more, or go deeper. Examples include verbal comments such as, "Do you want to talk about it?" or "That's interesting; go on." These messages all have one common characteristic: they are open-ended. They contain no evaluation of what is being said.

Active Listening. Silence, acknowledgments, and door openers do not demonstrate that the listener understands what the speaker has said. Active listening can help overcome this shortcoming. *Active listening* is the giving of feedback by mirroring the sender's message in an effort to demonstrate understanding of the other person's meanings and feelings. This approach makes the speaker feel that his or her ideas are respected, understood, and accepted. It also helps the speaker clarify personal feelings and can provide cathartic release. The technique also facilitates identification of the real issues and starts the problem-solving process. Here is an example of active listening in which one associate is talking to another:

Jim: I'm so fed up with the lack of appreciation I get from my boss. The more I do, the more she expects me to do. It never seems to end.

Lourdes: You feel frustrated with the constant workload and lack of appreciation by your boss.

Jim: Yeah, I do. I would be able to deal with the work if she would occasionally compliment me. She never gives me any positive feedback.

Lourdes: You'd like to hear her acknowledge your hard work.

Jim: I know it's not in her nature, but I need to feel appreciated to stay motivated. It's tough for me to work hard without a break or something. I would love to have an occasional celebration to recharge my batteries.

Lourdes: (Nods head.)

Jim: Maybe I'll take a long weekend and reward myself. I haven't had a vacation in a long time. I think it would do me good to get away for a few days.

Notice in this dialogue that Lourdes did not tell Jim what to do. She listened and reflected his feelings, which helped him determine what he was going to do. In the process, she kept the lines of communication open, while leaving the problem where it belonged—with Jim. Active listening can be a very powerful skill. Here are three examples of active listening responses:

"As I understand it, what you are saying is..."

"Do you mean that . . ."

"So your feeling is that . . ."

The key to effective paraphrasing is to listen closely to what the other person is saying and then capture the meaning of the message.

Another useful technique is to reflect the underlying feelings of the speaker by putting yourself in that person's shoes. This approach can be effective regardless of whether the other person has a problem or is extremely pleased about something. Here are three examples:

"I suppose that must make you rather anxious."

"It sounds like that upsets you quite a bit."

"It seems like you feel proud of your accomplishment."

There are seven important attitudes that are necessary for active listening.

1. Have a deep sense of trust in the ability of the other person to solve his or her own problem.

2. Be able to accept the feelings of the other person, despite the fact that they may be different from your own.

3. Realize that these feelings often are transitory and exist only for the moment, and that active listening helps the other person move from momentary feeling to momentary feeling.

4. Be willing to help the other person deal with his or her problem and make time for doing so.

5. Be able to "be with" the person who is experiencing the problem, but maintain a separate identity and do not get caught up in the feelings of this person to the point of losing your separateness.

6. Understand that when people begin sharing their problems or concerns, they often start out with a superficial or indirect statement; getting them

to focus on the real problem requires some encouragement and support-ive listening.

7. Be prepared to respect the privacy and confidential nature of sensitive communications by never gossiping or openly discussing people's prob-lems with others.[5]

Active listening is important because it offers a variety of benefits that can both promote and sustain the flow of ideas between the two parties. Some of the most important benefits are that active listening:

1. Encourages the other person to speak his or her mind fully.

2. Provides the speaker with a sounding board for solving problems.

3. Offers a motivation benefit to the speaker, who feels important in the eyes of the listener.

4. Encourages the speaker to think through his or her problem and not be quickly diverted.

5. Encourages the speaker to become more open and less defensive in com-munication.

6. Makes the speaker feel that his or her ideas are worthwhile and can be helpful in stimulating creative thinking.

7. Makes the speaker listen to his or her own ideas more carefully.

8. Provides the listener with a wealth of information on facts, attitudes, and emotions that were previously unexpressed.

9. Provides a growth experience for both the speaker and the listener.[6]

How to Communicate When You Own the Problem

When you own a problem, there are a number of ways to confront the situa-tion effectively. One of the most helpful is an assertive approach that is neither too aggressive nor too passive.

Effective Use of I-Messages

An *I-message* is often called a "responsibility statement." When a person uses an I-message, the individual takes responsibility for his or her own inner con-dition. In particular, I-messages meet three confrontive criteria for effective communication and change: (1) they have a high probability of promoting a willingness to change; (2) they contain minimal negative evaluation of the other party; and (3) they do not injure the relationship between the sender and receiver. In addition, I-messages foster honesty by presenting the sender as an individual who is interested in creating and maintaining a meaningful dialogue with the receiver. Here are three contrasts between I-messages and you-messages:

I-message	You-message
I get upset when you interrupt me because it breaks my train of thought.	When you interrupt me, you are being rude.
I feel impatient when you are late for our luncheon appointment and I waste my time waiting for you.	You always try to do too much before meeting me.
When I get this material after 3 P.M. on Thursday, I have to drop every-thing else in order to enter the data immediately and I feel resentful.	You need to plan your time bet-ter and stop goofing off.

I-messages differ from you-messages, such as "You are irresponsible," "You never pull your weight around here," or "You are inconsiderate." In most cases, you-messages provoke a defensive response and an argument. In contrast, I-messages are more likely to encourage an open dialogue because they are descriptive rather than evaluative, and they focus on communicating the speaker's feelings and needs to the other person. In some cases, simply becoming aware of the effects of one's behavior and the feelings it provokes can be enough to make people change their negative behaviors.

Use of Assertiveness

Assertiveness is the ability to communicate clearly and directly what you need or want from another person in a way that does not deny or infringe upon the other's rights.[7] Table 3.2 provides some important contrasts between nonassertive, assertive, and aggressive responses. A close reading of the assertive communications shows that the individual makes wide use of "I-messages." I-messages are clear codes about the speaker's inner condition (as opposed to you-messages, which blame the other person.) *Confrontive I-messages* have three components: (1) a specific and nonblaming description of the behavior exhibited by the other person; (2) the concrete effects of that behavior; and (3) the speaker's feelings about the behavior. Here are some examples, expressed in terms of these three components:

Behavior	Effects	Feelings
When you come late to our meetings	we have to spend valuable time bringing you up to date on where we are	and I resent this.
When you keep interrupting me	I lose my train of thought and don't get to make my point	and this makes me angry.

Table 3.2 A Comparison of Nonassertive, Assertive, and Aggressive Responses

	Nonassertive (No Influence)	Assertive (Positive Influence)	Aggressive (Negative Influence)
VERBAL	Apologetic words, veiled meanings, hedging; failure to come to the point. Rambling; disconnected. At a loss for words. Failure to say what you really mean. Qualifying statements with "I mean," "you know."	Statement of wants. Honest statement of feelings. Objective words. Direct statements, which say what you mean. "I" statements.	"Loaded" words. Accusations. Descriptive, subjective terms. Imperious, superior words. "You" statements that blame or label.
NONVERBAL General demeanor	Actions instead of words, hoping someone will guess what you want. Looking as if you don't mean what you say.	Attentive listening behavior. Generally assured manner, communicating caring and strength.	Exaggerated show of strength. Flippant, sarcastic style. Air of superiority.
Voice	Weak, hesitant, soft, sometimes wavering.	Firm, warm, well modulated, relaxed.	Tensed, shrill, loud, shaky; cold, "deadly quiet," demanding; superior, authoritarian.
Eyes	Averted, downcast, teary, pleading.	Open, frank, direct. Eye contact, but not staring.	Expressionless, narrowed, cold, staring; not really "seeing" others.
Stance and posture	Leaning for support, stooped, excessive head nodding.	Well balanced, straight on, erect, relaxed.	Hands on hips, feet apart. Stiff, rigid. Rude, imperious.
Hands	Fidgety, fluttery, clammy.	Relaxed motions.	Clenched. Abrupt gestures, finger-pointing, fist pounding.

Source: Elaina Zuker, *Mastering Assertiveness Skills: Power and Positive Influence at Work* (New York: AMACOM, 1983).

Knowing When to Shift Gears

While I-messages produce less defensiveness from others than do you-messages, it is obvious that no one welcomes hearing that his or her behavior is causing someone else a problem, no matter how the message is phrased. Even the best-constructed I-messages can cause the other person to feel hurt, embarrassed, defensive, angry, or sad. So it is important to stay alert to these reactions and know when to shift gears from confrontation back to active listening.

Manager: I get upset when you come late to these meetings because I have to fill you in on what you missed. (I-statement)

Associate: I was busy working on that new marketing brochure. I thought you told me that it was top priority. I've been working on it all week.

Manager: You thought that the brochure was more important than the meeting. (Active listening)

Associate: Yes, I did.

Manager: The brochure is important. However, I also want you to attend the meetings on time. (I-message)

Associate: I was trying to slip in quietly. I didn't think I interrupted you.

Manager: You seem a little surprised that it's such a problem to me even when you try to be quiet. (Active listening)

Associate: Well, now I can see your point about needing to fill me in and I'll try to get here on time in the future.

Manager: That would sure help me. Thanks.

Once the manager realized that the I-message was meeting resistance, the manager switched gears and used active listening. This tends to convey understanding to the other person, which makes the individual more receptive to your message.

Other Useful Communication Approaches

Regardless of who has the problem, there are some communication approaches that are useful in most situations and warrant discussion. Two of these are face-to-face communication and emphasis on a win-win approach.

Face-to-Face Communication

One of the most effective ways of communicating with people is on a face-to-face basis. If you have a concern with an associate's work performance, it often helps to speak to the individual directly. If your boss has left you a memo asking you to handle a particular assignment and you do not have time to squeeze this work into your schedule, see if it is possible to talk to him or her about it personally and present your reasons in a face-to-face meeting. If information, especially bad news, is conveyed in written form, it often gets a chilly reception. How would you feel if you received an interoffice memo transferring you to another department? Would you not have preferred that your boss called you in and told you directly that you were being transferred?

Face-to-face communication is also important in handling customer concerns. When someone registers a complaint about his or her bill or is upset because housekeeping made up the room but failed to leave a sufficient number of bath towels, he or she appreciates the help the hotel can provide in resolving the problem. However, customers like it even more when this assistance is provided in person. Before doing so, however, you must be sure to do your homework. For example, if you are going to have a face-to-face meeting with a guest, you must know the nature of the individual's problem and also know the steps, if any, that your associates have taken to resolve the problem. Armed with this information, you are then in a position to listen and offer assistance. Here is an example of how a manager can handle the situation of a guest who feels he is being overcharged:

Guest: Thank you for coming by to talk to me about my bill. There are a number of items here that I believe should be taken off.

Manager: I have already spoken with Miss Rodriguez, who filled in me in on your concerns. So I have a pretty good idea of the charges you are questioning. However, just to be sure we're on the same wavelength, would you put a checkmark next to them on the bill?

Guest: They are the six that I have marked just to the right of each charge.

Manager: I see. The first two deal with charges for items from the minibar. The next two are for phone calls. The last two are for city and local taxes that are assessed by governmental agencies and are passed on to all guests.

Guest: My concerns are these. I think the charge for liquor in the minibar is far too high. The phone calls were not mine. And I don't feel I should have to pay room assessments in addition to the room charge I have already paid.

Manager: Well, let me see how I can be helpful. Regarding the minibar charges, these rates are posted on the price sheet that is placed on the top of the minibar. This information was readily available to you. However, in this case let's consider the first drink a complimentary one and remove it from the bill. If you say these two phone calls are not yours, I'll have them deducted. The taxes, however, must remain because we are legally required by law to pass them along to you. We cannot roll them into the price of the room because we are legally required to provide full disclosure of all taxes.

Guest: Well, now that you've personally explained things to me and have been willing to meet me halfway, I agree. I'll pay the rest of the charges. Thanks for all of your help.

Manager: My pleasure. If you have any other problems, here is my business card. Call me any time.

Notice how the manager was able to diffuse the problem by personally meeting with the guest and discussing the matter. The individual did not talk to the guest over the phone or rely on the written bill to convey the message, "Here is your bill. Please pay it." The guest had concerns and the manager listened, explained, and accommodated the individual.

Communicating in Meetings

Sometimes it is necessary to communicate with groups in meetings. In these cases, it is important to remember that there is likely to be limited time for discussion because of the number of people in the group, so the information has to be carefully prepared and easily understood. Three of the most helpful rules for doing this are (1) make things simple by not communicating more than two or three important ideas; (2) communicate in small bites by introducing and then carefully explaining each of the ideas; and (3) present the information in a way that the participants can readily understand and/or apply.

Another useful technique when communicating with groups in meetings is to have an agenda and to distribute it to each person before the meeting. This lets everyone know the purpose and nature of the get-together. Additionally, agenda items should be carefully sequenced. For example, if there are five items and two of them are going to require more discussion than the others, these should be sandwiched in between simpler, easier-to-handle items. So the meeting should begin with an issue on which everyone can quickly agree, and then move on to another easy issue. Then one of the difficult items should be handled. This should be followed by another easy item, and the other difficult one should be addressed last. One reason for putting a difficult issue last is that most people like to finish meetings on time. So there is pressure on the group members to reach a decision on the matter, so that the meeting can finish as scheduled.

Nonverbal Communication

People frequently communicate without speaking. These forms of nonverbal communication usually fall into two categories: kinesics and proxemics. *Kinesics* is body language. Examples include facial expressions, eye contact, posture, and gestures. Research reveals that these forms of nonverbal communication are often more important than what is being said. For example, in the case of eye contact, researchers have found that many people believe that if the other person does not look them in the eye, it is a sign that the person is dishonest, uninterested, or lacking in confidence. Whether this is true or not, the finding helps explain why eye contact in U.S. society if so important.

Another example is provided by posture. The ways that people stand, walk, and carry themselves provide clues about their attitude. For example, when people are certain about what they are saying, they are likely to stand erect and move vigorously. When they are unsure of themselves, they are more likely to slouch or move tentatively. Without saying a word, people use posture to convey messages.

The same is true regarding gestures. Examples include shrugging one's shoulders (indicating that the person does not know something or is unsure of it), leaning forward toward the speaker (typically a sign of interest), or forming an OK sign with the thumb and index finger (an indication that the person agrees with what is being communicated).

Taken collectively, body language is often used to supplement verbal language. The same is true of *proxemics,* which is the use of physical space to convey information. A good example is where one person stands in relation to another. The closer the proximity, the more likely that the two individuals are friends or are conveying information that they do not want anyone else to hear. Another example is the way that people lay out their offices. An individual who places the visitor's chair on the opposite side of the desk from his own is conveying a more formal relationship than the individual who places the visitor's chair at the side of the desk so that the distance between the two people is reduced. Proxemics can also be used to convey status. For example, a hotel manager will have a larger office than lower-level associates. The size of the room lets everyone know that the manager is important. Additionally, corner offices or rooms with windows carry higher status, which in turn affects communication because people judge not only what is being said, but who is saying it.

A Win-Win Approach

Closely linked to the use of other communication approaches is the willingness to use a *win-win approach.*[8] Especially when you are dealing with potential conflict situations involving associates or guests, you want to be sure that your approach allows both of you to emerge feeling that the solution was a good one. In the situation described earlier, in which the hotel guest felt he had been overcharged, there were four potential outcomes: (1) lose-lose—both the manager and the guest could have been disappointed with the final results; (2) win-lose—the manager may have felt things went very well, but the guest was not satisfied; (3) lose-win—the manager may have felt that things went very poorly, but the guest was quite pleased with the outcome;

and (4) win-win—both sides could have felt that they came out ahead with the solution. Here are examples of each:

- Lose-lose: The manager grudgingly gave way on some of the bill while believing that the guest was taking advantage of the hotel; the guest, upset over the manager's unwillingness to be more responsive and cooperative, stormed out of the hotel and has never given it a nickel of his business since.

- Win-lose: The manager refused to budge on any of the items on the bill; the guest, in turn, refused to ever come back, in addition to encouraging his friends and associates never to use the hotel's services again.

- Lose-win: The manager allowed the guest to browbeat him into throwing out all of the disputed charges, resulting in the manager feeling he had been taken advantage of; the guest left feeling he had indeed gotten the best of the bargain.

- Win-win: The two individuals discussed the matter, the manager made some adjustments in the bill, and both sides agreed that this approach was acceptable.

This chapter has provided specific communication skills that are effective when dealing with problems. However, the skills are most helpful when you approach conflict with the intention of resolving it with a win-win solution. This solution must be acceptable to *both* parties.

SUMMARY

1. Communication is the process of transmitting meanings from sender to receiver. This process has eight key elements: ideas, encoding, transmission, noise, receiving, decoding, action, and feedback. Effective communication must address all eight elements if the intended meaning is to be properly conveyed and received.

2. One of the most effective ways of analyzing communication is by first determining if there is a problem and, if so, then identifying who has this problem. If the other person has the problem, the way to communicate effectively is different from when you own the problem. When the other person has the problem, it is important to avoid putting up typical road-blocks, such as those identified in Table 3.1, and to avoid committing common communication mistakes, such as poor empathy and improper inferences. It is also helpful to use assisting techniques such as silence, acknowledgments, door openers, and active listening.

3. When you own the problem, avoid using you-messages. It is more helpful to use I-messages and to be prepared to shift gears if the other person

becomes defensive. A confrontive message includes three parts: behavior, effect, and feeling.

4. In addition to the preceding methods, there are two other ways to achieve effective communication. One is to employ face-to-face communication. A second is to use a win-win approach in which all parties to the communiqué are agreeable to the final outcome.

KEY TERMS

communication	I-messages
empathy	assertiveness
inference	confrontive I-messages
acknowledgments	kinesics
door openers	proxemics
active listening	win-win approach

REVIEW AND APPLICATION QUESTIONS

1. George Wiley works at a very popular restaurant where management continually rotates work assignments. This week, for the first time, George was assigned to compiling the waiting list (the restaurant does not accept reservations) and calling people for their tables. By 8 P.M. the waiting time was around 90 minutes. At this point, a guest arrived with a large party and asked George, "Will the wait be very long? If so, I'd like to try one of the other nearby restaurants." George replied, "Compared to those others, it shouldn't be long at all." When the party was seated 90 minutes later, everyone in the group was angry; they told the server that they had been promised that the waiting time would be short. To prove their anger, they paid the bill but did not leave a tip. Since this is a rare occurrence at the restaurant, the server reported the incident to the restaurant manager, who in turn talked to George about what had happened. Based on the information in this story, what did George do wrong? Use Figure 3.1 to analyze the situation and identify where the problem occurred.

2. In the preceding story, who owned the problem? What communication mistakes were made in creating the problem? Be complete in your answer. What could the guest have done to prevent this situation? What could George have done to prevent this situation?

3. Bob Fitzgerald has come by to talk to Adrianne Forsythe and tells her, "I'm having all sorts of problems trying to tie my restaurant operations into the hotel's plan to upgrade its service quality. In particular, the decision to offer 24-hour room service is putting a major strain on my staff. I also need

more flexibility in salary negotiations with two of my chefs. As associate director of operations, you have the president's ear and I was wondering if you would talk to him for me and help resolve these problems." In this situation, who has the problem? What advice would you give to Adrianne regarding how to handle her communications with Bob? What should she be sure to do? What would you want her to avoid doing? Explain.

4. Sara Gomez walked out the front door of the hotel lobby and gave the claim check for her car to the valet. The individual looked at the ticket and sprinted away to the parking garage next door. After waiting 20 minutes, Sara asked one of the other valets when her car would be brought around. It took another ten minutes before someone finally brought the auto. As the individual waited for Sara to get into the vehicle, he said, "I'm sorry about the wait, but the valet who took your ticket was on his way to lunch and your car got lost in the shuffle."What is the communication problem here? How should it have been handled? If you were in charge of this end of the hotel's operation, what would you recommend to prevent this problem from recurring?

5. Sandy Bodwin arrived at her hotel at 6:10 P.M. Because she did not have a guaranteed reservation, she was told that her room had already been given to someone else and there were no other available rooms. Sandy did not know what to do. She was scheduled to attend a meeting at the hotel early the next morning. Because her plane had been scheduled to arrive at 3 P.M., she had not bothered to guarantee her room reservation. The reservations manager listened to Sandy's story and told her, "Stick around in the lobby for another 50 minutes and let's see if some of our other guests fail to arrive. We have a couple of guaranteed reservations that we're holding until 7 P.M. If one of those does not show up, I'll give you the room." Fortunately, this is what happened. The room was not as large as the one Sandy had reserved and it was located at the far end of the hotel, away from the conference rooms. However, she was happy with the arrangement and thanked the manager for his efforts. In what way did the manager use a win-win approach in helping solve Sandy's problem? How might the situation have ended up as a win-lose situation in which Sandy's problem was not resolved? How might the situation have ended up as a lose-lose situation for both parties?

SELF-FEEDBACK EXERCISE: WHAT TYPE OF LISTENER ARE YOU?

Read each of the following twelve statements, choose the response you would be most likely to use, and put an X next to that choice.

1. I'm sorry I was late getting to the restaurant this evening. I know how important it is for servers to be here on time, but the bus came early and I missed it and had to wait half an hour for another.

   _____ **a.** You'd better start getting here on time.

   _____ **b.** Does the bus often come early?

   _____ **c.** Everyone is late from time to time.

   _____ **d.** You seem upset over your tardiness.

2. I don't know when I'm going to get that special report done for the director of convention services. I'm already swamped with work.

   _____ **a.** You sound concerned over your workload.

   _____ **b.** Don't worry. Get to it as you go along.

   _____ **c.** How long have you been swamped with work?

   _____ **d.** All of us know the feeling, believe me.

3. Salary recommendations are to be submitted by next week. I wonder if I should talk to my team leader again to be sure that she remembers all of the important things I did this year.

   _____ **a.** Does she often change her mind when talked to?

   _____ **b.** Don't worry; a good person like you will also be well treated.

   _____ **c.** You appear concerned about your salary recommendation.

   _____ **d.** See if you can schedule a meeting with her for later today.

4. I'm beat. I don't think I can get anything else done today.

   _____ **a.** It happens to all of us. You can complete that work tomorrow.

   _____ **b.** Sit down and rest. You'll feel better in a little bit.

   _____ **c.** You sound exhausted.

   _____ **d.** What have you been doing that's got you so tired?

5. The word from upstairs is that there is going to be a restructuring of the entire operation and 10 percent of the workforce in this locale is going to be laid off. With my wife expecting our first child next month, this is the worst possible time for me to lose my job.

   _____ **a.** Why don't you ask the human resources manager if you're likely to be one of the 10 percent?

_____ **b.** Why do you think you might be one of the 10 percent laid off?

_____ **c.** Don't worry. Chances are you won't be affected.

_____ **d.** You seem nervous about the possibility that you might be one of the 10 percent to go.

6. I just had a call from the lawyer of the reservations clerk I terminated last week. The lawyer is threatening to bring a discrimination suit against us. He says his client was fired solely because she was a woman. This could be a real messy situation. You know how this organization hates lawsuits.

_____ **a.** You appear concerned that this situation could become messy.

_____ **b.** If she does, nobody can say it's your fault.

_____ **c.** You'd better call our own lawyer now.

_____ **d.** What could she base her lawsuit on?

7. Darn! Now I've got to fly down to Los Angeles and help coordinate that national convention program. I've been away from my family every week-end for a month. Pretty soon I won't have a family.

_____ **a.** Why don't you take them with you one of these times?

_____ **b.** A hotel manager's family has to realize that traveling is part of the deal.

_____ **c.** Relax. Next month you'll probably be able to stay home and make it up to them.

_____ **d.** You sound concerned about the effect that your traveling schedule is having on your family life.

8. If I take this promotion, I'll have to move to Pittsburgh, but I really love living here in Boulder. However, if I refuse the promotion, the company probably won't offer me another one for a long time. I just don't know what to do.

_____ **a.** You sound in conflict as to whether you should accept this promotion or not.

_____ **b.** This seems a big problem now, but in the long run everything will work out.

_____ **c.** Let's look at the pros and cons of living in Pittsburgh.

_____ **d.** What's so bad about Pittsburgh?

Part II   Understanding Yourself

9. Jerry is a constant complainer. If he isn't griping to me about the rest of his work group, he's complaining about his salary. He's really getting on my nerves.

_____ **a.** You seem irritated because Jerry complains to you so often.

_____ **b.** Don't let that bother you. Every office has a Jerry.

_____ **c.** Why do you think he's so unhappy?

_____ **d.** Complaints often point to larger general dissatisfaction.

10. I'm delighted I got this new job, but I'm worried I won't be able to learn quickly enough to keep up with everyone else.

_____ **a.** Everyone feels that way about a new job.

_____ **b.** You sound both happy and nervous about your new job.

_____ **c.** I'm sure your supervisor will help you learn quickly.

_____ **d.** What new things do you need to learn?

11. Performance evaluation time is always a difficult one for me. I'd like to give everyone a good rating, but I know it's not possible.

_____ **a.** Don't worry. We all feel that way.

_____ **b.** Just do the best you can.

_____ **c.** Performance evaluations seem to be challenging for you.

_____ **d.** What makes you feel this way?

12. Those people at table six are driving me crazy. They've changed their order three times and are now complaining about how long it's taking to get their food. I wish they'd lighten up.

_____ **a.** Relax. Three more hours and you're done for the evening.

_____ **b.** You seem upset over the way they're treating you.

_____ **c.** If it gets any worse, I'd talk to my supervisor and see if she can help out.

_____ **d.** Have you had problems like this before?

Scoring: Take the X you placed in each of the twelve scenarios and put it in the appropriate place on the following answer sheet. Then total the number of Xs you have in each column and put this number at the bottom of the column.

	Column I	Column II	Column III	Column IV
1.	___ a.	___ b.	___ c.	___ d.
2.	___ d.	___ c.	___ b.	___ a.
3.	___ d.	___ a.	___ b.	___ c.
4.	___ b.	___ d.	___ a.	___ c.
5.	___ a.	___ b.	___ c.	___ d.
6.	___ c.	___ d.	___ b.	___ a.
7.	___ b.	___ a.	___ c.	___ d.
8.	___ c.	___ d.	___ b.	___ a.
9.	___ d.	___ c.	___ b.	___ a.
10.	___ c.	___ d.	___ a.	___ b.
11.	___ b.	___ d.	___ a.	___ c.
12.	___ c.	___ d.	___ a.	___ b.
Total	___	___	___	___

Interpretation: Your totals show your preference for each of four common listening styles. The highest-totaled column is your favorite style; the lowest-totaled column is the style you like least. The styles are these:

Column I	Directing
Column II	Probing
Column III	Smoothing
Column IV	Active

Column I measures your preference for directing people and telling them how to deal with situations. Column II reports your preference for asking questions and learning more information. Column III reveals your preference for smoothing things over and putting people at ease. Column IV reports your preference for active listening, as reflected by statements that indicate you are listening and encourage the other person to continue talking.

CASE 3.1: NOT QUITE WHAT HE EXPECTED

When Phil Ewbanks met with the coordinator of conference activities of the Sky Mountain Resort hotel, he carefully reviewed all of his audiovisual and equipment needs. The coordinator, Terry Scandella, made an extensive list of everything that Phil would need for his one-day conference. In some cases, the equipment would remain in the room all day and Phil's people could use it at their leisure. In other cases, the equipment would be brought in and then taken out for use with other groups in the conference center.

Another area of concern to Phil was the timely delivery of food. Phil wanted a continental breakfast for all of the participants, coffee and soft drinks at 10 A.M. and 2:30 P.M., and a buffet lunch at noon. He felt very strongly that this food had to be delivered on time and in the quantities desired. Terry listened carefully and took notes. He then said to Phil, "I think I understand everything, but there are two things I'd like to review with you to ensure we're on the same wavelength. First, when do you need the VCR and monitor? Second, do you want us to bring the food into the room or do you want to adjourn and go out into the hallway to get the refreshments?"

Phil thought about these two questions for a minute and then told Terry, "Regarding the equipment, I'll need the VCR and monitor soon after we get started. The food, meanwhile, can be left outside the door except for the lunch, which I would like brought into the room and served to the participants at the conference table."

Terry wrote down these responses, thanked Phil for his assistance, and promised to have everything taken care of as requested. Unfortunately, this is not what happened. The program began at 8 A.M. sharp, and by 8:20 A.M. Phil was ready to use the VCR and monitor. However, the equipment was not on hand. It was being used by a group next door, and 20 minutes passed before it was available for Phil's group. Additionally, after the 10 A.M. coffee break the group met for another hour and then decided to take a five-minute break, go back outside, and get more coffee. To their dismay, they learned that the remaining food had already been picked up by the serving crew. However, Terry was able to have a few additional pots of coffee brought up and everyone seemed satisfied.

At the end of the day, Terry apologized for the inconveniences that had occurred and told Phil he would like to work with him again in the future. He then gave Phil an envelope, which Phil opened in the parking lot and found to contain the conference center's bill. The next morning Phil gave the bill to the head of accounting in his own firm. The individual seemed upset. "You must have given them the impression that we're out of money," she groused. "Usually we get a bill sent to us within ten days. Are you sure those guys at the conference center know what they're doing?"

1. Why was the VCR and monitor delivered late? What accounted for the communication breakdown? Use Figure 3.1 in explaining your answer.

2. What mistake did Phil make when he told Terry to leave the food outside the door? How did inference play a role here?

3. In regard to Terry's giving Phil the bill at the end of the day, who owns the problem? Why? What would you recommend this person do about the problem? Explain.

CASE 3.2: THE OPINIONATED SERVER

Last week Ted Phillips, his wife Joan, and their friends Bill and Maria Rodgers had dinner at a new local restaurant. Here is how part of their conversation with their server, Rita Dormand, went:

Rita: Hi. My name is Rita and I'll be your server this evening. Would anyone like a drink? We have a number of excellent house specials that are unique to us here at Jonesy's.

Ted: Thanks, but I think we'd all just like a glass of chablis.

Rita: Are you sure? I could have the bartender make up a couple of small glasses of some specialties and let you taste them. I just know you'd love them.

Ted: Thanks, but no thanks.

Rita: Okay. I'll be back with your drinks in a few minutes and then take your order.

Five minutes later Rita returned with the drinks. As she served them, she engaged the group in friendly banter. "You don't know what you missed," she told them. "Those specials are great." She then turned to the food order.

Rita: Before I take your order, let me tell you about our two specials. We have broiled Maine lobster with your choice of chowder, and we have prime rib with your choice of vegetables.

Ted: I think my wife and I will have the baked salmon entrée.

Bill: I'll have the broiled chicken.

Maria: I'll have the shrimp teriyaki.

Rita: Are you sure I can't interest you in either of the specials? They're really terrific and a better buy than the entrées.

Ted: Thanks, but no thanks.

Rita then left to put in the order, returning on two occasions to check on their drinks and see if she could interest them in one of the bartender's specials. She then brought their orders and, when they were finished, told them about the dessert menu.

Rita: We have a number of desserts, as you can see from the menu. But we also have a house specialty: a pecan pie that's baked according to a special recipe created by our founder.

Ted: Okay, let's give it a try. We'll have four orders.

Afterward, everyone agreed that the dessert choice had been an excellent one—and the tip reflected their feelings. However, on the drive home Ted summed up the feelings of the group when he noted, "I thought Rita tried hard, but I found her to be somewhat pushy." Everyone agreed, and Joan added, "If you don't know what you want to eat, she's the right person. But if you have any ideas of your own, you have to convince her you're serious or you're likely to be served what she thinks is best for you. She sort of reminds me of my mother when I was a child."

1. What was the primary problem in this case? Who owned this problem? Explain.

2. What communication mistakes did Rita make in dealing with her guests? Identify and describe two.

3. What recommendations would you make to Rita regarding how she can improve her communication skills? Identify and describe three.

ANSWERS TO BOX 3.1: "MARY'S ORDEAL"

1. True. The story states that she is director of human resources for a major corporation.
2. Inference. We do not know whether the professor received a hotel suite. We only know that the room had a queen-size bed.
3. False. She asked that the professor be picked up, but she never asked for a special limousine.
4. Inference. We do not know whether the hotel realized that the professor was arriving with his wife.
5. True. The story states this fact.
6. True. The story states this fact.
7. Inference. We do not know what she thought, but she certainly was surprised by the accommodations she received.
8. Inference. We do not know for sure who the six people were for whom Mary made reservations.
9. Inference. We know that there were other people in the limousine, but we do not know where they were going.
10. Inference. Mary is certainly leaning in this direction, but she has made no final decision regarding the matter.

ENDNOTES

1. Albert Aschaffenburg, "The Essential Skill," *Lodging,* November 1994, pp. 122–124.
2. Also see "Keeping the Lines Clear," *Lodging Hospitality,* June 1994, p. 14.
3. Also see Andrew D. Wolvin, "Communication in the Hospitality Industry," *International Journal of Hospitality Management,* Vol. 13, No. 3, 1994, pp. 195–199.

4. Richard M. Hodgetts, *Organizational Behavior: Theory and Practice* (New York: Macmillan, 1991), p. 412.
5. Adapted from Thomas Gordon, *Teacher Effectiveness Training* (New York: Peter H. Wyden, 1974), pp. 75–76.
6. Jane W. Gibson and Richard M. Hodgetts, *Organizational Communication: A Managerial Perspective,* 2nd ed. (New York: HarperCollins, 1991), pp. 72–73.
7. David A. Kolb, Joyce S. Osland, and Irwin M. Rubin, *Organizational Behavior: An Experiential Approach,* 6th ed. (Upper Saddle River, N.J.: Prentice-Hall, 1995), p. 173.
8. For more on this, see Mary Steinberg, "Win-Win Solutions," *Leader's Digest,* Fall 1995, p. 10.

Effectively Managing Change and Conflict

LEARNING OBJECTIVES

In the previous two chapters we examined personal insights and ways of communicating effectively. The overriding objective of this chapter is to look at ways that you can better understand and manage change and conflict. In addition to addressing the nature of individual change, we will consider approaches that you can use in dealing with resistance to both change and conflict. The last part of the chapter will focus on two complementary areas: management of stress and management of change. When you have finished studying all of the material in this chapter, you will be able to:

1. Define the term *change* and discuss typical examples of organizational change.
2. Identify how people respond to changes they like and dislike and discuss ways of overcoming resistance to change.
3. Define the term *conflict trigger* and discuss ways of resolving conflict.
4. Describe some of the ways of dealing with personal stress.
5. Relate some of the most useful steps in managing time effectively.

Understanding the Nature of Change

Change is any alteration of the status quo. Change occurs for many reasons. Quite often, hospitality organizations find that they must institute change because it is necessary to the survival or success of their enterprise. In all, there are four types of organizational change: anticipatory, reactive, incremental, and strategic. The first two are opposites of each other, as are the last two. They can be viewed this way:

anticipatory change ↔ reactive change

incremental change ↔ strategic change

An *anticipatory change* is based on expected developments. For example, as a hotel's busiest season approaches, more associates will be brought on board. The opposite of this is a *reactive change*, which is made in response to unexpected developments. For example, if the hotel suddenly finds that its major competitor in the nearby area has just reduced its rates by 10 percent to help pick up more business during the slack-demand months, the organization will have to react and make a countermove. An *incremental change* requires the organization to make small changes in order to stay on course. For example, as the hotel's new dining room extension opens next month, the organization will begin increasing its food purchases from outside vendors so that it can adequately serve the new customers. The opposite of this is a *strategic change*, which alters the overall shape and direction of the organization. For example, if the hotel decides to add a new wing and apply for a gambling license so that it can begin attracting a new market niche, this will be a strategic change for the organization.

Individual Change and You

Workplace changes such as those described in the previous section will eventually affect all associates. In some cases, people will look forward to these changes because they are viewed as beneficial. An example is a continuous-improvement training program that helps associates do a better job of providing customer service. In other cases, associates do not like changes and will either fight their implementation or give them weak support. The ways in which people respond to changes they like and those they dislike are markedly different. .

Response to Change. When people respond to change, most of them move through a series of stages. If they like the change, their behavioral pattern is similar to that in Figure 4.1(a), which has three stages. In stage A, associates have a positive attitude, morale, and desire to make the change work. In fact, the first phase of the process is often characterized by unrealistic optimism.

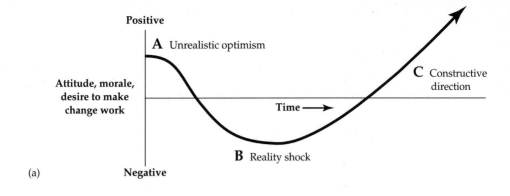

(a)

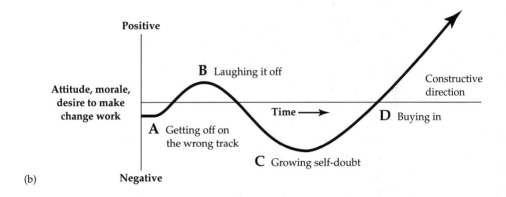

(b)

Figure 4.1 *(a) Responses to Changes that Are Liked; (b) Responses to Changes that Are Disliked*

Over time, however, this optimism typically gives way to stage B, the reality shock associated with the change. For example, while associates may be delighted to learn that a new computer system is being installed that will make their work much easier to perform, they will eventually realize that the change also means that they must master this system and learn how to use it effectively. As they do face up to this challenge, fortunately, they enter stage C, in which they accept the change and make it part of their daily operating procedure. As this happens, attitude and morale reach new heights.

When associates face changes that they fear or dislike, there are often four phases in the change process. Initially, in stage A, the changes are not viewed positively, and associates are apprehensive about them. However, this is often followed by stage B, in which associates laugh off the change and conclude that it will never last. Once they realize that the change is permanent, however, there is the growth of self-doubt and the belief that the change will be hard to implement, in stage C. Over time, fortunately, the associates begin to realize the benefits of the change, buy into the process, and accept and implement the change, in stage D. [See Figure 4.1(b).]

> When Rose Delgado learned that all of the associates at the front desk were to be cross-trained, she objected to the idea. "I know my job. Why should I learn everyone else's?" she asked. "They must be kidding about this cross-training idea." However, management was not. The company began a five-week rotation program, during which everyone who worked at the front desk of the hotel was required to spend a minimum of three days in each job. During the six months since the training ended, Rose's opinion has changed dramatically. "Customer comment cards indicate that our team at the front desk gives better service than any other in the hotel. I think a large part of this is because we are able to fill in for each other, and when one of us is inundated with work, another can jump in and help out. The cross-training has really paid off. I'm glad we did it."

Why Individuals Resist Change. There are a number of reasons why people resist change; it is important to be aware of how these can influence your own behavior. This section examines three of the most common.

One of the major reasons for resistance is surprise. Out of the clear blue, an announcement is made that significantly changes the status quo. How do most people respond? They resist by either fighting the change or simply failing to go along with it. For example, suppose that the central accounting department has sent a memo to all restaurant units indicating that financial information is now to be reported on a daily basis; these data are to be sent to headquarters via a special software package being provided to each unit. The restaurant managers have not been apprised of this change in financial reporting and they believe it will upset the way they currently run their operations. How will they respond? Many of them will ignore the request, while others will give minimal compliance. Why? Because the change was not discussed with them in advance; when people are negatively surprised they tend to resist complying with requests.

Closely linked to the previous reason is a desire for a safe, secure status quo. People like the way things are being done and do not want to change. The best way of getting them to change their minds is to show them how the new way of doing things will make life easier or more enjoyable for them. There must be a benefit for them or they will resist.[1]

A third common reason is that those who are being asked to make changes feel that they lack the experience, knowledge, or training to do the new job properly. In the preceding example, the accounting people provided each unit with a special software package that can be used to gather and submit the financial data. However, the unit managers may feel that they do not know how to use this software, nor does anyone else in their unit, so they are reluctant to comply. The accounting people should have first explained how the new data are to be sent to headquarters and then should have offered training to unit associates so that they would know how to carry out this task.

Do you ever resist change? Why? In answering these questions, take the quiz in Box 4.1 and then read the interpretation of your answers.[2]

Overcoming Resistance to Change

There are a number of ways that you can work to accommodate change.[3] Most of these involve support from your boss or the organization itself, but you can play a key role in this process. Here are five useful steps.

1. Find out what the change is all about and how it will affect you. Before you fight it, learn what you are up against.

2. Try to play a role in shaping the change. Participation and involvement often result in acceptance of changes because the individual who is being affected has had a hand in determining the nature and scope of the change.[4]

3. Find out what types of facilitation and support the organization is going to give you to help you deal with the change. If it is going to provide special training and/or compensatory time off, you may find that the change is acceptable to you.

4. Try to negotiate some of the terms of the change, such as getting the company to increase your salary, give you more time off, provide you with equipment, or identify you as a fast-track individual who is likely to be promoted in the near future. In this way, you are getting something for all of your trouble.

5. Work closely with the individuals who are calling for the change and get them to see how it will affect you and why you are resistant. This provides you with the opportunity to present your point of view and will often result in their willingness to modify the change to accommodate some of your concerns.

Dealing with Conflict

Conflict is opposition or antagonism toward other individuals or things.[5] Sometimes change brings about conflict, but in many cases it is a result of day-to-day situations. For example, a server may find that the guests who were just seated in his section have been driving all day and are now tired and hungry and want to hurry and eat so they can get back to their motel and go to sleep. In the process, however, they are rude to the individual and continually complain about everything from the food to the time it takes to be served.

Box 4.1
Job Changes and You

Read each of the following statements and decide the degree of resistance you would offer to the change. Indicate this resistance on a scale of 1 (no resistance) to 10 (strong resistance). An interpretation of your responses can be found at the end of the chapter.

_____ 1. I know my job and do it well, but the organization now wants me to learn a whole new computer program that supposedly will make my job easier, and this is going to take a fair amount of time to master.

_____ 2. I learned yesterday that starting tomorrow I am to keep detailed notes on customer service complaints and submit them to the front office every morning at 9 A.M.

_____ 3. I have been told that I am to be assigned to a work group responsible for reducing service time in the restaurant, but I have had no experience in how to carry out this type of work.

_____ 4. I'm to be moved to a new department after five years in my current job and I'm upset because I don't want to leave my old work associates with whom I have developed close, personal relationships.

_____ 5. My boss wants to transfer me to a new job in the department, but I don't think this transfer will be of any value to my career—and I'm sure he also knows this.

_____ 6. Everyone who has headed the customer relations department has been demoted because of poor performance, and I have just been asked to take on this job.

_____ 7. My boss just told me, in front of my peers, that I am going to have to volunteer as a team leader—or else.

_____ 8. My boss, whom I dislike intensely, has just told me that he needs the monthly cost control report by tomorrow, three days ahead of schedule.

_____ 9. I have been told to train a replacement for my job as soon as possible.

_____ 10. I have been asked to transfer to another department, but I love my current job and don't want to change.

In dealing with this situation, the server needs to avoid conflict. Before examining how this can be done, take the quiz in Box 4.2.

One way of avoiding conflict is to understand conflict triggers. A _conflict trigger_ is a situation that increases the chances of conflict.[6] There are many things that can do this. The quiz in Box 4.2 provides some examples. Here are five others:

Box 4.2
Dealing with Tough Customers

The following are nine real-life situations faced by restaurant servers and other associates. Would any of these situations create a conflict for you and, if you did not carefully control your feelings, result in your saying something unpleasant to the guest? Circle the number associated with each situation that might result in feelings of opposition or antagonism toward the customer.

1. A guest has ordered the breakfast special but wants you to substitute tomato juice in lieu of the grits and a pastry in lieu of the bacon. The restaurant has a "No Substitutions" notice at the bottom of the menu; you call this to the attention of the guest, while politely refusing his request. In turn, the guest insists that you get the manager and let him talk to the individual about the substitution. You look over your shoulder and see that the restaurant is packed with customers, there are at least 35 people waiting to be seated, and the manager is helping the staff up front deal with this overload. It is going to take some time before the manager can break away and talk to your guest, who continues to remain firm in his desire for substitutions.

2. A group of nine people has just been seated; as you hand out the menus, you can tell that they are angry over having had to wait 90 minutes for a table. When you ask them if they would like something to drink, they take their time ordering and then say, "We're assuming that since we had to wait over an hour, the first round of drinks is on the house, right?"

3. A diner ordered filet mignon with all the trimmings. After eating most of the steak, she calls you over and says, "This meat is inedible. I want you to take it back and get me another steak and this time I want it medium-rare, not well done like this one."

4. Three customers have finished looking over the menu; they ask you, "What's really good here and what should we stay away from?" You recommend all of the entrées on the left but suggest that they avoid five of the choices on the right unless they like heavily spiced food. The diners then order three choices from the group of heavily spiced foods. After they have finished approximately half of their dinner, they call you over and tell you that the entrées are terrible and suggest that you should have talked them out of these choices. They also believe that they are entitled to a refund on their bill.

5. A diner orders a well-done T-bone steak. You know that the cook believes that the only way to cook a T-bone is medium-rare or rare and you suggest that the guest opt for one of these. However, the individual waves you off and you write the order as requested. The chef cooks the steak rare and when the diner takes the first bite, he tells you that the steak is undercooked. You take it back and the chef reluctantly throws it on the grill for a few minutes. When you take the steak back to the

Box 4.2   Continued

diner, he takes another bite and insists that the meat is still not cooked properly and sends it back again. This time the cook leaves it on the grill for three minutes and you return with a medium T-bone for the diner. Again he calls you over and is becoming irate over the failure to get his food cooked the way he wants it.

6. A diner has looked over the menu and decides to order the Grand Pizza. However, as the individual begins eating it, he suddenly realizes that it has anchovies. He calls you over and says, "I don't eat pizza with anchovies. You're going to have to take this back and get the anchovies taken off." You politely open the menu and show the customer that the description of the Grand Pizza clearly states that it has anchovies. The customer responds, "Okay, but I didn't think it would have them all over the pizza."

7. A party of seven has been in the restaurant for over four hours. Approximately 40 minutes ago you gave them the bill; they have yet to look it over and decide how to pay. You go off duty in ten minutes and this is the last table you have to finish.

8. The guests at your table have finished their main course and ordered dessert. Before you can place this order, one of them says, "I'm assuming that dessert is on the house, the way it was the last time we ate here." You have no authority to give them free dessert, although you do know that when the restaurant opened four months ago, the manager gave free desserts to a number of guests in an attempt to build repeat business. You inform your guests that you are unfamiliar with this practice, so they insist on seeing the manager. When she arrives, she listens politely to their request and very tactfully declines. The guests order dessert anyway, but now their attitude has turned surly and somewhat abusive to you.

9. You are in charge of seating guests in the restaurant. The next available table is for six; reading down the waiting list, you call the appropriate group. Before they can be seated, however, the person in charge of the group says to you, "I don't care where you seat us, but don't put us next to any Hispanics or other minorities. I want to sit near White people."

1. *Ambiguous authority.* Unclear job boundaries can create conflict. For example, if a guest asks the bell captain for directions to a nearby restaurant, but the concierge is the individual charged with providing such assistance to guests, the concierge may feel that the bell captain is overstepping his or her authority.

2. *Communication breakdown.* When associates do not fully understand what is happening, they may face conflict.[7] For example, suppose a restaurant

places an announcement on the bulletin board that states that from now on all associates are to report for work 30 minutes before their shift is to begin. The company also intends to pay everyone for this extra 30 minutes, but that part of the message was left off by the typist.

3. *Unreasonable rules and procedures.* A rule that says the customer is always right, regardless of the situation, is likely to result in conflict between associates and the management. Associates know that sometimes the customer is wrong, and they will resent management's unwillingness to take their side when they are right.

4. *Status differentials.* The higher up in the organization a manager is, the greater the individual's status. So when the manager does something that is regarded as unfair, a conflict is often inevitable. For example, a manager of a large hotel who continually greets guests and ingratiates herself with them may help build customer goodwill. However, if the individual ignores associates or treats them condescendingly, they will lose respect for her and use covert measures to undermine her efforts.

5. *Unrealized expectations.* An organization that promises to promote its people based on work performance is likely to attract highly talented people. However, if these individuals are bypassed for promotion because the enterprise then begins allowing non-work-related performance to enter the picture, conflict will arise because of unrealized expectations.

Each of these triggers can bring about conflict or confrontation. It is important to be aware of these potential triggers in order to avoid them. Such action will also help you deal with stress, a topic that is examined in the next section.

Stress and You

Stress is a feeling of anxiety, pressure, and/or tension. When people are trying to manage change and conflict effectively, it is common for them to face stress; many people are at their best when under at least some degree of stress. How much stress is ideal? This depends on the person. It is useful to examine some of the reasons why some people feel high stress in situations in which other individuals feel moderate or low stress.

Individual Differences

A number of reasons help explain why some people are more affected by stress than are others. These can be explained in terms of demographic differences, irrational beliefs, and personality types.

Box 4.3
Your Beliefs and Attitudes

Indicate how true or false each of the following statements is for you.

	Mostly False	Somewhat True	Mostly True
1. I have to have the love and approval of almost everyone who is important to me.	_____	_____	_____
2. I must be thoroughly competent at most things I do.	_____	_____	_____
3. It is terrible when I am frustrated and things do not turn out the way I want.	_____	_____	_____
4. My emotions are controlled by external events and there is not much I can do about this.	_____	_____	_____
5. I find it easier to avoid difficult situations than face them.	_____	_____	_____
6. My past experiences affect me so strongly that I am unable to change how I feel or react.	_____	_____	_____
7. I need to have someone on whom I can depend and who will take care of me.	_____	_____	_____
8. I become upset over my own or other people's problems.	_____	_____	_____
9. There is one correct and perfect solution to every problem, and it should be found.	_____	_____	_____
10. The world should be fair and when it is not, I must be upset.	_____	_____	_____

Source: Albert Ellis and R. Harper, *A Guide to Rational Living* (North Hollywood, CA: Wilshire Books, 1961.)

Demographic Differences. *Demographics* is the study of the characteristics of human populations. When applied to stress, these demographics include age, education, and occupation. As people get older, they often encounter more stress because they are faced with greater responsibilities. A student in grammar school often feels far less stress than a student in college who realizes that good grades are critical to employment and early career success. A second demographic variable is education. Research shows that better-educated people often feel less stress because they are confident of their abilities and believe they can handle most situations. A third variable is occupation. Some jobs are far more stressful than others. A good example is hospitality jobs, where stress tends to be fairly high because of the demands that are placed on associates by customers.

Irrational Beliefs. *Irrational beliefs* are ideas to which an individual clings, even though they create stress for the person. Do you have any irrational beliefs? The quiz in Box 4.3 provides some insight into this question. Before continuing your reading, take the quiz.

Any of the answers in the quiz that you indicated were "mostly true" are likely sources of stress because they are irrational beliefs. Each of these beliefs serves as a magnifier of stress; it would be to your benefit to change these beliefs. These thought processes involve catastrophizing, overgeneralizing, expecting too much, or focusing on the negative. Here are some examples of the potential problems associated with each of the beliefs listed in Box 4.3:

This belief	Leads to:
Need for love and approval	Insecurity; social anxiety due to fear of rejection
Must be thoroughly competent	Perfectionism; depression; excessive criticism of one's self and others
Feel terrible when things do not turn out the way I want	Frustration; anger; a feeling of being out of control
Little control over personal emotions	Helplessness
Easier to avoid difficulties than to face risks	Procrastination; avoidance of risk taking
My past always affects me so that I cannot change how I feel	Making excuses for current behavior or emotions that are not acceptable; giving in rather than trying to change
Must depend on others	Excessive dependency; anger when others let you down
May become upset over problems	Extreme sensitivity
One correct solution for every problem	Rigid, obsessive-compulsive personality; fear of making decisions
World should be fair	Frustration; anger; hostility; depression

How can you deal with irrational beliefs? Once you are aware that your thoughts and beliefs about a stressful event can magnify your reaction, you can challenge your irrational or negative thinking and replace it with more rational, positive, and confident thoughts. This does not mean that tragic, painful, or upsetting situations will feel good. However, the event will not be made any more stressful than it has to be. An example of some old and new thinking is shown in the stress analysis chart in Table 4.1.

Personality Types. A third individual difference that helps account for stress is personality type. Basically, there are two: the Type A personality and the Type B personality. A *Type A personality* is characterized by a continually chronic struggle to get more and more done in less and less time. These individuals tend to be high achievers and have a high need for power. In the process, they tend to produce a type of psychological and physical havoc that can be detrimental to their health. A *Type B personality* is a patient, evenly paced person who pursues objectives in a systematic and fairly calm manner. There has been a wealth of research conducted on Type A and Type B people, and it has been determined that Type A behavior can be detrimental to one's health.[8] This is particularly true when a person's stress becomes too severe or lasts too long, for this can create problems. Figure 4.2 illustrates this. Notice that a person who is not under much stress can be bored and irritable; this individual is suffering from stress underload. Conversely, a person who is under too much stress can be irritable and accident prone; this individual is suffering from stress overload. If an individual has an optimal amount of stress, however, then the person tends to be highly motivated, mentally alert, and calm under pressure. For many people, stress underload is not a problem. The challenge is learning how to deal with stress overload.[9]

How vulnerable are you to stress? In answering this question, take the quiz in Box 4.4.

Burnout

Research shows that many people who work in the hospitality industry are overworked, and some are on the border of burnout.[10] *Burnout* is a response to chronic stress that results in emotional or physical exhaustion, or both.[11] For example, the National Institute for Occupational Safety and Health has found that some of the highest-stress jobs in the economy are those of waiters and waitresses.[12] One reason for this high burnout is that these individuals have limited control over their jobs, so they are continually subjected to stress that is imposed by others and that they cannot avoid.[13] Table 4.2 provides some comparisons of chronic stress and burnout, and illustrates the dangers associated with being subjected to prolonged periods of chronic stress.

Part II Understanding Yourself

Table 4.1 A Stress Analysis Chart

Stressful Event:

Yesterday I learned my position was being eliminated and there is nothing available
for me.

Old Way of Thinking	*New Way of Thinking*
(Magnify the Stressor)	(Filter the Stressor)
Irrational or negative talk	Rational or positive talk

1. This is the worst thing that could happen.
2. I'm a failure.
3. I'll never get another job.
4. They have no right to do this to me.

1. This is a setback, but only a temporary one.
2. I failed, but I can succeed again elsewhere.
3. If I look carefully, I'll find another job.
4. They have the right to run the company as they see fit.

Old Stress Reaction:

Physiological: nervous
Emotional: angry
Mental: worried about money
Behavioral: pacing the floor

Controlled Reaction:

Physiological: less tense
Emotional: hurt
Mental: thinking about options
Behavioral: none

Stress level (1–10)   9

Stress level (1–10)   6

Source: Adapted from Anthony R. Ciminero, *One Minute Stress Management* (Miami, Fla.: Private publication, 1986), p. 50.

Dealing with Stress

There are a number of steps that you can take in dealing with stress.[14] One is to watch your diet. A healthier approach to food, nutrition, and general diet can help reduce stress and keep you in generally good health. Most doctors agree that the average American eats too much salt, sugar, red meat, eggs, and butter. They recommend more consumption of fruit, vegetables, juices, water, dairy products made from skim milk, fowl, fish, whole-grain breads, and decaffeinated beverages.[15]

A second, and complementary, approach is physical fitness. Many hotels now have physical fitness centers because so many guests like the opportunity to work out when they are on the road. In fact, physical fitness has become something of a craze in the United States—and none too soon. Research reveals that most people, at best, get very little physical exercise. Yet exercise is one of the best ways to control stress and maintain good health. Individuals

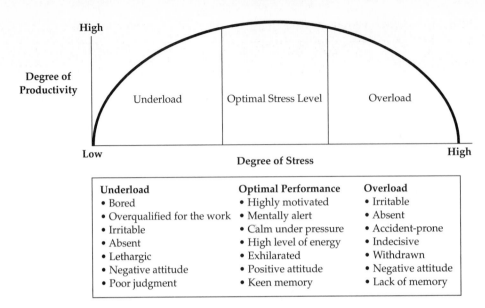

Figure 4.2 *The Underload/Overload Continuum*

who work out on a regular basis tend to have lower blood pressure, a lower heart rate, better muscle definition, and a more positive outlook on life. They are also less likely to suffer stress and burnout.

A third useful approach is mental relaxation, which consists of physical and psychological techniques that help people slow down. One of the most common is abdominal breathing, which calls for the person to place his or her hands on the abdomen, with fingertips touching, and breathe deeply for five to ten minutes twice a day. This procedure helps the person slow down and relax. Another technique is progressive relaxation, which requires the individual to lie down and slowly progress down (or up) the body, from head to toe, first stiffening the muscles and then relaxing them. After a few minutes, the entire body is relaxed. A third popular technique is transcendental meditation (TM), which requires the meditator to shut out all distractions and concentrate on a mantra, which is a single word or sound. For 15 to 30 minutes, the individual works to attain a physical and mental relaxation peak. Researchers have found that individuals who practice TM often need less sleep, fall asleep faster, use less coffee and aspirin, and are more self-confident and emotionally stable than they were before they started using TM.[16]

A fourth way to deal with stress is to learn how to examine your irrational beliefs and then replace them with more rational statements. The major techniques for mentally controlling your stress include the following suggestions:

■ Talk calmly to yourself.
■ Try to keep the stressful event in perspective.

Part II Understanding Yourself

Box 4.4
How Vulnerable Are You to Stress?

Read the following 20 statements and score each one from 1 (almost always) to 5 (never), based on how often each applies to you.

_____ 1. I generally eat at least one balanced meal a day.

_____ 2. Most nights of the week I get six to eight hours' sleep.

_____ 3. I am able to give and receive affection on a regular basis.

_____ 4. I have at least one friend or relative within 50 miles of where I live on whom I can rely.

_____ 5. At least twice a week I exercise vigorously.

_____ 6. I smoke less than a half pack of cigarettes a day.

_____ 7. I have fewer than five alcoholic drinks a week.

_____ 8. Based on medical charts, my weight is approximately where it should be.

_____ 9. My income is adequate to meet my basic expenses.

_____ 10. I attend club or social activities on a regular basis.

_____ 11. I am able to draw strength from my religious beliefs.

_____ 12. I have a good network of friends and acquaintances.

_____ 13. I have at least one friend in whom I can confide about personal matters.

_____ 14. I feel that I am in good physical health.

_____ 15. When I am angry or worried, I find that I am able to speak openly about these feelings.

_____ 16. I have regular conversations about domestic problems with the people who live in my house or residence.

_____ 17. At least once a week I do something for fun.

_____ 18. I do a good job in organizing my time effectively.

_____ 19. I drink fewer than three cups of coffee, tea, or cola a day.

_____ 20. I take quiet time for myself on a daily basis.

Scoring: Add the scores for each of the 20 items and then subtract 20. A score over 30 indicates a vulnerability to stress. You are seriously vulnerable if your score is between 50 and 75, and extremely vulnerable if it is over 75.

Table 4.2 Chronic Stress versus Burnout

Chronic Stress	Burnout
Feelings of fatigue	Chronic exhaustion
Feelings of anxiety	Hypertension
Dissatisfaction with job	Boredom and cynicism about work
Decline in commitment to job	Job commitment virtually nil; mental detachment from the organization
Moodiness	Impatience; irritability; unwillingness to talk to others
Feelings of guilt	Mental depression
Difficulty concentrating; tendency to forget things	Forgetfulness becomes more and more frequent; does not seem to know where he or she is.
Physiological changes such as increased blood pressure and heartbeat	Voicing of psychosomatic complaints

- Avoid catastrophizing, overgeneralizing, using unreasonable expectations, and focusing on the negative.
- Use "rational self-talk" to reinterpret any irrational beliefs.

Still another technique is to find yourself a mentor. A *mentor* is an individual who provides advice and assistance to a younger, junior member of the organization and who acts as a counselor and sponsor for the person. Mentors are particularly useful in helping a person deal with stress. Some organizations have formal mentoring programs in which young managers are assigned an experienced manager, who serves as the mentor. In other enterprises, it is up to each individual to seek out and cultivate an individual who will serve as his or her mentor. In either event, this is an excellent way of helping deal with the pressures of job-related stress.[17]

Managing Time Effectively

Closely linked with stress management is the need to manage time effectively. Quite often stress is created by a person's inability to get everything done in the allotted time. Is this typical of you? If so, there are a number of steps that you can take to correct the situation.

There are many ways to reduce the time needed to do things. This section examines five of the most helpful. Others are provided in Box 4.5.

Box 4.5
Ten Additional Rules of Time Management

1. Give yourself a reward, such as taking 15 minutes to drink a cup of coffee and work on your favorite crossword puzzle, after you have accomplished an important task.

2. Concentrate on doing just one thing at a time; this typically results in greater time efficiency.

3. Start with the most profitable parts of big projects and then move on to the less profitable segments of the task.

4. Try not to read word-for-word; skim over the material and look for the main ideas.

5. Generate as little paperwork as possible; for example, throw away nonessential papers as soon as you have read them.

6. Delegate as much work as possible and use experts with knowledge that can help you do things better and faster.

7. Put your waiting time to good use; if you are waiting in someone's outer office or waiting for a meeting to begin, take the opportunity to read or catch up on work that you have brought along with you.

8. If someone drops by and asks if you "have a minute," limit the amount of time you give this person; if the individual needs more time than you have available, schedule a meeting with the person for a time that is more convenient for you.

9. If you have to meet someone and the individual asks if you want to go to his or her office or vice versa, opt for going to the other person; you can always leave at your convenience, while if he or she comes to your office you have less flexibility in managing your time.

10. Do not waste time regretting failures or feeling guilty about what you did not get done today; schedule it for tomorrow and promise yourself that you will do a better job of managing your time.

First, create a "to-do" list. Write down the things that you need to accomplish today and organize your time so that you get these tasks finished. One of the best ways of doing this is to prioritize the work, so that the most important things are given first attention and minor tasks are addressed later on. This can be done by using an "ABC" priority system. Items marked A are important, high-priority items; B items are less important; and C items are done last.

Second, break work into small, easy-to-accomplish bites. A number of benefits are associated with this approach. One is that it gives continual feedback and helps you monitor performance. A second is that it is motivational because you can see your ongoing progress. Another is that people tend to work faster when they first start a task and again when they begin to wrap up the assignment. So by breaking work into a series of small tasks, you will work faster because your speed at the beginning and the end of each task will get you finished faster than if you worked on the job as one overall assignment and did not break it into smaller bites.

Third, use a work/reward approach to getting things done by first doing something that is difficult or demanding, then turning to something that is easy or rewarding to you. This time management strategy helps ensure that those tasks you do not like doing will be completed by being sandwiched between enjoyable tasks. This approach is particularly useful in dealing with a time management concept known as the *first law of operating priority*, which holds that when faced with simple and difficult chores, people are likely to opt for the simple ones first. When this happens, of course, the individual ends up accomplishing all of the easy tasks but few of the difficult ones. A work/reward approach helps overcome this problem—especially if it is tied to the ABC priority system discussed earlier.

Fourth, decide whether you are a morning person or an afternoon person. Your answer will help identify when you should be scheduling more difficult or challenging work. For example, if you are a morning person, choose the most demanding tasks and schedule most (if not all) of them for the morning; this is when you are at your best. This will leave the least difficult chores for the afternoon, when you are not as alert or sharp as you were earlier. This matching of your personality and work demands will help increase productivity.

Fifth, read standing up. People tend to read faster when they are in an uncomfortable position. So while your average reading time may be 250 words per minute when sitting down, it is likely to be in the range of 400 words a minute when standing up. Additionally, try to read things only once. If you start reading something such as a three-page memo, finish it. Do not put it aside after you have read the first page; when you go back, you will start at the beginning and end up reading the first page twice. If you continue reading the material piecemeal, you will find that you have read some parts of the memo three or four times. You can save time by reading things all the way through the first time.

The preceding recommendations, as well as those presented in Box 4.5, are particularly useful in managing your time. There is one more idea that can also be quite profitable to you. Before discussing it, however, take the quiz in Box 4.6 and then read the next paragraph.

The difference between the two lists is that the one on the left pinpoints others as the cause of the problem. The reason the manager did not get everything done was that he or she was being bothered by drop-in visitors, the organization's rules and regulations were too time consuming, and there were too many telephone interruptions. The list on the right is more personalized.

Box 4.6
What's the Difference?

Here are two lists that were put together by hospitality managers who felt that they had not done a good job of managing their time. Read and compare both lists and then answer the questions that follow.

List A	List B
1. Employees with problems kept coming by.	1. Tried to do too much in the allotted time.
2. There were too many telephone interruptions.	2. Set unrealistic time estimates.
3. There were too many routine tasks to be done.	3. There was too much personal procrastination.
4. I had to eat lunch.	4. A personal failure to listen.
5. There were too many interruptions by others.	5. A tendency to do it all myself.
6. Meetings being attended were poorly planned.	6. Inability to say no.
7. Mistakes by others took too much time to correct.	7. A refusal to let others do the job.
8. There is management by crisis throughout the organization.	8. General lack of personal organization.
9. Outside activities took too much time.	9. Delegated responsibility to others but did not give them the requisite authority to do the job well.
10. There were too many drop-in visitors.	10. A tendency to blame others for not getting everything done on time.

What is the difference between the two lists? What is present in the one on the left that is basically missing from the one on the right and vice versa? Write your answer below.

_____

_____

_____

_____

The manager is saying that because of personal errors or mistakes in judgment, not everything got done. The individual is also saying, "I assume responsibility for these mistakes." If you are going to be effective in managing your time, you also must be willing to accept personal responsibility. You must look at your work habits, find where they need improvement, and then take the necessary steps. A great deal of the conflict that people face in organizations today is a result of their inability or unwillingness to take responsibility for their actions. If they did so, they would save a great deal of time and effort. Remember—good time management begins with you!

SUMMARY

1. Change is any alteration of the status quo. There are a number of types of organizational change; including anticipatory, reactive, incremental, and strategic; each can affect individuals.

2. Individual changes relate directly to associates; there are a number of possible responses. As seen in Figure 4.1, depending on whether the change is liked or disliked, the pattern of responses can be markedly different. Some of the major reasons why individuals resist change include surprise, a desire for a safe status quo, and a feeling that the change will make demands on them to which they will be unable to adequately respond. Some of the ways of accommodating change include finding out what the change is all about and how it will personally affect the person, and playing a role in shaping the change.

3. Conflict is opposition or antagonism toward other individuals or things. These situations are often initiated by conflict triggers such as ambiguous authority, communication breakdown, unreasonable rules and procedures, status differentials, and unrealized expectations.

4. Stress is a feeling of anxiety, pressure, and/or tension. There are a number of reasons that help explain why some people are more affected by stress than are others. Examples include demographic differences, irrational beliefs, and type of personality. Individuals who are subjected to prolonged periods of stress can encounter burnout. A number of steps have proven helpful in dealing with stress, including diet, physical fitness, and mental relaxation techniques.

5. Closely linked with stress management is the need to manage time effectively. Some of the most effective ways of doing this include using a prioritized "to-do" list, breaking work into small bites that are easy to accomplish, using a work/reward approach to getting things done, deciding whether you are a morning or afternoon person, assigning work appropriately, and reading standing up.

KEY TERMS

change	demographics
anticipatory change	irrational beliefs
reactive change	Type A personality
incremental change	Type B personality
strategic change	burnout
conflict	mentor
conflict trigger	first law of operating priority
stress	

REVIEW AND APPLICATION QUESTIONS

1. Clara Verdall's department is likely to be reorganized within the next four months. This is an efficiency move by hotel management. What are some steps that Clara can take to help deal with any personal resistance to these changes? Offer her three suggestions for action.

2. A number of conflict triggers can increase the chances of conflict. In what way is each of the following a conflict trigger: ambiguous authority, communication breakdown, unreasonable rules and procedures, status differentials, and unrealized expectations? In each case, give an example.

3. Richard Phillips, a friend of yours, has received a poor evaluation from his boss. One of the comments on Richard's evaluation was, "He seems to have trouble getting along with others and is often in a poor mood." While Richard disagrees with these comments, you know him well enough to realize that the evaluation statement is accurate. In particular, Richard holds a number of irrational beliefs about himself and others. Referring to Box 4.3, you believe that numbers 3, 4, 6, 8, and 10 are particularly accurate. Based on this information, what conclusions can you reach about Richard? If you were trying to help him improve his future evaluation, what advice would you give?

4. Sarah Mullsen is a Type A personality. One of the individuals who works under Sarah's direct supervision, Tim White, is a Type B personality. What are some of the behaviors that help describe the way Sarah does things? Would Tim have trouble working with her? Why or why not? What do your answers relate about stress in the workplace?

5. Frances Conklin is a new supervisor in your work area. You have noticed that she often has trouble getting all of her work done because she is not a good time manager. What are four time management ideas you can give her that could help her get more done in less time? In each case, be sure to fully discuss your idea.

SELF-FEEDBACK EXERCISE:
ARE YOU A TYPE A OR A TYPE B PERSONALITY?

This self-feedback exercise is designed to help you determine whether you exhibit Type A or Type B behaviors. For each item, there are two alternatives: "a" and "b." Indicate which of the two is most descriptive of you by using the following scale:

If statement "a" is totally descriptive of you and "b" is not descriptive at all, give yourself 5 points.

If statement "a" is mostly descriptive of you and "b" is only somewhat descriptive, give yourself 4 points.

If statement "a" is slightly more descriptive of you than is statement "b," give yourself 3 points.

If statement "b" is slightly more descriptive of you than is statement "a," give yourself 2 points.

If statement "b" is mostly descriptive of you and "a" is only somewhat descriptive, give yourself 1 point.

If statement "b" is totally descriptive of you and "a" is not descriptive at all, give yourself 0 points.

1. a. On an average day, I usually work at a hectic pace.

    b. On an average day, I usually work at a relaxed pace.

2. a. I really hate days off. It means I don't get to do any job-related work.

    b. I enjoy days off. Getting away from the job is really relaxing.

3. a. I like fighting a deadline. It's one way I'm assured of getting the work done.

    b. I seldom have to fight deadlines. I pace myself so everything gets done on time.

4. a. My primary satisfaction comes from my work.

    b. My work is personally rewarding, but I also enjoy sports, social gatherings, time with family and friends, and so on.

5. a. I talk fast. Few people can say more in a minute or two than I can.

    b. I talk at a moderate rate. This is more than adequate to convey what I have to say.

6. a. I set very high standards for myself, and if I don't get things done according to my plan, I become quite upset.

b. I establish a reasonable amount of work, and if I get done, I am happy. I want to accomplish things, but I do not allow myself to get upset if I fall short.

7. a. When I play games, I play to win. It doesn't matter against whom I'm playing—young kids, novices, people less alert than I am to the rules and shortcuts—I want to emerge on top.

   b. I enjoy playing games but I don't always have to win. In fact, I try to find games in which I can obtain enjoyment just from the participation.

8. a. When I listen to people who are slow in speaking or who make their point in a roundabout fashion, I find myself wanting to complete the conversation for them or just walk away. They bore me.

   b. When I listen to people who are slow or rambling in their conversation, I try to get enjoyment out of what they are saying rather than the way they are saying it.

9. a. When I have to eat, I eat very fast. I know it may not be very good for my health, but by eating fast I can more quickly get back to other activities such as working.

   b. When I eat I like to take my time and enjoy the meal. This is one activity I really like to perform at a leisurely pace.

10. a. When I stop to think about it, I am always in a hurry even when I don't have to be.

    b. I seldom rush anywhere. I try to plan my daily calendar so that I know where I am supposed to be going and arrange things so that I can proceed at a reasonable pace.

11. a. I often try to do two things at the same time. Sure, it takes some getting used to, but I find that if I do things this way, I increase my output by almost 100 percent.

    b. I concentrate on doing one thing at a time. This way I know that I'm doing it right and won't have to repeat it later.

12. a. Even though I don't usually show it, I find that I'm often angry and upset at the way people behave and the way things get done. I know there is no sense getting angry, but underneath, I feel that way.

    b. I seldom get angry about things. People make lots of mistakes and sometimes things don't go my way. However, life is too short to spend it getting angry.

13. a. Waiting makes me nervous. When I have to wait, I find myself biting my nails, tapping my feet, scribbling on a pad, and so on.

    b. I do not enjoy waiting, but when it is necessary, I try to take the time to relax. If I do have a lot of work, I make it a point to bring some of it along with me so I can read or fill out papers at a leisurely pace.

14. a. I measure progress in terms of time and performance. For example, when I am given an assignment, I write down what I am to do and break it into time periods. Then I monitor progress closely. If I fall behind in something I am doing, I make it a point not to go home or go to sleep until I have completed the assignment for that day.

    b. I try to get things done in an agreed-upon time. However, I do not worry about progress on a hourly or daily basis. Rather, I realize that sometimes I will work faster than other times. So I try to keep up a good pace that ensures progress but is not excessively demanding.

15. a. When I go to bed, I cannot wait until morning so that I can get going again.

    b. When I go to bed, I try to get a good night's sleep without thinking about what I'll be doing first thing the next day.

16. a. I want people to respect me for what I do. Praise for my accomplishments is important.

    b. I want people to respect me for who I am. Even if I'm only an average worker, I'm entitled to respect.

17. a. I often find myself scheduling more and more work in less and less time.

    b. I set goals for myself, and when they are accomplished I sit back and relax.

18. a. When I speak I tend to overemphasize key words and speed up the delivery of the last few words in a sentence.

    b. When I speak I tend to talk at an evenly paced, moderate speed throughout.

19. a. When I engage in conversation, I find myself changing the topic to subjects that interest me. If I have to wait for a chance to talk, I pretend to listen while thinking of what I am going to say when the chance comes.

    b. When I engage in conversation, I try to listen to what the other person has to say and draw some enjoyment out of what I am hearing.

20.   a. I wear myself out by doing too much. Yet I enjoy it. When I fall into bed totally exhausted, this is a sign of a good day's work.

     b. I seldom wear myself out. If something does not get done today, I'll do it tomorrow. No job warrants wearing myself to a frazzle every day.

Scoring: Go back and review all of your answers. Make sure that on each of the 20, you have placed a score between 0 and 5. Now place your scores in the following key and add them.

1. ___	6. ___	11. ___	16. ___
2. ___	7. ___	12. ___	17. ___
3. ___	8. ___	13. ___	18. ___
4. ___	9. ___	14. ___	19. ___
5. ___	10. ___	15. ___	20. ___
___	+ ___	+ ___	+ ___ =

TOTAL ___

Interpretation: Compare your total to the following key. Most people are a mixture of Type A and Type B personalities. If you are a strong Type A personality, you might want to talk to some of your friends or classmates to see if they agree with you. If they do, you should carefully reread the material in the last part of the chapter to see if you can begin taking steps to "loosen up" a little.

0–19	You have a strong Type B personality.
20–39	You have a moderate Type B personality.
40–59	You have a mixture of Type A and Type B personalities; you do not exhibit any clear pattern.
60–79	You have a moderate Type A personality.
80–100	You have a strong Type A personality.

CASE 4.1: YOU CAN'T MAKE EVERYONE HAPPY

Helen Chen and Charles Sigourney work in the reservations department of a large cruise line. The company recently decided to reorganize operations, in order to increase overall efficiency. One of the things the firm has decided to do is change both of their jobs.

Helen is to be given additional training and increased responsibility, so she can more effectively handle customer service requests. The company has found that under the old organizational arrangement, there were too many people responsible for handling each reservation. Under the new arrangement, each reservations associate will handle all phases of a customer's reservation; if there is a problem, the client will then be able to interact directly with the one individual who took the reservation. Management believes that this will result in both better and faster service. Additionally, Helen will be given the authority to deal with customer problems and, where necessary, make changes or authorize refunds. For example, if a customer is dissatisfied with his or her accommodations because the individual was led to believe that a more spacious cabin would be provided, Helen would be authorized to give him or her a $200 credit toward any future cruise. Similarly, if a person were to become ill during the trip, Helen could okay a partial refund. By providing such authority to its reservations associates, the organization hopes to further increase customer satisfaction. Helen is delighted with these impending changes and cannot wait for them to be implemented.

Charles is to be given a new job. The company realizes that there will be customer problems, regardless of how efficiently the operation is organized. Charles's new job will call for him to identify these problems, categorize them, and then develop procedures for eliminating their recurrence or dealing with them most effectively. The job is critical to the firm's objective of providing high-quality customer service. However, Charles is not pleased with the assignment. He believes the work will not be as interesting or meaningful as his current job; he is thinking that he might be better off if he transferred to another department or found a job elsewhere. Before making a final decision, however, he intends to try the new job and see how well things work out.

Helen and Charles's boss, Marguerite Souchek, is aware of their feelings regarding the new assignments. She is delighted that Helen is optimistic about the job and hopes that Charles will feel the same way, once he has sunk his teeth into the new assignment. "We have tried our best to redesign these jobs so that everyone will be enthusiastic about their new work," she recently noted. "Unfortunately, you can't make everyone happy, and that's a fact of life that we're going to have to live with."

1. Over the next six months, how is Helen likely to respond to her new job? Use Figure 4.1 to help you answer this question.

2. Over the next six months, if Charles comes to like his new job, how is he likely to respond? Use Figure 4.1 to help you answer this question.

3. What advice would you offer to Charles in terms of dealing effectively with these new changes? Make three suggestions and explain each.

CASE 4.2: NEVER A DULL MOMENT

Martin Veintner has been a manager at a major hotel for almost two years, and during this time he has never received a very high performance evaluation. The main reason for these lackluster ratings is that Martin is viewed as ineffective in dealing with change, conflict, and stressful situations.

In an effort to improve Martin's performance, the hotel recently assigned Martin a mentor to help counsel and guide him. This person, Hank Trumble, began his mentoring by asking Martin about his personal beliefs and his philosophy of managing people. From these discussions, Hank identified six of Martin's most cherished beliefs. They include the following:

1. Martin thinks he must have the approval of those whom he manages; this desire influences the way he does his job.

2. He tends to blame others whom he sees as treating him unfairly and believes they should be punished in some way.

3. He becomes extremely frustrated when things do not turn out the way he wants.

4. He feels the need to worry about things, even if they are unlikely to happen.

5. He becomes easily upset over his own or other people's problems.

6. He believes that there is one correct and perfect solution to every problem and that it should be found and implemented.

Hank believes that one way of helping Martin improve his management of others is to examine and refute these six beliefs. He has raised this issue with Martin, but has met with a great deal of resistance. "There's nothing wrong with my beliefs about the world in general and people in particular," Martin told him. "I know what I know and it has gotten me this far, so why should I change my views?"

Hank is not giving up. He believes that if he works closely with Martin, he will be able to help him deal more effectively with others and, more important, with himself. He also believes that if Martin's beliefs change, he will become a more effective manager and will do a better job of coping with change, conflict, and stressful situations.

1. How are Martin's beliefs self-defeating? Explain your reasoning.

2. How are these beliefs having a negative effect on Martin and affecting his ability to deal with such typical job challenges as change and conflict?

3. If Martin changed his beliefs, would this help him more effectively manage his stress? Could it help him become a more effective time manager? Explain.

INTERPRETATION OF BOX 4.1: "JOB CHANGES AND YOU"

Review your answers and note all of those to which you gave a rating of 7 or higher. Then read the interpretations that follow that are associated with them.

1. This response measures your desire to maintain the status quo and maintain a safe, secure, stable environment.
2. This answer measures your willingness to fight changes that are suddenly thrust upon you with no advance warning.
3. This answer measures your unwillingness to assume responsibilities for which you feel you lack the appropriate skills and/or training.
4. This response measures the importance of emotional side effects on your willingness to change.
5. This answer indicates your willingness to fight change when you have a lack of trust in the individual who is promoting the change.
6. This response measures your fear of failure.
7. This answer indicates your willingness to oppose changes that are presented with a lack of tact.
8. This answer relates the likelihood of your opposing changes brought about by those with whom you have a personality conflict.
9. This response measures your opposition to changes that you feel threaten your job security.
10. This answer measures your willingness to oppose changes that break up your social group.

ENDNOTES

1. Also see "Are You a Proactive Change Manager?" *Lodging,* February 1995, p. 74.
2. Also see James Villas, "Turning the Tables," *Town & Country,* October 1994, pp. 42–44.
3. Caren Klein, "Coping with Resistance to Change," *Food Management,* April 1995, p. 44.
4. T. Quinn Spitzer, Jr. and Peter M. Tobia, "People-Wise Organizations: The Human Side of Change," *Management Review,* October 1994, pp. 44–47.
5. Richard M. Hodgetts, *Modern Human Relations at Work,* 6th ed. (Fort Worth: Dryden Press, 1996), p. 386.
6. Robert A. Kreitner, *Management,* 6th ed. (Boston: Houghton Mifflin, 1995), p. 518.
7. See, for example, "Challenge: How to Boost Employees' Communication & Problem-Solving Skills," *Food Management,* February 1995, p. 15.
8. R. Rosenmann, R. Brand, C. Jenkins, M. Friedman, R. Straus, and M. Wrum, "Coronary Heart Disease in the Western Collaborative Group Study: Final Follow-Up Experience of 8½ Years," *Journal of the American Medical Association,* No. 233, 1975, pp. 872–877; and Edward R. Ragland and Richard J. Brand, "Type A Behavior and Mortality from Coronary Heart Disease," *New England Journal of Medicine,* January 14, 1988, pp. 65–69.
9. John Soeder, "Handling the Heat," *Restaurant Hospitality,* April 1991, pp. 124–130.

10. Gary K. Vallen, "Organizational Climate and Burnout," *Cornell Hotel and Restaurant Administration Quarterly*, February 1993, pp. 54–59.

11. Richard M. Hodgetts, *Organizational Behavior* (New York: Macmillan, 1991), p. 344.

12. Reported in *U.S. News & World Report*, March 13, 1978, pp. 80–81.

13. Mort Sarabakhsh, David Carson, and Elaine Lindgren, "The Personal Cost of Hospitality Management," *Cornell Hotel and Restaurant Administration Quarterly*, May 1989, pp. 736.

14. Also see George A. Wolfe, "5 Ways to Handle Peak Work Periods," *Hotels*, September 1994, p. 22.

15. Adele Greenfield, "Staying Healthy in an Uptight Job," *HSMAI Marketing Review*, Spring 1995, pp. 54–56.

16. Reported in Hodgetts, *Organizational Behavior*, p. 353.

17. For additional insights see Lynn O'Rourke Hayes, "Remove the Mess, Reduce the Stress," *Restaurant Hospitality*, November 1993, p. 56.

CHAPTER FIVE

Developing Your Decision-Making Skills

LEARNING OBJECTIVES

One of the most important ways of gaining personal insights is to examine how you go about making decisions. Every day, customers present associates with situations that require careful evaluation and effective problem-solving decision making. The overriding purpose of this chapter is to examine the problem-solving process and ways that you can use your problem-solving skills to resolve a variety of situations. In particular, attention is given to such critical areas as perception, creativity, and personal decision-making styles. When you have finished studying all of the material in this chapter, you will be able to:

1. Identify and describe the problem-solving process.

2. Define the terms *perception* and *creativity* and explain their value in problem solving.

3. Identify your personal decision-making style.

4. Determine whether you are a left-brain or right-brain thinker.

5 Examine how you process information in arriving at decisions and relate some of the steps you can take in more effectively carrying out this activity.

The Problem-Solving Process

There is no universal approach to solving problems. However, there is a seven-step process that is typically used, in one form or another, for dealing with problems.[1] The problem-solving skills that you employ are related directly to this process, which is illustrated in Figure 5.1.

Identify and Define the Problem

Decision making begins with a definition of the problem. A problem can occur for one of two reasons. First, it can be a result of something that has gone wrong. For example, suppose that Maria Ruiz, who works in housekeeping, has shown up late for work three times this week. In this case, the symptom of the problem is Maria's tardiness. The reason is unclear and needs to be investigated. Possible reasons could include dissatisfaction with new work rules, a personal conflict with her direct superior, or a sick child at home who needs her attention.

A second common type of problem is a result of something that needs to be done. For example, suppose that over the last three months the Surfside Hotel's five major competitors have all introduced van service to and from the airport. During this same period, Surfside's occupancy rate, which is typically much higher than any of the competitors, has slipped sharply; many of its guests have told the hotel manager that airport van service is a very attractive feature. In this case, the problem is obvious.

It is important to remember that the identification and definition of a problem is the most important step in the problem-solving process. It is also important to remember that the *cause* of the problem must be addressed, not the symptom. For example, the guests at Surfside may be disappointed with the hotel's lack of airport service. However, this is the symptom. What you need to do is eliminate the reason for this negative feeling.

Gather and Analyze Relevant Facts Regarding the Problem

The next step is to gather data about the problem. In this process, you must ask: What do I need to know about this problem in order to solve it? In the case of the Surfside Hotel, for example, you could talk to the guests and/or have the customer satisfaction questionnaire revised in order to gather information on the value of van service to and from the airport.

Develop Alternative Solutions to the Problem

From the information that is gathered, alternative solutions to the problem need to be formulated. What are some of the most likely ways to resolve the problem? Sometimes you will be able to develop these alternatives personal-

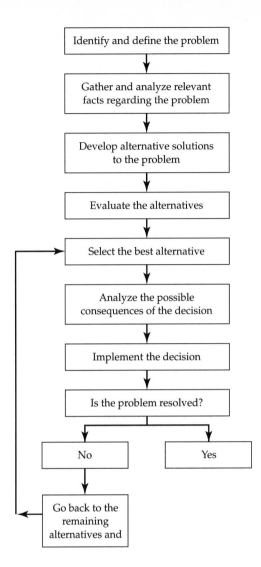

Figure 5.1 *The Problem-Solving Process*

ly; other times, input from guests or other associates is needed. In the case of the airport van service, the choices may be fairly obvious. You could rent or buy a van to provide the service; or you might make an arrangement with the airport taxi service and pay a fixed fee for every trip the service provides to incoming and departing guests; or your hotel could look into a similar arrangement with a van company.

Evaluate the Alternatives

Now you have to decide which of these alternatives will best solve the problem. In making this decision, you must balance two criteria: service and cost.

You will want to provide a service that is at least as good as that of the competition. At the same time, you will want to weigh the expense of the service. In carrying out this process, it is common to rank the choices in terms of both criteria. In this way, you know which alternative provides the best service and which costs the least money.

Select the Best Alternative

This step is obvious: you must choose the best alternative. Of course, this is sometimes more difficult than it initially appears because trade-offs are involved. For example, suppose your evaluation is the following:

Alternative	Ranking in terms of service (1 is best)	Ranking in terms of cost (1 is best)
Buy a van	2	2
Rent a van	3	3
Use a taxi service	1	4
Use a van service	4	1

This evaluation shows that it would be best for you to buy the van; when the two rankings for each alternative are totaled, buying the van has the lowest number (4) and is thus the best choice. This decision will result in better service for the customers than will most of the other alternatives, and the van will cost the hotel less money than most of the other alternatives. On the other hand, it is important to remember that this alternative does *not* provide the best service (the taxi does) nor is it the least expensive (the van service is). So there are trade-offs being made in arriving at the final decision.

Analyze the Possible Consequences of the Decision

Once you have chosen the best alternative, it is important to analyze the consequences of the decision. This is particularly important in terms of anticipating problems that might occur during implementation. For example, what will you do if the van breaks down? And what about the fact that at some point in time the van may be coming back to the hotel with a full contingent of passengers just as another group of guests is exiting the airport terminal and walking to the pick-up site? Obviously these guests are going to have to wait until the van has dropped off its passengers and returned to the airport. So there is often a downside to decisions; you must decide how these can be minimized.

Implement the Decision and Evaluate the Results

Based on all of the analysis, you must now put the decision into action. Sometimes this step involves a modification of the alternatives. In any event, once the decision is implemented, you must gather information on how well things are going and be prepared to make additionally required changes. Here is what happened at the Surfside Hotel.

> After analyzing the alternatives, the hotel manager decided to buy a van and offer 24-hour airport service. At the same time the hotel struck a deal with the airport taxi service. If the van was not at the airport or could not arrive within five minutes of the time a passenger was ready to leave for the hotel, the taxi service would pick up the passenger. Before doing so, however, the driver would call the dispatcher and ensure that the van was not in the nearby area. If the van was at the airport (or arriving in a few minutes) the driver would direct the passenger to the pick-up zone. Only if the individual insisted on taking a cab and paying for it would the driver accept the fare. The same arrangement is used from the hotel to the airport. If the van will not be available for at least five minutes, the hotel will call for a cab for the guests.

Since this new strategy was implemented, Surfside has found business increasing, and guest comments about the service are all positive. Of course, if the problem had not been resolved, the hotel would have had to go back and try again by selecting and implementing the next best solution (see Figure 5.1).

Developing Useful Problem-Solving Skills

Now that we have examined the problem-solving process, we want to look at developing problem-solving skills. Two areas warrant consideration: perception and creative thinking. The two are interrelated because people's perceptions often influence their ability to think creatively—and when they learn to think creatively, they often have different perceptions.

Perception

Perception is a person's view of reality.[2] Customer service is a good example. The Surfside Hotel believes that it is giving better airport service now than ever before. However, suppose an individual is walking to the pick-up site, but the driver does not see her and drives off. How does this guest view the hotel's van service? Extremely poorly. On the other hand, 90 percent of all the customer feedback cards may report that the hotel is doing an excellent job of providing van service. What we have here is a perception gap. Most people like the service, but not everyone. This idea can be further reinforced by interpreting some perception pictures. Figure 5.2 presents four pictures. Look at each picture and write down your answer to the question. When you are finished, compare your answers to those of others who are taking this quiz. Did

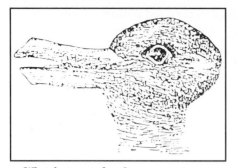

a. What do you see here?

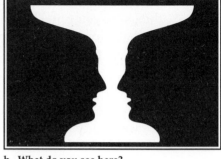

b. What do you see here?

c. What do you see here?

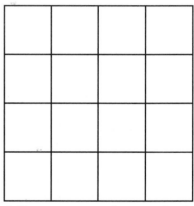

d. How many squares do you see here?

Figure 5.2   *Perception and You*

you all see the same thing? Where did you differ? After you have examined the similarities and differences in response, turn to the end of the chapter and find out what most people "see" in the pictures.

An understanding of perception is an important key in unlocking an answer to the question: How do you solve problems? This is because you are limited by your view of reality. However, it is not necessary to stay within these confines. If you learn how to think creatively, you can expand your perceptions and improve both the quantity and quality of your problem-solving decisions.

Creative-Thinking Process

Creative thinking is the ability to see things in new, imaginative ways. This process is particularly useful in problem solving because it is closely linked to all of the seven steps that we examined earlier.[3] The linkage is as follows:

Creative Thinking	Problem Solving
1. Personal need	1. Identify and define the problem.
2. Preparation	2. Gather and analyze relevant facts.
3. Incubation	3. Develop alternative solutions.
	4. Evaluate the alternatives.
4. Illumination	5. Select the best alternative.
	6. Analyze the possible consequences of the decision.
5. Verification	7. Implement the decision.

Personal Need. *Personal need* refers to the inner drive of an individual to be creative in solving a problem. In many hospitality-related situations, associates are often called on to be original or develop spur-of-the-moment solutions. When this need arises, the creativity process begins.

> When Margaret and Frank Reardon arrived at the Grand Marquis Hotel, it was already past 10 P.M. Their plane had been delayed by bad weather, and the drive from the airport had been slow because of ice on the roads. As they approached the check-in desk, Frank took a credit card out of his wallet, placed it on the counter, and said to the reservations clerk, Toni Addams, "Drs. Margaret and Frank Reardon. We have a one-night reservation." Toni quickly surveyed the guest list and saw that the reservation had not been guaranteed for late arrival. However, she also saw that they were the main speakers at the medical conference that was scheduled to begin at 8 A.M. the next morning. Apparently the conference arrangement people had failed to consider the fact that they might be arriving late. All of the rooms were already filled and because of the bad weather, Toni was sure that the Reardons would not want to be transported to another hotel at this time of the night. So without saying a word about the problem, Toni asked the couple to sign in.

Preparation. Obviously Toni has a problem that will require a creative solution. This is where *preparation,* the second phase of the creative-thinking process, enters the picture. Some people think that creativity is like a bolt out of the blue. In truth, creative people report that they spend a great deal of time preparing to be creative. During this period, they are saturated with information and learn how to use these data to generate new, original solutions. In Toni's case, she has been a reservations clerk for four years and has had to deal with a wide variety of problems. So she has had ample preparation.

Incubation. The *incubation* state is marked by the unconscious mind working on the problem. The data the individual has gathered about the problem and the problem itself sit in the person's mind, while he or she mulls things over or simply lets the mind take over the problem-solving process. This is often a quiet period during which little physical activity takes place.

As soon as the Reardons had finished registering, Toni asked them if they would like to have a small bite to eat in the hotel's all-night restaurant while she took care of their room reservations. Since they had not eaten in almost six hours, they welcomed the suggestion. As they left, Toni began thinking about how she could resolve the room dilemma.

Illumination. *Illumination* is that stage of creative thinking when the solution to the problem is discovered. Sometimes the individual may gradually work out the solution. In other cases, especially if it is a small problem, the entire solution may become obvious all at once.

As Toni began thinking about where she could put up the Reardons for the evening, it occurred to her that at the north end of the penthouse was a meeting room that could be sealed off from the rest of the unit. There was a full bathroom there and, if furniture could be brought up, the area could be turned into a temporary bedroom.

Verification. The last step in the creative-thinking process is *verification*, which involves implementing the solution and making any necessary modifications. Sometimes creative solutions do not work quite the way they are envisioned, but with some minor changes they can be made to work correctly. It is at this point that the problem solver begins "tweaking" the solution to fit the situation.

Toni called the penthouse and talked to the guest, who happened to be another member of the conference the Reardons would be addressing. After Toni explained the situation, the guest readily agreed to having the north end sealed off and turned into a bedroom for the evening. Toni then called the assistant manager, told him what she had done, and asked him to oversee preparation of the room. Within 30 minutes the project was complete. The assistant manager then went to the restaurant, where the Reardons were just finishing their coffee. "The hotel manager has asked me to personally look after you," he told the Reardons. "I have had a special room set up for you in the penthouse and would be happy to take you there whenever you're ready."

Things appear to be working out well. However, notice that Toni asked the assistant manager to help out; he will be with the Reardons when they go to their room. If there is anything else that needs to be done to improve the situation, the assistant manager can see that it is done.

Brainstorming

In the preceding example, one individual (Toni) did most of the creative thinking (although the assistant manager certainly helped out by going to the dining room and welcoming the Reardons). Sometimes, however, creative decisions are best made by groups. This is particularly true when the problem affects all of the members and they may be able to collectively resolve it. One of the best known approaches for doing this is *brainstorming,* a technique that encourages individuals to work collectively to generate a unique or creative approach to problem solving. There are two basic psychological phenomena that are common to group participation in creative thinking:

1. There is an effort to produce as many ideas as possible with no attempt to restrict or restrain what people say. Free association of ideas is what counts, and a group can generate more ideas than an individual can.

2. There is a chance to shape the opinions and ideas of the group and, in turn, to be shaped by them. This further stimulates each individual to contribute to the group effort.

A number of guidelines and procedures are used in conducting brainstorming sessions. The following are six of the most useful: (1) hold the session to about 40 to 60 minutes in length; (2) do not have more than 10 to 12 people in a session; (3) do not reveal the problem before the session begins; (4) state the problem clearly but not too broadly; (5) use a conference table that allows the participants to see and communicate easily with each other; and (6) if the matter being discussed involves a physical product, such as a registration form, a serving tray, or a cellular phone, have one in the room so the participants can examine it.

The procedures used in brainstorming will vary slightly, depending on the specific method employed.[4] The most common is the *freewheeling method,* in which individuals call out ideas regarding how the problem can be resolved; others in the room can either build on these ideas or offer different ones. In either event, one individual is assigned to write down the ideas on a flipchart or a board, so that everyone can see what is being said and use this to generate additional ideas. One of the primary benefits of the freewheeling approach is that it helps generate a "charged" atmosphere in which each individual tries to outdo the others by offering creative ideas.

Another approach is the *round-robin method,* in which each group member in turn contributes an idea. When a group member has nothing to contribute, he or she simply says "pass." The process continues until everyone has passed. One of the primary benefits of the round-robin method is that it gives everyone a chance to participate on an equal footing and reduces the chances of a couple of people dominating the meeting.

One of the best ways of practicing your problem-solving skills is by combining perception and creativity. Box 5.1 offers such an opportunity.[5]Complete this exercise before continuing to the next section.

Problem-Solving Approaches

People solve problems in a number of different ways. Some individuals are very methodical and analytical. They gather information and systematically formulate logical solutions. Other people are very sporadic and unstructured. They gather a wide array of information and brainstorm their way to creative solutions.[6] Each uses a different approach, yet each is successful. To better understand why this is true, it is necessary to examine (1) decision-making styles, (2) left-brain and right-brain thinking, and (3) how people think and process information.

Decision-Making Styles

Everyone has a unique decision-making style that reflects the individual's personality and preferred way of doing things.[7] This preferred style greatly influences the way the person makes decisions and solves problems. You can see this more clearly by looking at two major activities of decision making: information gathering and data evaluation. Each of these activities is quite different from the other and has its own set of orientations.

Information-Gathering Orientation. Information gathering involves two psychological functions: sensation and intuition. Individuals who are *sensation types* like to solve problems in standard ways. These individuals do well in routine work; they are quite effective at lower levels of the hierarchy. When they work with standard, familiar problems, they are typically assertive and fast-paced, and they like to use a "let's get it done now" approach. However, if sensation types have to learn new skills or complicated details, they often become impatient or frustrated.

> Pablo Guzman is responsible for inventory control in all three restaurants in a large hotel complex. For the last four years he has used a specially designed inventory reporting form that he created. Two weeks ago, however, Pablo received a new, more detailed form from the organization treasurer with a note explaining that in the future the company wants all inventory data reported on this form. Additionally, while Pablo's form was completed three times a week, the new form is to be filled out and sent back to the treasurer's office by noon every day. Pablo believes that the new form is not only more complicated but not as useful as his own. So he has ignored the new

Box 5.1
Using Your Perception and Creative Flexibility

The following five problems are designed to help you improve your perceptual and creative skills. In no more than five minutes, read and complete each of the assignments. After this time, form into groups of four to six individuals and choose one person to direct the brainstorming session and to write down the answers. Then using the freewheeling approach, answer each question. When you are finished, compare your answers to those at the end of the chapter.

1. Interpret the following message: 2TTTT

2. Make an equilateral triangle (all sides equal) by connecting the three dots.

3. Add one word to each of the three words below to create a commonly known word or word combination. In all three cases, the word you add must be the *same.*

           PORT   MOTOR   PET

4. Three men went to a ballgame. Each treated his two sons to the price of admission. In all, they bought seven tickets. Nobody had a pass and everybody saw the game seated. Explain.

5. Study the pattern of the following numbers:

$$\frac{1 \qquad 4}{0 \quad 2 \ 3}$$

Now fill in the numbers 5, 6, 7, 8, and 9 either above or below the line according to the set pattern.

---

form and continued to submit his own. Yesterday he received a phone call from the treasurer's secretary. The treasurer would like to see Pablo in his office at 3 P.M. today.

Why is Pablo not using the new inventory control form? Because he is a sensation type. He wants to get things done quickly and easily—and the form he designed is a lot easier for him to complete the one that he received from the treasurer. So he is dragging his heels and has not been complying with the directive to change forms.

Individuals who are *intuitive types* like to solve new problems. In fact, doing the same thing over and over again bores them, and they are likely to become impatient and make snap decisions in handling such routine problems. Intuitive decision makers rely on hunches, nonverbalized cues, spontaneity, and an openness in redefining and reworking problems until they are solved. These individuals also keep the total picture in mind and modify or alter their approaches in an effort to continuously focus on the major problem.

> When Pablo arrived at the treasurer's office, he was certain that he would be asked to explain why he was not using the new inventory form. However, the issue never came up—at least directly. Instead, the treasurer spent his time talking about the value of the new inventory form and how it would help computerize financial controls. "A lot of our people don't like the new form," he told Pablo, "and I know there are some problems with it. However, to make it easy on everyone, I'm assigning Karlene Carter to your unit for the next three weeks. She has carefully analyzed both your form and our new one. I've asked her to work with you, use both forms, and then modify ours so that it is as simple and easy to use as yours." The treasurer then sent for Karlene, introduced her to Pablo and said, "I know the two of you have a lot to talk about, so I'll let you get going." On the way back to Pablo's office, Karlene explained how excited she was to be working in inventory control and to have the opportunity to combine the two forms into one easy-to-use report. "I've got a million ideas. I can't wait to get started and tailor-make this form into one that everyone in the organization will want to use!"

Is Karlene an intuitive type? She certainly is. Notice how she wants to create a new form that combines the best of the current ones. She seems open to new ideas, spontaneous, and willing to redefine and rework the current materials to create a new, better inventory control form.

If an individual is high on sensation, he or she will be low on intuition. These two psychological functions represent extreme orientations used by individuals in gathering information, and they can be represented as in Figure 5.3.

Evaluation Orientation. Evaluation orientation involves two psychological functions: thinking and feeling. These are opposite extremes used in evaluating information. (Again, see Figure 5.3.)

Thinking types tend to be unemotional and uninterested in the feelings of others. Their decisions are controlled by intellectual processes based on external information and generally accepted ideas and values. These people usual-

Information-Gathering Orientations

High	Balanced	High

Sensation   Intuition

Evaluation Orientations

High	Balanced	High

Thinking   Feeling

Figure 5.3 *Information Gathering and Evaluation Orientations*

ly organize information well and seldom reach a conclusion before carefully considering all important options. Thinking types make excellent hospitality managers who function well in situations in which personal feeling has to be secondary to making the right decision.

> Steve O'Bannion is in charge of all front-door operations at a major hotel. When a guest drives up to the hotel, Steve's associates are responsible for welcoming the individual and providing valet parking. The hotel outsources these two functions to Steve's company, so that its associates can devote their time to in-house services. The tourist season at the hotel will come to an end next week, and for the next three months the hotel will have only a 50 percent occupancy. As a result, Steve has told all of the part-time help that he hired at the beginning of the season that they will be laid off for 90 days. "I'll hire you back when business picks up, but for the moment I don't need you any more," he told the assembled group. "Friday will be your last day." A little later in the morning one of the part-timers, Joel Steinmetz, came to see Steve to ask if he could keep him on for a few more weeks until he could find another job. He told Steve, "I signed a one-year lease on my apartment and I can't make the payments if I don't have a job." Steve told Joel that he was sorry, but "I've got a business to run and I have to keep my expenses to a minimum."

Is Steve a thinking type? He certainly is. He did not become angry at Joel, but he did make it clear that Joel could not keep his job. The fact that Joel had signed a lease was not an issue for Steve. He focused strictly on the job at hand, knew the number of people he needed to provide the guest services, and was not going to be dissuaded from his objective of running an efficient business.

Feeling types like harmony and pleasant environments. They tend to be sympathetic and relate well to others. They also enjoy pleasing people and believe that much of the inefficiency and ineffectiveness in the organization is a result of interpersonal difficulties.

When Joel realized that he was going to be let go by Steve O'Bannion, he talked to the hotel concierge, one of his friends. The individual told Joel to speak with the assistant manager, Rita Chang. "She is a very nice person and is always trying to help people. I'm sure she would hire you for a few weeks. There has got to be a lot of work that still has to be done, even though the season is coming to an end. Go and ask her." Joel took his friend's advice and went immediately to Rita's office and spoke with her. After explaining that he had worked for Steve for the last six months, Rita said, "Well, you certainly know a lot about how we operate, so you'll be able to hit the ground running. I'm going to send you over to Bob Fitz in human resources. He'll have you fill out all the necessary paperwork. Then you're to report to the grounds maintenance manager. He's always understaffed because some people around here don't particularly like him, so he's last on their list for assistance. We need to start putting this place back together, especially the golf course, which needs a lot of work. I know that they'll need you for at least a month, and in the interim you can look around for additional work." Joel thanked Rita and hurried over to Bob's office.

Is Rita a feeling type? Yes, she is. Notice how she immediately related to Joel and granted his work request. Additionally, she assigned him to the grounds maintenance group because she felt that this group did not get sufficient resources to do its job well.

A Composite Picture. What type of decision maker are you? Before examining your profile, keep in mind that psychologist Carl Jung believed that an individual tends to be dominant in only one of the four functions (sensation, intuition, thinking, or feeling), which is backed up by one of the functions from the other set of paired opposites. For example, an individual can be high in sensation, followed by thinking. Or the individual can be high in intuition, followed by feeling. The four basic decision style combinations are sensation/thinking, sensation/feeling, intuition/thinking, and intuition/feeling. These are referred to as basic decision styles.[8]

A number of tests have been developed for measuring decision-making styles. Box 5.2 provides one that has been specially developed to measure your preferences for sensation/intuition and thinking/feeling. Take this test and complete the scoring key before continuing your reading.

Remember that your decision-making style will be a reflection of the type of work you do as well as your personal interests; so there can be changes in your approach, depending on the job-related demands that are made on you.

Box 5.2
What Type of Decision Maker Are You?

The following statements are presented in pairs (a and b). In each case you are to rate your preference for the statements by allocating a total of 10 points. For example, if you strongly agree with statement 1a and do not agree at all with statement 1b, give statement 1a all 10 points and give statement 1b a zero. If you like statement 1a better than statement 1b, then give statement 1a more of the 10 points than you give to statement 1b. Follow this approach in evaluating each of the twelve paired statements. Remember that each pair must have a *total* of 10 points.

I prefer to:

_____	1a. use methods that I know are effective in getting the job done.
_____	1b. try using new methods that require approaches that I have not used before.
_____	2a. make decisions about people in the organization based on facts and the systematic analysis of situations.
_____	2b. make decisions about people in the organization based on empathy and my feelings and understanding of their needs and values.
_____	3a. think about possibilities when formulating decisions.
_____	3b. think about actualities when formulating decisions.
_____	4a. draw conclusions based on unemotional logic and careful step-by-step analysis.
_____	4b. draw conclusions based on what I feel and believe, and based on my past experiences.
_____	5a. make decisions by looking at the big picture and trying to imagine how everything fits together.
_____	5b. make decisions by looking at the factual details that are available and letting these guide my actions.
_____	6a. solve problems by thinking through a solution.
_____	6b. solve problems by letting my feelings guide me.
_____	7a. rely heavily on ideas when making decisions.
_____	7b. rely heavily on facts when making decisions.
_____	8a. help others explore their feelings.
_____	8b. help others make logical decisions.
_____	9a. carry out carefully crafted, detailed plans and do so with precision.
_____	9b. design plans without necessarily carrying them out.
_____	10a. use common sense and conviction to make decisions.
_____	10b. use data, analysis, and objective reasoning to make decisions.

Box 5.2   Continued

_____ 11a. make decisions by imagining what might be and let this influence my judgment.

_____ 11b. make decisions by examining details of the actual situation and let this direct my judgment.

_____ 12a. experience emotional situations and discussions.

_____ 12b. use my ability to analyze situations.

Scoring: Place each of your answers to the quiz in the following scoring key. For example, if you gave an 8 to statement 1a and a 2 to statement 1b, place an 8 next to the 1a in Group 2 and a 2 next to the 1b in Group 1.

Group 1	**Group 2**	**Group 3**	**Group 4**
1b. ___	1a. ___	2a. ___	2b. ___
3a. ___	3b. ___	4a. ___	4b. ___
5a. ___	5b. ___	6a. ___	6b. ___
7a. ___	7b. ___	8b. ___	8a. ___
9b. ___	9a. ___	10b. ___	10a. ___
11a. ___	11b. ___	12b. ___	12a. ___
Total ___	___	___	___
Intuitive	Sensation	Thinking	Feeling

Interpretation: Group 1 measures your preference for the intuitive type of decision making. Group 2 measures your preference for the sensation type of decision making. Group 3 measures your preference for the thinking type of decision making. Group 4 measures your preference for the feeling type of decision making.

As noted in the text, most people have two high scores. One is typically for intuitive or sensation decision making; the other is for thinking or feeling decision making. Identify the decision style that is most representative of you by placing a checkmark next to it:

_____ sensation/thinking

_____ intuition/thinking

_____ sensation/feeling

_____ intuition/feeling

Remember that your highest score identifies the first of these two styles and your second highest score identifies the other. Write down your two highest-scoring styles and the accompanying number for each, based on this test.

Type	**Score**
1. _____	_____
2. _____	_____

Additionally, researchers have found that there is a link between a person's decision-making style and whether the person is left-brain or right-brain oriented. So before we conclude our discussion of information-processing styles, we need to look at how you think and integrate this into the overall problem-solving process.

Left-Brain, Right-Brain Thinking

Closely related to your decision-making style is the way in which you process information. Research shows that some people tend to use the left side of their brain more than the right, while others are just the opposite. *Left-brain dominance* is the tendency to be factual, analytical, methodical, and structured. *Right-brain dominance* is the tendency to be intuitive, creative, improvisational, and unstructured.[9] Table 5.1 provides some contrasts between these two brain hemispheres.

Left-brain people tend to make decisions in a sequential way. They start by defining the problem, move on to conducting a rational, methodical analysis of the causes, and then generate solutions for solving the problem. These individuals are extremely effective in screening out extraneous information, and they rely most heavily on logic and facts. Right-brain people are different in their analytical approach to decision making. They tend to have a broader focus, often pick up cues in the environment around them, and combine facts in a more creative way. Both types of individuals can be very effective in making decisions, but there are times when one approach provides a better answer than the other. And sometimes a combination of the two is even more effective!

> Tim Walters and Pam Mandley work at a five-star restaurant in the Chicago area. Customers book reservations weeks in advance in order to eat here, and the restaurant owner prides herself on the establishment's first-class service. Every week customers are contacted and asked to fill out a brief questionnaire regarding their experiences at the restaurant. Three months ago Tim and Pam were given a composite of the latest responses. To their surprise, over 40 percent of the diners said that it takes too long to be served. The owner asked Tim and Pam to devise a strategy for eliminating this problem. Their investigation revealed that the average diner had to wait 55 minutes from the time the server took the order until the food was delivered to the table. From their interviews with customers, Tim and Pam also determined that 30 minutes was the maximum amount of time that people were willing to wait.
>
> Based on this information, Tim and Pam worked closely with the dining room staff to redesign the work flow in the kitchen, so that orders could be handled more efficiently. In the process, they had

Table 5.1 Specialized Brain-Hemisphere Functions

Left Brain	Right Brain
Recognize and remember names	Recognize and remember faces
Respond to verbal instructions	Respond to visual instruction
Dislike improvising	Like to improvise
Solve problems systematically	Solve problems playfully
Solve problems logically	Solve problems intuitively
Respond to logic appeals	Respond to emotional appeals
Deal with one problem at a time	Deal with several problems at a time
Not psychic	Highly psychic
Produce logical ideas	Produce humorous ideas
Seldom use metaphors	Often use metaphors
Give information verbally	Give information with movement
Depend on words for meanings	Interpret body language

some of the stoves and other appliances resituated and the aisles widened. Under this new arrangement, customer waiting time was reduced to 38 minutes. However, followup customer surveys indicated that the diners still reported that it took too long for service. This is when Pam suggested another change. At the front of the dining room was a large, regal clock that is mounted on the wall and can be seen by everyone. Pam had the clock removed and replaced with a large painting of a pastoral setting. Since this change, the number of customers reporting that service is too slow has dropped from 46 percent to 4 percent, and 31 percent of the diners rate the restaurant as excellent in "provides prompt service."

When Tim and Pam worked on redesigning the flow of work in the kitchen and cutting the waiting time for service, what type of thinking were they using? They were employing left-brain thinking. They systematically, logically, and sequentially analyzed the problem and formulated solutions. However, when this approach did not fully solve the problem, Pam used right-brain thinking to generate an additional change. Who would have thought that the clock was part of the reason that people felt service took too long? Obviously, many of the diners looked at it and noted how long they were waiting. Additionally, it is possible that the clock resulted in the customers exaggerating how long they waited. In either event, Pam's decision to remove the clock also removed the diners' perception of how long they were waiting.

Table 5.2   The Range of Decision Styles in Human Information Processing

| | Left Hemisphere ← Decision Style → Right Hemisphere | | | |
	ST Sensation/Thinking	NT Intuition/Thinking	SF Sensation/Feeling	NF Intuition/Feeling
Focus of attention	Facts	Possibilities	Facts	Possibilities
Method of handling things	Impersonal analysis	Impersonal analysis	Personal warmth	Personal warmth
Tendency to become	Practical and matter-of-fact	Logical and ingenious	Sympathetic and friendly	Enthusiastic and insightful
Expression of abilities	Technical skills with facts and objects	Theoretical and technical developments	Practical help and services for people	Understanding and communicating with people

Source: Adapted from William Taggart and Daniel Robey, "Minds and Managers: On the Dual Nature of Human Information Processing and Management," *Academy of Management Review,* April 1981, p. 190.

Thinking and Processing

The story of Tim and Pam is useful in pointing out that the way people think (left-brain, right-brain) typically plays a role in how they process information. This is illustrated in Table 5.2, which brings together decision styles and brain dominance.

After you have read the information in the table, go back to the results of Box 5.2 and look at the type of decision maker you are. If you are a sensation/thinking or intuition/thinking type, you are likely to be a left-brain thinker. If you are a sensation/feeling or intuition/feeling type, you are likely to be a right-brain thinker. Is this true for you? You can answer this question by turning to the end of the chapter and completing the self-feedback exercise. Do this now; after you compute your score on this exercise, read the next paragraph.

Most people find that Table 5.2 accurately reflects their information processing style: left-brain thinkers tend to be sensation/thinking or intuition/thinking types, and right-brain thinkers tend to be sensation/feeling or intuition/feeling types.[10]

A second important idea conveyed by Table 5.2 is that individuals have to be flexible in their processing style. Since they face a wide variety of technical and human-oriented questions, they will be more effective if they can change their style to fit their problems. Sometimes a hospitality manager has to be a good planner; other times the individual has to be a coach or mentor; still other times the person has to be an empathetic listener. No one style is best in every situation. This can be illustrated by looking at the way a manager might use each of the four styles in Table 5.2 when responding to an associate whose performance has been marginal.

Manager's Style	Response	Characteristic of the Response
Sensation/ thinking	Improve your performance or you're fired!	Factual, impersonal, practical
Intuition/ thinking	If your performance does improve, you will be transferred to another position.	Possibilities, impersonal, ingenious
Sensation/ feeling	You need to change; what can we do to help you?	Factual, personal, sympathetic
Intuition/ feeling	You can improve your performance; let me suggest an approach	Possibilities, personal, insightful

Today researchers are studying how and why left-brain-dominant people process information differently from right-brain-dominant people. They are also interested in integrated and mixed problem-solving strategies. An integrated problem solver uses the left *and* right hemispheres simultaneously without a clear preference for either. If pressured to express a preference, individuals do tend to favor one over the other. However, the strong connection between the two hemispheres indicates that the real preference is for using both together. A *mixed* problem-solving strategy is used by individuals who use *either* a left- or right-dominant strategy, depending on the situation. So there are actually four categories of problem-solving strategies: right-brain, left-brain, integrated, and mixed.

Regardless of your style, however, it is possible to make up for deficiencies by teaming up with someone who can complement your approach. For example, in our earlier story, Tim and Pam initially used a left-brain approach to solve the customer service problem. Then Pam used a right-brain approach to generate an additional strategy that ended up resolving the problem. Although the story did not clearly spell out whether Tim was a left-brain thinker or whether Pam was an integrated or mixed thinker, one thing is certain: Pam provided important additional input to the solution. This is something that you also can do; and to the extent that you are a left- or right-brain thinker, you can learn to think from the other side of your brain—if you practice doing so. A good example is provided by Box 5.3, which gives you an opportunity to use your creative skills.

Box 5.3
Thinking Creatively

This test does not measure intelligence or mathematical ability. It is designed solely to provide you the opportunity to use your creativity and to think from both sides of your brain. As you work to solve each of the puzzles, try to use both logic and creativity. Consider some of the possible answers to the problem and then use mental brainstorming to help you arrive at the correct solution. Take 20 minutes to solve as many of these problems as you can. Then join together with other individuals who are taking the quiz, share answers, and collectively brainstorm the remaining problems. If you are a left-brain thinker, team up with at least one right-brain thinker, and vice versa.

Instructions: Each line below contains the letters of words that will make a correct phrase. Your task is to fill in the missing words.

Examples: 12 M. in a Y.   12 months in a year

88 P. K.   88 piano keys

1. 26 L. of the A.   _____

2. 4 Q. in a G.   _____

3. 54 C. in the D. (with the J.)   _____

4. 12 S. of the Z.   _____

5. $200 to P. G. in M.   _____

6. 9 P. in the S. S.   _____

7. 18 H. on a G. C.   _____

8. 90 D. in a R. A.   _____

9. 24 H. in a D.   _____

10. 13 S. on the A. F.   _____

11. 7 W. of the W.   _____

12. 57 H. V.   _____

13. 60 S. in a M.   _____

14. 5 F. on one H.   _____

15. 29 D. in F. in a L. Y.   _____

When you have finished, compare your answers with those at the end of the chapter. Most people get only six of these right when working alone. They pick up five more when they join a group and add those that other members have figured out. And they get two more when working collectively with the other group members in a brainstorming session. How well did you do?

SUMMARY

1. There is no universal approach to solving problems. However, there are seven steps that are typically used: (1) identify and define the problem; (2) gather and analyze the relevant facts regarding the problem; (3) develop alternative solutions to the problem; (4) evaluate the alternatives; (5) select the best alternative; (6) analyze the possible consequences of the decision; and (7) implement the decision and evaluate the results.

2. In developing useful problem-solving skills, two areas play an important role: perception and creative thinking. Perception is a person's view of reality. Creative thinking is the ability to see things in new, imaginative ways. In particular, the five steps in the creative-thinking process (personal need, preparation, incubation, illumination, and verification) are closely linked to the steps in the problem-solving process.

3. There are a number of ways to generate creative solutions to problems. One of the most helpful is brainstorming, which allows groups of individuals to apply their creative ideas to solving a problem.

4. There are a variety of ways in which people solve problems. These activities can be examined in terms of two major activities: information gathering and data evaluation. Information gathering involves two psychological functions: sensation and intuition. Sensation types like to solve problems in standard ways. Intuitive types like to solve problems using new approaches. Data evaluation involves two other psychological functions: thinking and feeling. Thinking types tend to be unemotional and uninterested in the feelings of others. Feeling types like harmony and pleasant environments. Most people tend to be dominant in only one of the four functions (sensation, intuition, thinking, or feeling) which is backed up by one of the functions from the other set of paired opposites.

5. Closely related to individuals' decision-making styles is the way in which they process information. Research shows that some people tend to be left-brain dominant, while others are right-brain dominant. Still others tend to be whole-brain and draw on both sides of their brain in processing information. Left-brain-dominant people tend to be factual, analytical, methodical, and structured. Right-brain-dominant people tend to be intuitive, creative, improvisational, and unstructured. Research shows that sensation/thinking and intuition/thinking people tend to be left-brain-dominant, and sensation/feeling and intuition/feeling people tend to be right-brain-dominant. These preferences tend to greatly affect the way individuals process information.

KEY TERMS

perception	freewheeling method
creative thinking	round-robin method
personal need	sensation types
preparation	intuitive types
incubation	thinking types
illumination	feeling types
verification	left-brain dominance
brainstorming	right-brain dominance

REVIEW AND APPLICATION QUESTIONS

1. How does the problem-solving process work? Identify and describe the seven steps.

2. Leona Rosenzweig, who is in charge of the housekeeping department of a large hotel, has found that three of the associates responsible for cleaning the large suites in the tower area have been leaving 30 minutes before their shift is up. Leona discovered this yesterday when she saw one of their friends clocking out the three associates and demanded to know what the individual was doing. What problem does Leona face? What are the symptoms of this problem? How can the problem-solving process be of value to Leona?

3. In what way does perception affect a person's problem-solving skills? Give an example.

4. What is meant by the term *creative thinking*? In what way is this process similar to that of problem solving?

5. Paul Ranfler would like to improve the layout of his hotel's lobby and make the area more attractive to guests. In what way could brainstorming be of value to him? Whom would you recommend that Paul include in the design of the session? Explain your reasoning.

6. If Paul Ranfler conducts a brainstorming session, what advice would you give to him? Help him run an effective session.

7. Sandra Carlson's problem-solving approach is that of sensation/thinking. Don Manguez's approach is that of intuition/feeling. How would you describe the way in which each individual goes about solving problems?

8. Referring to the two people in question 7, would they complement each other in arriving at effective decisions or would they get in each other's way? Explain your reasoning.

9. Referring to Sandra Carlson and Don Manguez in questions 7 and 8, which one do you think is left-brain dominant? Which is right-brain dominant? What do your answers tell you about the way in which they will process information and solve problems?

10. If a person is a left-brain thinker, what types of hospitality-related problems would the individual be effective in solving? If the individual is a right-brain thinker, what types of hospitality-related problems would the person be effective in solving? Compare and contrast the two.

SELF-FEEDBACK EXERCISE: ARE YOU A LEFT-BRAIN OR A RIGHT-BRAIN PERSON?

As noted in the chapter, some people tend to be left-brain dominant, while others are right-brain dominant. The following questions are designed to help you determine which you are. Before answering the 25 questions, however, keep in mind that this exercise is designed only to provide you with some preliminary information regarding your perception of the type of decision maker you are. Also remember that many people are not totally left- or right-brain dominant, but rather use an integrated or mixed decision-making process. The following does not measure the latter two strategies. It provides feedback only on your preference for left- or right-brain thinking.

Answer each of the following as accurately as you can. It is a forced-choice test, so circle the letter of the option you like best (or dislike least), but remember to answer each one.

1. When you solve problems, your basic approach is:
   a. logical, rational
   b. intuitive

2. If you wrote books, which type would you prefer to write?
   a. fiction
   b. nonfiction

3. When you read, you read for:
   a. main ideas
   b. specific facts and details

4. Which of these types of stories do you most like to read?
   a. realistic
   b. fantasy

5. When you study or read:
   a. you listen to music on the radio
   b. you must have silence
6. How do you prefer to learn?
   a. through ordering and planning
   b. through free exploration
7. How do you like to organize things?
   a. sequentially
   b. in terms of relationships
8. Which of these phrases better describes you:
   a. almost no mood changes
   b. frequent mood changes
9. Do you enjoy clowning around?
   a. yes
   b. no
10. How would you describe yourself?
    a. generally conforming
    b. generally nonconforming
11. Are you absentminded?
    a. frequently
    b. almost never
12. What types of assignments do you like best?
    a. well structured
    b. open-ended
13. Which is most preferable to you?
    a. producing ideas
    b. drawing conclusions
14. Which is the most fun for you?
    a. dreaming
    b. planning realistically
15. Which of these would be most exciting for you?
    a. inventing something new
    b. improving on something already in existence
16. What type of stories do you prefer?
    a. action
    b. mystery

17. Which do you like better?

   a. cats

   b. dogs

18. What do you like better?

   a. creating stories

   b. analyzing stories

19. Do you think better:

   a. sitting up straight

   b. lying down

20. If you could be either, which would you prefer to be?

   a. a music composer

   b. a music critic

21. Could you be hypnotized?

   a. yes, quite easily

   b. no, I don't think so

22. Which would you prefer to do?

   a. ballet dancing

   b. interpretive impromptu dancing

23. Which are you better at?

   a. recalling names and dates

   b. recalling where things were in a room or picture

24. When it comes to getting instructions, which do you prefer?

   a. verbal instructions

   b. demonstrations

25. When getting verbal instructions, how do you generally feel?

   a. restless

   b. attentive

Scoring: Compare your answers to the following key. Circle your response to each, and then add up the total of circled responses in each column.

	Column I	Column II
1.	b	a
2.	a	b
3.	a	b
4.	b	a
5.	a	b
6.	b	a

	Right Brain	Left Brain
7.	b	a
8.	b	a
9.	a	b
10.	b	a
11.	a	b
12.	b	a
13.	a	b
14.	a	b
15.	a	b
16.	b	a
17.	a	b
18.	a	b
19.	b	a
20.	a	b
21.	a	b
22.	b	a
23.	b	a
24.	b	a
25.	a	b
Total	____	____
	Right Brain	Left Brain

Interpretation: Column I measures your perceived preference for using right-brain functions, while Column II measures your perceived preference for using left-brain functions. If you want more information on the way you perceive yourself as a decision maker, go back and reread Box 5.1. Right-brain thinkers tend to have scores of 16 or more in Column I. Left-brain thinkers have scores of 16 or more in Column II. Whole-brain or balanced thinkers, who are able to think from both sides of their brain, have scores of 15 or less in both columns.

CASE 5.1: AND NEXT YEAR WILL BE EVEN BETTER!

Rich Sleshing is not much of a partygoer. So when he was called into the bank president's office, he hardly suspected that the president was going to put him in charge of the annual Christmas party. "Let's do something different this year," the executive told Rich. "Every year we go to a local hotel and have a sit-down dinner, followed by a dance. Do you think you could break this pattern? You can have 30 percent more budget than last year." Rich promised to try to live up to the president's expectations.

Upon leaving the president's office, Rich immediately called his sister-in-law, Janice, who is the executive assistant for a major executive in town. He discussed his situation with her, and Janice gave him the number of Sue Shapiro. "She handles all of our parties. The woman knows how to put these events together. Give her a call."

Three days later Rich and Sue met for lunch to discuss his ideas for the bank's Christmas party. "I was thinking that perhaps we should rent a place like a big hall and have the dinner and dance there. Or maybe we could have a dinner cruise on one of the yachts that go out to the breakwater and return. What do you think?" Sue listened quietly but said nothing. When he was finished, Rich asked for her ideas. As she talked, Sue made notes so that she could review everything with him when she was finished.

> I like what you're trying to do, Rich, but you have to put more pizazz into the party. You're keeping the dinner and dance, but just moving the location. For the budget you have available, you can do a lot more. I suggest renting an indoor amusement park over on the beach. We would decorate the entrance in a Christmas theme, and let everyone enjoy the rides and the games for free. The food would consist of hot dogs, sodas, and other amusement-park fare. Then, before the evening wrapped up, everyone would gather in front of the stage at the north end of the park, where the president could talk to the associates for a few minutes and wrap up the party.

Rich thought her idea was a lot better than his, and he agreed to put her in charge of all arrangements. He could not have made a better choice. At the end of the party, the president thanked everyone for coming to the get-together, praised all of them for their hard work, and called the party "the best one we've ever had." Everyone agreed. On the way out of the park, Rich's boss told him, "The president loved what you did. He told me he can't wait to see what you're going to do for next year's party!"

1. How does Rich process information? Is he a sensation or an intuitive type? Is he a thinking type or a feeling type? Explain.

2. How does Sue process information? Is she a sensation or an intuitive type? Is she a thinking type or a feeling type? Explain.

3. Why did the president like the party? What was he looking for that Rich and Sue provided? In your answer, include a brief discussion of creativity.

CASE 5.2: HE'LL BE COMING BACK

The guest in Room 664 had called down to the main desk three times within the past 90 minutes. The man's first concern was that the room was too dark and he had trouble reading. Housekeeping changed the bulbs in all four room lamps, sharply increasing the illumination. Thirty minutes later the man called again. Something was wrong with the television picture. An electrician arrived within five minutes and reported to his boss that the set was working fine, but the guest was still not pleased. The manager had a replacement television brought in immediately. Forty minutes later the man called again and said the toilet was making noise. The plumber arrived within seven minutes, looked over the unit, and made some minor adjustments. However, the toilet did not make any noise and everything appeared to be in working order.

Peter Nance arrived for his shift a few minutes after the guest's last call. Karl Krueger, whom he was replacing, explained what had been going on. "Brace yourself for more calls," he told Peter. Ten minutes later the next one came. The guest said that the ventilation system was making noise. Rather than sending someone to check it out, Peter went up, introduced himself, and asked about the problem. As he turned the air conditioner off and on a few times and listened to the noise from the unit, the guest talked continuously. "You know, this is my fifth stay at this hotel. I always get a room on the ocean side. This is my first time facing inland. Could that have something to do with the way the air-conditioning unit is working?" Peter told him he was not sure, but he would see that the problem was resolved.

Peter then returned to the front desk and asked the room clerk if there were any available units on the ocean side. He learned that all of them had been booked, but one of the guests had just called and canceled. Peter responded, "Okay, take our guest in Room 664 and move him into that room and send someone up to move his things. I'll call and tell him we're moving him."

When he heard the news, the guest was elated. He was also impressed when a basket of fruit arrived an hour later, compliments of the hotel. As he checked out a few days later, he told Peter, "This was a very enjoyable stay. Thanks for all of your help. You'll be seeing me again."

1. What was the guest's problem? Why was Karl unable to solve this problem?

2. How did Peter process the information in this case? Is he a sensation or intuition type? Is he a thinking or feeling type? Explain.

3. In comparing Karl's approach with Peter's, which of the two used a more left-brain solution? Which used a more right-brain solution? Explain.

ANSWERS TO FIGURE 5.2: "PERCEPTION AND YOU"

a. The most common answer is that this is a bird with a big beak. The second most common answer is that it is a rabbit (the bird's beak becomes the rabbit's ears).

b. The most common answer is that these are the profiles of two people facing each other. The second most common answer is that it is a vase or a goblet. (The faces are in black; the vase or goblet is in white.)

c. Answers to the third picture vary. Some people see an old woman; some see a young woman. If you see only one of these women, have someone else look at the picture and see if he or she can find the other woman. The old woman is looking directly to your left; the young woman is also looking to your left, but is looking back behind her, so that you can see only the left side of her face.

d. Answers for the number of squares varies widely. The most common is sixteen (four down and four across). Another answer is seventeen (add to the sixteen the large square containing all sixteen smaller squares). From here the answers continue up to 30. These other thirteen squares include: (a) the four quadrants of the large box; (b) five more boxes of four (including the one in the middle of the large box and the four at the box edges, inset from the corners); and (c) four boxes of nine small squares. If you add these (5 + 4 + 4 = 13) to the original seventeen, you end up with 30.

ANSWERS TO BOX 5.1: "USING YOUR PERCEPTION AND CREATIVE FLEXIBILITY"

1. There are a number of common answers. The two most popular are "two for tea" and 240.

2. You have to draw the triangle outside of the dots:

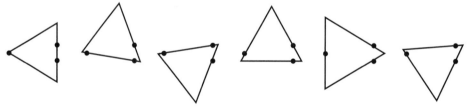

3. The word is CAR: CARPORT, MOTORCAR, CARPET

4. The answer is that a grandfather took two of his sons to the ball game and they, in turn, each took two of their sons. The answer can be drawn diagrammatically in this manner:

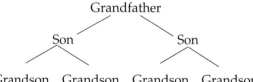

5. There are a number of answers to this problem. Most of them use a mathematical ratio in determining whether to place the number above or below the

line. For example, the most popular answer is to put 5, 6, and 7 below the line and 8 above, and continue this pattern: one down, one up; two down, one up; three down, one up, and so on. Any of these patterns are acceptable. However, the individual who developed this puzzle created it for *children*. Here was the recommended answer for the children:

$$
\frac{\quad 1 \qquad 4 \qquad 7 \qquad}{0 \quad 2\ 3 \quad 5\ 6 \quad 8\ 9}
$$

Can you identify the logic? (Remember that the game is designed for children, so do not be too analytical or mathematical in your approach.) The answer is in the next paragraph, so before you continue reading, answer this question: What is the logic that results in the numbers being put below or above the line?

The answer is probably simpler than you thought. The numbers below the line are created with circles or arcs, while those above the line are created with straight lines.

ANSWERS TO BOX 5.3: "THINKING CREATIVELY"

1. 26 letters of the alphabet
2. 4 quarts in a gallon
3. 54 cards in the deck (with the jokers)
4. 12 signs of the zodiac
5. $200 to pass Go in Monopoly
6. 9 planets in the solar system
7. 18 holes on a golf course
8. 90 degrees in a right angle
9. 24 hours in a day
10. 13 stripes on the American flag
11. 7 wonders of the world
12. 57 Heinz Varieties
13. 60 seconds in a minute
14. 5 fingers on one hand
15. 29 days in February in a leap year

ENDNOTES

1. Jane Whitney Gibson, *The Supervisory Challenge,* 2nd ed. (Upper Saddle River, N.J.: Prentice-Hall, 1995), chapter 4.
2. Richard M. Hodgetts, *Modern Human Relations at Work,* 6th ed. (Fort Worth: Dryden Press, 1996), p. 79.
3. Richard M. Hodgetts, *Management Fundamentals* (Hinsdale, IL: Dryden Press, 1980), pp. 84–86.

4. Jane Whitney Gibson and Richard M. Hodgetts, *Organizational Communication: A Managerial Communication,* 2nd ed. (New York: HarperCollins, 1991), p. 163.

5. Also see Arthur B. VanGundy, *Idea Power: Techniques & Resources to Unleash the Creativity in Your Organization* (New York: American Management Association, 1992).

6. Richard M. Hodgetts, *Organizational Behavior* (New York: Macmillan, 1991), p. 381.

7. Also see Andrew J. DuBrin, *The Breakthrough Team Player* (New York: American Management Association, 1995).

8. See William Taggart and Daniel Robey, "Minds and Managers: On the Dual Nature of Human Information Processing and Management," *Academy of Management Review,* August 1981, p. 190.

9. Jacquelyn Wonder and Priscilla Donovan, *Whole-Brain Thinking* (New York: Morrow, 1984).

10. Ibid., p. 191.

PART THREE

Understanding Human Resource Management

This part of the book addresses the human resource management (HRM) activities that are carried out in hospitality organizations. In the four chapters that compose Part III, you will learn about the "nuts and bolts" of HRM. These activities are critical to the success of industry enterprises because they help ensure that the most qualified associates are hired, trained, and retained.

Chapter 6 examines the ways that firms recruit, select, and orient their associates. In addition to looking at the ways in which companies forecast the supply and demand of associates for their enterprises, attention is directed to the specific steps used to select new hires: screening processes, interviews, and reference and background checks. In discussing this overall process, attention is also given to legislation that helps direct what companies can and cannot do in this hiring process, as well as to identifying and discussing some of the most common types of tests that are used in screening new hires. In this chapter you also will learn some of the most useful guidelines for effect interviewing, and will have the opportunity to examine some of the specific programs that companies use to orient new associates.

Chapter 7 focuses on training, development, and appraisal of associates. All of this begins with a needs analysis that helps identify the specific types of training and development that will be required by the associates. In studying this area, you will learn about team training and cross-functional training, and the way that companies evaluate the costs and measure the results of their training efforts. Attention is also directed to performance appraisal methods used to evaluate how well associates are doing and pinpoint areas for improvement. In studying this material, you will find out how organizations train their managers to sidestep common evaluation errors, and how these enterprises are now using personal development plans to help improve the performance of their associates.

Chapter 8 looks at the ways hospitality organizations motivate their associates. In addition to learning about some of the most useful theories of motivation, you will study some of the specific approaches that enterprises use to motivate their own people. Particular attention will be given to the importance of money and other financial considerations, and then psychological rewards will be examined. In the process, you will be given the chance to determine how important financial and psychological rewards are in motivating you. The chapter concludes with an examination of how the results of motivation efforts are evaluated by organizations and how this information is used to ensure that associates continue to remain enthusiastic about their jobs and optimistic about their future with the organization.

The last chapter in this part of the book examines ways to create effective associate relations. Hospitality firms do more than just hire, train, and motivate their associates. They also develop programs for providing them with personal assistance and establish rules and guidelines for handling discipline-related issues. In Chapter 9 you will learn about counseling and the use of power to create effective associate relations. You will also become familiar with employee assistance programs and know why these programs are becoming more popular than ever. You will also find out how much authority organizations have to discipline their associates, as well as to dismiss those who do not measure up to expectations.

When you have finished reading the chapters in Part III, you will know a great deal about the HRM functions and activities that are carried out in the hospitality industry. You will also be able to link this information with that in Part II and be able to answer the question: How can the HRM process help me become a better associate by drawing on my strengths and eliminating or sidestepping my weaknesses?

Recruiting, Selecting, and Orienting Associates

LEARNING OBJECTIVES

Some of the most important human resource management activities include recruitment, selection, and orientation of associates. The overriding objective of this chapter is to examine the nature of these activities. The first part of the chapter will examine how hospitality firms determine the supply and demand of associates for their operations. Then we will focus our attention on how applicants are selected through the use of screening procedures such as testing, interviewing, and background checks. The last part of the chapter will address the orientation process used to familiarize new hires with the organization, the job, and the challenge. When you have finished studying all of the material in this chapter, you will be able to:

1. Define the term *recruiting* and explain how human resources planning is carried out in hospitality organizations.

2. Compare and contrast the objectives of preliminary screening with those of secondary screening and discuss the role played by selection testing.

3. Explain how selection interviewing is conducted and describe some of the mistakes that interviewers make in this process.

4. Describe the role and importance of reference and background checking.

5. Define the term *orientation* and describe some of the common objectives and components of these programs.

157

Recruiting

Recruiting is the process of locating and attracting qualified job applicants. In recent years the hospitality industry has found itself having to compete vigorously for entry-level associates as well as for managerial talent. The National Restaurant Association projects that there currently is a shortfall of as many as one million workers at the entry level in the food service industry. In particularly short supply are 16- to 24-year-olds.[1] At the managerial level, hospitality organizations are continually looking for associates to help them meet the demands created by expansion and growth. In dealing with these challenges, hospitality enterprises are now carefully forecasting their human resources needs and identifying sources from which they can recruit the needed talent.

Human Resources Planning

Human resources planning is the process of determining the organization's human resources needs and developing a strategy for meeting these needs. There are a number of ways that this is done. One is a "top-down" approach, in which upper-level management estimates the number of people it will need over the next couple of years and uses this information to allocate associates for the departments and units in the organization. Another approach is the "bottom-up" approach, in which lower-level departments estimate their personnel needs for the next few years; upper-level management combines these estimates and arrives at a final figure. In practice, most organizations use a combination of the top-down and bottom-up approaches in determining how many people to hire. Figure 6.1 illustrates how this is done.

The primary objective of human resources planning is to balance supply and demand. This requires consideration of a wide range of variables, including (1) market conditions, such as increased competition in the form of new goods and services; (2) economic conditions, such as increased inflation or economic growth; (3) demographic conditions, such as labor shortages due to slackening population growth or lack of trained associates; and (4) technological developments, such as the introduction of machinery and equipment into the industry that results in the need for specially trained associates. One of the major considerations in this process is that of determining sources to tap in filling both new positions and those of individuals who are moving on to other jobs. This is a particularly challenging problem, given the current difficulty of attracting and keeping qualified hospitality associates.[2]

Sources of Supply

There are a wide variety of recruiting sources that organizations can tap, and because of the growing shortage of associates it is becoming more common to

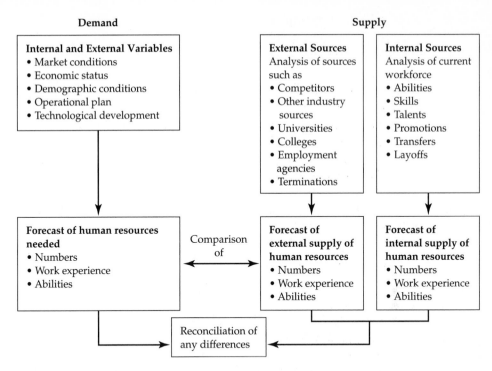

Figure 6.1 *Forecasting Human Resources: Supply and Demand*

Source: Richard M. Hodgetts and K. Galen Kroeck, *Personnel and Human Resource Management* (Fort Worth: Dryden Press, 1992), p. 41.

find hospitality firms casting their hiring nets ever wider. In general, there are two major sources of recruitment: internal and external.

Internal Sources. *Internal recruitment* is the process of promoting or transferring associates within the organization. Common approaches include (1) posting job openings so that associates can apply for them, (2) asking managers to recommend people for available positions, and (3) creating search committees to help identify internal candidates. There are a number of benefits associated with promoting from within. One is that the people are already familiar with the organization's operations, so it takes less time to train and develop them. A second, related reason is that the enterprise is already familiar with the person's work performance and this makes it easier to slot the individual into a job where he or she is likely to do well. A third reason is that the approach is motivational and lets associates know that if they do a good job, the organization is not hesitant about promoting them.

External Sources. *External recruitment* is the process of hiring individuals from outside the organization. Common approaches include (1) recommendations and referrals from individuals who know someone who might be persuaded to join the organization, (2) newspaper and trade publication advertising, and (3) college recruiting. There are a number of advantages of using external recruitment. One is that it offers a far wider pool of potential applicants from which to choose. A second reason is that there may not be anyone inside the company who can meet the demands of the new job opening. A third reason is that no enterprise that seeks to rapidly expand and grow can rely exclusively on its current workforce; the firm needs to supplement this labor pool with outside people.

In order to generate interest from external candidates, hospitality organizations are currently using a number of different approaches.[3] One is to link themselves with colleges and universities (often referred to as "adopt-a-college" strategies) and spend a good deal of time nurturing this relationship, as well as interviewing and hiring graduates. Another approach is the use of imaginative advertising to attract applicants.

> One recent Pizza Hut solution was to mail 2,000 small gift boxes to potential management-trainee recruits. Printed on the box were the following questions: "What are you meant to make of this?"; "What customer-driven company encourages you to run your own business?"; "What market is looking for the very best managers?"; "Who believes good management is about innovation, flair, and creativity?"; and "Who rewards you well with a very competitive basic salary and big incentive bonus?"
> Inside the box was a small, beautifully wrapped bag of flour, and the intriguing words: "Well, you've got to start somewhere. Call Amanda at this number . . . ."[4]

A third approach is geographic advertising that extends a radius of 200 to 300 miles from the organization. The reason for this wide net is that a large percentage of hospitality associates are now willing to travel a great distance to relocate.[5]

A fourth approach is the use of search firms. These enterprises can be particularly helpful in identifying management talent on a nationwide basis.[6]

Selection

The selection process entails a series of important phases including initial screening, secondary screening, interviewing, and reference and background checking. Then, based on the results of these phases, a hiring decision is made.

Initial Screening

Initial screening is the process of quickly eliminating applicants who are unlikely to be successful on the job. An organization that has three openings and 27 applicants will use this process to whittle down the list to a small number, say five or six. The problem with this approach is that it is more negative than positive. The person doing the screening is looking for reasons to take people off the list rather than to leave them on. In doing so, of course, it is important that applicants not be discriminated against; there are a wide number of laws with which human resources associates should be familiar. Table 6.1 briefly lists seven of the most important, as well at noting their purposes, to whom they are applicable, and the groups responsible for their enforcement. However, even working within these guidelines, it is possible to eliminate those who are unqualified.

One of the simplest ways of doing this is to have applicants fill out an application form. This will provide the organization with a host of information including education, past work experience, and skills. When these do not match the attributes needed for the job, the individual can be quickly screened out. Those remaining now go on to the secondary screening process.

Secondary Screening

Secondary screening is the systematic paring of the list of applicants who have passed the initial round. The first screening is often carried out in a perfunctory manner. In the secondary round, however, the process is more positive and focuses on choosing the best of those who still remain. If there is any testing to be done, it is typically conducted at this point.

Selection Testing. There are a wide variety of tests used in the hospitality industry. Examples include professional tests, demonstration tests, and situation tests. Before briefly examining these, it is important to remember that all tests should have both validity and reliability.

Validity and Reliability. Validity means that a test measures what it is intended to measure. For example, a personality test designed to identify individuals who are able to interact well with others and handle high degrees of stress could be extremely useful when choosing restaurant servers or front-desk associates for a hotel. If the test is valid, it will help the organization pick out those who are best able to do this from those who are not. However, if the test is not well designed and administered, many individuals who do not interact well with others or handle stress effectively may get very high scores. In this case, because the test lacks validity it is not doing a good job of identifying those who have the desired behaviors and those who do not.

Reliability means that test measures are consistent. So if an individual scored high on a particular screening test and was asked to retake the test, the person would again score high if the test was reliable.

Well-designed tests are *both* valid and reliable. However, it is important to remember that if a test is reliable, this does *not* guarantee that it is also valid.

Table 6.1 Select Legislation Relevant to Human Resource Management

Act or Law	Purpose	Application	Enforcement
Title VII of the Civil Rights Act of 1964 (as amended by the Equal Employment Opportunity Act of 1972)	Prohibits discrimination in employment based on sex as well as on race, color, religion, or national origin. Prohibits discrimination in hiring, firing, wages, fringe benefits, classifying, referring, assigning, promoting, training, or apprenticeships	Most employers of 15 or more employees, public and private employment agencies, labor unions with 15 or more members, and joint labor-management training programs (exemptions: Native American tribes and religious institutions with respect to religion)	Equal Employment Opportunity Commission (EEOC) and state and local agencies
Age Discrimination in Employment Acts of 1967 and 1975	Prohibits discrimination on the basis of age against any person above age 40 in hiring, firing, compensation, or other conditions of employment	All public employers, private employers of 20 or more, employment agencies serving covered employers, and labor unions with more than 25 members	EEOC and U.S. Department of Labor
Equal Pay Act of 1963 (amendment to the Fair Labor Standards Act)	Prohibits unequal pay for men and women who work in the same establishment and whose jobs require equal skill, effort, and responsibility	All employers covered by the Fair Labor Standards Act	EEOC

Americans with Disabilities Act of 1990	Forces organizations to provide reasonable accommodation to disabled, disfigured, psychologically impaired, and persons with HIV virus	All employers with more than 15 employees	EEOC
Immigration Reform and Control Act of 1986	Requires employers to screen employees systematically for the right to work in the United States but not discriminate on the basis of national origin in the process	All employers	Immigration and Naturalization Service of the Dept. of Justice, EEOC, and Department of Labor
Pregnancy Discrimination Act of 1978	Pregnant women and new mothers must be treated the same for all employment-related purposes, including receipt of benefits under fringe-benefit programs	All Title VII employers	EEOC
State/local civil rights laws	Regulate discrimination by employers (particularly those not covered under federal law)	Varies	State civil rights division (agency name varies)

Source: Richard M. Hodgetts and K. Galen Kroeck, *Personnel and Human Resource Management* (Fort Worth: Dryden Press, 1992), pp. 64–66.

Consider the following situation of a job applicant who is asked the following three questions on a written test designed to find out how well the person can interact with hotel clientele:

1. When you greet a new guest, you should first: (a) shake hands with the individual; (b) call the person by name; (c) tell the person your name.

2. If a guest asks you where he can find the gift shop, you should: (a) give him a map of the hotel and point out the location of the shop; (b) give him detailed, verbal instructions; (c) drop whatever you are doing and escort him to the shop.

3. If a guest tells you that she is not pleased with the service in the restaurant, you should: (a) give her a credit for her most recent restaurant charge; (b) listen to her and take detailed notes; (c) ask her to tell you the three things that she liked least about the service.

In identifying individuals who can work well with hotel clientele, are these questions valid? The answer is: Only if they can help distinguish between those who would be effective from those who would not be effective. Quite obviously, the problem with this quiz is that it is unlikely to do a very good job of screening applicants because most people are not going to answer the question based on what they would do but rather based on what they think the company wants them to say. So the validity of the quiz is highly questionable. On the other hand, is the quiz reliable? The answer is: Yes, because the answers that were given would not change if the individual took the quiz again (assuming, of course, that the person did not know what the best answers were) and so the score would be the same. So a test can be reliable *without* being valid. This is why it is important for human resource management associates who are responsible for testing and screening to ensure that their tests do indeed measure what they are designed to measure!

Types of Tests. Many different types of tests are used in screening hospitality associates. In each case, the objective is to quickly separate applicants with good potential from those who are less likely to be as productive. Three of the most common types are professional tests, demonstration tests, and situation tests.

A *professional test* is designed to select individuals for areas such as management staff, production staff, service staff, and beverage staff by identifying their professional knowledge and familiarity with the technical basics of the position for which they are applying. These tests are not designed to automatically eliminate individuals with no prior knowledge of the position, but they do help management identify those who will need additional training if they are chosen for that job. Recently graduated hospitality majors, for example, often lack specific job information that can be obtained only through work experience. The professional test is often used as only one of several screening devices.

A *demonstration test* is designed to identify proficiency in a specific job-related skill and to measure the practical aspects of job performance. These tests are also useful in verifying the applicant's ability to meet physical requirements such as moving, lifting, coordinating, and so on.

> Anne Gardner recently applied for a job as a pastry chef in a popular local restaurant. Along with the three other applicants, Anne was asked to create a dessert for the dinner menu. Having just returned from a special course she had attended, Anne was able to make a chocolate mousse with a thick, rich base made from low-calorie ingredients. Each serving contained 33 percent fewer calories than the typical mousse. Her dessert proved to be the most popular one of the evening, and Anne began work the next day.

Anne was given a demonstration test and she passed with flying colors. Was the test valid? It certainly was: it was job related and identified her ability to create a dessert. Was the test reliable? Of course. Anne will be able to reproduce her famous chocolate mousse and make it a standard offering on the dessert cart.

A *situation test* is one that presents the applicant with a challenging job-related situation and asks the person how he or she would handle the matter. Quite often these situations have no one right answer. They are designed to provide insight into the individual's ability to think clearly, establish priorities, and handle stress.

During his screening interview, Roberto Garcia was asked to write answers to a number of different questions. One of them was the following:

> How would you handle this situation: You are the only person at the check-in desk; it is just after midnight and it has been raining heavily for four hours. Suddenly the lobby doors open and a woman with two infant children enters and walks quickly to the desk. "I know I'm late," she says, "but the weather is terrible. I had a room reserved until 6 P.M., but I'll take anything you can give me." You quickly scan the computer screen and see that every room is filled.

The question is designed to see how Roberto can improvise a solution. Obviously the hotel does not want him to send the lady and her children out into the weather. What other alternatives are available? How can he accommodate the guest, given that there are no available rooms?

Based on the test results, the organization will decide which individuals warrant further consideration. These people will then be given selection interviews.

Selection Interviewing

The *selection interview* is quite common; most organizations employ it in some form. Unfortunately, it is often not conducted well and there are a number of shortcomings associated with it. Researchers have found six problems with screening interviews:

1. The accuracy of the interview tends to depend on the skill of the interviewer, and many individuals are not very effective in interviewing.

2. Interviewers tend to be best at assessing motivation and intelligence, but not very good at determining honesty or leadership potential.

3. In many cases, decisions are made during the first five minutes of the interview.

4. Many interviewers commit a number of errors when evaluating applicants, including weighing negative information more heavily than positive information; having stereotyped beliefs about the applicant's sex, race, and age; and having incorrect beliefs about the type of person who is right for the job.

5. Interviewers tend to talk more when they like the candidate, and thus fail to obtain important information.

6. Interviewees who are asked to come back for a second interview tend to adjust the interview to meet the needs of the situation, knowing when to be dominant and when to allow the interviewer to take over.[7]

There are a number of ways to improve interviewing effectiveness.[8] One is to be aware of the types of questions that are legal (proper) and illegal (improper) and refrain from asking the latter. A close review of these (see Box 6.1) reveals that many are commonly broached with interviewees with no intention of being discriminatory; however, they should not be asked at all. Before continuing, take the quiz in Box 6.1 and check your answers.[9]

How can associates do a better job of interviewing job applicants? There are a number of useful recommendations. Box 6.2 sets forth ten of the most helpful.[10] In addition, it is important to decide whether to use a structured or unstructured interview. A *structured interview* employs a set of established questions, each designed to determine some job-relevant characteristic of the applicant.[11] An *unstructured interview* focuses on specific objectives while allowing the interviewee to determine the questions that he or she will ask and to influence the direction that the interview will take.

Regardless of the type of interview, in recent years interviewers have begun relying more and more heavily on situational questions. A *situational question* describes a scenario—typically a problem likely to occur on the job—and asks applicants what they would do in that situation. These questions are designed to help evaluate how well applicants can express themselves, examine problem situations and offer recommendations, and think on their feet.

Box 6.1
What Can You Ask?

When employers screen prospective employees, there are many questions that they cannot ask of the applicants. Here are 20 questions that are commonly posed. Identify each as proper (P) or improper (I). (*Hint*: More than half of them are improper.) Answers are provided at the end of the chapter.[12]

P I 1. Have you ever been arrested and, if so, for what reason?

P I 2. If you are hired, can you provide proof of citizenship, visa, or alien registration number?

P I 3. How old are you?

P I 4. Do you have any physical handicaps that could prevent you from performing this job?

P I 5. Are you married?

P I 6. What type of work experiences have you had?

P I 7. Did you receive an honorable discharge from the military?

P I 8. What courses did you study in school?

P I 9. Are you able to read, write, or speak any foreign languages?

P I 10. Where did you learn to speak Spanish (or whatever language in which the individual indicates he or she is fluent)?

P I 11. Have you ever worked for our company before?

P I 12. Have you ever worked for our main competitor, [name of company]?

P I 13. If you have children, who will take care of them when you are at work?

P I 14. Did you graduate from college? If so, what was your major area of study?

P I 15. Your name sounds German. Do your ancestors come from Germany?

P I 16. Would you please list all of the organizations, clubs, societies, and lodges to which you belong?

P I 17. Are you currently pregnant?

P I 18. Do you and your spouse plan to start a family in the near future?

P I 19. What does your spouse do for a living?

P I 20. If you were offered this job, what salary (or range) would you expect?

Situational questions are often quite effective in distinguishing those who have true self-confidence from those who merely express bravado in the interview situation.

Another approach, similar to the use of situational questions, is the use of probing questions that require the applicant to carefully think through the

Box 6.2
Guidelines for Effective Interviewing

A number of guidelines have been found to be particularly beneficial in interviewing because they result in the use of more consistent, accurate procedures and produce better outcomes. These include the following:

1. Identify a set of "musts" regarding the characteristics that the person who is hired for the job should have.

2. Prepare for the interview by developing a set of structured questions that are relevant to the job "musts" and confine the interview to these questions. Also consider using situational questions; they often provide considerable insight into the candidate's likely performance.

3. Establish rapport with the candidate by clarifying information contained in the job application form or résumé, or by making small talk for a few minutes. This procedure helps put the individual at ease.

4. Use open-ended questions that elicit more than a mere "yes" or "no" response.

5. Avoid leading questions, such as, "Did you major in hospitality because you like to work with people?"

6. Ask self-evaluation questions that require the applicant to discuss past successes and failures, present strengths and weaknesses, and future objectives and limitations. Better candidates tend to be more specific in their answers.

7. Use intentional pauses to find out how the applicant deals with silence. Although this strategy may make the applicant uncomfortable, it can provide additional insight into the person's behavior and ability to handle stress.

8. Keep control of the interview and work to steer it away from discussions of topics that are not job relevant.

9. Wind down the interview by giving the applicant the opportunity to ask questions. In responding, be honest and candid and portray the job as realistically as possible.

10. Close the interview by thanking the candidate and providing information about what will occur next in the process. Then, after the candidate leaves, evaluate the individual on those areas that were identified as "musts."

response and then phrase it in his or her own words. In some cases, organizations will have already identified common responses to these questions and know the type of individual they are looking to hire. Figure 6.2 provides an example of one such screening approach, in which the organization is looking for individuals with extroversion, pride, responsibility, and energy—four characteristics it has found to be of critical importance.[13]

Screening Interview

Name: _____

Position: _____

Extroversion	**Applicant Response**
As a member of the restaurant staff, how would you help develop repeat business?	*Positive response:* Specific answer that shows personal action or interaction; *e.g.* learn and use their names, ask questions, make suggestions, make sure food always looks and tastes great. *Negative response:* Be friendly, give good service.
If I asked your best friend to describe you, what would he/she say?	*Positive:* People-oriented answers; *e.g.* outgoing, lots of fun, friendly, positive. *Negative:* Nice person, good worker.
If you saw someone you thought you recognized but weren't quite sure, what would you do?	*Positive:* Go up and ask, make an effort to talk to them. *Negative:* Just keep walking, wait until I was sure.

Pride

What qualities do you need to be a great (position) in a restaurant?	*Positive:* Like people, work hard, do more than expected, smiling, flexible, patient, lots of stamina, good work habits, attention to detail, good communicator. *Negative:* Be nice.
Is it difficult for you to carry on "small talk" with people?	*Positive:* No, not at all. *Negative:* Sometimes, depends on the situation.
What recent accomplishments do you take great pride in?	*Positive:* Specific advancement toward a goal; *e.g.,* completed courses, finished a difficult project, job advancement, family success. *Negative:* Don't have any specific goals.
What are some reasons for your successes?	*Positive:* My personality, optimism, positive self-image, want to succeed. *Negative:* Just lucky, I don't know.

Responsibility

What would your previous employers say about your work?	*Positive:* Hard worker, dependable, ideal employee, valuable, would rehire. *Negative:* Did a good job.
What would you do to make a negative situation positive?	*Positive:* Find out what the problem was and fix it. *Negative:* Get a manager, stay calm.
What kinds of people irritate you?	*Positive:* Lazy, negative, complainers. *Negative:* I like everyone, I don't pay attention to them.
How do you decide what to do with your time off?	*Positive:* Make lists, organize, get right at things. *Negative:* Don't do it very well, go with the flow.

Energy

What activities have you been involved in during the past two years?	*Positive:* Participative activities; *e.g.* aerobics, sports, volunteer work, charities. *Negative:* Not many, I just work.
What motivates you to get your job done?	*Positive:* Money, recognition, pride in my work. *Negative:* Making people happy.
How do you feel about doing more than one activity at a time?	*Positive:* Like it, it's a challenge. *Negative:* Want to do only one thing at a time.

Figure 6.2   *The Foolproof Foodservice Selection System*™

Source: Reprinted by permission of John Wiley & Sons, Inc. from *Foolproof Foodservice Selection System* by Bill Marvin. © 1992 John Wiley & Sons, Inc.

Research shows that employment interviewing has not demonstrated high predictive validity. On the other hand, it will undoubtedly continue to be a common selection procedure; and among organizations that interview large numbers of applicants every year, there is a growing trend toward using computerized[14] and videotaped interviews.

In computerized interviews, applicants interact with a terminal and, depending on their responses, different questions appear on the screen. When the interview is over, the computer generates a report regarding the information that was obtained. Sometimes this process is referred to as data-based interviewing. Because of the extreme cost savings, computerized interviewing is likely to increase in popularity with many organizations over the next decade.[15]

Another interviewing practice catching on in some organizations is the use of videotaped interviews. This allows interviewers to stop and replay critical parts of the interview, to watch tapes whenever they want, to discuss questions and answers with other managers, and to document interviewing practices.[16]

These are all important developments in helping organizations improve the reliability of their interviewing process. While they add increased time and cost to the screening of applicants, they can be particularly useful in improving selection and, in the long run, saving money for the hospitality organization.

Reference and Background Checking

Reference checking is a common employment practice. For many reasons, organizations need to verify information given to them by job applicants. In particular, background investigation has become a crucial personnel function because of the increase of misrepresentation of work experience on applications and résumés.[17] As a result, there has been a growing need for this service, and a number of companies now provide it to organizations that do not have the resources to conduct their own investigations.

Unfortunately, research on the validity of reference checking is not very encouraging. In particular, because of the fear of lawsuits, many employers are reluctant to provide more than minimal information such as job title and dates of employment. This is not particularly helpful, since many companies would like to know a lot more about the person they are considering for the job. Some of the most common questions include:

Why did this individual leave your employ?

What type of worker was he or she?

Would you hire the individual again?

How would you rate this person on a scale of one to ten?

Was there anything that this individual did that caused you to question his or her honesty or integrity?

The reason that these questions go unanswered is that companies are afraid of being sued. A close look at a few of these questions helps show why this can be a very potent legal threat. Consider the first question. Suppose that the individual had been caught stealing money but was allowed to resign. Could the company say that it fired the person for stealing? It really did not fire the person; he or she was allowed to resign. Additionally, the firm may not have put this information in the employee's personnel file; so there may be no record of stealing. If the case went to court, the lack of written information would weigh heavily against the firm.

Similarly, consider the second question, which asks what type of worker the individual was. This is difficult to answer and is likely to involve qualitative judgments that could come back and haunt the firm. If the individual is said to be "fairly reliable," what does this mean? If the person is described as "one of the better workers we had in that department," what does this mean? Again, because of the negative spin that can be placed on these statements, many firms prefer not to give out anything but standard information such as job title, dates of employment, and so on.

Another troublesome area is that of recommendations. Research studies reveal that individuals writing letters of recommendation seldom give out negative information. This makes it difficult to distinguish among applicants, since everyone appears to be of exceptional quality.

Recent evidence suggests that organizations should provide special training to those who conduct reference and background checks. This can help them become more astute at carrying out this function and better protect the firm from legal entanglements.[18]

Applicants who pass the reference and background checks constitute the hiring pool. In many cases, they will be immediately hired. In some cases, however, the organization will not yet have positions for them, and they will be placed on a waiting list. This approach is particularly common when promoting from within. As the company pinpoints the areas where it will be needing people, it will begin developing an internal pool of talent on which it can draw to fill these needs. Then, as the positions become open, the firm can tap this preselected pool.

Other Considerations. The selection process described thus far has detailed the basic steps used by hospitality organizations when selecting associates. However, this process is typically supplemented by other considerations and guidelines,[19] including the following:

1. Where possible, promote from within; this increases morale and helps maintain associate loyalty.

2. Hire and promote individuals who are likely to stay with the organization; otherwise, you end up giving people training and experience that they will be taking to the competition.

3. After the initial screening process eliminates those who do not meet the minimum requirements, be more careful about paring the applicants; use a double elimination process so that a person has to score poorly in two areas before he or she is dropped from further consideration.

4. When interviewing candidates, be sure that the interviewers know the job requirements and have discussed among themselves the types of questions that will be asked. In this way, the interviews will cover all of the important areas and not focus on just a few.

5. Try to look beyond the résumé and other factual data and ask: How well do this individual's personality and interests mesh with those of the organization? A lack of experience can be a drawback, but if the applicant seems to have the right chemistry, experience may be a secondary consideration.

6. When hiring from within, look for input from people in the organization who have worked with the person; in the case of an outside applicant from the industry, use external networks to find out how well this person has done and why the individual is interested in changing jobs.

7. Remember that no candidate is likely to be perfect, so focus on whether the individual can meet the major demands of the position and, through experience and training, compensate for his or her deficiencies.

8. Hire for tomorrow as well as today. Ask yourself: Does this person have the ability and desire to grow with us, or will the individual be unable to meet the future challenges with which we will be confronted?

Orientation

Orientation is the process of introducing new associates to their work group, their supervisor, and their tasks.[20] There are a number of reasons why orientation has become a major part of the hiring process in hospitality organizations. In particular, effective orientation programs have been found to (1) reduce turnover, (2) lessen the anxiety associated with job failure, (3) increase associate satisfaction, and (4) reduce the time needed for new associates to start performing productively.[21]

Turnover and Profit

One of the primary reasons for developing an effective orientation program is that high turnover rates increase the costs of recruiting, screening, and selecting while sharply reducing profit and productivity.

> Marriott International, which annually loses about 60 percent of the front-line staffers in its flagship Marriott Hotels, Resorts, and Suites division, estimates that it costs as much as $1,100 to recruit and train each replacement. The total bill runs into the millions each year. Says division human resources vice-president Richard Bell-Irving: "When someone leaves, it messes up your employee teams, messes up your productivity, and messes up the service you provide to your guests."[22]

There are a number of different costs that go up when turnover rates are high. Some of the expenses directly related to turnover include (1) advertising and recruiting, (2) management and clerical time devoted to the selection process, (3) orientation and training, and (4) overtime for current associates. Some of the indirect costs associated with turnover include (1) lack of productivity of new hires; (2) the potential loss of reputation and goodwill; (3) increased accidents, waste, and breakage; (4) a lack of teamwork, which can be developed only with a stable staff; and (5) decreased motivation among the existing staff.[23]

Depending on the size of the organization, these costs can run into the millions of dollars annually. In one study of six restaurant companies, Robert Woods and James Macaulay found that annual associate turnover averaged 96 percent, with the range extending from 50 percent on the low side to 150 percent on the high side.[24] Table 6.2 reports the estimated cost of turnover among the hourly associates and the managers in these six restaurants.

What is particularly interesting about turnover costs is that many organizations fail to evaluate their impact carefully.[25] However, those that do are able to see the link between turnover and profitability and can begin making the

Table 6.2 Estimated Cost of Turnover in Six Restaurant Companies

Chain Number	Number Employed	Number Turning Over	Turnover Percentage	Cost
Hourly Associates				
1	1,500	2,250	150%	$ 5,600,000
2	9,000	9,900	110	24,700,000
3	7,500	9,375	125	23,400,000
4	900	720	80	1,800,000
5	1,300	975	75	2,400,000
6	1,650	825	50	2,000,000
Managers				
1	100	65	65	650,000
2	750	375	50	12,000,000
3	700	420	60	4,200,000
4	75	30	40	300,000
5	80	40	50	400,000
6	140	42	30	420,000

Source: Robert H. Woods and James F. Macaulay, "Rx For Turnover: Retention Programs That Work," *Cornell Hotel and Restaurant Administration Quarterly*, May 1989, p. 81.

necessary changes.[26] There are a number of ways that this can be done.[27] One of these is the development of an effective orientation program.

Objectives and Components

Effectively created orientation programs are designed to accomplish a number of objectives. Typical examples include:

- Explain the history and philosophy of the company.
- Communicate the mission and goals of the organization.
- Explain personnel practices and standards.
- Make clear what the firm's expectations are regarding service excellence.
- Make new associates feel both welcome and comfortable.
- Reduce first-year turnover and absenteeism.

- Instill a sense of pride and enthusiasm in the new associate.
- Build teamwork, commitment, and loyalty.

In accomplishing these objectives, hospitality organizations use a wide variety of approaches. Table 6.3 shows the major daily components of orientation programs for six properties in the United States: four luxury hotels, a casino hotel, and a resort.[28] A number of these components are similar for all six. For example, each program has a welcome, introduction, or overview; a discussion of history, philosophy, vision, values, or culture; presentation of policies and procedures; a property tour; fire, safety, and security training; basic customer service training; and an explanation of benefits. At the same time, there are a number of differences. For example, three use the orientation programs to complete such tasks as processing identification cards, fitting uniforms, and assigning lockers; the other three complete these administrative tasks before the orientation program begins. Two of the programs have an advanced customer service training component designed to supplement their basic cross-cultural training. So despite the fact that there are common elements throughout all of the programs, there are also individual components designed to handle the specific needs of each organization.

Program Implementation and Innovation

While the orientation program is typically conducted by the human resource management staff, all of the hotels in this study incorporated management associates to assist in the program. They found that new associates are more likely to identify with fellow associates. Additionally, participation by the new nonmanagerial associates was required by all the organizations, and most also required their new managerial hires to attend. In fact, two of the companies had another management orientation to supplement the basic program.

In addition to the information provided in Table 6.3, some of the programs introduced a variety of innovative approaches. These included (1) spreading orientation over a period of days or weeks, rather than having it compressed into one, two, or five days; (2) using signers for the hearing impaired; (3) having translators available for non-English-speaking newcomers; (4) providing cultural-diversity training; and (5) using specially trained associates as instructors. In each case the objective was to create a program that addressed both technical (job duties and other organizational considerations) and social (interaction with the people and the new setting) concerns.

In addition, it is important to realize that today's orientation programs are quite different from those that were popular in earlier decades. Here is an example of the contrasting messages of each:

Table 6.3 Major Daily Components of Six Orientation Programs

Case 1 Day 1	Case 2 Day 1	Case 3 Day 1
Welcome	Welcome	Welcome
Overview of history, philosophy, values of the company and the property	History, philosophy, values of the company and the property	History, values, marketing of the property
Introduction of GM and executive committee	Introduction of GM and planning committee	Executive welcome, introduction of key executives
Rules, policies, and procedures	Review of employee handbook (policies and procedures)	Policies, procedures, and grooming standards
Property tour	Property tour	Map exercises and scavenger hunt (property tour)
Fire and safety procedures	Fire and safety training	Fire, safety, and security training
Service-excellence training (customer service)	Customer-service training (service standards)	Guest-services training (customer service)
Benefits		Employee-relations practices and benefits
		Review of relevant laws (*e.g.,* drinking age)
Introduction of newcomers to immediate supervisors	Begin department orientation (training) component	Question-and-answer session

Day 2

Benefits

Case 4 Day 1	Case 5 Day 1	Case 6 Day 1
Welcome	Welcome	Welcome
History, vision, and values of the company and the property	Overview of history and mission of the company	History, philosophy, culture of the company and the property
Introduction and welcome by the GM	Review of the mission statement and property by the GM	
Review employee handbook (policies and procedures)	Review of the employee handbook and explanation of the role of the human resources department (policies, procedures, and benefits)	
Property tour	Property tour	Property tour
Fire, safety, and security training		

Table 6.3 Continued

Case 4	Case 5	Case 6
Day 1	Day 1	Day 1
Guest-service standards (customer service)		Initial customer-service training
Benefits		
Complete administrative processing, including photo IDs, locker assignments, and uniform fittings	Completion of administrative processing, including photo IDs and uniform	Completion of administrative processing, including photo IDs and time cards
		Explanation of future projects (company expansion plans)
Day 2	Day 2	Day 2
Department orientation	Explanation of the roles various departments play:	Benefits
Position orientation		Fire and safety training
Day 3	—finance and accounting	Advanced customer-service training
	—food and beverage	
Achieving total customer responsiveness (advanced customer-service training)	—rooms	Policies and procedures
	—engineering	Compensation
Job skill training (additional departmental and position training)	—security and fire safety	Begin departmental orientation
	—condominiums	
	—sales and marketing	
Day 4		
Cross-cultural training		
Day 5		
Overnight stay as a guest in the hotel		
Evaluation of overnight-guest experience in light of customer-service standards (customer-service training)		

Notes:

Company-specific descriptions used by individual properties for the major components of their orientation programs were retained except in those cases where doing so could jeopardize the anonymity of the property.

In some cases the sequence of the components was rearranged to facilitate comparison across the orientation programs (cases 1–6).

Orientation-program days (days 1–5) do not necessarily correspond to newcomers' first five days of employment. In case 2, for example, the explanation of employee benefits occurs on the second day of *orientation*, which is actually on or about day 60 of *employment*.

Source: David J. Kennedy and Florence Berger, "Newcomer Socialization: Oriented to Facts or Feelings?" *Cornell Hotel and Restaurant Administration Quarterly*, December 1994, pp. 64–65.

Past Programs	Today's Programs
Welcome.	Welcome.
This is our company philosophy.	We were expecting you.
This is what we expect of you.	We like you; that's why we hired you.
These are our rules, policies, and procedures.	We know you're nervous; it's only natural.
This is a great place to work.	We expect you to ask us a lot of questions.
	We're here to answer those questions.
	We're going to teach you coping and stress-management techniques.
	We're going to help you build a support network so you can learn how things are done here.
	We're going to do everything we can to help you be comfortable and successful.

In bringing about this new focus, hospitality organizations are also working to introduce new changes into their orientation programs and use these innovations to create a strong initial bond between themselves and the participants. Some of these include:

1. Carefully designing the program so that it includes a balance of providing factual information and fostering an atmosphere that is conducive to learning appropriate skills and being able to process personal feelings.

2. Creating the program components so that they directly address what new associates are going to experience emotionally.

3. Avoiding giving the participants too much information during the program, so that they end up suffering from information overload and are unable to adequately process all they are learning.

4. Making all new associates go through some form of orientation before they begin work.

5. Carefully choosing the instructors who will be conducting the orientation and ensuring that all of them understand their role in the program.

6. Giving associates an opportunity to meet executives of the organization, ask questions, and learn what these managers have planned for the future.

7. Developing an evaluation system for determining how well the program is going, the impact it is having on the bottom line, and those changes that need to be made to increase the program's effectiveness.

Orientation is a critical step in helping reduce turnover and ensuring that associates are both motivated and productive. A follow-up step consists of providing the associates with the necessary training and development they need to continue these efforts. This will be the focus of attention in the next chapter.

SUMMARY

1. Recruiting is the process of locating and attracting qualified job applicants. In determining the number and type of people that will be needed, hospitality organizations typically formulate a human resources plan that is closely linked to the recruitment process.

2. Selection of associates often involves a series of phases. Initial screening is used to eliminate those who are clearly not qualified for the job. Secondary screening is used to further pare the list through the use of testing and interviews. Those who remain at this point are then further screened through the use of reference and background checks. At the end of this process, the organization has a preselected pool of talent on which it can draw.

3. The turnover rate in many hospitality organizations is extremely high; this has a severe effect on both profit and productivity. In dealing with this problem, an increasing number of firms are now developing orientation programs that address both the technical and social aspects of the job. As a result, associates are better prepared to meet the challenges they confront and the turnover rate is sharply reduced.

KEY TERMS

recruiting
human resources planning
internal recruitment
external recruitment
initial screening
secondary screening
validity
reliability

professional test
demonstration test
situation test
selection interview
structured interview
unstructured interview
situational question
orientation

REVIEW AND APPLICATION QUESTIONS

1. The Grand View Hotel has just finished an expansion project that has doubled the number of rooms and added a large formal dining room. At present, the hotel has a staff of 722 and believes that it will need to hire at least 400 additional people over the next year. What types of external recruit-

ment would be of most value to the hotel? Should it also consider internal recruitment in its plans? Why or why not?

2. Cruise Away, a major cruise line, has a turnover rate of over 100 percent. The firm is continually recruiting and, on average, hires 24 associates a week. Every day the human resources department receives a host of job applications. In paring this list, what steps should the company take during the initial screening process? What steps should it take during the secondary screening process? In each case, discuss two steps.

3. Last month, Regina Fuentes applied for a job with a national restaurant chain. One of the screening tools is a personality test that is designed to measure whether the applicant can work effectively with guests and other associates. Regina took the test and was told that she did not receive a high score. She was then allowed to take the test again, but once more her score was low. Based on this information, is the test reliable? Why or why not? Based on this information, is it possible to say whether or not the test is valid? Explain.

4. Richard Miksich is a new interviewer in the human resources department. This is his first job and he has had very limited interviewing experience. What are four guidelines you could offer Richard regarding how to improve his interviewing effectiveness?

5. One of the most useful guidelines for effective recruiting is, "Look beyond the résumé and the screening tests." What does this statement mean? Do you think it is a good piece of advice? Why?

6. You are interviewing for a job with a large hotel that is in the process of revising its orientation program. The interviewer asks, "If you were designing an orientation program, what would it look like? What are three components that would be included?" What would you tell the interviewer?

SELF-FEEDBACK EXERCISE: WHAT ARE YOU LOOKING FOR IN A JOB AND IN THE SELECTION PROCESS FOR GETTING ONE?[29]

There are many ways to attract applicants to the hospitality industry. One is by offering jobs that people find to be both interesting and enjoyable. Another is by creating a selection and screening process that is not overly burdensome. This self-feedback exercise provides information related both to jobs and to the selection systems used to screen applicants. Following are ten attributes related to job content and ten more related to the selection system. Read each group of ten and rank them from 1 (most important) to 10 (least important). When you are finished, follow the instructions in the scoring key to help answer the question: What are you looking for in a job and in the selection process?

Job Content Attributes (Rank from 1 to 10)

_____ a. A comfortable working environment.

_____ b. A company that provides good benefits.

_____ c. The opportunity to assume responsibility.

_____ d. Working close to where I live.

_____ e. Company-paid insurance coverage.

_____ f. Time off when I want it.

_____ g. Advancement within the organization.

_____ h. A company of which I can be proud.

_____ i. A boss who praises good performance.

_____ j. Work that is varied and not boring.

Selection System Attributes (Rank from 1 to 10)

_____ a. Completing a short (not lengthy) application blank.

_____ b. Being asked interview questions that relate to the job.

_____ c. Being given important information about the job during the interview.

_____ d. Being allowed to express myself during the interview.

_____ e. Not having an interview that follows a strict pattern.

_____ f. Not having to take a bunch of psychological tests.

_____ g. Not having to complete an honesty test.

_____ h. Being interviewed by the manager, not the assistant.

_____ i. Receiving a prompt follow-up after the interview.

_____ j. Not having to answer questions that are personal in nature.

Scoring: For both groups of responses, enter your answers in the following key; then subtract each answer from the average response that researchers received from a large sample of college juniors and seniors at three major universities. In computing the difference, do not use a minus or plus sign.

Whether your answer is higher or lower than the average, simply enter the difference (*e.g.,* 8 minus 4 = 4; 6 minus 10 = 4).

	Job Content Attributes				Selection System Attributes		
	Your Answer	Average Response	Difference		Your Answer	Avergae Response	Difference
a.	_____	6	_____	a.	_____	9	_____
b.	_____	4	_____	b.	_____	5	_____
c.	_____	1	_____	c.	_____	1	_____
d.	_____	10	_____	d.	_____	3	_____
e.	_____	7	_____	e.	_____	7	_____
f.	_____	9	_____	f.	_____	10	_____
g.	_____	3	_____	g.	_____	8	_____
h.	_____	5	_____	h.	_____	4	_____
i.	_____	8	_____	i.	_____	2	_____
j.	_____	2	_____	j.	_____	6	_____
		Total	_____			Total	_____

Interpretation: Look at the individual differences and the overall difference between your answers and the average responses. This will provide you with feedback regarding the job content attributes and selection system attributes that are important to you and how similar or different your responses are when compared to those of the average college student. Your answers will also help you better understand why hospitality organizations need to be flexible in their recruiting and screening techniques; what appeals to some applicants will not appeal to others. You can see this by comparing your individual and overall responses to those of others in the class, and noting the differences between your answers and theirs.

CASE 6.1: A MATTER OF TEST

Marianne Shortelle works for the human resources department of a large hotel chain. Although she has been on board for only six months, the company has given her a wide range of interesting and challenging jobs. One of her recent assignments is to review the hotel's applicant-screening process and identify ways that the company can do a better job of identifying potential entry-level managerial talent.

One of the screening techniques that has attracted Marianne's attention is testing procedures. From what she can glean from conversations with people who have been in the department for quite a while, these tests are designed to identify two characteristics that are critical to the success of entry-level managers: intelligence and the desire to achieve. Marianne has personally completed copies of both tests and had the results evaluated by the department. She was informed that if she had applied for an entry-level managerial position, she would have passed with flying colors.

Marianne was pleased with this news, but decided to dig a little further and look at the performance record of individuals who had taken this test between 36 and 48 months ago to see how well they have worked out in the organization. She discovered that 32 of the people who did well on the test are still with the hotel and 28 of them are doing extremely well. The other four have had only mediocre performance evaluations.

Before concluding her investigation, Marianne also decided to examine the files of individuals who were not hired because of poor test scores. It took her two weeks to locate 27 of these people, all of whom were now working for one of four major competitors. In 24 of these cases, the individuals had been promoted at least twice and appeared to be on their way to very successful careers.

Marianne is now examining her information so that she can draw conclusions regarding the value of the company's current tests. She has mentioned this to one of her associates in the department and the individual seemed surprised. "There's nothing wrong with the two tests we are administering," he told Marianne. "Those who do well on them also tend to do well in the company."

1. Based on the information in this case, are the screening tests valid? Why or why not?

2. Are the screening tests reliable? Defend your answer.

3. What recommendations would you make to Marianne regarding the continued use of these tests? Explain.

CASE 6.2: AVOIDING AN UNMITIGATED DISASTER

For the last two months the human resources (HR) department of a cruise line has been actively recruiting and screening applicants for a wide variety of job vacancies. The department is not very large, so it has decided to get outside assistance for conducting the screening interviews. A group of six managers drawn at random from throughout the company have been asked to come to the HR area next Thursday, where they will spend two days interviewing those candidates who have passed the initial screening and testing phases. The decision to use these managers was made by the president of the company, who rejected an HR request to hire outside interviewers to help in the process. "Heck," he told the head of HR, "we don't need outside help. Who knows more about our company than our own people? Let's bring in some of our managerial staff and let them help screen the candidates. If anyone knows the type of people we need around here, it should be our managers."

The head of HR, Elizabeth Sloan, is not sure that the president knows what he is talking about. "Effective interviewing is a lot more than just sitting across the table talking to someone," she told her assistant, Ted Sieracki. "We need to be sure that these individuals understand how to ask the right questions, as well as being aware of the questions that they should not ask. In addition, there are all sorts of mistakes that are commonly made in the interviewing process and I don't want these managers to make any of them. I think the first place to start is by calling a meeting with them and discussing the procedures that they should be following during the interviewing process." Ted agreed and placed a call to each of the managers who will be conducting the interviews. All six are scheduled to meet with Elizabeth and Ted later this week.

In the interim, Elizabeth and Ted intend to outline an agenda for the meeting, along with a list of "dos and don'ts" that they feel are critical to effective interviewing. Some of the topics that they want to discuss with the managers include the following:

- Formulation of the overall objectives for the interviews.
- Identification of information that is critical to an effective evaluation of the candidate.
- Questions that are to be avoided because they are considered improper (if not illegal).
- Ways to establish rapport with candidates.
- How to formulate questions that elicit the desired information.
- How to avoid leading questions.
- How to use intentional pauses to find out how the applicant deals with silence.
- How to keep control of the interview and work to steer it away from discussions of topics that are not job relevant.
- Effective ways to wind up the interview and close on a positive note.

Elizabeth believes that if the managers understand how to do all of these, the interviews will indeed be effective. If not, in her words, "then we are going to have an unmitigated disaster."

1. If you were helping Elizabeth Sloan in this process, what are some of the questions you would want the managers to avoid asking? List five of them.

2. Would you recommend that the managers use situational questions? Why or why not?

3. What are some other common mistakes that researchers have found that interviewers make? Would you include any of these in your discussions with the managers? Why or why not?

ANSWERS TO BOX 6.1: "WHAT CAN YOU ASK?"

I   1. No inquiries related to arrests are permitted, although inquiries concerning specified convictions that relate reasonably to fitness to perform the particular job for which the person is applying are proper.

P   2. It is proper to ask this question in order to determine whether the applicant is prevented from lawfully becoming employed because of visa or immigration status.

I   3. Unless this is job related (and in most cases it is not), the question is improper.

P   4. This question is designed to help screen out those who are unable to do the job; it is proper to ask the person if there are any reasons that he or she would fall into this category.

I   5. This is not a job-related question and should be avoided.

P   6. It is acceptable to ask about work experience in order to determine the person's suitability for the job.

I   7. It is improper to ask about the type or condition of military discharge.

P   8. This answer can help the person doing the screening learn more about the applicant's skills and abilities.

P   9. Here, also, the person doing the screening is learning more about the applicant's abilities.

I 10. This question is not job related and should not be asked.

P 11. The company has a right to ask about previous work experience, and in this case might want to know why the individual initially left the firm.

P 12. Again, this is background information that is not considered private and is fertile ground for questions.

I 13. This is none of the organization's business and, like questions about other personal family matters, should be scrupulously avoided.

P 14. This is background information that a prospective employer is entitled to know.

I 15. It is improper to ask any questions related to the applicant's lineage or ancestry.

I 16. These types of questions should not be asked, unless there is a job-related reason for doing so—and there usually is not.

I 17. It is a violation of the individual's right of privacy to ask this question.

I 18. This question invades the person's privacy and should not be asked.

I 19. This is not a job-related question.

P 20. This is job related and can be asked.

ENDNOTES

1. "Aggressive Recruiting of Entry-Level People," *Managers,* June 1994, p. 26.
2. See Judy Liberson, "Prized Chefs," *Lodging,* May 1995, pp. 56–60; and Stephen Michaelides, "The Incredible Shrinking Labor Pool," *Restaurant Hospitality,* January 1995, p. 116.
3. Milford Prewitt, "Management Shortage Prompts Desperate Recruitment Tactics," *Nation's Restaurant News,* April 3, 1995, pp. 7–9.
4. Sarah Taylor, "Where Did Everyone Go?" *Caterer & Hotelkeeper,* March 1995, pp. 60–61.
5. Mary Williams, "Staff Will Move to Jobs, Says Survey," *Caterer & Hotelkeeper,* November 1994, p. 14.
6. Kathleen Cassedy, "Desperately Seeking Superstars," *Lodging,* November 1994, p. 88.
7. Richard M. Hodgetts and K. Galen Kroeck, *Personnel and Human Resource Management* (Fort Worth: Dryden Press, 1992), p. 240.
8. Milford Prewitt, "Personnel Expert: Top-Notch Interviewing Key to Hiring," *Nation's Restaurant News,* June 19, 1995, pp. 67–68.
9. For additional questions, see William P. Fisher, "I Could Get in Trouble For That?" *Nation's Restaurant News,* June/July 1995, p. 39.
10. Also see Howard Feiertag, "Good Interviewing Techniques Are Crucial to Success," *Sales Clinic,* November 7, 1994, p. 14.
11. See, for example, Michael T. MacHatton, "Quality Personnel Selection: Using a Structured Interview Guide to Improve Selection of Managers," *Hospitality Research Journal,* Vol. 18, No. 1, 1994, pp. 77–98.
12. For additional insight into this area, see Julia Lawlor, "Don't Ask That Question," *Sales & Marketing Management,* March 1995, p. 76.
13. For another example, see Louis A. Birenbaum, "Hiring for a Spa: Building a Team with Group Interviews," *Cornell Hotel and Restaurant Administration Quarterly,* February 1990, p. 55.
14. Don Allen, "Finding the Right Fit," *HR Focus,* April 1995, p. 15.
15. For more on this, see Mitchell B. Brooks, "Interviewing Face-to-Interface," *Personnel,* January 1990, pp. 23–25; and Christopher L. Martin and Dennis H. Nagao, "Some Effects of Computerized Interviewing on Job Applicant Responses," *Journal of Applied Psychology,* Vol. 74, 1980, pp. 72–80.
16. Mark A. Johnson, "Lights, Camera, Interview," *Human Resource Magazine,* April 1995 , pp. 66–68.
17. Ben R. Furman, "Solid Screening Procedures Minimize Workplace Crime," *Hotel & Motel Management,* June 5, 1995, p. 29.
18. Hodgetts and Kroeck, *Personnel and Human Resource Management,* p. 240.
19. For more on these types of insights see Joseph N. DePalma, "Dos and Don'ts for Improving Staffing Average," *Hotel & Motel Management,* September 23, 1991, p. 41; and Fred L. Conner, "Looking Beyond Their Résumés," *Cornell Hotel and Restaurant Administration Quarterly,* November 1990, pp. 112–113.
20. Richard M. Hodgetts, *Modern Human Relations at Work,* 6th ed. (Fort Worth: Dryden Press, 1996), p. 306.

21. Ibid.
22. Ronald Henkoff, "Finding, Training, & Keeping the Best Service Workers," *Fortune*, October 3, 1994, p. 114.
23. Loret Carbone, "Less Employee Turnover: The Hidden Key to Profitability," *Nation's Restaurant News*, March 20, 1995, p. 50.
24. Robert H. Woods and James F. Macaulay, "Rx for Turnover: Retention Programs That Work," *Cornell Hotel and Restaurant Administration Quarterly*, May 1989, p. 81.
25. Gerald L. White, "Employee Turnover: The Hidden Drain on Profits," *HR Focus*, January 1995, pp. 15–17.
26. Stephen Chapdelaine, "Business Culture Linked to Profitability," *Restaurants USA*, November 1994, pp. 40–43.
27. Noel C. Cullen, "Protect the People Investment: Reduce Turnover," *Chef Magazine*, October/November 1994, pp. 22–25.
28. David J. Kennedy and Florence Berger, "Newcomer Socialization: Oriented to Facts or Feelings?" *Cornell Hotel and Restaurant Administration Quarterly*, December 1994, pp. 58–71.
29. The information in this self-feedback exercise can be found in Mark D. Fulford and Richard J. Wagner, "Making Non-Career Jobs Attractive to Younger Workers," *FIU Hospitality Review*, Fall 1994, pp. 71–78.

CHAPTER SEVEN

Training, Developing, and Appraising Associates

LEARNING OBJECTIVES

The first step in creating a team of talented associates is to recruit and hire the right individuals. The process by which this is done was described in Chapter 6. The overriding objective of this chapter is to examine how hospitality organizations go about training, developing, and appraising their associates. These processes are designed to ensure that the talents of the organization's associates are fully tapped. The first part of this chapter will examine the nature and substance of training and development. Then attention will be focused on how organizations can properly evaluate associates and create follow-up plans for ensuring that everyone has the opportunity to employ his or her talents. When you have finished studying all of the material in this chapter, you will be able to:

1. Define the terms *training* and *development* and explain how a needs analysis is conducted.
2. Describe the most typical types of training programs used in the hospitality industry, including skills training, cross-functional training, team training, and games.
3. Discuss how organizations go about determining the costs of their training programs and evaluating their effectiveness.
4. Define the term *performance appraisal* and discuss some of the most common methods used to appraise associate performance.
5. Describe some of the most common performance appraisal rating errors and how they can be addressed.
6. Discuss the role and importance of personal development plans in the evaluation of associates.

The Nature of Training and Development

Training is the process of providing associates with specific skills or helping them correct deficiencies in their current performance.[1] *Development* is the process of providing associates with the experience and attitudes needed for success in the future.[2]

Typically, training is directed toward teaching people how to do things such as fill out a monthly cost control report, greet a customer at the check-in desk, or provide service to a party of six.[3] Because of its restricted focus, training is typically carried out at the lower and intermediate levels of the organization, where "how to do it" information is of major importance.[4]

Development is usually carried out at the managerial level and is used to help improve and fine-tune performance. Some of the most common reasons for conducting development programs include (1) reducing or preventing managerial obsolescence by keeping individuals up to date, (2) increasing the overall effectiveness of the managerial force, (3) strengthening management's overall satisfaction with its jobs, and (4) preparing managers for future positions of increased importance.

Most hospitality organizations spend far more of their time and money on training than on development. There are three reasons for this. One is that there are more people who need training than who need development. The second is that training helps improve current performance and maintain customer satisfaction, objectives that are critical to the success of every hospitality organization. The third is that the benefits from training can be realized more quickly than those from development. Of course, the specific types of training and development that will be needed will be determined by the situation.[5] This is why all effective programs begin with a needs analysis.

Needs Analysis

There are a number of ways that needs analyses can be conducted. One of the most common is for the organization's training department (or those responsible for formal training) to design orientation training as well as follow-up programs that are needed on the job. These latter programs are typically developed from managerial and performance feedback. Managers are asked to provide information regarding the types of training their associates need; work performance is used to identify areas where improvements are needed.

In addition, organizations often conduct brainstorming sessions among managers and trainers in order to identify new training programs that will be needed. These programs are often based on an evaluation of what competitive firms are doing, as well as feedback from customers and clients regarding services they would like to see introduced and/or improved. Quite often, these programs are tied to those that are currently being offered, so the overall philosophy of the training remains the same. A good example is provided by the Radisson hotel chain. The company's guest service training is wrapped around three principles. Here is how the company explains each:

1. Show a *Yes I Can!* attitude.
   This means not only responding to customer requests, but also looking for opportunities to anticipate customers' needs and exceed their expectations. It means that no customer request is too small or unimportant. It also means that we will try to respond to every request in a way that will delight that customer.

2. Take personal responsibility.
   This means that when you start something with a customer, you see it through to the end. This means following through on your promises and following up to make sure the customer was satisfied.

3. Use teamwork.
   No one serves the customer alone. We all need each other's help to provide the best possible service. Working together to serve the customer is what teamwork is all about. We develop and build teamwork by treating each other as customers.[6]

Working within its training philosophy, the company will design programs that meet its specific needs. In doing so, there are a number of options.

Typical Types of Training Programs

Depending on the associate's job and how long the individual has been with the organization, a variety of common programs are used for training purposes.[7] At the Marriott Corporation, for example, all new recruits attend an eight-hour initial training session and are then assigned a "buddy" to serve as a mentor for the next 90 days. During this time period, new associates also attend refresher training programs designed to extend their knowledge and make them even more effective in providing guest services.[8] Some of the most commonly used types of training include skill training, cross-functional training, team training, and games.[9] The following sections examine these.

Skill Training. *Skill training* is designed to teach trainees how to do things such as serve a table, handle a room reservation, or deal with a customer problem. This training typically provides the participants with a series of "dos and don'ts" so that they leave the session with a clear understanding of what they need to know and how to use this information. For example, in the case of customer problems, Radisson Hotels International works to help its associates turn the problem into an opportunity. In doing so, trainers not only set forth a list of steps to be followed, but get the participants involved in discussing the process and describing how they would use it in handling on-the-job situations. Here are the eight steps that the trainer will follow in presenting this information *and* getting the participants involved in the training process:

1. Hand out copies of the ABCs pocket reference card and review the ABC approach to turning problems into opportunities:

   ■ **Apologize for the problem**—Say, "I'm sorry you're having this problem." Show the customer you are willing to take responsibility for solving the problem.

   ■ **Be understanding**—Recognize how the customer is feeling. If the customer is angry, try to deal with that anger before trying to look for a solution. For example, "I can see you're angry. I'd like to help solve the problem."

   ■ **Correct the problem quickly**—The faster you can resolve the problem, the better. Solving a problem on the spot is the best. If not, make sure the problem is solved within the next few hours. If it takes a long time to solve the problem, keep the customer informed about your progress.

   If it can't be solved—

   ■ **Discuss what the customer wants done**—Ask what other options or alternatives would be acceptable.

   ■ **Explain what actions you will take**—State which of the options or alternatives you are willing to take and explain your reasons. In some cases, you may need to negotiate a solution if the customer's request is unreasonable. Also, be careful about overpromising.

   ■ **Follow through on the solution you've agreed upon**—Make sure you take responsibility to do what you promised.

2. Explain that each person will describe a problem one of their customers has had (or could have). Tell them not to reveal how it was solved (or could be solved).

3. Invite people to tell their stories, in turn. They can use the "Using the ABCs" Worksheet and/or pocket reference card if they are helpful.

4. After each person shares their story, conduct a group discussion on solutions to that challenge.

5. Ask the person whether the problem in their story has already been solved. If it has, ask how. If not, ask the person which of the possible solutions mentioned he or she plans to use.

6. Thank the person for sharing their ideas and/or experiences.

7. Repeat steps 3 through 6 for each person.

8. Conclude the meeting by making the following points:

- Everyone's commitment to the *Yes I Can!* Principles and Service Standards will prevent many of the problems mentioned from ever occurring.

- When a problem or difficult situation is handled well by using the ABCs, we end up with a more loyal customer than if the problem had never occurred in the first place.[10]

When people leave this training session, they have acquired the skills needed to address customer concerns, they know how to handle these situations.[11]

Team Training. *Team training* is designed to promote effective intragroup cooperation for the purpose of increasing productivity. Today an increasing number of hospitality organizations are offering team training; they are realizing that high-quality service is more often a result of effective team performance than of effective individual performance. This training focuses on a number of critical behavioral areas, including the ability to communicate well, willingness to cooperate with others, and the ability to put group goals ahead of individual goals. These ideas are instilled in the participants in a number of ways. One is through lecture and discussion. A second is with case studies, in which the participants analyze a situation that calls for teamwork and then discuss the steps that need to be achieved in creating the environment for effective teamwork. A third is through outdoor experiential exercises, such as low-level risk activities.

> Last week Rich Sanders and the other six members of his work team participated in a "ropes" course. All of the members were taken to a nearby field, blindfolded, and positioned near each other. Then the trainer told them, "I have a large, thick rope that I am going to distribute to each of you. You are to hold out your hands, palms up, and I will place the rope in your hands. When everyone is holding on to his or her part of the rope, I will signal you to begin. You have thirty minutes to form yourselves into a square. You may talk to each other, but do not take off your blindfold and do not drop your part of the rope."

> For the next half hour Rich and his friends figured out who had the beginning and end parts of the rope. They also realized that the trainer had positioned them in such a way that they needed to straighten out the rope (it was criss-crossed) and form themselves into a semicircle. Once this was done, they needed to figure out how to create a square. During the exercise there was a large amount of talking (and yelling), but at the end of the 30 minutes they were still unable to form a square. When they took off their blindfolds, they realized that they were in an oval-shaped formation.

> For the next hour the group discussed the activity and examined how it could have done a better job of creating the square. The team members concluded that there were too many people calling out directions and there was

no one who took sufficient directive leadership. They also discussed the need for better teamwork, a willingness to follow directions, and the need for clear, concise communication. At the end of the training session, everyone agreed that they had gained some important insights into teamwork.

The preceding story is a good example of how hospitality organizations can create better teams. In particular, by getting the members involved in a situation that requires teamwork, the trainer is better able to introduce and reinforce the ideas that are critical to the process.

Cross-Functional Training. *Cross-functional training* is the process of teaching individuals to carry out operations in areas other than those directly assigned to them. This can be done in a number of ways. One of the most common is through the use of *job rotation,* which is the process of teaching associates a variety of different tasks by moving them from one job to another. In this way, associates will be able to carry out a number of jobs and, if someone is absent from work due to illness or temporarily away from his or her work station, another associate can fill in and perform the job. At the Ritz-Carlton hotel in Dearborn, Michigan, for example, there is a two-week cross-training program during which participants are taught how to perform tasks in a number of different areas, including front-office agent, reservations agent, and concierge.

One of the reasons why cross-functional training within a particular functional area has become so important in recent years is that when all members of a team know how to perform all of the team's tasks, the group is likely to have high work productivity. There are three reasons for this: (1) everyone knows how to carry out all of the tasks, so if someone is late or needs help, the other team members can provide it; (2) it is possible to rotate work assignments so that job boredom is reduced; and (3) the group begins to build strong esprit de corps because of the trust and reliance they have in each other. In addition, when associates are given cross-training in other departments, it expands their knowledge and can help prepare them for potential growth careers.

> Last week there was a major international convention at the D'Aville Hotel. At one point there were over 125 people waiting to check in. However, thanks to the cross-training program that the hotel instituted last year, the hotel staff was able to get everyone registered and up to their rooms within 45 minutes of the time they joined the check-in line. This was an improvement of 30 minutes over the previous year. Commenting on the staff's performance, the hotel manager noted, "When it took us an hour and fifteen minutes to get people into their rooms last year, we knew we had to improve our performance markedly. Thanks to our new cross-functional training program, we've been able to do just that."

Games. Many organizations also develop (or purchase) games that are designed to introduce and/or reinforce important concepts.[12] These games often involve group participation, so that the team members working in harmony are required to make decisions or formulate a course of action that will help resolve a particular problem or create an opportunity for the organization. Sometimes these games are generic and reinforce a particular idea, such as the need for teamwork. Other times these games are specially designed and are company specific. A good example is provided in Box 7.1. The purpose of this game, developed by the Radisson Corporation, is to help reinforce in the participants the proper way to respond to a particular situation.[13]

The most important part of this training is not the activities in which the participants engage, but the processing of the results when the game is completed. The trainer will always conclude by spending some time having the group answer questions such as: What was the purpose of this game? What did you learn? What behaviors are you going to take away and use in your own job? By answering these questions, the trainer helps establish a link between what the participants have been doing in the game and what they can learn from this activity that can be useful to them on the job.

Cost of Training

A major issue that is often raised concerning training programs is whether the benefits justify the cost.[15] Is training a good investment? There are a number of ways to answer this question.[16] One is to look at what the competition is doing. If they are spending more and more money on training, they are likely to be developing a more productive workforce; the only way to keep up is by also offering training. Of course, it is possible that their training dollars are being wasted, but many organizations are unwilling to take this chance. So they also offer training.

A better way to judge whether or not training pays off is to ask organizational associates who are able to evaluate the impact of the training. In one recent study, George Conrade and his associates examined the perceptions of managers with ten or more years of lodging industry experience. These property managers were asked to indicate whether they felt training had any influence on a wide number of operational factors, including consistent service delivery, associate knowledge, and repeat business. The managers were also asked to indicate whether their responses were a result of (1) experience, (2) information they gathered from reading books or taking courses, or (3) both of these. The results are reported in Table 7.1 and show that property-level managers overwhelmingly believe that training pays off.

Before concluding this discussion of training, it is important to realize that the initial costs of developing and providing initial training can be quite high. Table 7.2 provides some data related to training budgets in the industry. On the positive side, training benefits accrue when there are a large number of people to be trained, so that the cost per participant drops sharply, and when

Box 7.1
Jeopardy: Can You Ask the Right Question?[14]

Hospitality organizations have developed a number of clever training programs that get the participants involved and help reinforce important ideas. The following examples are drawn from a *Jeopardy*-related game (you are given the answer and must determine the question) that has been constructed by Radisson Hotels International. The game is played after instructional training as a fun way to evaluate and reinforce the learning. On the left are answers and on the right are questions. Your task is to match the right answer with the correct question, and to do so within five minutes. Be sure to time yourself. In all, there are fifteen answers that must be matched with their correct questions. Ready? Go!

Answer		**Question**
a. Recommend an hors d'oeuvre or nonalcoholic beverage	_____	1. What could you offer to do if you saw a guest running late for a meeting?
b. Offer to help with the banquet setup	_____	2. What can you do to go beyond what the customer expects?
c. Customer and associate satisfaction.	_____	3. What should you do when a customer's concerns are not directly under your control?
d. Offer alternatives.	_____	4. What could a server do when the the kitchen is out of the soup of the day?
e. Look at luggage tags or check the guest register.	_____	5. What is a cost of a lost customer?
f. Call the guest's client.	_____	6. What is the most important competitive factor for Radisson?
g. Walk the customer to her meeting in the conference room.	_____	7. What is the result of great service?
h. Thank a co-worker for neatly sorting linens.	_____	8. What can a kitchen steward do to help the wait staff?
i. Call for reservations and arrange for transportation.	_____	9. What can you do for a customer who can't find her way to a meeting?
j. Service differentiation.	_____	10. What could a busperson do for a person eating a messy meal, such as ribs?
k. Lost revenue.	_____	11. What are easy ways to find out a guest's name?

Box 7.1   Continued

l. Involve others in the solution.

_____ 12. What can a concierge do for a guest rather than giving him or her a brochure and directions?

m. Suggest a soup the customer might like even better than creamed asparagus.

_____ 13. What should we do when what the customer asks for is not possible?

n. Do more than a competing hotel would in the same situation.

_____ 14. What can a laundry worker do to show appreciation to a fellow employee?

o. Bring an extra napkin.

_____ 15. What could a bartender do for a customer who has obviously had too much to drink?

Write down the time it took you to complete this exercise. Then compare your answers to those at the end of the chapter and see how well you did.

Source: Courtesy Radisson Hotels Worldwide

the training begins to produce bottom-line results. Unfortunately, many organizations fail to look at the long-run benefits associated with training and, as a result, they end up shortchanging themselves. This can be avoided if the company carefully evaluates its programs and assesses where the training is proving useful and where it is not cost effective.

Measuring the Payoff. Hospitality organizations can measure the effectiveness of their training programs in a number of ways. One is through customer feedback. What are clients saying about the level of service? What are the most common concerns? Are they the same as those in the past, or have the training programs designed to deal with these problems had a positive effect, so that the current client concerns are different ones?

A second way of measuring the payoff is to ask the participants the value that training has had for them and the additional types of training they would like. These responses are often quite useful in pinpointing whether or not associates feel they are learning useful concepts as well as highlighting new areas to be targeted for training.

A third way is to examine the cost of doing business and evaluate the impact that training is having on efficiency and profitability. It is sometimes difficult to establish a direct link between training and bottom-line results, but it is often possible to draw general conclusions regarding the overall value of the training.

Table 7.1 Perceptions of Property-Level Managers Regarding the Influence of Training

Is this factor influenced by training?	Yes	How Do You Know?		
		Experience	*Study*	*Both*
Consistent service delivery	99	84	5	11
Employee knowledge	97	85	7	9
Repeat business	96	84	5	11
Management knowledge	95	84	4	13
Employee skill	94	90	4	6
Profits	94	77	11	12
Suggestive selling	94	83	9	8
Management skill	93	84	6	10
Professional development	92	76	12	12
Motivation level	91	89	3	8
Reduced operating costs	90	78	11	11
Employee attitude	87	92	2	6
Employee turnover	87	79	12	9
Empowerment	86	79	9	12
Management attitude	86	89	2	9

Note: Numbers indicate percentage or respondents in agreement.

Source: George Conrade, Robert Woods, and Jack Ninemeier, "Training in the U.S. Lodging Industry: Perception and Reality," *Cornell Hotel and Restaurant Administration Quarterly,* October 1994, p. 18.

A fourth way is to compute how much it costs to train a person and determine whether this cost is likely to be recovered through increased efficiency. Table 7.3 provides an example drawn from a major hospitality organization that trains 25 associates a week in effective team management. The average cost per trainee was $1,165.52 for the first 25 participants. After this first session, however, costs dropped sharply; there were one-time expenses that applied only to the first program (development costs of $11,150), and the charge for audiovisual equipment would eventually be eliminated because the equipment would be paid for over time. So the cost of the second program was ($29,138 − $11,150 = $17,998/25) $719.52 per participant. Additionally, if the organization were to find that 35 people could be trained at the same time, the cost would drop even further, *e.g.,* $22,998/35 = $657.09.

Improving the Design

The last step in effective training and development is to determine whether the design of the programs should be changed and, if so, what modifications

Table 7.2 Average Training Budgets by Organization Size

Organization Size (Number of employees)	Seminars/ Conferences	Hardware	Outside Services
100–499	$ 8,418	$ 5,117	$ 4,619
500–999	16,554	9,630	8,308
1,000–2,499	46,169	17,347	18,658
2,500–9,999	77,975	78,508	40,287
10,000 or more	636,190	622,378	342,028

Custom Materials	Off-the-Shelf Materials	Total Outside Expenditures	Facilities/ Overhead
$ 3,228	$ 5,181	$ 26,563	$ 15,242
7,461	8,671	50,624	11,219
12,444	17,362	111,981	21,743
54,470	75,340	326,580	137,413
385,243	361,537	2,347,377	983,083

Source: B. Filipczak, "Training Budgets Boom," *Training,* October 1993, p. 42. Reprinted with permission from the October 1996 issue of *Training* Magazine © 1996. Lakewood Publications, Minneapolis, MN. All rights reserved. Not for resale.

should be made. Research shows that learning tends to be greatly improved if participants are actively involved in the process.

Susan Chang just returned from a two-day training program during which she learned how to greet customers, confirm their room reservations, and get them checked into the hotel within a four-minute window. During the first day of the program, the trainer described the hotel's customer service philosophy and discussed the most effective ways of processing people who are checking in. After answering questions from the group, the trainer then divided everyone into groups of three. One individual played the role of the guest who was checking in, a second assumed the role of the reservations associate, and the third videotaped the roleplay. When the roleplay was completed, the group then played back the tape, analyzed how well the reservations associate followed the rules and guidelines set forth by the trainer, and discussed how things could have been handled more efficiently. Then the team members shifted roles and did it again. After all three individuals had had a chance to be the reservations associate, they made a list of the things they did incorrectly and how they would address these mistakes in the future. The group then met in a plenary session with all of the other trainees, and collectively shared their mistakes

Table 7.3   Training Cost Breakdown: A Practical Example (25 Participants)

Direct Costs

Instructor (5 days × $200 per day)	$1,000
Fringe benefits (25 percent of salary)	250
Materials: $50 per participant ($50 × 25)	1,250
Room and audiovisual equipment (5 days × $50 per day)	250
Total direct costs	$2,750

Indirect Costs

Clerical and administrative salaries	$800
Fringe benefits (25 percent of salary)	200
Pre- and postlearning materials	225
Total indirect costs	$1,225

Development Costs

Fee to purchase program	$5,000
Instructor training	
Registration fee	2,500
Travel and lodging	2,400
Salary	1,000
Benefits (25 percent of salary)	250
Total development cost	$11,150

Overhead Costs

General organization support, top management's time (10 percent of direct, indirect, and development costs)	$1,513

Compensation for Participants

Participants' salaries and benefits (time away from job)	$12,500
Total training cost	$29,138
Cost per participant	$1,165

and steps for ensuring that they did not happen again. When completing her evaluation of the program, Susan wrote, "I learned a great deal about how to check in guests because I got to assume this role and see others doing it also. This hands-on experience and feedback was extremely valuable to me."

Box 7.2
Avoiding the Pitfalls

A host of common training mistakes are often committed by hospitality organizations.[17] By avoiding these errors, businesses can save time and increase profitability. Six of the most common are the following:

1. *Not understanding the value of training.* Training can reduce mistakes, increase customer satisfaction, and lead to greater revenue and profit. As a result, much of the money spent on training is returned to the organization within the first year.

2. *Not knowing how to train effectively.* Trainers usually have to learn how to do their jobs. This is why it can be particularly useful to start the training effort by identifying those who will be doing the training and having them attend a "train the trainer" course where they can learn these skills.

3. *Failure to plan training and set goals.* Training should be offered in a systematic way, beginning with a needs analysis and the identification of training targets that are both clear and measurable. Without such a plan, the entire process can be haphazard.

4. *Failure to use available training tools.* Some programs need to be developed from scratch and carefully tailored to the needs of the organization. In many cases, however, training instruments, films, and other materials can be purchased or rented and can save a great deal of training time and money.

5. *Not training for the future.* Training should be an ongoing process, but many organizations train only when they identify a specific, immediate need. They fail to train for the future, so all of their efforts are designed to help the company get where it needs to be in the next 30 days. Training should be for tomorrow as well as for today.

6. *Not adequately measuring training effectiveness.* Many organizations do not know whether their training is effective because they have not developed adequate measurements. It is critically important to identify the types of feedback that can be used in evaluating training and then take the steps that will be necessary to gather this information and evaluate the results.

Other useful steps for effective training include (1) a carefully crafted, comprehensive plan that addresses the current and future needs of the organization, (2) training programs designed with the specific needs of the organization in mind, and (3) diligent selection of the participants (especially for follow-up training) for these programs. At the same time, it is important to sidestep common mistakes that are made in training. Box 7.2 identifies and describes six of these.

Performance Appraisal

Performance appraisal is the systematic observation, evaluation, and description of work-related behavior. The purpose of performance appraisal is to determine how well associates are carrying out their tasks and to decide what action to take as a result of these findings. These appraisals are often linked to training and development. For example, if an individual is rated as poor in ability to communicate well with others, the person will be scheduled for training in communication skills as well as, perhaps, one-on-one developmental meetings for personal assistance in this area. In carrying out this appraisal process, organizations often rely on a variety of appraisal methods.

Appraisal Methods

While there are many types of appraisal methods, three of the most common are graphic rating scales, paired comparison, and critical incidents. The first two are heavily objective, while the latter is more subjective.

Graphic Rating Scales. The *graphic rating scale* technique consists of evaluating people along a series of continua that measure such things as work quality, work quantity, and other performance-related dimensions. Figure 7.1 provides an example.

The graphic rating scale is the most widely used appraisal method and offers a number of important advantages, including the following: (1) the technique is relatively inexpensive to develop; (2) it can be applied across a wide range of jobs; and (3) it can easily be used to quantify performance. On the other hand, there are a number of potential drawbacks, including the following: (1) there can be interpretation errors so that how one manager rates an individual on work quality may be different from the way another manager would rate the same individual; (2) a standard graphic rating scale may not apply to all of the jobs for which it is being used; and (3) because it is easy to complete, the possibility of consistent errors (such as rating everyone in the same way regardless of individual performance) tends to be common.

Despite its limitations, many hospitality organizations find that the graphic rating scale is easy to use and can be applied in a wide variety of jobs. As a result, it enjoys great popularity.

Paired Comparison. The *paired comparison* evaluation involves comparing each associate who is being rated against all of the others on the basis of work-related factors. Table 7.4 provides an example of how this can be done in terms of both work quantity and work quality. Since most hospitality organizations rate their people on far more than these two factors, the manager might fill out as many as seven or eight paired comparisons. However, when the individual

Part III   Understanding Human Resource Management

ASSESSMENT	S = SIGNIFICANT STRENGTH M = MEETS EXPECTATIONS P = PROBLEM AREA X = NOT APPLICABLE	Please check (✔) the appropriate box.			
PRODUCTIVITY		**S**	**M**	**P**	**X**
1. QUALITY: Meets internal/external customer requirements (specs and schedule) with minimum scrap/rework.					
2. PRODUCIBILITY: Meets output goals while doing it right the first time.					
3. MEETING DEADLINES: Promptly completes assignments in order to meet quality and producibility goals.					
4. PLANNING AND ORGANIZATION: Develops and evaluates course(s) of action with realistic objectives and time frames.					
5. CONTROL OF COSTS/BUDGETS: Works within budget and suggests cost-cutting improvements.					
6. DECISION MAKING: Makes decisions and takes responsibility for them; avoids procrastinating.					
7. PROBLEM SOLVING: Diagnoses problems quickly. Accurately recommends or implements effective solutions. Documents analyses and results.					
INTERACTIVE SKILLS					
8. ORAL COMMUNICATION: Maintains or enhances the self-esteem of others, listens and responds with empathy, transmits information clearly. Answers inquiries accurately and in a timely manner.					
9. WRITTEN COMMUNICATION: Produces concise, readable reports, memos, and so forth in a timely manner.					
10. TRAINING AND DEVELOPMENT: Improves job performance through training and seeks opportunities for growth through special assignments.					
11. TEAM BUILDING: Stresses and develops cooperation among coworkers, internal customers, and suppliers.					
12. PROJECT LEADERSHIP: Gives clear directions, explains reasons for decisions, solicits coworker input to maximize group capabilities.					
ADDITIONAL RESPONSIBILITIES					
13. SAFETY EFFECTIVENESS: Maintains a clean, safe, and accident-free work environment. Obeys all safety rules.					
14. ETHICAL CONDUCT: Promotes, supports, and adheres to all policies, procedures, and business conduct guidelines.					
15. ATTENDANCE: Present at work on time every scheduled day and does not leave early.					
16. PROFESSIONAL DEVELOPMENT: Strives to improve own level of competence, keeps abreast of new developments, and continues educational pursuits.					

Figure 7.1 *Graphic Rating Scale: An Illustration*

ASSESSMENT

EXPLANATION OF S AND P RATINGS: Provide specific behavioral examples of each strength or problem area.

ACTION PLANS FOR THE COMING PERIOD (BASED ON THIS REVIEW) TO CORRECT PROBLEM AREAS:

ACTION PLANS FOR THE COMING PERIOD TO MEET AGREED UPON PERSONAL AND BUSINESS OBJECTIVES:

EMPLOYEE REVIEW:
Please check (✔) the appropriate box.
☐ I am in agreement with the evaluation.
☐ I am in agreement with the evaluation with the exceptions noted below.
☐ I disagree with the evaluation as noted below.
Comments:

Signatures _____   _____   _____
               Employee   Appraiser   Date

Reviewed by (AFTER APPRAISAL DISCUSSION COMPLETED)

                               _____   _____
                                      Name   Date

Figure 7.1 *Continued*

Source: Martin Levy, "Almost Perfect Performance Appraisals," *Personnel Journal*, April 1989, pp. 78, 80.

Table 7.4 Paired Comparison Method for Rating Associates

On the Basis of Work Quantity

Associates Being Rated

As compared to:	Anderson	Brown	Carpenter	David	Evans
Anderson		−	+	−	+
Brown	+		+	+	+
Carpenter	−	−		−	−
David	+	−	+		+
Evans	−	−	−	−	

Evans has the highest ranking for work quantity

On the Basis of Work Quality

Associates Being Rated

As compared to:	Anderson	Brown	Carpenter	David	Evans
Anderson		−	+	+	+
Brown	+		+	+	+
Carpenter	−	−		+	+
David	+	−	−		−
Evans	−	−	+	+	

David has the highest ranking for work quality

Note: A plus (+) indicates "higher than" and a minus (−) indicates "lower than." The individual with the greatest number of pluses is the one with the highest ranking.

is finished, there is an overall ranking of the associates from best to poorest. For example, if there is a group of six associates being ranked on five factors, the individual receiving the highest ranking on a factor could be given six points, the next highest-ranked person would receive five points, and so on. Then, after all the individual scores are totaled, the associates would be ranked on the basis of overall points. If there is a tie, the factor that is regarded as most important (for example, work quality) would serve as the tie breaker in determining the final order.

A number of advantages are associated with the paired comparison method, including the following: (1) it is easy to use; (2) the number of factors that are included can be increased without much difficulty; and (3) there is a clear ranking of associates from first to last. On the other hand, some of the major drawbacks to this method include the following: (1) the manager may feel that two associates are equal on a particular factor, but must choose between them; (2) the manager may not remember everyone's performance on all of the factors being evaluated; and (3) there is a built-in bias in that the difference between the best and poorest worker may be very small, but on a list of ten associates it appears that the first one is far superior to the last one.

While it is not as popular as the graphic rating scale, paired comparison is widely used because of its simplicity and the fact that it discriminates between the best and poorest performers. Additionally, it can be very effective in helping identify those with the most promotion potential.

Critical Incident Technique. The *critical incident technique* is the documentation of instances of associate performance in which particularly effective or ineffective behavior is observed. Many years ago when the method was first put into use, supervisors carried a notebook, making entries about observed behaviors. Current use of the technique is more refined, but the basic approach remains the same: reporting of observed job-related behaviors.

Some of the primary advantages of the critical incident technique include (1) a strong focus on job-related behaviors and (2) a written record that can be used for evaluation purposes. Some of the primary disadvantages of the technique include the following: (1) emphasis is given to particularly effective and ineffective behavior and not to average or routine work-related behaviors; (2) not all of an individual's extremely effective and ineffective behaviors are likely to be recorded; and (3) more recent performance is often weighed more heavily than performance earlier in the evaluation period. Despite these shortcomings, however, the critical incident approach still remains a popular, although often complementary, method of evaluating performance.

Rating Errors

While all managers try to be objective in their appraisal, many managers are guilty of rating errors caused by various forms of bias. Some of the most common include the halo error; the severity, leniency, and central tendency errors; the contrast error; the similar-to-me error; and the recency error. The following sections briefly describe each.

Halo Error. The *halo error* occurs when a rater generalizes his or her limited knowledge about a person to other, unrelated characteristics of that person and forms attributions as to the causes of the person's performance. When committing the halo error, the rater fails to distinguish among the different aspects of performance. For example, a supervisor may know that an associate is punctual, and on that basis may form a "halo" conclusion or attribution that the individual must also be motivated, dependable, and productive.

The halo error can also occur as a generalized negative impression of the associate. All performance might be attributed to some cause that the supervisor generalizes about the associate. For example, the manager may assume a lack of interpersonal skills or poor productivity because of the associate's dress habits. For example, "Maria is such a poor dresser that she must also have a difficult time getting along with her co-workers."

Severity, Leniency, and Central Tendency Errors. *Severity errors* occur when a rater tends to rate associates too low, with few or no associates identified as outstanding. The best associates are rated as average or slightly above average, while average associates are assigned below-average ratings. This error discriminates against the best associates.

Leniency errors occur when the rater rarely assigns unsatisfactory ratings and rates most associates as above average or excellent. The rater gives the poorest associates average ratings, and in so doing discriminates against the best associates. This error has been a primary problem for many organizations, and in dealing with it they have turned to use of the paired comparison method, described earlier.

Central tendency errors occur when a rater does not use the extreme rating scale categories—for example, by giving the best associates a score of six to eight on a ten-point range. Raters who commit this error restrict the range of ratings, so the best associates are assigned slightly above-average ratings and the poorest associates are given slightly below-average ratings.

The leniency, severity, and central tendency errors cause problems in hospitality organizations especially when pay and promotions are based on performance appraisal. One problem is that neither outstanding nor unsatisfactory associates are clearly identified. The appraisal system is also unfair when some associates are rated by severe raters, some by central tendency raters, and others by lenient raters. When ratings by different raters are compared with each other in making evaluation decisions, it is neither accurate nor fair to all associates, and can cause substantial discontent in the workplace.

Contrast Error. The *contrast error* occurs when a manager fails to rate each associate independently. As a result, the rating of one associate inappropriately influences the evaluation of another associate. For example, the rater may first evaluate an exceptional associate and then evaluate an average associate. The average associate, in contrast to the exceptional associate, is assigned a below-average rating. The contrast error can also bias ratings upwardly. For example, when an average associate is rated immediately after a very poorly performing associate, the average individual is assigned a high rating because, in contrast, the person appears to be quite good.

Similar-to-Me Error. The *similar-to-me error* occurs when a rater assigns higher ratings to those he or she believes exhibit traits and behaviors that are similar to the rater. Conversely, research shows that associates who are viewed as "different from me" end up getting poorer ratings.[18]

Recency Error. The *recency error* occurs when the rater fails to consider performance across the entire rating period. Instead, the individual recalls only recent performance and bases ratings on these latest observed behaviors. For example, consider the supervisor who begins looking closely at the performance of his or her associates only a few weeks prior to annual evaluations and noting critical incidents that can be incorporated into the evaluation. In this case, recent performance will be a primary factor in determining how well the associates are rated.

Dealing with Rating Errors. There are a number of ways that these rating errors can be addressed. One is to carefully train the managers and other raters regarding how to observe and evaluate performance. In this way, everyone is looking for the same behaviors and reporting their observations in a similar way. In particular, attention must be focused on job-related behaviors. For example, a manager may feel that a college degree is important for managerial success in the hospitality industry today. However, this is not a job-related behavior and should not be a criterion in the evaluation process. By making raters aware of their own biases and focusing their attention on the factors to be evaluated, organizations can reduce rating errors.

A second, and related way, is to clearly enunciate the factors that are being evaluated so that everyone has the same understanding of them. For example, what is meant by "job quantity" and "job quality"? When this question is answered, all of the managers who are rating their associates on these bases will be looking at the same behaviors and will be interpreting these behaviors in the same way. This, in turn, will help ensure that the ratings are consistent.

A third way is to discuss common rating errors, describe how and why they occur, and outline what can be done to prevent their recurrence. This is a particularly useful strategy for training individuals who are new to the evaluation process and are looking for assistance and guidance. It is also beneficial for those who have been evaluating associates for some time and may have fallen into common rating-error problems. In this case, managers can review their evaluations and look for obvious errors such as severity, central tendency, and leniency. Other errors, such as the halo error, the contrast error, and the similar-to-me error, are more difficult to identify since they require greater personal analysis and may be hidden from the view of outside observers. Nevertheless, by examining past evaluations, it is possible to help managers improve their rating objectivity and generate evaluations that are more useful to the organization.

Personal Development Plans

In recent years, some hospitality organizations have begun moving away from standard performance evaluations and replacing them with personal development plans. Most performance evaluations focus on identifying what associates have done right and wrong and provide an overall evaluation that, among other things, can be used by higher-level management for salary and promotion decisions. A *personal development plan* (PDP) is a performance-related guide that focuses on finding new and better ways to develop associate skills so as to improve guest service, enhance job satisfaction, and reduce turnover. A good example is provided by Bristol Hotels, which uses the form in Figure 7.2 to determine whether individuals meet standards (MS) or need improvement (NI).

In employing the PDP, the Bristol manager will prepare goals based on technical skills (those required to perform routine tasks associated with the position), interpersonal skills (how the associate interacts with staff members and guests on a verbal and/or written basis), and supervisory skills or self-management skills (how well the associate organizes his or her time, acts responsibly, or leads others).[19] The objective of this exercise is to help identify what the associate is expected to do and to help the individual continually improve his or her performance through a process of ongoing development. In all, there are five key steps that are followed. In the case of a food and beverage (F&B) manager who is going to be helping develop a banquet server, these steps include:

1. The F&B manager lists the technical, interpersonal, and managerial goals required of a new banquet server as soon as the server is hired.

2. Shortly after the hire date, the manager outlines how the server will be trained to achieve the goals outlined in Step 1.

3. About 90 days after the hire date, the manager will evaluate the server's performance against the goals from Step 1 as either "meeting standards" or "needs improvement." Written feedback is recorded in the section titled "Review Comments."

4. After the manager has completed Step 3, the associate will record his or her comments on the form, some of which will be the result of the review meeting with the manager.

5. During the second half of the review, a new PDP will be prepared. Goals marked as "needs improvement" will be carried forward, new objectives that build on goals already achieved will be added, and a new development outline will be prepared for each goal (as in Step 2).

This cycle (steps 1–5) will be repeated for each performance review period. As a result, associates will learn how to improve as well as how to build on their past successes and further develop their skills and abilities. Commenting on the value of the PDP, the president of Bristol Hotels has noted:

Bristol Hotel Management Corporation Personal Development Plan

Performance Review/Comments:

_____   _____
Name   Position

Technical Skills (Performing the routine of the job)   MS NI

_____ ☐ ☐
_____ ☐ ☐
_____ ☐ ☐
_____ ☐ ☐
_____ ☐ ☐
_____ ☐ ☐
_____ ☐ ☐
_____ ☐ ☐
_____ ☐ ☐
_____ ☐ ☐
_____ ☐ ☐

Communication/Interpersonal Skills (Interacting & communicating with people in completing job assignments)

_____ ☐ ☐
_____ ☐ ☐
_____ ☐ ☐
_____ ☐ ☐
_____ ☐ ☐
_____ ☐ ☐
_____ ☐ ☐
_____ ☐ ☐
_____ ☐ ☐
_____ ☐ ☐
_____ ☐ ☐
_____ ☐ ☐

Self Management/Supervisory Skills (Acting responsibly, making decisions, organizing time, etc.)

_____ ☐ ☐
_____ ☐ ☐
_____ ☐ ☐
_____ ☐ ☐
_____ ☐ ☐
_____ ☐ ☐
_____ ☐ ☐
_____ ☐ ☐
_____ ☐ ☐
_____ ☐ ☐
_____ ☐ ☐

_____   _____   _____   _____
Employee's Signature   Date   Dept. Mgr. Initials   Manager (Print Name)

                                                                                        P-002-A
_____   _____   12/95
Manager's Signature   GM's Signature

Figure 7.2   _Bristol Hotel Company Personal Development Plan and Evaluation_
Courtesy: Dianna DeLorenzi, Bristol Hotel Company.

Bristol Hotel Management Corporation Personal Development Plan

Performance Goals:

Type _____ Date_____

_____   _____
                Name   Position

Goals For Developing
Technical Skills (Performing the routine of the job)   Target Date

_____ _____
_____ _____
_____ _____
_____ _____
_____ _____
_____ _____
_____ _____
_____ _____
_____ _____
_____ _____
_____ _____
_____ _____

Goals For Developing
Communication/Interpersonal Skills (Interacting & communicating with people in completing job assignments)

_____ _____
_____ _____
_____ _____
_____ _____
_____ _____
_____ _____
_____ _____
_____ _____
_____ _____
_____ _____
_____ _____
_____ _____
_____ _____
_____ _____

Goals For Developing
Self Management/Supervisory Skills (Acting responsibly, making decisions, organizing time, etc.)

_____ _____
_____ _____
_____ _____
_____ _____
_____ _____
_____ _____
_____ _____
_____ _____
_____ _____
_____ _____
_____ _____

_____ _____   _____ _____
Employee's Signature   Date   Dept. Mgr. Initials   Manager (Print Name)

_____   P-002-A
Manager's Signature   12/95

Figure 7.2   *Continued*

We don't have a lot of rules, bureaucracy, approval levels, or even a formal chain of command. The PDP matches up well with [the hotel's] long-standing philosophy of giving employees authority to make decisions on their own and be very responsive to guests' needs. You need smart, competent people to make this approach work, however. With the PDP, we have found a way to identify, develop, and reward such people in our organization. The talent and potential were there all along. We just weren't tapping into it in the best way we could. Now, the company is building on its strengths and getting a very nice return on its investment.

Introducing the PDP has helped create an environment where our company's mission to exceed guest expectations has a direct relationship to an individual's success with the . . . organization. Our service has always been good; now, we have a way to make it consistently outstanding.[20]

SUMMARY

1. Training is the process of providing associates with specific skills or helping them correct deficiencies in their current performance. Development is the process of providing associates with the experience and attitudes needed for success in the future. In determining the types of training and development programs that are needed, hospitality organizations typically begin with a needs analysis.

2. A number of types of training programs are popular in hospitality firms. Some of these include skill training, cross-functional training, team training, and games. In determining whether these programs are worth the cost, there are a variety of ways of measuring effectiveness, including asking customers, talking to training participants, and computing the cost per trainee and determining whether this money is likely to be recovered through increased efficiency.

3. Performance appraisal is the systematic observation, evaluation, and description of work-related behavior. There are many types of appraisal methods. Three of the most common are graphic rating scales, the paired comparison method, and the critical incident technique.

4. While all managers try to be objective in their appraisal, many are guilty of rating errors caused by various forms of bias. Some of the most common include the halo error; severity, leniency, and central tendency errors; the contrast error; the similar-to-me error; and the recency error. These errors can be addressed in a number of ways. One is by carefully training managers and other raters regarding how to observe and evaluate performance. A second is by clearly enunciating the factors that are being eval-

uated so that everyone has the same understanding of them. A third is by discussing these errors, describing why they occur, and pointing out ways that they can be prevented.

5. In recent years, some hospitality organizations have begun moving away from standard performance evaluations and replacing them with personal development plans (PDPs). These plans focus on finding new and better ways to develop associate skills so as to improve service, enhance job satisfaction, and reduce turnover. Because of their emphasis on improving associate abilities, rather than simply evaluating past performance, PDPs may well prove to be a growing trend in the area of performance evaluation.

KEY TERMS

training	critical incident technique
development	halo error
skill training	severity error
team training	leniency error
cross-functional training	central tendency error
job rotation	contrast error
performance appraisal	similar-to-me error
graphic rating scale	recency error
paired comparison	personal development plan

REVIEW AND APPLICATION QUESTIONS

1. A small restaurant chain is in the process of developing a training program for its restaurant associates, in particular the servers. What types of training would you recommend that they include in the program? What would you like to see the servers learn as a result of having attended this program?

2. Of what value is team training? Cross-functional training? Would every hospitality organization benefit from these types of training? Explain.

3. A major hotel chain would like to evaluate its supervisory training program in order to determine how much it costs to train each participant. What types of expenses should the hotel be sure to include in its calculations? Be as complete as possible.

4. When evaluating its associates, why would a hospitality organization opt to use the graphic rating scale rather than the paired comparison method? When would it prefer the paired comparison method over the graphic rating scale? Explain.

5. The manager of a large local hotel has been reviewing the performance evaluations of all associates in the organization and has found that on a scale of 1 to 10, the average score on all eight factors on which associates are measured is 9.96. Based on this information, which rating errors might be present? Identify and describe two. What type of performance evaluation would you suggest that the hotel use in order to prevent this from happening in the future?

SELF-FEEDBACK EXERCISE: CAN YOU SPOT THE ERROR?

On the left is a list of performance evaluation errors. On the right are examples of each error. Match the two lists by placing the letter accompanying the error on the left next to the example on the right. (Hint: In three cases the error on the left can be found more than once.) Answers are provided at the end of the exercise.

a. Halo error   _____ 1. Margaret's people all receive excellent evaluations, except for a few who are rated as good; no one receives any lower rating than this.

b. Severity error   _____ 2. Roberta's performance evaluations are often most heavily influenced by how well the individual has performed in the last 60 days.

c. Leniency error   _____ 3. George rates all of his people as "average" or "needs improvement." No one ever gets a "superior" or "good" rating.

d. Central tendency error   _____ 4. Paul never gives poor evaluations to his people, nor does he ever give excellent reviews. Everyone is rated as "acceptable."

e. Contrast error   _____ 5. Barbara is always on time for work; her boss likes this, so he always gives her a high performance evaluation.

f. Similar-to-me error   _____ 6. Joanne has a college degree in hotel and restaurant management from a major southeastern university and always gives highly favorable ratings to individuals who graduated from this university.

g. Recency error

_____ 7. Exceptionally good associates do not like to work for Barney because he gives everyone an average evaluation score, regardless of how well they perform.

_____ 8. Everyone who works for Ruth tries to do an exceptional job in the weeks just prior to annual evaluations because this performance tends to influence their evaluations more than anything else they do.

_____ 9. Bob always starts off rating his best associate first and, as a result, the second person always tends to get a lower evaluation than he or she deserves.

_____ 10. Exceptionally good associates like to work for Clara because she gives only a few excellent or good evaluations and this helps them stand out from their peers.

Answers

1. c	6. f
2. g	7. d
3. b	8. g
4. d	9. e
5. a	10. b

CASE 7.1: SHE'LL KNOW IT WHEN SHE SEES IT

Joel Bruckner and his partner Sidney Mueller have purchased seven hotels over the last decade, and in each case they have made the hotel more profitable than ever. Last month they bought a 700-room hotel on the Gulf Coast and are currently in the process of remodeling it and getting it ready for a grand opening. At the same time, they have hired Richard McKenzie to manage the operation. Richard has had fifteen years' experience with two of the nation's largest hotel chains and has an excellent record of performance. In addition to his other duties, Richard will be overseeing the human resource management function, including training and development. The hotel has a total of 425 associates, including groundskeepers, maintenance, and restaurant associates.

Richard is a strong believer in training. "Most hotels offer similar ameni-ties," he says, "so the secret to success is to do things better than the competi-tion does them. This is where training comes in. Anyone can serve a table or check in a guest, but the best restaurants and hotels differentiate themselves from the others." In keeping with this philosophy, Richard has asked Margaret Dunlap, the head of human resources, to provide him with a training and development plan for the next two years of operation. Richard would like to see the type of training the associates are scheduled to receive, who will be getting the training, and how Margaret intends to measure the effectiveness of the various programs. He would also like to know the types of development programs Margaret is going to suggest for the managerial staff.

Margaret knows that the next two weeks are going to be very busy as she develops the plan that Richard has requested. In particular, she is hoping to give her training and development programs an extra degree of panache. "I don't want to suggest the same old run-of-the-mill training that we've seen in hospitality organizations for the last ten years," she told her assistant. "I want this training to be more comprehensive, more useful, and more interactive for the participants." When her assistant pressed her for more clarification, Margaret admitted that she did not know for sure what the training should entail. However, she assured her assistant, "I'll know it when I see it." Her assistant is now in the process of helping design these programs, but feels uncomfortable with the guidance given to her by Margaret. "I know she'll know it when she sees it, but I'm the one whose creating the program pro-posals and I'm not sure *I'll* know it when I see it. I wish I had more guidance on this assignment."

1. What types of training programs would you recommend to Margaret's assistant? Describe two of them.

2. What types of development programs would you recommend for the managers? Briefly explain the content of one of them.

3. Would it be possible to measure the effectiveness of these training and development programs? How?

CASE 7.2: THE CONFUSED VICE-PRESIDENT

Julie Schatzner is the newly appointed vice-president of operations for a cruise line. She has three managers who report directly to her and they, in turn, manage departments of between 13 and 26 people and are directly responsible for the performance evaluations of these associates.

In order to acquaint herself with the individuals who work directly for her, as well as their subordinates, Julie has been reading through the performance evaluations of the last three years. She has noticed a major difference in the way the three managers evaluate their people.

One of the managers, Rusty Daubnes, has thirteen people in her department. These individuals, like those in all other departments, are evaluated on a graphic rating scale that has ten factors. Rusty gave a rating of 10 on all factors to nine of her people, and the other four had received a 9 on between two and four of the factors and a 10 on the remaining factors. As a result, Rusty recommended everyone in her department for the maximum raise.

Tony Suarez has 21 people in his department and of these, 16 received a score of 7 on all ten factors. Two of the remaining five individuals received an average score of 6 on all ten factors and the other three received an average score of 8.2. As a result, Tony broke his group into three categories and asked for a slightly above-average raise for those with the 8.2 score, an average raise for those with a score of 7, and a slightly below-average raise for those with a score of 6.

Barbara Minter has 26 people in her department. The breakdown of scores from her group was as follows: two received an average score of 7.2; eighteen received an average score of 6.1; and six received an average score of 5.3. Barbara recommended the first group be given an above-average raise, the second get an average raise, and the third group be given nothing.

Julie is somewhat confused by the evaluations because they seem to fluctuate so radically. The associates in all three departments appear to be getting their jobs done, but their evaluations are quite different. As a result, Julie has decided to talk to the three managers and try to determine the approaches they use in evaluating the associates and assigning their ratings. For the moment, Julie finds herself confused.

1. What type of performance appraisal instrument is the graphic rating scale? How is it used? Describe the instrument and its application.

2. What performance evaluation error does each of the three managers appear to be making? In each case, describe the error.

3. How can these three errors be eliminated? What steps would you recommend that Julie take? Explain.

ANSWERS TO BOX 7.1: JEOPARDY: CAN YOU ASK THE RIGHT QUESTION?"

1. f	6. j	11. e
2. n	7. c	12. i
3. l	8. b	13. d
4. m	9. g	14. h
5. k	10. o	15. a

ENDNOTES

1. Luis R. Gomez-Mejia, David B. Balkin, and Robert L. Cardy, *Managing Human Resources* (Upper Saddle River, N.J.: Prentice-Hall, 1995), p. 293.
2. Richard M. Hodgetts and K. Galen Kroeck, *Personnel and Human Resource Management* (Fort Worth: Dryden Press, 1992), p. 372.
3. Ken Golder, "Comprehensive Hotel Sales Training: An Industry *Must*," *HSMAI Marketing Review,* Summer 1994, pp. 49–52.
4. Also see K. Michael Haywood, "Effective Training: Toward a Strategic Approach," *Cornell Hotel and Restaurant Administration Quarterly,* December 1992, pp. 43–52.
5. See Michelle Neely Martinez, "Disney Training Works Magic," *HR Magazine,* May 1992, pp. 53–57.
6. *Yes I Can!* Participant workbook. Radisson Hotels International, 1993, p. 7.
7. See Edward Watkins, ed., "Hyatt Stays in Touch," *Lodging Hospitality,* September 1990, p. 43–48.
8. Ronald Henkoff, "Finding, Training, and Keeping the Best Service Workers," *Fortune,* October 3, 1994, p. 116.
9. Kimberley J. Harris and Debra Franklin Cannon, "Opinions of Training Methods Used in the Hospitality Industry: A Call for Review," *International Journal of Hospitality Management,* Vol. 14, No. 1, 1995, p. 86.
10. Leadership Guide, Radisson Hotels International, 1993, p. 69.
11. For additional insight into this topic, see Karen Seelhoff, "Skills Training Gets the Job Done," *Lodging,* April 1995, p. 143.
12. Also see Werner Mendel, "Corporate Training by Adventure Learning," *Cornell Hotel and Restaurant Administration Quarterly,* June 1993, pp. 31–33.
13. Christine Lynn, "Training Methods Utilized by Independent Restaurant Managers," *FIU Hospitality Review,* Spring 1994, pp. 51–56.
14. Leadership Guide.
15. For additional insights to training, see Golnaz Sadri and Peggy J. Snyder, "Methodological Issues in Assessing Training Effectiveness," *Journal of Managerial Psychology,* Vol. 10, No. 4, 1995, pp. 30–32.
16. Jack Hayes, "Investment in Training Will Pay Dividends," *Nation's Restaurant News,* October 11, 1995, pp. 72, 94.
17. Some of this information can be found in E. Ray Swan, "10 Common Training Mistakes," *Hotels,* August 1994, p. 20.
18. Hodgetts and Kroeck, *Personnel and Human Resource Management,* p. 340.
19. For more on this, see John Beckert and Kate Walsh, "Development Plans Replace Performance Reviews at Harvey Hotels," *Cornell Hotel and Restaurant Administration Quarterly,* December 1991, pp. 72–80.
20. Ibid., p. 80.

CHAPTER EIGHT

Motivating Associates

LEARNING OBJECTIVES

One of the most important functions of human resource management (HRM) is the effective motivation of associates. How can associates be motivated to do the best possible job? The answer is multifaceted; the overriding objective of this chapter is to examine some of the ways that motivation can be created and sustained. The first part of this chapter will study the nature of motivation, with particular attention given to select theories of motivation. The second part of the chapter will examine motivation among hospitality associates, with specific consideration given to programs and techniques used by various organizations. When you have finished studying all of the material in this chapter, you will be able to:

1. Define the term *motivation.*

2. Compare and contrast content, process, and learning theories and describe some specific examples of each.

3. Discuss the importance of money and other financial forms of motivation, including incentive programs.

4. Describe how hospitality organizations create an overall motivation program that combines financial and nonfinancial motivators.

5. Explain the role and importance of feedback in measuring and evaluating the effect of an organization's motivation efforts.

The Nature of Motivation

The word *motivation* comes from the Latin verb *movere,* which means "to move." In terms of HRM, motivation has been described or defined in a number of ways. Here are some examples:

Motivation represents an employee's desire and commitment and is manifested as effort.[1]

Motivation is the set of forces that cause people to behave in certain ways.[2]

Motivation is a process that starts with a physiological or psychological deficiency or need that activates behavior or a drive that is aimed at a goal or incentive.[3]

Motivation is the willingness to exert high levels of effort toward organizational goals, conditioned by the effort's ability to satisfy some individual need.[4]

Each of these definitions reinforces the Latin meaning: for some reason(s), when people are motivated they will do something, *e.g.,* work longer hours, put out additional effort, attain greater levels of performance. What causes motivation? There are a number of ways to answer this question. The following sections present a series of select motivation theories that shed light on this subject.

Select Theories of Motivation

A wide array of motivation theories help explain how and why people act as they do. The following sections examine three general groups: content theories, process theories, and learning theories.

Content Theories

Content theories of motivation attempt to explain the subject in terms of *what* arouses, energizes, or initiates behavior. Two well-known content theories are the two-factor theory of motivation and need-achievement theory. Both help explain what motivates people.

Two-Factor Theory of Motivation. The *two-factor theory of motivation* explains the process in terms of two categories: hygiene factors and motivators. This theory is based on the research of Frederick Herzberg and his associates, which was conducted among 200 engineers and accountants.[5] Using semi-structured interviews, the researchers asked the respondents to recall a time when they felt exceptionally good about their job and a time when they felt exceptionally negative about their job. The data were then examined and divided into two categories.

In one category the researchers put those responses that did not create job satisfaction but were useful in preventing dissatisfaction. These factors were external to the work itself and included company policies and administration, technical supervision, salary, interpersonal relations, and working conditions. The researchers labeled these *hygiene factors* because, like hygiene (brushing and flossing one's teeth, for example), they do not make things better but they do prevent things from getting worse.

In the other category the researchers put those responses that were associated with positive feelings about the job and related to the content of the work itself. Examples included achievement, recognition, responsibility, advancement, and the work itself. These were called *motivators* because they were critical in building high levels of job satisfaction and motivation.

The two-factor theory holds that hygiene factors will not motivate associates, but they will prevent job dissatisfaction. In Herzberg's words, "Managers need to give hygiene and shut up about it." Since salary is a hygiene factor, the theory argues that management should not continually point out how much money the associates are being paid because, at best, money is only a short-run motivator. The theory also holds that hygiene creates a zero level of motivation and this level continuously escalates. So the salaries and working conditions of associates today must be increased and improved in the future in order to prevent associate dissatisfaction. At the same time, the key to successful motivation is found in the "satisfiers" that make the job worth doing. If associates are given recognition, increased responsibility, and a chance for advancement and growth, they will be motivated.

In comparing hygiene factors and motivators, it is readily obvious that hygiene relates to external factors that are given by management (better supervision, better working conditions), while motivators are internal factors that are given to one's self (a feeling of achievement, pride generated from recognition). Simply put, the two-factor theory argues that management does not really motivate associates; rather, it creates the right environment for associates to motivate themselves. Additionally, the theory postulates that many of the things that organizations do for their associates, including giving them salary raises and increased benefits, are not motivational but simply prevent associates from becoming unmotivated.

The two-factor theory is particularly useful because it points out that not everything management does has motivational potential. The theory also reinforces the fact that psychological rewards (how associates feel about themselves and the work they do) are more potent than physical rewards (the financial rewards they get for doing their jobs). Keep in mind, of course, that money may be a far more important motivator for some industries and some associates. Herzberg's theory cannot be blindly applied. Consider yourself. Which of the two is more important for you: hygiene factors or motivators? Take the quiz in Box 8.1 and find out.

Box 8.1
What Motivates You?

Many factors motivate people at work. Following is a list of 20 factors. Read the list and then decide the importance of each. Use the following key to distinguish between those that are extremely important and those that hold little appeal.

5 = Extremely important
4 = Important
3 = Indifferent
2 = Not very important
1 = Of no importance

_____ 1. Interesting work
_____ 2. Impressive job title
_____ 3. Good retirement program
_____ 4. Challenging tasks
_____ 5. Increased responsibility
_____ 6. Recognition for a job well done
_____ 7. Extra days off with pay
_____ 8. Bonus pay
_____ 9. Good wages
_____10. Job feedback on performance

_____ 11. A feeling of importance
_____ 12. A chance to achieve
_____ 13. A feeling of competence
_____ 14. Guaranteed cost of living
_____ 15. Good working conditions
_____ 16. Generous expense account
_____ 17. Pride in the job
_____ 18. Health insurance coverage
_____ 19. A chance to exercise personal initiative
_____ 20. Window in the office

Group A		Group B	
_____	2.	_____	1.
_____	3.	_____	4.
_____	7.	_____	5.
_____	8.	_____	6.
_____	9.	_____	10.
_____	14.	_____	11.
_____	15.	_____	12.
_____	16.	_____	13.
_____	18.	_____	17.
_____	20.	_____	19.
Total _____		Total _____	

Interpretation: Remember that you gave a 5 to factors that are extremely important and a 1 to factors that are of no importance, so the group with the _higher_ total is the one that includes the factors that have the greatest overall motivational appeal for you. Group A consists of physical rewards (money, working conditions, and job security), while Group B consists of psychological rewards (interesting work, job challenge, and a feeling of competence). If the total of your two lists is close, you have an equal need for both types of rewards. Most people have a higher total in Group B than in Group A. In further analyzing your own responses, look at those factors to which you gave a 5. This will help you identify the types of things that have the greatest motivational appeal to you. You might also compare your totals with those of other students in the class to see what other patterns of response were elicited by this exercise.

Need-Achievement Theory. Another content theory useful in understanding HRM in the hospitality industry is *need-achievement theory*, which attempts to describe and explain people's desire to achieve and the means they use in doing so. This theory is closely linked to the work of David McClelland, who has identified three characteristics of high achievers:

1. They like situations in which they take *personal* responsibility for finding solutions to problems. Rather than wanting to win through chance or luck, they want to rely on their own abilities, talents, and drive.

2. They tend to be *moderate*-risk-takers rather than high- or low-risk-takers. They find little satisfaction in low risks; and they realize that success in high-risk situations is more a matter of luck than of skill or personal achievement.

3. They like *feedback* so they can assess their performance. This allows them to make the necessary changes to ensure that they continue to succeed.

Need-achievement theory has a practical side. People can learn to be high achievers, and McClelland and his associates have developed programs for doing this. In particular, there are four steps that individuals need to follow. First, it is important for them to get feedback on their performance so that successes can be reinforced and failures can be abandoned or prevented in the future. Second, it is important for people to choose successful role models and to emulate the way they do things. Third, individuals should try to modify their self-image and imagine themselves as needing success and challenge. Fourth, people must control their self-talk by thinking and talking to themselves in positive terms.[6]

Unlike the two-factor theory of motivation, need-achievement theory offers a more practical approach to both understanding and applying motivation ideas. The theory can also be used in conjunction with other motivational theories in increasing associate performance.

Process Theories

Process theories of motivation focus on *how* behavior is initiated, redirected, and halted. Unlike content theories, which are primarily descriptive, process theories are action-oriented. Two of the best examples are provided by goal-setting theory and equity theory.

Goal-Setting Theory. *Goal-setting theory* holds that an individual's objectives will influence his or her work behavior. Specifically, some of the research findings regarding goal setting include the following:

1. Clear and specific goals tend to result in greater performance than does "doing the best you can."

2. Goals that are attainable but difficult to achieve tend to lead to higher performance than do easy goals, providing that the individual accepts these more challenging targets.

3. When individuals participate in setting their own goals, they tend to accomplish more than when these goals are assigned to them.

4. When individuals are provided with frequent feedback regarding how well they are doing, their output tends to be higher than when such feedback is not given.[7]

Goal-setting theory, by itself, is insufficient to understanding the motivation process. However, in conjunction with other approaches, it helps point out the benefit that specific and challenging goals can have in encouraging people to do their best.[8]

Equity Theory. *Equity theory* is a motivation theory that holds that in order to be motivated, individuals must believe that the reward-to-work ratio is fair. Sometimes this theory is referred to as "social comparison" theory because it involves people trying to answer the question: How well am I doing compared to others in this organization? Obviously they tend to compare themselves with others who are doing similar work or holding similar positions and hope to conclude that they are doing at least as well as, if not better than, the objects of their comparison.

The answer to the comparative question can be any one of three: (1) the reward-to-work ratio is lower than that of others; (2) the reward-to-work ratio is the same as that of others; or (3) the reward-to-work ratio is greater than that of others. When the first conclusion is reached, the individual will feel he or she is not being properly rewarded and will take steps to bring the reward-to-work ratio back in line. This often takes the form of securing more rewards or doing less work. Of course, if neither of these two alternatives is feasible, the individual may simply stop making comparisons with these other people because there is nothing the person can do to bring about equity (at least in his or her own mind). Or the individual may quit or get a job elsewhere in the organization, where the perceived reward-to-work ratio is equitable.

Equity theory involves personal perception. For example, an associate may be receiving higher pay than his fellow associates, but believe that he is worth even more. In this case the reward-to-work ratio is still out of balance. Another associate may be receiving the same pay as everyone else in the group, but believe that she is getting less. In both cases, these individuals believe that they are being treated inequitably even though this is not true.

Research related to equity theory reveals that perceived fairness plays an important role in the motivation process. If associates believe that they are being shortchanged, even if they are not, this will have a negative impact on their work performance. In particular, equity theory is useful to the study of motivation because it helps explain why management must continually assess each associate's view of perceived fairness.[9]

Learning Theories

Learning theories of motivation help explain how behavior is comprehended, reinforced, weakened, and terminated. The essence of learning theories can be found in Thorndike's *law of effect*, which holds that people are more likely to do things for which they are rewarded and avoid those things that will bring about discomfort or punishment.[10] Thus *learning* is a relatively permanent change in behavior that results from reinforced practice or experience.[11]

While there are a host of learning theories, those that are of most value to our study of human resource management are learning-intervention strategies. These are strategies designed to shape desired behavior by providing rewards for doing things well and withholding rewards when things are done poorly. In all, there are four learning-intervention strategies.

Learning-Intervention Strategies. The four basic learning-intervention strategies are positive reinforcement, negative reinforcement, extinction, and punishment. *Positive reinforcement* is the use of rewards to strengthen behavior. The important thing to remember about this strategy is that a positive reinforcer for one person may have no value for another person.

> The Wellington Arms Hotel has a quality incentive program that awards points for outstanding performance. Everyone who earns 300 points in a twelve-month period receives an all-expenses-paid trip to London for five days. José Barrero has never earned more than 140 points in any of the three years in which the program has been in effect. This year the hotel expanded the program and is offering cash bonuses in lieu of the trip. José has earned 327 points during the first nine months of this year and is well on his way to a 500-point year!

Was the trip to London a positive reinforcer for Jose? Apparently not, since he never came close to winning the award. However, when the hotel began offering cash bonuses, his performance increased sharply, indicating that these bonuses are indeed positively reinforcing his behavior.

Negative reinforcement strengthens desired behavior while bringing about the termination or withdrawal of some aversive condition. Negative reinforcement gets people to do things in order to avoid some form of embarrassment or punishment.

> Margaret Challing has a department meeting every Monday morning at 8:30 A.M. Because she knows that people are sometimes a little late, she begins these meetings at 8:32 A.M. sharp! This allows everyone two

extra minutes to get to the conference room and find a seat at the table. If anyone comes in late, Margaret will stop the meeting and ask the person why he or she is late. This tactic is so embarrassing that no one is ever tardy anymore.

Margaret uses negative reinforcement. The only way to avoid being the focus of her attention is to arrive on time—and everyone does.

Extinction is the failure to reinforce behavior and thus encourage its termination. In the preceding example, if Barney shows up late and seems quite pleased that Margaret has singled him out for attention, her efforts at using negative reinforcement will be ineffective. Apparently Barney likes the attention, so Margaret is actually encouraging this behavior by giving him positive reinforcement. Once she realizes this, Margaret could begin ignoring his tardiness and thus use extinction to reshape Barney's behavior.

Punishment is the use of aversive stimuli such as reprimanding someone for poor performance. The major problem with punishment is that it focuses on behavior that is wrong, but does not provide assistance in correcting the situation. For example, if Richard chastises Ann for poor performance and then tells her, "You have to do better," this action may hurt her feelings and make her angry, but it does not show her how to do a better job. For this reason, effective hospitality managers avoid the use of punishment or couple it with a helping strategy. For example, Richard could follow up his comments to Ann by reviewing steps she will need to take to improve her performance. Of course, if she continues to do poorly, Richard may give her a poor performance evaluation or terminate her, but that would be only after other methods prove ineffective.

In gaining some additional insights regarding how to use reinforcement principles, complete the self-feedback exercise at the end of the chapter and compute your score. When you are finished, continue on to the next section.

Motivating Hospitality Associates

Motivation theory can be extremely useful in helping formulate a strategy for getting associates to do things. In doing so, however, it is important to focus the effort by answering the question: What *really* motivates people? Fortunately, there is sufficient research in the hospitality industry to answer this question—and the answer is somewhat different from that in industry at large. Simply put, money—or in Herzberg's terminology, hygiene factors—seems to be of far more importance than anything else. There are a number of facts that support this statement. One is the salaries paid to chief executives in the hospitality industry. Every year the top ten executives earn an average of over $1 million, including salary, bonus, and other compensation.[12] Research

Table 8.1 Work Factors Ranked by Hospitality and Industrial Workers

Work Factor	Hospitality Workers	Industrial Workers
Good wages	1	5
Job security	2	4
Opportunities for advancement and development	3	6
Good working conditions	4	7
Interesting work	5	1
Appreciation for a job well done	6	2
Loyalty to employees	7	8
Feeling "in on things"	8	3
Tactful disciplining	9	9
Sympathetic personal help	10	10

1 = what respondents want most from their organization

10 = what respondents want least from their organization

Source: Tony Simons and Cathy A. Enz, "Motivating Hotel Employees," *Cornell Hotel and Restaurant Association Quarterly*, February 1995, p. 23.

studies at the lower levels of the industry also support the importance of monetary rewards as strong motivators.

The Importance of Money

Over the last four decades there has been a wealth of research related to motivational factors. Much of this research was conducted among industrial workers, and the findings were consistent: psychological rewards such as interesting work, full appreciation for work done, and a feeling of being "in on things" ranked at the top of the list, while good wages, job security, and good working conditions ranked in the middle. Recent research conducted among hospitality associates, however, has found a substantially different set of responses. Table 8.1 reports the results of a study conducted among 278 associates from twelve different hotels located in the United States and Canada.

The responses in the table show that good wages, job security, and good working conditions are three of the top four work factors as ranked by hospitality associates. More important, the data contrast sharply with those from industrial settings, showing that motivational factors are not universal across all businesses. Hospitality associates are far more motivated by monetary rewards. These findings are not unique. Studies earlier in this decade conducted among associates at Caribbean hotels[13] and Las Vegas casino dealers[14] uncovered similar results. In both cases, good wages and working conditions were the top two preferences among the respondents.

What is particularly interesting about the results in Table 8.1 is that the 278 respondents covered a wide continuum of individuals from the industry, so the researchers were able to isolate a number of demographic factors and determine their impact on the responses. For example, age was a causal variable. Respondents over the age of 30 ranked job security as second in importance, while those under the age of 30 ranked it sixth in importance. Aside from this, the responses were fairly similar, with good wages being first on both lists. The researchers also found that the rankings were not affected by gender; both men and women reported almost identical rankings for all ten factors. However, there was a difference in responses when analyzed by department. These data are presented in Table 8.2.

Table 8.2 shows that good wages are at or near the top of the list in most cases. However, each of the departments is different in terms of its individual ranking. The food and beverage servers ranked good wages, good working conditions and job security as three of their top four choices, a pattern that was similar for the survey group at large. On the other hand, the human resources respondents put psychological rewards (opportunity for advancement and interesting work) highest on their lists. At the same time, there was some overall similarity in the responses. For example, all seven groups ranked the last four factors in the table at the bottom of their lists, with sympathetic personal help being the last choice for all of them. While there are a number of ways of interpreting the data, one thing is certain:

> What management *can* do is to take employee desires into account to create an environment where high effort, properly channeled, will give employees some measure of satisfaction. For many hospitality employees, this optimum motivation environment may involve some form of cash incentive and potential for advancement. For others, it will focus on security and good working conditions. In most cases, a positive respectful work environment has the potential to facilitate employee retention and generally also to set the stage for excellent performance, particularly in back-of-the-house areas. Useful consideration can also emerge from considering the age and department affiliation of different employees.[15]

Other Financial Approaches

Many hospitality motivation programs do not rely solely on wages; rather, they incorporate some form of financial package that is tied directly to performance and/or commitment to the organization. Two good examples are the currently popular "cash-for-college" programs and incentive plans that are closely linked to profit and growth objectives.

Table 8.2 Work Factors Ranked by Associates in Various Hotel Departments

Work Factor	Food & Beverage Servers	Rooms, Front Desk	Housekeeping	Accounting Control	Sales, Marketing	Back-of-the House Food & Beverage	Human Resources
Good wages	1	1	2	1	2	1	3
Job security	3	4	1	4.5	4	5	6
Opportunities for advancement and development	2	2	5	2	1	4	1
Good working conditions	4	5.5	3	4.5	5	2	4
Interesting work	6	5.5	4	3	3	3	2
Appreciation for a job well done	5	3	6	6	6	6	5
Loyalty to employees	7	7	7	8	8	7	7
Feeling in on things	9	8	8	7	7	8	8
Tactful disciplining	8	9	9	9	9	9	9
Sympathetic personal help	10	10	10	10	10	10	10
Number responding	52	50	54	58	25	23	16

1 = what respondents want most from their organization
10 = what respondents want least from their organization
Source: Tony Simons and Cathy A. Enz, "Motivating Hotel Employees," *Cornell Hotel and Restaurant Association Quarterly*, February 1995, p. 26.

Cash for College. A number of hospitality organizations now offer their associates an opportunity to earn money for college tuition and books. An example is a local Burger King franchise in western Michigan, which gives scholarships of up to $2,500 to associates who want to further their education beyond high school. The only restriction is that associates have to show the franchise their grades and must pass the courses. Associates who participate in this program accumulate one scholarship dollar for every hour they work.

The program developed as a result of a Department of Labor study, which found that fast-food workers were not using their employment as an end in itself; rather, these associates were using their jobs as a stepping stone to other employment or to further their education. This led the franchise operator to realize that if he offered scholarship assistance, he was likely to attract college-bound people and could hold on to them far longer than the average fast-food franchise. This is exactly what has happened. West Michigan Burger King's turnover rate is two-thirds lower than the fast-food industry average. There are a number of reasons for this. Here is one.

> Shalanda Couch, a 22-year-old criminal justice major at Grand Valley State College, has participated in the Cash for College program since its 1987 inception. By the time she finished high school, Couch already had accumulated enough scholarship money to pay for her first two years at college. Some four years later, she now looks forward to graduating debt-free and attending law school.
>
> If Burger King had not offered the scholarship program, Couch admits she probably would not have stayed there as long as she did. "After three years I probably would have looked for a different job that paid more money," she said.
>
> Since the restaurant helped so much with her college bills, she decided to stay seven years, far longer than the average tenure in the industry.[16]

Another example is provided by Chick-Fil-A, a 370-unit fast-food chicken chain based in Atlanta. Chick-Fil-A offers a $1,000 scholarship to all associates who work an average of 20 hours a week or more and are recommended by their supervisor. This program has been particularly useful in retaining these individuals; today more than 20 percent of the company's 370 operators qualified for the scholarship when they were crew members.[17]

Incentive-Based Rewards. Another popular motivation program is that of performance-driven incentives, which often include more than just financial rewards such as a bonus. A good example is a Domino's incentive entitled "Rookie Meets Rookie." This program allows the top two qualifying rookie managers from each region to spend three days, all expenses paid, in Lakeland, Florida, the spring training camp of the Detroit Tigers. During their stay, the managers attend an exhibition game and meet the team's rookies. Another program is called "20/20" and targets stores with average weekly sales of $20,000 or more. In order to win the incentive of a vacation for two to Bermuda or Hawaii, the store managers must increase average weekly sales by 20 percent or more.[18]

Another example is provided by Ralph & Kacoo's, a six-unit dinner-house company headquartered in Baton Rouge, Louisiana. The company sets three sales ranges for each of its six restaurants' daily sales and pays these bonuses on a quarterly basis. If a unit falls within the first range on a given day, every associate who punched in that day is awarded an extra hour of compensation at time-and-a-half. If the restaurant falls within the next highest range, all associates are awarded two extra hours of compensation. If the highest range is achieved, all associates get three extra hours.[19]

A third example is offered by the Hard Rock Café, where as many as three times a year the company president will walk into a unit and ask the managers to nominate and the staff to vote for the best associate of the quarter. The winner is given an all-expenses-paid, one-week trip to Hawaii.[20] In most organizations, however, incentives are not spontaneous. They are a result of a plan that has been communicated to the associates. For example, at the Peasant Restaurants, headquartered in Atlanta, the general manager of the year receives a trip for two to Europe. In order to win the incentive, the individual must meet the demands of the company's five-part formula: (1) have the five highest scores overall on regional inspections; (2) have the highest scores on dining experience as rated by the corporate staff; (3) have a superior training program; (4) have an accurate and timely administrative record; and (5) post positive sales growth.[21] At Chi Chi's of Louisville, Kentucky, the company annually awards 22 trips to field managers who increase liquor sales during Cinco de Mayo festivities. In addition, there are five $1,000 employee of the year awards, five $100 employee of the quarter awards, and five $25 employee of the month awards. Meanwhile, at Wendy's, the company gives quarterly cash bonuses to managers who meet a variety of performance goals related to sales, profits, and cost control.[22]

Still another good example is provided by TravelMasters, a travel agency headquartered in Tyler, Texas. The company is well known for its ability to continually revise and revamp its incentive programs so as to maintain associate motivation. In fact, the company has been so successful in its creative efforts that it has won *Travel Weekly's* Travel Agency Achievement Award three times in recent years. One of the company's incentive programs is called Cruise Quest, a type of board game that rewards agents for selling cruises. As soon as an agent closes a sale and collects the deposit, the individual may participate in the game by rolling the dice and is instantly rewarded with cash.

> The game operates on several tiers, and cash bonuses become greater as the agent goes along. At the end, agents answer a bonus question

for prizes. First prize is a free eight-night cruise, including [airfare], for the agent and a companion; second prize is a four-night cruise, and third prize is a three-night cruise.[23]

Cruise sales increased by 56 percent during the first year that the company implemented Cruise Quest. The main reason for its success, according to management, is that the incentive system rewards agents for closing the sale, which is the primary activity on which it wants the agents to focus their efforts. The company has also won awards for other cruise incentives, including one that rewards agents with points based on the length of the cruises they sell. In all, there are six levels at which agents can redeem points for prizes, ranging from a Disney vacation to gift certificates. Moreover, as the motivational potential of a particular program begins to wear off, TravelMasters replaces it with a new program designed to sustain a high motivational level.

Creating an Overall Program

Of course, financial incentives are not the only forms of motivation; most hospitality organizations have incentive programs that combine monetary and psychological rewards. Moreover, many have found that praise and recognition are often more powerful and more long-lasting rewards than mere money.

Use of Praise. Giving associates recognition for a job well done is a key aspect of most motivation programs, and there are a number of ways that this is done. At the Ritz-Carlton hotels, for example, any associate can send a "First Class" card—a three-by-five-inch card designed with the company logo—to express his or her appreciation to anyone else in the organization for a job well done.[24] These cards are typically tacked to bulletin boards in associate offices and work stations, so everyone who comes by can read the kind comments made by fellow associates. At Checkers, a fast-food franchise, the company uses its company display sign to congratulate associates who have done a good job. Everyone who drives past the unit can see the individual's name prominently displayed on the sign.[25] At the Radisson hotel chain, associates are given recognition awards for outstanding helpfulness, courtesy and service. Figure 8.1 provides an example.

Combination Approaches. Most hospitality organizations use a combination approach to motivation, employing both financial and psychological rewards. For example, in addition to their First Class card, the Ritz-Carlton uses "Lightning Strikes," which are monetary rewards granted by members of the Executive Committee to any associate for outstanding service. In addition, associates who submit the best ideas for improvement are listed on a bulletin

Service Recognition Award

This award is presented to:

JOHNNY QUINTANILLA
NAME

FRONT OFFICE
DEPARTMENT

for outstanding helpfulness, courtesy and service as an employee
of the **Radisson Mart Plaza Hotel**

APRIL 25, 1995
AWARD DATE

Figure 8.1
Courtesy Radisson Hotels Worldwide.

board and given a buffet dinner for two, and those who generate the greatest number of useful ideas are honored at quarterly receptions.[26]

Another example is provided by Don Shula's Hotel & Golf Club in Miami Lakes, Florida. The club has a well-designed "MVP Program" for choosing one associate every month as the Most Valuable Player. Associates are eligible based on what the club refers to as "raving fan service." All individuals who are nominated are given a special MVP T-shirt, have their picture in the Miami Lakes paper, and have their name listed on the Team Café Information Board. So even those who do not win the monthly first prize are recognized and honored. The winner receives one paid day off during the month, a $50 prize, a personal picture posted in visible areas around the property, lunch with senior-level management, a framed certificate, and a nomination for Team Player of the Year. The associate who is chosen as Team Player of the Year receives a weekend pass for two at Walt Disney World, weekend accommodations for two nights, $250 spending money, a $50 certificate for any merchandise on the property, lunch with senior-level management, a picture in

Table 8.3 Typical Rewards for Outstanding Performance

Plaques	Logo items	Special luncheon
Trophies	• hats	Dinner with spouse or
Certificates	• shirts	friend
Chief executive officer	• pens	Local trip
letter	• mugs	Distant trip
Honor roll	• coasters	Day off
Letter to personnel file	• decals	Ticket to special event
Picture in company	• paperweights	Cash
newspaper	• desk sets	Gift certificate
Use of limousine	Banner for office	
Savings bond	Special parking space	
	Lapel pin	
	Piece of jewelry	

the Miami Lakes paper, and a picture on the Team Café Information Board. A close analysis of the awards for Player of the Month and Player of the Year reveals that there is far more psychological than monetary reward involved, and the latter are not very large amounts. This is because the Shula organization realizes that motivation is an internal process and recognition is often more powerful than mere money.

Other Rewards. In addition to the preceding examples, there are a host of other rewards that hospitality organizations use to motivate their associates. Some of the most common are reported in Table 8.3, while others are more creative. Examples include:

- Giving an associate a day off and allowing the individual to choose a member of the management team to do his or her job for the day.
- Giving an associate a subscription to the magazine of his or her choice.
- Having a senior-level manager bake a batch of chocolate-chip cookies to reward someone for outstanding customer service.
- Having the associate's car washed in the parking lot during the lunch hour.
- Giving out $100 rewards every quarter to those associates who admit mistakes they made on the job.
- Keeping a large box filled with all sorts of gifts in a public area and allowing an associate to choose one based on some accomplishment that the individual has performed.

- Sending a $20, $50, or $100 bill to a spouse with a thank-you note for the associate's outstanding work performance.
- Paying for a housecleaning service for an associate's home.
- Passing out silver dollars for good work.
- Giving an associate $20 on the spot for handling a particularly troublesome customer relations problem.[27]

Evaluating the Results

One of the most critical aspects of effective motivation is the proper reinforcement of associates. There are a wide variety of ways of doing this; Box 8.2 describes some of them.[28] Another is getting feedback on how well things are going and making necessary changes. Many hospitality organizations rely on survey feedback from their associates to help them in this process. Table 8.4 provides some examples of feedback from associates who were asked to rate their employers for *Restaurant Business*'s Employers of Choice awards. The magazine mailed 1,000 surveys to randomly selected unit-level associates for each participating chain. The associates were asked a variety of questions covering topics ranging from salary to work satisfaction to how well they are trained by the organization. A close look at the table reveals that each of the six chains that had the highest overall rankings did a very good job of making their organization a place where people like to work. Most important, the surveys provide feedback for evaluating current performance and making necessary changes.

This approach is also useful in helping compare the success of motivation tools and techniques with those being used in other industries and geographic locations. For example, research reveals that the hospitality industry does not do a very good job of providing fringe benefits to its associates. On the other hand, American hospitality firms tend to be far more effective in motivating their associates than are counterpart companies in most other countries. One recent survey found that U.S. hospitality firms offered more opportunities for exercising leadership skills than did those from most of the other surveyed countries. Additionally, when compared to these other nations, American firms had higher overall associate satisfaction with salary, training, and promotions than any of the other countries except the Netherlands. These data are reported in Table 8.5 and clearly show that the motivation programs employed by American hospitality organizations such as those described in this chapter are proving to be highly effective. In particular, when ranked from first to last in each of the categories in Table 8.5, American firms, on average, rated very high on salary, promotion prospects, job satisfaction, and the nature of the work. So these firms are offering their associates a good mix of both physical and psychological rewards—the key to effective motivation!

Box 8.2
Ten Useful Ways to Motivate Associates

There are a number of ways that managers can motivate their associates. Ten of the most helpful are the following:

1. *Empower people.* Give your associates the authority to do things without always having to check back and get an okay before proceeding. This approach saves time and helps build associates' self-esteem.

2. *Get associates involved in matters that affect them.* By getting associates' opinions and input, it is easier to motivate them to go along with changes. When associates have had a voice in shaping what is to be done, they are more likely to support the effort.

3. *Set a good example.* If you want people to go the extra mile, you have to be willing to do it yourself. Associates tend to emulate the behavior of their managers. To the extent that you do things well, they will also.

4. *Set standards.* No one likes to be told what to do, but quite often it is necessary to set quantitative standards and strictly adhere to them. Associates may not like to be told to be at their work stations by 8 A.M. and to take only a fifteen-minute coffee break in the morning. However, by sticking to these standards, you ensure that everyone is treated equitably, which is often a motivational factor. Most associates do not mind if you work them hard, just as long as you work all of them hard.

5. *Give them the numbers.* Let associates know how well they are doing and what else needs to be done. When management shares information related to costs, productivity, sales, profits, and growth, associates can begin to see the impact of their efforts and feel more involved in things—and this will help build their motivation to perform better.

6. *Offer praise.* Praise can be administered in a number of different ways from verbal to written, but they all have the same effect. People like to be appreciated and they want to hear this message loud and clear.

7. *Talk up the benefits.* Many people are looking for jobs that have benefits and a fairly good pay scale. When these are available, emphasize them strongly; a good benefit package not only attracts good people but helps retain them.

8. *Challenge the associates.* Work that is challenging requires extra effort and gives people the opportunity to use their abilities and talents; this approach can be very motivational. This is particularly true if associates are talented, well trained, and capable of meeting the challenge. Where possible, replace simple tasks with ones that stretch the associates and give them an opportunity to achieve and feel good about themselves.

9. *Let associates know how well they are doing.* There is no better way to keep associates interested and motivated than by giving them feedback on their performance and showing them where they are doing well and poorly. This approach serves to rein-

Box 8.2   Continued

force good behavior and provide a basis for correcting poor behavior.

10. *Treat everyone fairly.* Managers who show favoritism tend to lose the respect and support of those who are not treated fairly. On the other hand,

when everyone is treated equitably, this serves to build an environment in which associates feel that they can succeed on their own merits. This, in turn, helps create and sustain a positive motivational environment.

SUMMARY

1. Motivation is a set of forces that cause people to behave in certain ways. A number of motivation theories help explain how and why people act as they do.

2. Content theories of motivation attempt to explain the subject in terms of what arouses, energizes, or initiates behavior. One well-known content theory is the two-factor theory of motivation, which describes the process in terms of two categories: hygiene factors and motivators. Hygiene factors prevent dissatisfaction, while motivators create satisfaction. The theory is particularly useful in reinforcing the fact that psychological rewards are more potent than physical rewards. Another content theory is need-achievement theory, which attempts to describe and explain people's

Table 8.4   Associate Responses to Selected Motivation-Related Questions

Company	How Good Is the Pay?	How Good Are the Benefits?	How Good Are Advancement Opportunities?	How Well Trained Are You?	Overall, What Do You Think of the Company?
Hard Rock America	3.8	4.2	3.7	3.9	4.2
Restaurants Unlimited	3.4	3.7	3.5	3.8	4.1
Applebee's	3.3	2.8	3.4	3.9	3.9
Marriott	3.1	3.1	3.5	3.3	3.8
T.G.I. Friday's	3.1	3.7	3.4	3.7	3.7
McDonald's	3.0	3.1	3.5	3.7	3.8
All companies in survey	3.0	3.0	3.3	3.5	3.7

Note: Answers are ranked on a scale of 1 (least important) to 5 (most important).

Source: Ron Sympson, "Can We Talk?" *Restaurant Business,* March 1, 1995, p. 66. Reprinted with permission of Cahners Communication.

Table 8.5 Satisfaction with Salary, Training, and Promotions in Selected Countries

	Australia	Finland	France	United Kingdom	Hong Hong	Netherlands	Sweden	United States	Average
The nature of work	67%	72%	89%	71%	73%	76%	81%	76%	75%
Salary	45	34	39	39	32	70	40	54	45
Promotion prospects	42	28	39	47	42	45	34	51	44
Working conditions	60	61	69	63	59	69	60	67	64
Training opportunities	42	39	42	45	44	48	33	55	44
Relevance to education	60	72	58	55	56	64	46	61	53
Job satisfaction	43	68	52	60	66	69	77	70	64
Line management	65	68	66	70	68	69	58	71	68
Colleagues	67	76	82	82	75	91	67	67	78

Source: Oxford Brookes University and International Hotel Association, Paris, "Class of 1990 Responds to Job Satisfaction Survey," *Hotels,* March 1995, p. 56. Reprinted with permission of Cahners Communication.

desire to achieve and the means they use in doing so. The theory also sets forth steps that people can take to increase their desire to achieve.

3. Process theories of motivation focus on how behavior is initiated, redirected, and halted. One of these theories is goal-setting theory, which holds that an individual's objectives will influence his or her work behavior. In addition, the theory encourages managers to have clear, specific goals for associates, let associates participate in the goal-setting process, and provide associates with frequent feedback regarding how well they are doing. Another process theory is equity theory, which holds that in order to be motivated, individuals must believe that the reward-to-work ratio is fair. Because people often compare what they are getting against what others are getting, managers have to realize that perceived fairness is critical to the motivation process.

4. Learning theories help explain how behavior is reinforced, weakened, and terminated. While there are a host of learning theories, those that are most valuable in the study of human resource management are learning-intervention strategies. These are based on the judicious application of positive reinforcement, negative reinforcement, extinction, and punishment.

5. In the hospitality industry, researchers have found that money is a strong motivator. So also are other financial approaches, including "cash-for-college" programs and incentive-based awards. In putting together a comprehensive motivational package, however, most organizations opt for a combination of monetary and psychological rewards, including praise, recognition, and financial awards.

6. In order to ensure that their motivation programs are working well, organizations have to get and evaluate feedback. Areas in which they need to have such information include salaries, benefits, advancement opportunities, and the associates' overall perception of the company. Research shows that American hospitality firms tend to do a very good job in most areas, when compared to international firms.

KEY TERMS

motivation
content theories of motivation
two-factor theory of motivation
hygiene factors
motivators
need-achievement theory of motivation
process theories of motivation
goal-setting theory

equity theory
learning theories of motivation
law of effect
learning
positive reinforcement
negative reinforcement
extinction
punishment

REVIEW AND APPLICATION QUESTIONS

1. A local hotel is in the process of designing a new incentive program for its associates. Four factors being given major attention are salary, incentive pay, an annual awards banquet, and rapid promotion. Which of these is more important than the others? Defend your answer.

2. A cruise-line company has decided to develop a motivation program designed to help its associates become high achievers. What are four steps that the company should teach the associates in order for them to increase their high-achievement drive?

3. Charlie's, a large local restaurant, is the most popular one in the city. The restaurant has over 500 associates and prides itself on being a good place to work. Recently the company's management has heard complaints that some of its people feel they are being paid less than others who are doing the same work. This is simply not true. In response, the restaurant is thinking about publicly listing the salaries of all associates. Would this be a useful step in dealing with this emerging equity issue? Why or why not?

4. Every morning there is a meeting of operating associates of the National Cruise Line company; it is imperative that everyone be there on time. For the last two weeks, Gladys Edelmann, a new associate, has been late every day; her boss, Sheldon Bendricks, has decided that something has to be done. How could Sheldon use learning intervention strategies to deal with the issue?

5. Mindy's is a rapidly growing restaurant chain in the Southwest. The company currently has 44 units and is planning to open 60 more over the next three years. The firm would also like to develop an effective motivation program that will attract good associates and retain current associates. What are some things management should keep in mind as it develops this motivation program? Offer four useful suggestions.

SELF-FEEDBACK EXERCISE: HOW EFFECTIVE ARE YOU IN USING REINFORCEMENT PRINCIPLES?

Following are a dozen situations with which you might be confronted on the job. In each case you are offered four responses you can make to the situation. In choosing one, keep in mind the principles of reinforcement theory as well as your general understanding of how to motivate hospitality associates. Here are the four responses you can make:

a. I'd praise the individual for what he or she did and make it a point to include it in his or her performance evaluation.

b. I'd praise the individual for doing a good job.

c. I'd ignore the situation.

d. I'd tell the person that this performance is unacceptable and bring formal sanctions against him or her if it happens again.

Read each of the following situations carefully and then decide which one of the above responses is appropriate. Put your answer to the left of the number.

_____ **1.** Andy has come in late for the third day in a row. You talked to him about it yesterday and he promised it would not happen again. It has.

_____ **2.** Mary has just submitted a detailed, complex report on time. It looked as if she would be late with it, but she stayed at the office until 8 P.M. yesterday to ensure that it got in on time.

_____ **3.** Although most of the restaurants in the chain barely made quota, Paul's had sales of 10 percent over quota. This is the third year in a row that his unit has done better than expected.

_____ **4.** Usually Eileen does an excellent job. Last week, however, two customers complained to the manager that she was abrupt in her treatment of them.

_____ **5.** You were tied up with the hotel owner and missed a luncheon with a potentially large account. Jay, your assistant, realized the situation, took control of things, and convinced the client group to hold their annual convention at your hotel next year. Going past Jay's office, you stick your head in to talk to him.

_____ **6.** Bob and Steve both work in an area where food and chemicals are stored. There is a strict no-smoking policy in this area. You show up there unexpectedly and find them smoking.

_____ **7.** For the third day in a row, Jeanne is waiting to see you about the same problem. The air conditioning unit in her office is broken, and it will be the end of the week before maintenance can get to it. You informed her of this on both of her previous visits.

_____ **8.** You've just received a memo that Karl's suggestion regarding how to reorganize the office workflow will save the firm $10,000 this year. He is being sent a check for $500 and the memo is to inform you of his good work.

_____ **9.** During the weekly departmental meeting, Tim was not prepared to present his report. This is the fourth week in a row that he has been unprepared.

_____ **10.** Roberta has been working toward reducing tardiness in her department by 7 percent. The latest quarterly figures show that her department's tardiness rate is down by 12 percent.

_____ **11.** Carol was on the West Coast yesterday closing a business deal with a major client. You would have liked her to be with you at this morning's meeting, but you know the West Coast deal had priority. To your surprise, she took the red-eye special, arrived five minutes before the meeting, and made an excellent defense of your long-range proposal, which was accepted by top management.

_____ **12.** You have just received a call from a regional manager, who informed you that Hank, a usually reliable person, is supposed to be making a presentation to a customer in fifteen minutes, but Hank is nowhere to be found. As you hang up the phone, you see Hank in the outer office. He tells you he is terribly upset, but he simply forgot about the scheduled presentation.

Scoring: Notice that the four responses available to you offer four types of reinforcement: positive, negative, extinction, and punishment. Undoubtedly you employed all of these in handling the twelve situations. How well did you do? In answering this question, compare your responses to the answers of 145 hospitality managers, who created the following scoring key. In each case, circle the letter for your answer to each question. Then total the four columns and add these four numbers to get your overall score.

Question	A	B	C	D
1	-2	-1	0	+2
2	+2	+1	-1	-2
3	+2	+1	-1	-2
4	-2	-2	+2	0
5	+2	+2	0	-2
6	-2	-2	0	+2
7	-2	-2	+2	+1
8	+1	+2	-1	-2
9	-2	-2	0	+2
10	+2	+2	-2	-2
11	+2	+2	-2	-2
12	-2	-2	+2	-2
Total	____ +	____ +	____ +	____ = ____

18–24	Excellent
11–17	Good
6–10	Average
5 or less	Poor

CASE 8.1: ACTUAL VERSUS DESIRED

The Darby Hotel fell on hard times during the early 1990s and was recently sold to a group of investors who have been very successful in turning operations around. One of the first things they did was call the associates together and talk about their plans for the future. The new management intends to refurbish major portions of the hotel, increase the number of rooms, and build a large banquet area adjacent to the golf course. The company also intends to begin reviewing all jobs and hiring more people to fill the ranks that have been depleted over the last three years. An initial review of operations reveals that the hotel is understaffed by about 21 percent.

The company is also going to carefully review the results of a survey that it gave to the associates last week. This survey asked the associates to rank ten factors in terms of current status and desired status, giving 1 to the most important factor and 10 to the least important factor. Here are the results of the survey.

Factor	Current Status	Desired Status
Wages	8	1
Working conditions	2	9
Incentive pay	7	2
Job security	6	5
Loyalty to associates	5	8
Tactful disciplining	1	10
Willingness to listen to associates	3	7
Effective recognition for performance	9	4
Interesting, challenging work	4	6
Opportunities for advancement	10	3

1. What do the data reveal about the current status of the company's motivation strategy?

2. In terms of Herzberg's two-factor theory of motivation, what conclusions could you reach?

3. What suggestions would you make to management regarding changes that should be implemented?

CASE 8.2: STARTING FROM SCRATCH

When Gloria and Tina Shapiro opened their diner, they had no idea that one day they would be in charge of a rapidly growing fast-food chain. All they knew for sure was that it was impossible to get a hamburger, fries, and a thick shake the way they used to be able to back in the 1960s. So they decided to open a restaurant and call it "The '60s."

On opening day they did over $4,000 of business; by the end of the first week, they knew that they had a successful operation. Over the last three years, Gloria and Tina have expanded their operation and opened fourteen more units in the nearby area. Sales have been increasing by 248 percent annually and the Shapiros are now in the process of putting together a management team to help them run their rapidly growing organization. They are also looking to develop an incentive package that can help them reduce associate turnover. Many of their new hires are high-school and college students who are looking for part-time jobs; other associates need to take any job they can find while they are waiting for something better to come by. As a result, annual turnover is 184 percent.

Gloria and Tina would like to sharply reduce this turnover and offer their associates a career opportunity. "We are a growing business," Gloria recently noted, "and there is going to be a wealth of opportunity for anyone who stays with us. Additionally, we need to hire a team of associates who can help us grow, and this won't happen if we have to continually replace our workforce every six months." As a result, the Shapiros are now in the process of designing an incentive package; they have asked the associates to submit ideas for consideration. One of the most common submissions has been a "cash-for-college" suggestion that would result in associates being able to build a nest egg to pay for tuition, books, and related expenses. Another suggestion is an incentive program tied to unit performance factors such as increased sales, reduced operating costs, and positive customer service feedback. A third suggestion is an annual recognition dinner to acknowledge those who have done outstanding work and to reward them for their efforts.

Gloria and Tina plan on using these ideas to help create an overall program that will provide a wide array of incentives to associates. Most of the current suggestions are financially focused, but the owners intend to also include nonmonetary rewards. The major challenge they now face is that of sorting through all of the suggestions and creating a well-designed, effective program. They hope to have a preliminary design completed within 90 days and have the overall program introduced and in effect within six months.

1. How important are monetary incentives for associates in the hospitality industry? Defend your answer.

2. Are any of the current suggestions discussed in the case of practical value to the Shapiros? Explain.

3. In addition to the suggestions in the case, what other recommendations would you make to the Shapiros? Offer at least three additional factors that they should be sure to include in their program.

ENDNOTES

1. David A. Whetten and Kim S. Cameron, *Developing Management Skills: Motivating Others* (New York: HarperCollins, 1993), p. 26.
2. Ricky W. Griffin, *Management,* 4th ed. (Boston: Houghton Mifflin, 1993), p. 366.
3. Fred Luthans, *Organizational Behavior,* 7th ed. (New York: McGraw-Hill, 1995), p. 141.
4. Stephen P. Robbins, *Organizational Behavior,* 6th ed. (Upper Saddle River, N.J.: Prentice-Hall, 1993), p. 205.
5. Frederick Herzberg, Bernard Mausner, and Barbara Block Snyderman, *The Motivation to Work* (New York: Wiley, 1959).
6. For more on these ideas, see David C. McClelland, "Business Drive and National Achievement," *Harvard Business Review,* July–August 1962, pp. 99–112; David McClelland, "Achievement Motivation Can Be Learned," *Harvard Business Review,* November–December 1965, pp. 6–24; and Robert L. Helmreich, Linda I. Sawin, and Alan S. Carsrud, "The Honeymoon Effect in Job Performance: Temporal Increases in the Predictive Power of Achievement Motivation," *Journal of Applied Psychology,* May 1986, pp. 185–188.
7. For more on this, see Richard M. Hodgetts, *Organizational Behavior: Theory and Practice* (New York: Macmillan, 1991), pp. 142–144.
8. For more on this theory, see John R. Hollenbeck and Howard J. Klein, "Goal Commitment and the Goal-Setting Process: Problems, Prospects, and Proposals for Future Research," *Journal of Applied Psychology,* May 1987, pp. 212–220; A. M. Mento, R. P. Steele, and R. J. Karren, "A Meta-Analytic Study of the Effects of Goal Setting on Task Performance: 1964–1984," *Organizational Behavior and Human Decision Processes,* Volume 39, 1987, pp. 52–83; and Edwin L. Locke, Gary P. Latham, and Miriam Erez, "The Determinants of Goal Attainment," *Academy of Management Review,* January 1988, pp. 23–29.
9. Also see Luthans, *Organizational Behavior,* pp. 160–162.
10. Edward L. Thorndike, *Animal Intelligence* (New York: Macmillan, 1911), p. 244.
11. W. Clay Hamner, "Reinforcement Theory and Contingency Management in Organizational Settings," in Richard M. Steers and Lyman W. Porter (eds.), *Motivation and Work Behavior* (New York: McGraw-Hill, 1983), p. 118.
12. See, for example, Peter Romeo, "Who Made the Most?" *Restaurant Business,* July 1, 1994, pp. 62–63.

13. Kwame Charles and Lincoln Marshall, "Motivational Preferences of Caribbean Hotel Workers: An Exploratory Study," *International Journal of Contemporary Hospitality Management,* Vol. 4, No. 3 (1992), pp. 25–29.

14. Richard Darder, "Six Steps to Creating a Positive Motivational Working Environment," *International Gaming and Wagering Business,* March 1994, pp. 17–18.

15. Tony Simons and Cathy A. Enz, "Motivating Hotel Employees," *Cornell Hotel and Restaurant Association Quarterly,* February 1995, p. 26.

16. Donald J. McNerney, "Fast-Food Franchise Serves Up Cash for College," *HR Focus,* February 1995, p. 13.

17. Paul Frumkin, "Employee Incentives Pay Off," *Restaurant Business,* August 10, 1988, p. 129.

18. Ibid.

19. Ibid.

20. Jeff Weinstein, "Personnel Success," *Restaurants & Institutions,* December 9, 1992, p. 113.

21. Ibid.

22. Ibid., p. 108.

23. Felicity Long, "Motivating Employees via Incentives," *Travel Weekly,* June 8, 1995, p. 48.

24. Richard M. Hodgetts, *Blueprints for Continuous Improvement* (New York: American Management Association, 1993), p. 95.

25. Susie Stephenson, "Talk about Recognition!" *Restaurant and Institution,* December 15, 1994, p. 70.

26. Hodgetts, *Blueprints for Continuous Improvement,* p. 95.

27. For additional examples, see "Pretty Nifty Rewards," *Restaurants & Institutions,* January 1, 1995, pp. 111–112.

28. Also see Susie Stephenson, "12 Ways to Motivate Employees," *Restaurants & Institutions,* October 15, 1994, p. 112; and Lynn O'Rourke Hayes, "Get Off Your Butt and Motivate Someone," *Restaurant Hospitality,* July 1993, p. 64.

CHAPTER NINE

Creating Effective Associate Relations

LEARNING OBJECTIVES

A variety of human resource management (HRM) functions are carried out in hospitality organizations. In the last three chapters, seven of these have been examined: recruiting, selecting, orienting, training, developing, appraising, and motivating associates. In addition, human resources programs are used to help create effective associate relations. The ways in which this is done are the focus of this chapter. In particular, we will consider associate counseling, the effective use of power, the development of employee assistance programs to help with various personal and work-related problems, such as substance-abuse, child-care programs, and the creation of effective discipline strategies. When you have finished studying all of the material in this chapter, you will be able to:

1. Define the term *developmental feedback* and describe how managers use this feedback to deal with nonperformance.

2. Describe the five bases of power and examine how power can be used to create effective associate relations.

3. Relate the most common types of *employee assistance programs* and other support efforts by hospitality organizations and discuss the value they provide to these firms.

4. Define the term *discipline* and discuss the five steps involved in administering this process.

Developmental Feedback

Developmental feedback is a process by which supervisors convey information to associates regarding work performance that needs improvement. This feedback process has three stages: prediscussion, discussion, and postdiscussion.

Prediscussion

In the prediscussion stage, the supervisor prepares for the meeting with the associate by reviewing the associate's performance and deciding how to address the nonperformance issue. At this stage, the manager will typically write down things he or she wants to convey, as well as determine how to position the discussion so that everything goes smoothly. The manager will also convey the reason for the meeting to the associate in a nonthreatening way such as, "Karl, you and I need to discuss our expectation of providing check-out service within five minutes of the time a guest gets on line. I've noticed that this target is not being met. When would be a good time for us to sit down and talk?" In this way the manager gives the associate something to think about, while letting the person know that the meeting will be focused on looking for ways of improving performance and will not be used to "chew out" the individual.

Discussion

When the two meet, the manager will immediately set a pleasant tone and put the associate at ease. Then the problem will be discussed in terms of what can be done to improve the situation. In many cases, the associate will provide information regarding why it is difficult to get the work done within the assigned time limit—and these will indicate that the problem goes beyond just this person. For example, the associate may say, "The computer system is so slow that I cannot handle more than one person a minute. So if there are more than five people on line, I can never get to all of them within five minutes." In particular, the manager will avoid questions that put the associate on the defensive. Instead, the manager will focus the discussion on how things can be improved. Examples include: What do you think needs to be done? If we do this, do you believe we can resolve the problem? How long do you think it will take to implement your ideas? Would you be willing to work with us on planning and implementing this solution?

Once the manager gets the associate to agree on a plan of action, the meeting will begin to wind down. Before concluding, however, the manager will review what has been discussed and what the associate has agreed to do. The manager will then express confidence in the associate's ability and set a time to meet again and review the associate's progress.

Postdiscussion

The postdiscussion meeting is designed to examine how well things are going and to pinpoint any areas that might still need improvement. For example, the manager might say, "Now that we have upgraded the computer system and installed new software, I see that we have reduced the average waiting time from nine minutes down to six minutes. What else do you think we can do to get to our goal of five minutes?" Perhaps the major problem is that it is taking Karl longer than anticipated to master the new software and all he needs is a little more time. In any event, the postdiscussion meeting serves to review progress and set the stage for any follow-up meeting that may be warranted. It also gives the manager an opportunity to provide reinforcement to the associate for the job he or she is doing and encourage the person to continue his or her efforts.[1]

The Role of Power

When managers provide developmental feedback and other forms of assistance, they must know how to use power effectively. There are a number of forms of power; each has value in creating effective associate relations.

Power is the ability to influence someone to do something that he or she would not otherwise do. Hospitality managers typically rely on one or more of the commonly cited bases of power: reward, coercive, legitimate, referent, and expert.

Reward power is based on the follower's expectation of receiving something that he or she wants. For example, in many organizations, associates who comply with company rules and are productive members of the work group are given annual salary raises. Reward power can be particularly helpful when used to point out the benefits of doing things a particular way. It is also an excellent form of positive reinforcement.

Coercive power is power based on fear. This power is present whenever associates believe that their boss has the power to punish them, and the boss is willing to exercise this option. Coercive power can take many forms. In a hospitality organization, a manager can use coercive power to punish those who are not complying with orders or procedures by using an either/or approach, *e.g.*, "Improve your performance or you will be fired."

> Ruth Moeller works the front desk at the Balmoral Hotel, which prides itself on fast, courteous service. One of the hotel's latest customer service programs is called "Ten or $10" and refers to the promise that a guest who waits on line for more than 10 minutes to check in or check out will be given a $10 credit. Over the past two weeks, Ruth's performance has not been good. She has been slow and

has made a number of mistakes that resulted in guests having to wait on line for 15 to 20 minutes. Ruth's immediate boss, Charles Vanderfield, has talked to her twice in the past four days and has told her, "If your performance does not sharply improve over the next week, it will seriously affect your promotional opportunities with us." Ruth is trying very hard to do things right. However, her mother is scheduled for surgery next week and Ruth continues to be preoccupied with this problem.

Charles's handling of this situation is an example of how coercive power is used. Obviously, it is not a very effective method because it presents things in an "either/or" way, *i.e.,* either improve or suffer the consequences.

Legitimate power is power vested in the manager's position or role in the hierarchy. All managers have legitimate power; the further up the hierarchy, the greater the power of the officeholder. Legitimate power has degrees of both reward and coercive power. For example, managers typically decide which of their subordinates are to be promoted and/or given salary increases. At the same time, these managers can use coercive power to discipline and punish by denying promotions and salary raises to associates as well as to terminate their employment. Depending on how legitimate power is used, managers can use it to create a number of different results, both positive and negative. Here is an example of a positive outcome:

> Because of a hiring freeze, Terri Falcone agreed to take on added responsibility in order to ensure that the Christmas season was successful. Fortunately, it turned out to be the most profitable in the hotel's history. However, now Terri is being asked to continue her increased workload for the next six months while the human resources department tries to fill vacant positions. Her boss, Sally Olafson, called her in for a meeting yesterday and gave her the opportunity to talk about how she felt regarding her work assignment. Terri welcomed the opportunity to express her displeasure and concern over what she feels is management's lack of concern for her situation. When she was finished, Sally told her that she was going to receive an excellent performance evaluation, and was in line for a major promotion. "I know the last four months have been tough," she told her, "but this will soon be behind you and I'm going to assign two more people to your department to help relieve some of the added pressure. In the meantime, I'd like you to hang in there and continue your outstanding performance." By this time, Terri was feeling much better and promised Sally that she would give it her best effort.

Sally's approach was effective because she gave Terri a chance to express her concerns and then, using her legitimate power, made it clear that she was going to see that she was rewarded (combination of legitimate and reward power).

Referent power is power based on the follower's identification with the leader. This is sometimes referred to as charismatic power and is possessed by individuals who are loved, respected, and/or trusted by their associates. In the preceding example, Sally asked Terri to do her best in a difficult situation, and Terri agreed to do so. There are a number of reasons why Terri may have agreed to the request. One of them may well be that she feels that Sally is trustworthy and she admires Sally's leadership style. She feels Sally would never let her down and will be in her corner when it comes time for promotions. As a result, Sally has referent power. When this occurs, *what* people have to say is not as important as *who* is saying it.

Expert power is based on competence. A manager who is seen as capable of analyzing, implementing, and controlling tasks that have been assigned to the group will often have expert power. The associates will look to the individual to provide them with the competence or direction needed to get the job done. Expert power can be acquired in a number of different ways. Two of the most common are experience and formal training.

> For the past two months Claudia Hernandez and her associate, Richard McDermott, have been meeting every week to briefly discuss Richard's career progress with the cruise line. Claudia has sent Richard to a series of management training programs over the past year and given him a wide assortment of assignments designed to prepare him for promotion. Now Richard has been offered a position with a major competitor, but Claudia feels the opportunities are better if Richard stays put. "I'm on the promotion committee," she explained to him yesterday, "and I know the credentials that are necessary for moving up. You're getting them and if you stay with us, there is no limit to how high you can go. That's why I've been sending you to all of these courses and getting you special assignments that will help tap your leadership potential." Earlier today Richard called the competitive firm and told them he was going to be staying in his current job.

Did Claudia use expert power to direct Richard? She certainly did; and her use of this power was particularly effective in getting Richard to see his opportunities with the company and agree to stay.

The effective use of power is only one way that hospitality managers can help create effective associate relations. Another is through the use of employee assistance programs. Before looking at these programs, however, take a few minutes now and analyze your own approach to using power by completing the self-feedback exercise at the end of the chapter.

Employee Assistance Programs and Other Support Efforts

In addition to providing developmental feedback, many hospitality organizations have created employee assistance programs and other forms of support help. An *employee assistance program* (EAP) is designed to help associates deal with both personal and work-related problems. Examples include alcohol abuse or dependency, career development difficulties, depression or burnout, emotional difficulties, family issues, literacy, personal financial problems, and stress-related problems. In addition, organizations provide other support efforts such as child care. The following sections examine two of the most common forms of assistance now being offered: substance-abuse assistance through the use of an EAP, and child care through special programs developed by hospitality firms.

Substance Abuse

The two major types of substance abuse in the hospitality industry are alcohol and drugs. As in other industries, substance abuse has a major effect on productivity. Recent research reveals that 25 percent of American workers have personal knowledge of co-workers who use illegal drugs on the job, and drug abuse costs U.S. businesses $60 billion annually in decreased productivity.[2] The hospitality industry is not immune from the effects of such abuse. Vincent Eade conducted a survey of hotel and restaurant associates who were recently treated for drug abuse and found that alcohol, marijuana, sedatives, heroin, and cocaine/amphetamines were most common.[3] Of these, approximately half of the respondents reported that alcohol was their first drug of choice. This is not surprising, given the role that alcohol plays in the hotel and restaurant business. However, regardless of the type of substance abuse, hospitality organizations are increasingly beginning to create EAPs to help their associates deal with these problems.[4]

Types of Programs. Any hospitality organization can implement an EAP. However, most programs serve as referral agents and are rarely involved in the actual treatment of associate problems. Instead, community agencies are used and, depending on the company's benefit package, costs are covered by insurance or are paid by the employer on a sliding-fee schedule. Moreover, if a company is not large enough to support its own EAP, a consortium of businesses in a community may organize and share the costs. This is often done through the Chamber of Commerce or other trade association.

In general, there are two types of programs: internal and external.[5] An internal program designates a staff person as an EAP specialist. This individual typically works in the HRM department and is skilled in helping associates deal with personal and work-related problems. The main advantage of this approach is that it gives the organization control over the program. The main drawback is that associates may feel there is a lack of confidentiality and may be reluctant to use the EAP's services. An external program allows associates to contact outside experts and receive assistance from them, while the bill for these services is paid by the organization. The main advantage of this approach is its confidentiality.

Whether a hospitality organization uses an internal or external program, the success of the effort will depend heavily on the EAP specialist. Today, due to regulations set by insurance companies and state government, specialists must meet minimum requirements and be licensed or certified. Additionally, notes one expert in the area:

> Care should be taken when choosing an EAP agency or specialist. The EAP will have access to important company information, so integrity of all members of the agency's staff is important. If the program is national, it is important to find out how it gets its community referrals. Does it randomly select agencies from the Yellow Pages, or does it make on-site inspections, check staff credentials, and monitor performance?
>
> It is important to know who will be working with the company. What is the person's education and experience? Will the person be able to relate to the employees and understand the special demands of a foodservice business?[6]

Developing the Program. Most organizations start a drug-abuse program by developing a written policy emphasizing their commitment to a drug-free workplace.[7] It is also common to find management following up by developing a program that helps enforce this policy. While many approaches are used in doing this,[8] the following eight are typical steps in the process.

First, emphasis is placed on performance. Rather than training supervisors to become counselors, the company will teach them to focus on work results. Then, if someone's performance begins to decline, the supervisor can confront the individual; if it appears that the associate has a drug-related problem, he or she can be given the opportunity to get assistance through the EAP. While this is a good initial step, it is important to realize that in many cases job performance does not suffer very much from initial drug abuse. It is not until much later in the process that the problem becomes clearly obvious. (See Figure 9.1.) By teaching the supervisor to pick up initial signs of performance decline, organizations are often able to minimize the negative effects of this problem.

Second, anyone who is recommended to the EAP or who goes on his or her own is guaranteed total confidentiality. Whatever happens from this point

Stage	Absenteeism	General Behavior	Job Performance
I Early	Tardiness Quits early Absence from work situations ("I drink to relieve tension")	Complaints from fellow employees for not doing his or her share Overreaction Complaints of not "feeling well" Makes untrue statements	Misses deadlines Commits errors (frequently) Lower job efficiency Criticism from the boss
II Middle	Frequent days off for vague or implausible reasons ("I feel guilty about sneaking drinks"; "I have tremors")	Marked changes Undependable statements Avoids fellow employees Borrows money from fellow employees Exaggerates work accomplishments Frequent hospitalization Minor injuries on the job (repeatedly)	General deterioration Cannot concentrate Occasional lapse of memory Warning from boss
III Late Middle	Frequent days off; several days at a time Does not return from lunch ("I don't feel like eating"; "I don't want to talk about it"; "I like to drink alone")	Aggressive and belligerent behavior Domestic problems interfere with work Financial difficulties (garnishments, etc.) More frequent hospitalization Resignation; does not want to discuss problems Problems with the laws in the community	Far below expectation Punitive disciplinary action
IV Approaching Terminal Stage	Prolonged unpredictable absences ("My job interferes with my drinking")	Drinking on the job (probably) Completely undependable Repeated hospitalization Serious financial problems Serious family problems; divorce	Uneven Generally incompetent Faces termination or hospitalization

(left margin label: Alcohol Addiction Line)

Figure 9.1 *Observable Behavior Patterns of Alcohol Abuse*

Source: Gopal C. Pati and John J. Adkins, Jr., "The Employer's Role in Alcoholism Assistance," *Personnel Journal*, July 1983, p. 570.

on is between the associate and the EAP staff. The supervisor's only job is to monitor the associate's work behavior and keep track of changes.

Third, management throughout the organization totally supports the effort and makes it clear that associates with problems should seek help from the EAP and that doing so will not affect their career opportunities with the firm. If there is a union in the company, these individuals also strongly support the effort.

Fourth, associates are given training to teach them responsibility for their health. This helps them recognize the early signs of problems such as high stress, extreme tension, increased drinking, reliance on drugs as sedatives, and so on.

Fifth, supervisors and managers are trained to identify common symptoms of overwork, drug dependency, and the like. In the latter case, for example, how does a manager know when an associate is drinking too much? One human resources expert put it this way:

> This is a difficult question to answer, but there are some signs for which the individual can remain alert. Among white-collar workers, these include such things as elaborate (and often bizarre) excuses for work deficiencies, pronounced and frequent mood swings in work pace, avoidance of the boss and associates, and increased nervousness. Among blue-collar workers, the clues include a sloppy personal appearance, signs of a hangover, frequent lapses of efficiency leading to occasional damage to equipment or material, increased nervousness, and increased off-the-job accidents. Perhaps the biggest problem managers face in dealing with alcoholics is that they are skillful in denying the problem, especially when confronted by the boss.[9]

By learning about the habits and customs of alcoholics, managers become better able to deal with them. Do you know much about alcoholics? Before continuing, take the quiz in Box 9.1.

Sixth, organizations promote EAP services to family members as well. The logic is simple: If someone has a spouse or child who has a problem, this can affect the associate's work performance. By including family members in the EAP coverage, the firm helps associates do a better job.

Seventh, self-referral is promoted. If associates feel that they have personal or work-related problems and can benefit from the EAP's assistance, they are encouraged to seek help. Moreover, as associates learn more about the program and become convinced that it is a totally confidential assistance service, self-referrals tend to increase.

Eighth, regular follow-ups and evaluations of the EAP ensure that the program is effective. One of the most common measures is to compare organizational performance both before the EAP was created and now, and to notice changes in areas such as tardiness, absenteeism, turnover, work errors, acci-

The following twelve statements about alcoholics are either true or false. Read each carefully before making your choice. Answers are provided at the end of the chapter.

T F **1.** When a food service associate is suffering from alcoholism, approximately 25 percent of the individual's wages are lost to unproductive work time such as absenteeism, unnecessary overtime, tardiness, sick leave abuse, health insurance claims, and disability payments.

T F **2.** It is estimated that approximately 12 percent of the hospitality workforce is affected by personal problems related to alcoholism or drug abuse.

T F **3.** Approximately 30 percent of alcoholics are women.

T F **4.** Approximately 25 percent of alcoholics are white-collar employees.

T F **5.** Around 20 percent of alcoholics in the workplace are professional or managerial personnel.

T F **6.** Almost 25 percent of alcoholics in the workplace have completed or attended college.

T F **7.** Alcoholics usually miss a lot of work.

T F **8.** Alcoholics drink all the time.

T F **9.** Alcoholics are usually middle-aged or older.

T F **10.** Alcoholics have low-level, dead-end jobs.

T F **11.** Alcoholics have below-average intelligence.

T F **12.** Alcoholics typically drink in public, so it is fairly easy to spot them.

dents, and feedback from those who have received services. Based on the results, the hospitality organization will then decide what changes, if any, to make in the EAP.

EAPs are extremely useful in creating effective associate relations. In particular, they help hospitality firms assist associates in dealing with problems that often require professional assistance.

Child Care

Another type of support effort that is becoming popular in hospitality organizations is child-care programs. Today it is increasingly common to find both parents working. As a result, child care is a growing concern for associates; organizations that can offer some form of employee assistance in child care stand to benefit in both the selection and retention of quality associates.[10] There are many ways in which this can be done. The three main approaches include (1) offering services, (2) supplying information, and (3) providing financial support. Table 9.1 describes some of these options and provides examples of hospitality organizations that offer each.

Services. Child-care services take a variety of forms. One of the most common is on-site day care. An example is the Opryland Hotel in Nashville, Tennessee, which has an on-site center that operates from 5 A.M. to midnight. Management reports that turnover among associates who use the center has decreased by 19 percent.[11]

Despite these benefits, many hospitality organizations are unable to offer child-care services because the cost is too high both to them and to their associates. In addition to the expense of the facility, which can run $100,000 and up, there is the out-of-pocket cost for the parents. These fees typically range from $75 to $250 per week. In some cases, organizations will provide the benefit for free. However, in those cases where it is being at least partially funded by the parents, research shows that a company typically needs around 2,000 employees in order to support a day-care center. This is why many centers are confined to corporate headquarters and are not found in individual properties.

One major exception is when several employers join together and collectively support the center. For example, three Hawaiian hotels have now combined their financial resources to fund the cost of the $1.5 million Mauna Lani School, which serves their child-care needs. Another exception is when the hospitality organization creates a partnership with a public agency and collectively sponsors a child-care center. For example, the Twin Towers Hotel and Convention Center in Orlando, Florida, has collaborated with its local school board to open a satellite school at the hotel. The arrangement turned out to be a good deal for both groups.

> The school district, which was facing capacity constraints, gained an additional location, and the hotel contributed the real estate, utilities, and the children's lunches. The hotel gained an on-site public school and after-school program staffed by public-school teachers for its employees' children in pre-K, kindergarten, and the first grade. Parents benefit because they are near their children and only have to pay for the after-school program. Spearheaded by the hotel's managing director . . . the program is credited with reducing turnover and increasing morale.[12]

Supplying Information. Some organizations are unable to provide child-care services, but they do provide information to their associates regarding how to obtain such assistance. They do this by putting associates in contact with community-based referral networks. For example, Marriott has a nationwide referral program for its associates.

Table 9.1 Child-Care Options

Options	Descriptions	Pros	Cons	Examples
Offering Services				
• On-site day care	• Care is provided on or near the employer's property, perhaps by a contracted operator.	• Decreases lateness, absenteeism, and turnover. Helps recruitment.*	• May be expensive for the employee. Its quality must be monitored. May raise issues of co-worker equity.	• Opryland Hotel • Marriott headquarters • Sands Hotel, Casino, and Country Club
• Consortium-sponsored day care	• Employers join forces to finance day care, frequently run by a contracted operator.	• Reduces costs and liability.	• Policy and procedures must be agreed upon. Raises co-worker equity issues. Location may pose problems.	• Mauna Lani School
• Public-private partnerships	• The employer joins forces with a public agency.	• Reduces costs.	• Same as above.	• Twin Towers Hotel and Convention Center
Supplying Information				
	• The employer provides information about community services, helping the employee learn about what kind of care to look for, where to look, and how to evaluate it. The employer may hire a full-time administrator and may offer seminars and family support.	• Low cost. No liability. Serves many employees. Serves communities.	• Narrow in scope. Doesn't lower absenteeism. Isn't a recruiting tool.	• Marriott • General Mills

Providing Financial Assistance

• Flexible spending accounts	• The employee pays for child care with before-tax dollars.	• Low cost. Reduces the employee's taxes. No equity/co-worker issues.	• Restrictive regulations. May be hard for small employers to administer.	• International Dairy Queen
• Cafeteria benefit plans	• Employer sets total of benefit package and available options and employees select their own levels of contribution(allocation) for the benefit(s) desired.	• Low cost. Employees can select their child care. No equity issues.	• Confusing to employees. Complex to administer.	• General Mills
• Subsidies and discounts	• The employer subsidizes the child-care provider, negotiates a discount with a day-care center, or reimburses the employee.	• Low cost. Employees can select their child care.	• Doesn't provide for evening-shift workers if community centers are used. Considered taxable income.	• Brinker-International • BBD Consultants • KFC

*All options may provide these benefits by reducing the employee's worries and obligations about child care.

Source: Janet H. Marler and Cathy A. Enz, "Child Care Programs That Make Sense," *Cornell Hotel and Restaurant Association Quarterly,* February 1993, p. 62.

A referral system strategy is the most common child-care benefit. In particular, it is a low-cost option. Unfortunately, the approach also has limitations. For example, a referral system is of no value to individuals who live in areas where there is no day care available, and the system generally does not help those who need part-time care or care during odd hours. So the value of the referral system is based heavily on the demographic characteristics of the associates.

Financial Assistance. In addition to (or instead of) the preceding two options, some hospitality organizations provide their associates with financial assistance. One of the most common is flexible spending accounts, which are benefits that have been created by tax legislation. The benefits allow associates to pay for child care with before-tax dollars and thus reduce taxable income. The associate can designate the amount of money to be set aside for child-care assistance (typically no more than $2,400 annually) and can use this fund to pay for the service. Many companies offer this option, including Marriott, International Dairy Queen, and Kentucky Fried Chicken.

Another common option is the cafeteria benefit plan, which allows associates to select the benefits they want, while allowing the company to control its level of contribution. Young people can choose to spend more of their benefits for child care, while older associates can opt for more health insurance coverage.

Still another approach is subsidies given by the company. For example, BBD Consultants, a 20-unit Burger King franchisee in Grand Rapids, Michigan, pays associates a subsidy of $1 an hour, up to $32 a week, for child care. A related form of assistance is discounts that are negotiated between the company and community centers or day-care chains. For example, Brinker International (parent company of Chili's, Romano Macaroni Grill, and Regas Grill) offers employee discounts through contracts with a Kansas City day-care chain and a nationwide children's learning center.

Research reveals that day care is one of the fastest-growing needs of hospitality associates. So it is likely that more and more firms will begin developing programs for providing this service.

Effective Disciplining

While hospitality organizations offer a variety of programs designed to create effective associate relations, they always maintain control of their operations. They want to create high associate satisfaction, but they do not intend to let the associates do whatever they want. Effective discipline is another major area of attention in creating effective relations.

Table 9.2 Types of Problem Employees

Type	Primary Goal	Secondary Goal
Type I—does not intentionally violate the rules, does so unintentionally and infrequently.	To correct the behavior, to inform and train.	To maintain the individual's motivation.
Type II—will violate the rules when he or she considers some treatment unfair; will occasionally violate the rules.	To correct the behavior and to avoid discipline problems with others.	To identify and deal with why the person feels treated unfairly. Otherwise, future problems will occur.
Type III—Will violate the rules whenever he or she can get away with it, generally creates problems, and is often disciplined.	To avoid discipline problems with others.	To document the use of discipline (toward eventual termination).
Type IV—Is not so much a problem employee as an employee with a problem.	To get help for the individual and to provide a reason to use that help	To document if the individual is unwilling to seek help or the problem recurs.

Source: Reprinted by permission of the publisher from *Management Solutions,* February 1987 © 1987. American Management Association, New York. All rights reserved.

Discipline is any action designed to correct associate deviations from organizational rules, procedures, policies, and norms. The term carries the connotation of punishment, but quite often this is not the case. Table 9.2 illustrates this idea. Notice that each type of associate in the table requires a different type of discipline or assistance, administered in a helpful, constructive way.[13] In fact, sometimes problems do not require disciplinary action; they can be handled through effective mediations by the manager. When discipline is required, of course, the manager must decide which type to use.

Types of Discipline

Hospitality organizations employ two basic types of discipline: negative and positive. Both are commonly used in hospitality firms.

Negative Discipline. *Negative discipline* is the use of punishment to ensure compliance with organizational rules and regulations. It is best expressed with the cliché, "Do it or else." This approach is still common in organizations where it is considered easy to replace anyone who leaves and the enterprise lacks a high regard for its associates.

One of the major shortcomings of negative discipline is that it often results in people doing the minimum amount of work. For example, if managers penalize everyone who comes to work late, the associates will all come in on time but may stretch out their breaks. If management sets a minimum amount of work and fires everyone who fails to comply, associates will produce at, or slightly above, this minimum. Negative discipline often results in associates avoiding punishment, having a negative attitude toward management, and looking for ways to beat the system. The approach does not create the enthusiastic, wholehearted support needed for maximum organizational effectiveness. Another shortcoming of negative discipline is the legal aspect. In some cases, management is legally restricted from taking disciplinary action against associates. Take the quiz in Box 9.2 and see if you can identify when management's actions are legally justified and when they are not.

Positive Discipline. *Positive discipline* is the use of two-way communication to convey desired changes in work behavior and to provide guidance to associates in taking this corrective action. Positive discipline, often called constructive discipline, creates a willingness on the part of associates to accept and abide by the organization's rules, procedures, policies, and norms. The approach is based on the belief that most people want to do a good job and when they make a mistake or break a rule, it either was unintentional or was done for a good reason. When the organization uses positive discipline, the associate and the boss discuss the infraction of the rules before taking action. Positive discipline involves a five-step process: (1) the manager and the associate meet in private; (2) the manager points out the rule violation or improper behavior; (3) the manager gives the associate a chance to explain the behavior; (4) a decision is made regarding what to do; and (5) the decision is implemented.

Positive discipline does not rule out the use of penalties or sanctions. In fact, during the process the manager usually writes out what is being discussed and agreed upon. If the associate does not improve performance, the employer can justify using stronger measures. However, positive discipline proceeds from the assumption that the individual may have a good reason for breaking the rule and that all of the facts should be examined before a decision is made. Thus it is often discipline without punishment.

Administration of Discipline

The effective administration of discipline requires the balancing of organizational interests with the protection of the rights of individuals. In doing this, hospitality organizations typically follow five specific steps.

Box 9.2
What Do You Think?

Each of the following statements or explanations is totally true and both the individual and the organization agree with the facts. Given this information, can the company legally fire the person, or will the associate find the courts coming down on his or her side? In each case, vote for the organization (O) or the associate (A) by placing an X next to your choice. After you are finished, check your answers with those that are provided at the end of the chapter.

1. Joe Barnathan was dismissed from his job in the kitchen of a prominent restaurant because he broke one of the major safety rules regarding the handling of flammable materials. Joe admits that he made this mistake, but notes that just about everyone else in the department has done the same thing from time to time, and this is the first time that anyone has ever been dismissed. The company admits that it has failed to enforce the rule in the past, but has decided to make an example of Joe and to uniformly enforce the rule in the future.
   ____O   ____A

2. June Wardberg was fired from her job last month because her work was judged unsatisfactory for the third consecutive quarter. Over the past four years the company has fired 27 people for poor work performance, and all of them were women. In June's lawsuit, she has asked for reinstatement because the organization has a bias against women.
   ____O   ____A

3. Barbara Findlay refused to help move some heavy equipment because she was afraid that she could be injured in the process and feared for her safety. The company has countered by saying that Barbara's safety was not an issue and she was fired for failure to follow orders.
   ____O   ____A

4. Toni Hount works in the accounting office and often is called upon to handle large sums of money. The company recently discovered that there was a shortage of $2,600; the person conducting the investigation for the firm called Toni in for an interview regarding the matter. Because the company is unionized and she is a member, Toni asked to have a union representative present during the interview. Her request was denied and Toni was eventually let go because the company concluded that she knew, or should have known, some material facts regarding the shortage. Toni has countered by filing a lawsuit in which she claims that she should not have been interviewed without a union rep present, so she is entitled to reinstatement and back pay.
   ____O   ____A

5. Pablo Sanchez received three warnings regarding coming late for work. After the third warning, as described in the employment manual, he was dismissed. Pablo has brought suit against the company. His lawyer argues that three warnings are insuf-

Box 9.2   Continued

ficient and Pablo should have received at least five warnings before any action was taken.

___O ___A

6. The Monmouth Parke Hotel has a rule against smoking on the job by any associate. Last week Roberta Clarion was found smoking and was dismissed. Her lawsuit charges that it is illegal to prevent associates from smoking on the job because this is a personal freedom that is protected by law; she has asked the court to reinstate her.

___O ___A

7. Paula Franke admits that she lost her temper and screamed at a customer. However, she argues that this is insufficient grounds for dismissal and has asked the court to overturn the company's rule regarding dismissal for careless treatment of customers and force the company to give her back her job.

___O ___A

8. Chuck Ronstadt has worked in the maintenance department for six years and has frequently failed to follow safety procedures. For the first time ever, last month he had an accident. Upon investigation, the company found that he had not followed procedures, and it fired him. Chuck argued that he had not been following these procedures for years; he claims that this proves that the procedures are unnecessary, so he should be reinstated.

___O ___A

Rules and Regulations Must Be Specific. Management often feels that rules and regulations are vital to the effective operation of the organization. For example, it may insist on courteousness to all guests, the following of safety procedures in the maintenance area, and no smoking anywhere on the property. Other common rules relate to absenteeism, tardiness, theft, protection of equipment, and insubordination. Whatever the rules and regulations, they must be spelled out clearly and specifically. Any ambiguity can result in rule violations and, worse perhaps, lawsuits from associates who charge discrimination. Any time there is doubt regarding what a rule means, the courts are likely to side with the associate.

Rules and Regulations Must Be Communicated. Associates have to be made aware of the rules and regulations. In doing this, hospitality organizations typically use employee handbooks, memos, verbal communiqués from superiors, or some combination of these approaches. The written document is particularly important; it provides physical evidence should legal action be brought by an associate who claims lack of knowledge about a particular rule or practice. Written communication is also important because it serves as a basis for explaining and clearing up any misunderstandings about the rules and regulations.

Enforcement Must Be Consistent. The organization cannot arbitrarily decide to discipline 10 percent of those found to be violating a particular rule. Violations must be documented and everyone who breaks the rules must be treated in the same way.[14] Of course, the organization can use a system of progressive discipline under which continual violations of the rules result in sterner punishment and eventually lead to dismissal. However, the penalties must be tied directly to the offense (first time, second time) and not to the individual who committed it. One way of ensuring consistency is through training programs and meetings at which discipline cases are discussed and management actions are reviewed. This approach familiarizes managers with ways to deal with specific cases effectively and consistently, since they are aware of what has been done in the past.

Individual Circumstances Must Be Considered. Extenuating or mitigating circumstances must be fully weighed. For example, danger to one's health and safety can constitute an extenuating circumstance and limit the right of the organization to discipline associates who fail to comply with orders. Similarly, an associate who has been on vacation and returns to work unaware that a new rule has been implemented regarding leaving the work area without authorization cannot be expected to follow the rule. Another mitigating circumstance is job seniority. Some hospitality organizations rigidly enforce safety rules and fire those who break them. However, if an associate has worked for the company for 25 years and commits an infraction, he or she is unlikely to be severely punished because the individual has so much to lose that the courts are likely to modify the penalty. For example, an associate who is 58 years old and has 30 years' longevity is unlikely to find another job that pays the same salary as what he or she is earning currently. As a result, unless the infraction is extremely serious, the organization is likely to find the courts siding with the associate or suggesting that the two parties work out a solution that is acceptable to both.

Progressive Discipline Should Be Employed. *Progressive discipline* is the administration of discipline in a series of gradually increasing penalties for repeated violations of rules and procedures. (The major exception to progressive discipline is the commitment of a major infraction, such as stealing funds, deliberately destroying property, or using narcotics on the job. In these cases hospitality organizations often dismiss the individual outright.) The first time an associate breaks one of the rules, the penalty is minor. However, continual violations result in increased penalties. Here is an example:

First violation: An oral warning not noted in the associate's employment record..

Second violation: An oral warning noted in the associate's employment record.

Third violation: A written warning noted in the associate's employment record.

Fourth violation: A suspension from the job for a predetermined time—usually one day to two weeks, depending on the severity of the infraction.

Fifth violation: Discharge from the job.

Some firms use a variation of this example by setting minimum and maximum penalties for disciplinary action. For example, the first offense for tardiness, a minor infraction, might result in as little as an oral warning or as much as a written notification in the personnel file. The second infraction would carry a more severe penalty such as at least a written notification in the personnel file and as much as a day off without pay. This progression would continue to the point where the minimum penalty was dismissal, although it is important to remember that hospitality organizations often have appeal systems that associates can use to reverse discipline findings and overrule managers who are too zealous in their application of these rules. In recent years, some personnel consultants have recommended modifying progressive discipline through what they call corrective discipline.

Corrective discipline is based on the use of shared responsibility. Both the superior and the associate assume a role in ensuring that the associate performs appropriately. The main idea behind the approach is that through early identification of any problems, clear communication regarding what the associate is doing wrong and how the person should change the behavior, and positive reinforcement to encourage the individual to keep doing things well, punitive discipline can be reduced in all but a small number of cases. The progressive discipline steps are still used, but their purpose is to reinforce positive discipline. Only in severe cases such as stealing, fighting, or drug use is punitive discipline employed, and in all cases the company will carefully check to be sure that it has acted prudently and in good faith. One attorney who is very active in representing management clients in the restaurant, hotel, and service industry has recommended that companies develop a checklist for ensuring that this is done. This entails answering the following questions:

1. Was the associate informed about the possible disciplinary consequences of his or her conduct?

2. Was the company's rule, policy, or order that was violated reasonably related to efficient and safe operations?

3. Was the associate given an opportunity to tell his or her side of the story? Was there a thorough investigation?

4. Was the investigation conducted fairly and objectively?

5. Did the investigation produce substantial proof (facts) of guilt?

6. Has the discipline for this offense been applied evenhandedly to all associates, without favoritism?

7. Is the degree of discipline reasonable for the offense, taking into account:
   - the seriousness of the offense?
   - the frequency of the offense?
   - time lags between infractions?
   - the associate's overall record?
   - any extenuating circumstances?

A no answer to any of these questions could well be a legitimate cause for the manager to reassess his or her proposed action and, where appropriate, to correct any managerial deficiencies prior to the administration of the discipline.[15]

Employment at Will

While the preceding policies limit management's right to discipline associates, organizations still hold a great deal of power, as seen by the doctrine of employment at will. *Employment at will* holds that associates are retained through the goodwill of the organization. This doctrine covers all associates who do not have written contracts spelling out their conditions of employment. If a hospitality organization decides to terminate an individual, it is often within the firm's employment-at-will rights. At the same time, however, legislation over the years has limited the right to discharge associates for certain types of reasons. Additionally, the courts have used both tort and contract theories to avoid applying the employment-at-will doctrine.

Tort Theories. A *tort* is a civil wrong other than a breach of contract. It is based on the understanding that everyone in society owes certain duties to every other person. When tort theory is used to set aside the employment-at-will doctrine, it is done not because of some specific agreement or contract, but based on the court's interpretation of what society itself determines to be right or wrong. For example, the courts have ruled that it is wrong to discharge people for reasons that violate public policy. Examples include being discharged for (1) protesting cigarette smoking by other employees, (2) failing to participate in price-fixing schemes, (3) refusing to support the employer's lobbying efforts, and (4) telling the local police the name of another associate who is suspected of criminal wrongdoing.[16] Companies found guilty of wrongful discharge can be sued and, in many cases, plaintiffs have won substantial financial settlements.[17]

Contract Theories. A *contract* is an agreement between two or more parties that is intended to be legally binding. Contracts can be written or oral and usually cover the terms, conditions, and duration of employment. A common example of a written contract is an employee handbook that states that all associates will be placed on probation before they are discharged. An example of an oral or implied contract is the statement, "At this hotel we never fire anyone. If you do make a mistake, we always give you a chance to straighten things out."

Some courts have ruled that employers have an obligation of good faith and fair dealing with associates. For example, in one case a firm was prevented from firing an individual in order to prevent the person from collecting a bonus. In another case, the court ruled that a female associate could not be discharged for refusing to date her supervisor. The courts have held that every contract contains an implied covenant of good faith and fair dealing, and neither party can do anything that will injure the rights of the other to receive the benefits of the agreement.

Current Status of Employment at Will. The result of the latest court rulings on employment at will point to three facts. First, every hospitality organization should determine the level of job security that it wants to offer its associates. Second, this decision should be communicated in writing to the associates. Third, these policies should be uniformly and consistently followed. Some of the most helpful suggestions for drafting employee handbooks or personnel manuals include:

- Do not say, "These benefits provide financial security now and in the future." Instead say, "These benefits will help you become financially secure."

- Do not say, "Many of the programs and benefits are designed to increase in value as your length of service with the company and your salary grow." Say instead, "If you continue as an associate with the organization, many of these benefits are designed to increase in value along with your length of service. Other benefits are dependent upon your salary, so they will increase if your salary increases."

- Do not say, "When you retire"; say, "If you retire."

- Always qualify statements with the words "under the present plan" if you want the option to change that policy in the future.

- Always say what you mean.

- Always make it clear that the actual health, insurance, and benefit program descriptions will supersede those in the handbook and that the statements in the handbook are only summaries.

- Pay particular attention to sections in the employee handbook referring to promises of internal promotion, competitive pay, salary reviews and performance appraisals, safety, compliance with state statutes, and regulations.

Additionally, many human resources experts recommend that employee handbooks, policy manuals, application forms, and other printed materials contain disclaimers stating that these materials cannot be construed as contracts or legally binding associate rights. State courts have almost always acknowledged that these disclaimers provide a sufficient defense for overturning the "implied contract" exception.

Documentation and Dismissal

Before concluding this discussion of discipline, it is important to note that there are times when associates can be dismissed. In doing so, however, effective documentation must be maintained.

Organizations use two types of documentation: anecdotal and formal. *Anecdotal documentation* is informal in nature and consists of taking notes related to the associate's performance. Each entry in the manager's log is designed to report on the effects of a meeting or conversation held with the associate. This form of documentation is not given to the human resources department or to the associate. It is primarily used to keep track of conversations in the early stages of the performance improvement process. The danger here is that these informal notes can be subpoenaed in the event of an investigation.

Formal documentation begins with a written warning and becomes a part of the official record. A copy is placed in the associate's personnel file and a second copy is given to the individual. If the organization is unionized, a copy is also given to the union representative. An example of such a document is provided in Figure 9.2.

Formal documentation is important when an associate files a grievance and a manager must testify before a labor arbitrator or produce evidence as part of an investigation. The document shows that the associate was put on formal notice regarding work performance and told that things needed to improve. Today, formal documentation is a vital part of the discipline and dismissal process.

SUMMARY

1. Developmental feedback is a process by which supervisors convey information to associates regarding work performance that needs improvement. This feedback process has three stages: prediscussion, discussion, and postdiscussion.

```
To:       Barbara Wilson
From:     June Cantrell
Subject:  Written warning
Date:     February 11, 1998

As we discussed this morning, in the four months you have been with us,
you have been late on fourteen occasions, ranging in length from 5 minutes
to 55 minutes. We have spoken about this problem on three different occa-
sions and you still continue to be late. Since our last conversation three
weeks ago, you have been late five times.

Your tardiness creates problems for the other people in your department
who must cover for you. In addition, when you do arrive, others in your
department must take time from their assignments to tell you what they
have done in expediting your work.

You have indicated to me that you would take an earlier bus so that you
would arrive on time. However, you apparently have not done this.

This memo should be considered a written warning regarding your tardi-
ness. If you are late again during the next four weeks, you will be subject to
disciplinary action. We will meet one month from today to review your
attendance record.
```

Figure 9.2 *Formal Documentation*

2. In creating effective associate relations, managers use five types of power: reward, coercive, legitimate, referent, and expert. Reward power and expert power have proven to be the most useful.

3. In addition to providing effective counseling to associates, many hospitality organizations also have employee assistance programs (EAPs). An EAP is designed to help associates deal with both personal and work-related problems. One of the areas EAPs are helpful in addressing is that of associate substance abuse. There are many such types of programs, but they always begin with the organization developing a written policy and then getting everyone involved in the effort to create a drug-free workplace. Child-care programs, which are also becoming increasingly popular, come in many different forms. The three main approaches are: (a) offering services, (b) supplying information, and (c) providing financial support.

4. Discipline is any action designed to correct associate deviations from organizational rules, procedures, policies, and norms. There are two basic

types of discipline: negative and positive. Effective organizations use positive discipline because of its long-range benefits. They also administer discipline in a fair and logical way, including developing specific rules and regulations, communicating them to everyone, enforcing them consistently, taking individual circumstances into account where necessary, and employing progressive steps of disciplinary action. Today management's right to discipline has been limited by the courts but, in the main, employment at will is still a very viable concept. Hospitality organizations have the right to dismiss associates for poor performance or violations of rules and regulations.

KEY TERMS

developmental feedback	negative discipline
power	positive discipline
reward power	progressive discipline
coercive power	corrective discipline
legitimate power	employment at will
referent power	tort
expert power	contract
employee assistance program	anecdotal documentation
discipline	formal documentation

REVIEW AND APPLICATION QUESTIONS

1. When and how would a manager use developmental feedback? Why is this form of feedback particularly useful in developing effective associate relations?

2. Research shows that the most effective managers use reward power and expert power the most and coercive power the least. Why is this so? Be sure to define and discuss all three types of power in your answer.

3. The Landover Grand Hotel would like to establish an employee assistance program for dealing with drug abuse. What steps would you recommend to them in developing this program? Additionally, what would be the benefits of having an external, rather than internal, program? Be complete in your answer.

4. A major cruise line is in the process of creating a child-care program for its associates. In particular, the company would like to provide financial assistance to those who want this program. What types of assistance can the cruise line offer? Identify and describe two types.

5. What are two examples of situations where a hospitality organization cannot fire an associate, even if management would like to do so? In each case, explain why the individual cannot be fired.

6. Despite legal limitations, the doctrine of employment at will is still alive and well. What does this statement mean? How much authority does management have to dismiss associates? Are there any guidelines the organization should follow in doing this? Explain.

SELF-FEEDBACK EXERCISE: WHAT TYPE OF POWER DO YOU PREFER TO USE?

Read each of the following situations and decide what you would do in each case by placing a 5 next to the action you would most likely follow, a 4 next to your second favorite choice, and so on, down to a 1 next to your least favorite choice. Then enter your answers on the answer sheet and total the columns. An interpretation of the exercise is provided at the end.

1. Someone from your department has to be transferred to the company's hotel in Buffalo. You know that no one wants this assignment, but since it must be done, you are determined to send the best-qualified associate, Janet Franz. You know that Janet is going to object to the assignment, but you are determined to stick to your guns. Indicate your order of preference for each of the following approaches to this problem.

_____ a. Remind Janet that this new job pays 20 percent more than she is currently making and could be an important step in her promotion to higher-level management.

_____ b. Point out that you have analyzed the abilities, talents, and performance evaluations of all the associates, and that you feel she is best qualified for the job.

_____ c. Tell her that if she does not take the job, her future career in the hotel chain could be in jeopardy.

_____ d. Remind her that you have always given her good advice in the past, and then recommend that she take this appointment.

_____ e. Point out that as the manager it is your job to make these decisions, and this is your decision.

2. The hotel at which you are working opened last week and has been inundated with business. Revenues are likely to be 40 percent greater than forecasts. Unfortunately, there is not yet sufficient staff on hand to take care of this unexpected business, and you are having to assign people to work one

extra day every two weeks for the foreseeable future. This week will be Bill Harper's turn, and you know he is not going to be pleased with the news because he wants to spend more time with his family. Indicate your order of preference for each of the following approaches to this problem.

_____ **a.** Tell Bill that these assignments are part of the job, and if he does not like it he can secure employment elsewhere.

_____ **b.** Tell Bill that your job is to make staffing decisions, and you have just done so.

_____ **c.** Point out to Bill that these extra work assignments are a result of unexpected business that will result in more financial opportunities for him.

_____ **d.** Explain that you have examined the situation carefully and this is the only way to handle the situation, at least until you are able to hire more people.

_____ **e.** Remind Bill that you would never ask him to work extra if there other ways of resolving the problem.

3. The district manager is going to be in your office a week from today. You would like to present a special report designed to inform her about how well your unit is doing. The best qualified person for writing and presenting this report is Harry Wondell. What approach would you use in getting Harry to write the report?

_____ **a.** Tell Harry that you are delegating this job to him and ask him to have the report ready to discuss with you in five days.

_____ **b.** Remind Harry that you have often made these types of presentations and that they were important in helping you get where you are today.

_____ **c.** Tell Harry precisely what you would like him to present to the district manager, review the data with him, and then ask him to give you a preliminary presentation the day before the district manager arrives so you can offer any suggestions for improvement.

_____ **d.** Tell Harry when you want the report ready, and point out that if the presentation is not effective it could be bad for his career.

_____ **e.** Explain to Harry what needs to be done, thank him for his help, and tell him that you will write a special memo acknowledging his contribution and put it in his personnel file.

4. You need extra funding for equipment in your department. If you get it, you will be able to increase work output by 15 percent. However, your boss has very little discretionary money and will be reluctant to buy this equipment. How would you go about persuading him to do so?

_____ a. Remind him that you have built a reputation as a highly productive manager, and this purchase is a wise one.

_____ b. Focus your presentation on the fact that senior-level managers like him who are unable to achieve productivity increases are being let go.

_____ c. Remind your boss that you were hired to increase departmental productivity, and this request is directly in line with the authority that has been delegated to you.

_____ d. Point out that if your unit's productivity goes up, the boss's chances for promotion will also rise.

_____ e. Explain that you have examined a wide variety of ways to increase productivity, and this is the most efficient of all.

5. You want Roberta Garcia to apply for a company-sponsored training program. You have not yet talked to her about it, but you believe that it will be good for her career. How would you go about selling her on the idea?

_____ a. Explain that you have evaluated her performance and believe that this training will be helpful to her in carrying out her assignments.

_____ b. Remind her that promotion out of her current position requires additional training such as the program you are recommending.

_____ c. Point out that you would never recommend training that you yourself have not had.

_____ d. Note that you are required to choose people periodically for these training programs, and you have chosen her.

_____ e. Tell her that if she does not take this training, she is likely to be laid off the next time the company has a cutback.

Scoring: Transfer your answers to the following answer sheet by placing the number for each choice next to the appropriate letter. For example, if you placed a 5 next to choice "a" in situation 1, put a 5 next to the "a" in Column I. If you placed a 3 next to choice "b" in situation 1, put a 3 next to the "b" in Column II. After you have entered all of your answers to situation 1, go on to situation 2, and so on. In each case, your row should contain a 5, a 4, a 3, a 2, and a 1. When you finish entering all of your answers, add each of the five columns.

	Column I	Column II	Column III	Column IV	Column V
Situation 1	_____ a.	_____ b.	_____ c.	_____ d.	_____ e.
Situation 2	_____ c.	_____ d.	_____ a.	_____ e.	_____ b.
Situation 3	_____ e.	_____ c.	_____ d.	_____ b.	_____ a.
Situation 4	_____ d.	_____ e.	_____ b.	_____ a.	_____ c.
Situation 5	_____ b.	_____ a.	_____ e.	_____ c.	_____ d.
Total	_____	_____	_____	_____	_____
	Reward	Expert	Coercive	Referent	Legitimate

Interpretation: Column I indicates your use of reward power. Columns II through V represent expert, coercive, referent, and legitimate power, respectively. The higher the column number, the greater your preference for that particular type of power. Research shows that the most effective managers use reward power and expert power the most and coercive power the least. Referent and legitimate power are of moderate importance. What do your answers reveal about your use of power?

CASE 9.1: SOMETHING HAS TO BE DONE

The Royale Excelsior Hotel is the largest hotel in a major southwestern city. In recent years the Excelsior has found itself facing growing competition from new hotels that, while smaller, have managed to carefully target both the tourist and the convention business. As a result, the Excelsior's revenues have slowly begun to decline. The manager of the Excelsior, Eleanor Robbins, has promised the board of directors that this situation will be turned around. Eleanor began with an analysis of operations. To her dismay, she has learned that turnover and absenteeism at the hotel are much higher than she realized. Many associates come to work late, and in some cases do not show up at all. When Eleanor pressed her staff as to why these behaviors were not corrected, she learned that substance abuse among the associates is a growing problem and the staff does not know how to deal with it. She also learned that 25 percent of the associates are married with young children, and these family responsibilities take up a large amount of their time.

After conferring with the director of the human resources management (HRM) department, Eleanor has decided to undertake a two-pronged strategy. First, consideration will be given to creating an employee assistance program (EAP) to deal with substance abuse. There are a number of steps that must be taken before this program can be implemented, but Eleanor is determined to create a plan of action within the next 60 days and have substantive progress made toward implementation within 120 days. In particular, she wants to know what will be involved in creating an EAP and how much all of this will cost. For this reason, she has put together a committee that is headed by the director of HRM.

Second, Eleanor has created a second committee to identify the types of child-care needs that the associates have and to find out the various kinds of services that are available for meeting these needs. The chairperson for this committee is a woman with two small children who has been working for the Excelsior for seven years. Eleanor would like the committee to gather all of the needed information and submit its report within 60 days. In particular, the manager wants to know the various options that are feasible and to determine the cost of implementing each.

In order to ensure that progress is made on both of these programs, Eleanor has been meeting with each group on a weekly basis, and has been in close touch with the chairman of the board of directors. She recently told the chairman, "I'm glad we carried out that analysis of operations. It brought to light a lot of things I didn't know about. However, I think there is still time to correct these problems and create even more effective associate relations. The important thing we have to keep in mind is that we cannot overlook these problems. Something has to be done about them—and soon! I'll be able to tell you more when I get the reports from the committees."

1. If the hotel decides to create an EAP, what is the first step it should take?

2. In addition to the preceding step, what are six other steps that the hotel will have to take in order to create an effective EAP? Identify and briefly describe each.

3. Is the creation of a child-care program likely to be a productive idea? Why or why not?

CASE 9.2: MATTERS OF DISCIPLINE

It seems to David Wanright that things at his company's restaurant units are not going very well. In the past 90 days the company has dismissed nine associates; there are four more against whom disciplinary action is pending. This has not been good news for the company's senior-level management and they have asked David to look into what is going on. "The last thing we want is to end up in a lawsuit by some disgruntled associate who is suing us for wrongful dismissal," David's boss told him. "On the other hand, if associates break the rules, then we have to enforce discipline fairly and firmly. So go talk to the managers in the units where there is disciplinary action pending and find out what you can about those four cases."

David spent the last six days talking to the managers and associates who are involved in the pending disciplinary cases. He has taken this information and condensed it to two sentences per situation. On the basis of these facts, which neither side disputes, he is going to recommend that the action either be pursued against the associate or dropped. Here is what he learned about each of the four cases:

Case 1: Margaret Connelly has had a history of tardiness; over the last six months she has been late a total of 24 times. The company's policy is that anyone who is late five times in one month will be dismissed and Margaret has been late five times in the last three weeks.

Case 2: George Simpson, a parking valet, went to a birthday party and had a couple of drinks before reporting for work. While parking one of the cars, George had an accident that resulted in $2,400 damage to a guest's vehicle.

Case 3: Kim Fong works in the maintenance department and was assigned the job of rewiring a sophisticated electronic panel. Kim told his boss that he lacked the necessary equipment for doing this type of work and that without such equipment the job could prove extremely hazardous; so he refused to do it.

Case 4: Maria Suarez had an accident in the kitchen. She failed to follow one of the basic safety rules and, as a result, a large amount of damage was done to the kitchen.

1. If you were advising David, how would you recommend that each of the four cases be resolved? In each case, explain your answer.

2. In those cases where associates are to be dismissed, how would you recommend that the organization handle the matter?

3. In ensuring that there is not a continual repeat of discipline-related problems, what guidelines would you recommend that the restaurant follow? Describe each.

ANSWERS TO BOX 9.1: "ALCOHOLICS: WHAT DO YOU KNOW ABOUT THEM?"

1. True.
2. True.
3. False. Approximately 50 percent are women.
4. True.
5. False. Around 45 percent are professional or managerial personnel.
6. False. Around 50 percent have completed or attended college.

7. False. Most alcoholics rarely miss work. Unless they are in an advanced stage of the disease, they show up regularly.
8. False. Most alcoholics schedule their drinking for weekends and after work.
9. False. Alcoholism can occur at any age; many alcoholics are under the age of 30.
10. False. Many alcoholics have challenging upper-level jobs that carry a great deal of responsibility.
11. False. There is no relationship between intelligence and alcoholism.
12. False. Alcoholics often keep their drinking secret from associates and employers.

ANSWERS TO BOX 9.2: "WHAT DO YOU THINK?"

The following answers are based on court decisions in recent years.
1. Associate. The courts have held that rules must be consistently and uniformly applied. If there is a select enforcement of them, the individuals who are negatively affected are entitled to restitution. Of course, if the company announces to all of its associates that in the future the rule will be enforced uniformly and proceeds to do so, then those who break the rule in the future can be dismissed.
2. Associate. The courts have consistently held that if only women are fired (or any other select group), this constitutes discrimination by the organization.
3. Associate. The courts have held that if someone is in fear for his or her safety, the organization must allay these fears or assign the work to someone else. Associates cannot be required to perform tasks that they truly believe can result in personal injury.
4. Associate. The courts have ruled that if an individual asks for union representation, this request must be granted in order to ensure that the individual is accorded fair treatment.
5. Organization. If the procedures for dismissal are clearly spelled out in writing, provide for warnings prior to dismissal, and do not discriminate against any particular group, the company is justified in sticking to its guns and terminating those associates who fail to adjust their behavior after the predetermined number of warnings.
6. Organization. The company has a right to set a no-smoking rule and enforce it.
7. Organization. The company has a right to establish rules of business conduct toward customers and enforce them.
8. Associate. The courts have held that failure to enforce rules can affect associates' view of their importance and result in confusion regarding their implementation. On the other hand, if the company had vigorously enforced these rules all along and dismissed Chuck the first time he violated one of them, then it could continue to dismiss individuals who failed to follow procedures.

ENDNOTES

1. For more on this, see Thomas K. Connellan and Ron Zemke, *Sustaining Knock Your Socks Off Service* (New York: AMACOM, 1993), pp. 161–167.
2. Vincent H. Eade, "Drug Abuse in the Hospitality Industry," *FIU Hospitality Review,* Fall 1993, p. 81.
3. Ibid., pp. 81–86.
4. "Choosing an EAP," *St. Louis Business Journal,* May 3–9, 1993, p. 18C.
5. James Peters, "How to Set Up an Employee Assistance Program," *Restaurant Business,* October 10, 1988, p. 90.
6. Ibid., p. 99.
7. Karen Cheney, "Deal a Blow to Drug Use," *Restaurants & Institutions,* March 15, 1995, pp. 121–126.
8. For example, see Margaret Coshan, "An EAP Can Be Part of the Solution," *Canadian Business Review,* Summer 1992, pp. 22–24.
9. Richard M. Hodgetts, *Modern Human Relations at Work,* 6th ed. (Fort Worth: Dryden Press, 1996), p. 391.
10. Janet H. Marler and Cathy A. Enz, "Child Care Programs That Make Sense," *Cornell Hotel and Restaurant Association Quarterly,* February 1993, p. 61.
11. Kathy Seal, "Child-Care Centers Finding Their Place in the Lodging Industry," *Hotel and Motel Management,* December 17, 1990, p. 1.
12. Ibid., p. 66.
13. Joseph Seltzer, "Discipline with a Clear Sense of Purpose," *Management Solutions,* February 1987, pp. 32–37.
14. See, for example, Daniel M. Shideler, "Documenting Disciplinary Situations," *Supervisory Management,* July 1989, pp. 15–20.
15. This information can be found in Keith Warren, "Progressive Discipline," *Hospitality Human Resources,* May 1995, p. 5.
16. Richard M. Hodgetts and K. Galen Kroeck, *Personnel and Human Resources Management* (Fort Worth: Dryden Press, 1992), p. 427.
17. Deborah L. Jacobs, "Getting Mad, Then Getting Even," *New York Times,* July 1, 1990, Section F, p. 21; William E. Fulmer and Ann Wallace Casey, "Employment-at-Will: Options for Managers," *Academy of Management Executive,* May 1990, p. 102; Angelo J. Genova, "Personal Liability for an Employment Termination," *Management Solutions,* December 1988, pp. 26–28; and Julius Steiner, "Good Supervision: The Best Defense against Wrongful Discharge Claims," *Management Solutions,* July 1988, pp. 28–31.

Understanding Customers

This part of the book focuses on the customer (or guest) and helps explain the link between the associate, which was the focus of Part II, and the HRM process, which was the focus of Part III. If you have the personality and interest to be a hospitality associate, and you have been properly trained and motivated, then you are in a position to apply your skills and knowledge in the workplace. The four chapters in this part will help explain how this is being done in effectively running hospitality organizations.

Chapter 10 examines how customer needs are identified and addressed. In this chapter, particular attention is given to the importance of providing quality service and the costs associated with failing to do so. Consideration is also given to the importance of first impressions as well as to the five dimensions of service: personal reliability, tangibles, responsiveness, assurance, and empathy. Each of these five is defined and described in length. The last part of the chapter examines how organizations effectively handle complaints by learning to size up the situation and take the necessary action.

Chapter 11 examines the international customer, an individual who is becoming increasingly important in the industry. And because these customers come from many different countries, it is important to have a basic understanding of the nature of culture. This topic is covered in the first part of Chapter 11. Then the five most important cultural dimensions—power distance, individualism, masculinity, uncertainty avoidance, and time orientation—are examined in detail. In the process, you will learn that there are a great many international differences because of culture. The last part of the chapter looks at ways of doing business in three selected countries: China, India, and France. At this point, you will learn some of the "dos and don'ts" of doing business in these cultures, and see that what works well in one country often has little or no value in another. The specific culture of each nation must be studied so that the needs of the customers are directly addressed.

The focus of Chapter 12 is on developing outstanding service. In addition to discussing the three laws of service, the first half of the chapter addresses the behavioral ABCs of service. In this chapter you will learn how organizations focus their service quality strategy by niching their market and using value-added services such as unconditional guarantees. The last part of the chapter examines how firms ensure that they stay on track through the use of effective service recovery and the empowerment of associates.

Chapter 13 examines some of the ways that hospitality firms are now working to maintain their total quality service initiatives. The service paradigm is changing, and what was competitive service a few years ago is now passé. Organizations need to focus on developing and retaining quality associates and reducing the costs associated with improved service. Some of the strategies used in this process are discussed in the chapter, including cost analysis, cause-and-effect diagrams, flow-charting, and cross-training. Attention is also given to empowerment, a topic examined in Chapter 12, but this time the focus is more detailed. In the last part of the chapter, you will learn how organizations obtain feedback on the results of their total quality service efforts and how they use this information to measure progress. You will also become familiar with the tests for effective rewards and the ways that companies are now rewarding their associates for providing total quality service.

When you are finished studying all of the material in this part of the book, you will understand how hospitality firms are now focusing their efforts on the guest and doing everything they can to not just meet the individual's needs but go beyond—thus creating what is popularly called customer delight! You will also understand your role and that of human resource management activities in helping create and sustain outstanding levels of customer service.

CHAPTER TEN

Identifying and Addressing Customer Needs

LEARNING OBJECTIVES

In the hospitality industry, service is the key to success; this success is a result of how well the customer feels his or her needs are being met. The overriding objective of this chapter is to examine some of the major ways that hospitality organizations go about identifying and addressing customer needs. There are a number of critical parts in this process, beginning with the careful formulation of a service philosophy or credo and concluding with the delivery of a service that is perceived by the customer to at least meet minimum expectations. The first part of this chapter will address some of the ways that organizations create the "right" service philosophy. Then attention will be directed to dealing with pitfalls to outstanding service. The second part of the chapter will look at what customers want and how the five dimensions of service can ensure customer satisfaction. The last part of the chapter is devoted to ways of effectively handling complaints. When you have finished studying all of the material in this chapter, you will be able to:

1. Relate the role and importance of creating the right customer service strategy.

2. Compute the financial cost associated with providing poor service.

3. Explain the five dimensions of effective customer service and show how each can be achieved.

4. Take proper action in dealing with disgruntled customers.

Meeting the Quality Challenges

Competition in the hospitality industry has increased significantly in recent years. Today there are hotels and restaurants for every pocketbook, and if customers do not like the way they are being treated, they have the luxury of going elsewhere. Moreover, lost customers cost the company money. In ensuring that this does not happen, customer service has become a critical issue. Figure 10.1 illustrates this idea by showing how, over time, the amount of market share captured by offering unique product features begins to decline, while the share captured by customer service continues to increase. The logic is fairly straightforward. Firms in the hospitality industry that provide unique offerings find that the competition soon copies their approach. As a result, these offerings are expected by the customer and become "generic." For example, in the 1980s some major hotels started to offer cable television, pay-per-view movies, king-size beds, minibars, and smoke-free accommodations. Today, all major hotels offer these features. And business travelers, who are one of the most profitable segments of the hotel business, are far more demanding. A recent sample survey of these individuals asked them to list those amenities that they regarded as minimum in order for a hotel to increase its share of the corporate market segment. Their responses included (1) an "office-friendly" guest room, (2) an up-to-date business center, (3) a health club, (4) a lounge for breakfast and refreshments, (5) a special check-in desk, and (6) a casual restaurant and optional sports bar.[1] Today most hotels that cater to the business market offer these features. So it is no longer possible for hotels to differentiate themselves on product offerings over the long run. The only way to excel is by providing customer service that is tailored to the specific demands of the clientele. This is the key to success.

At the same time, hospitality organizations know that it is not enough to simply get a customer's business; getting the client to come back again and again for repeat business is the key to a profitable enterprise.[2] This presents firms with a quality challenge: How can they provide the best products and services at the most attractive prices? The best-run firms are meeting this challenge in a number of ways. One is by creating the right philosophy to guide the associates.

Create the Right Philosophy

Quality begins with the associates. Every individual who works for a hospitality organization must understand the values, beliefs, and overriding objectives of the enterprise. In this way, everyone is working from the same set of beliefs. One way in which this is done is by creating mission statements or guiding philosophies and then disseminating these to the associates so that

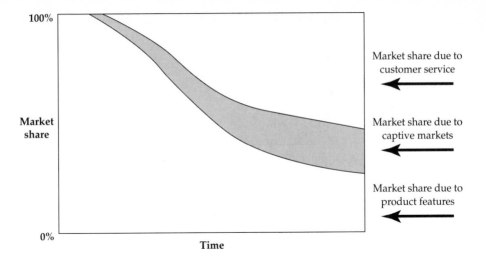

Figure 10.1 *How the Three Major Factors Contribute to Market Share*

Source: Reported in Joan Koob Cannie and Donald Caplin, *Keeping Customers for Life* (New York: AMACOM, 1991), p. 43.

everyone understands what is expected of them. At Radisson Hotels, for example, all associates learn the organization's service goal and strategy.

Customer service goal: To win our customers' future business and loyalty.

Customer service strategy: To create opportunities to delight customers by anticipating their needs and exceeding their expectations.

At the Ritz-Carlton, the company has stated its credo in three sentences and then distributed this credo on a card that all associates carry with them. It reads:

The Ritz-Carlton Hotel is a place where the genuine care and comfort of our guests is our highest mission.

We pledge to provide the finest personal service and facilities for our guests who will always enjoy a warm, relaxed yet refined ambience. The Ritz-Carlton experience enlivens the senses, instills well-being, and fulfills even the unexpressed wishes and needs of our guests.

At Red Lobster the company states its philosophy in six words:

The guest is our first priority.

These service-driven statements are often very general, but this is particularly helpful in ensuring that associates remember the main idea, which is then made operational by teaching the associates how to implement the philosophy. For example, at the Ritz-Carlton, associates are taught to follow the organization's three steps of service:

A warm and sincere greeting. Use the guest's name, if and when possible.

Anticipation and compliance with guest needs.

Fond farewell. Give them a warm good-bye and use their names, if and when possible.

At Red Lobster, four rules support the organization's customer service philosophy:

1. *No food waits.* All food is walked immediately by whoever is in the alley to any table in the restaurant.

2. *If you're not proud of it, don't serve it.* If the food is cold, the presentation is poor, or the drink has not been properly poured, it is not brought to the table.

3. *You make it right.* If a food or drink is not properly prepared, the server will ask that it be redone. If items are over/underportioned or improperly prepared, the individual will take action to fix it before bringing the order to the guests.

4. *Teamwork—smiling, friendly service.* Together all associates create a place and an experience that encourages the guest to keep coming back by working as a team, depending on each other, giving guests a dining experience that exceeds their expectations, and undertaking a commitment to doing what it takes to deliver for each guest.[3]

Many other well-run hospitality organizations follow the same pattern by carefully and simply spelling out what they expect associates to do in order to deliver quality service. At the Sheraton Hotels, there is a four-step guest satisfaction system:

1. Every time you see a guest, smile and offer an appropriate hospitality comment.

2. Speak to every guest in a friendly, enthusiastic, and courteous tone and manner.

3. Answer guest questions and requests quickly and efficiently, or take personal responsibility to get the answer.

4. Anticipate guest needs and resolve guest problems.

Determine the Cost of Poor Service

A second important step in meeting the quality challenge is to answer the question: How much does it cost our organization when we fail to provide

Table 10.1 Calculating the Cost of Poor Service for a Hospitality Organization

Lost Revenue	Cost to the Organization
1. Amount that the average customer spends in one year	_____
2. Number of customers lost each year	_____
3. Revenue from lost customers (#1 × #2)	_____
4. Lost revenue from potential customers who are dissuaded from doing business with the organization because of the poor experience of others (#3 × 10)	_____
Other Costs	
5. Time spent redoing things that were done incorrectly the first time	_____
6. Time spent apologizing to customers	_____
7. Telephone and mailing costs associated with apologizing and/or explaining things to customers	_____
8. Cost of liability insurance	_____
9. Legal costs	_____
10. Cost of collections from customers who refuse to pay	_____
Total costs (#3 through #10)	_____

good service? Research shows that the cost of losing a customer can be extremely high, while the profit associated with keeping a customer can be extremely rewarding. Table 10.1 provides a worksheet for determining how much it costs a hospitality organization every time it loses a customer.[4] Notice that the fourth entry under "Lost Revenue" measures how much money is lost because disgruntled customers talk to others about their bad experiences and the latter, in turn, do not do business with the organization. Research reveals that a customer who receives bad service is likely to talk to ten others about this negative experience. So a dissatisfied customer often costs the hotel or restaurant much more than the revenue that the individual would have spent there in the future. The customer has an impact on others as well.

Deal with the Pitfalls to Outstanding Service

There are a number of reasons why hospitality organizations fail to provide outstanding service. One or two of these alone can create problems. Unfortunately, many enterprises face far more of them and fail to make the necessary adjustments. The following sections examine two major categories that account for many of the most common pitfalls to outstanding service.

Inflexible Policies and Rules. One of the major reasons for poor service is company policies and rules. These are often established to promote efficiency, but end up hurting customer service.

> When Margaret Beadle and her two young children checked into the Oceanside Hotel, it was almost 10 P.M. They had driven over 400 miles that day and had encountered bad weather most of the way. Since they had wanted to get to the hotel as quickly as possible, they had not stopped for dinner. As they were checking in, Margaret asked, "What time does your dining room close?" The associate replied, "We stop serving at 9:30 P.M. and close at 10 P.M. I'm afraid you're too late, but there is a restaurant four miles down the highway, and they are open until 11 P.M." Because of the lateness of the hour and her unwillingness to get back on the road, Margaret bought the children some snacks from the hotel's vending machines to tide them over until morning. Over the past five years, she and the children have come through this area on a number of occasions, but they never stay at the Oceanside anymore.

What did the hotel do wrong? It closed the restaurant when there were guests who wanted to eat. What could the associate at the check-in desk have done? He should have contacted the restaurant associates and asked if they could fix something for Margaret and her children. Perhaps they would have been content with sandwiches and milk. However, the front-desk associate allowed policies and rules to dictate customer service.

The preceding story also reinforces two related pitfalls to customer service. One is excessive job specialization, in which everyone has a specific job and each individual does no more than this job requires of him or her. The associate at the front desk did not call the restaurant and serve as a liaison for the customer; he remained within the job description. The other pitfall is a failure to coordinate the service process. Associates need to act as a team and collectively work to provide service. This was not done in the case of Margaret Beadle.

Another pitfall related to policies and rules is the failure to give sufficient authority to the associates so that they can resolve customer problems. For example, the associate at the front desk may not have called the restaurant because he knew that those associates had no authority to stay open past 10 P.M. Everyone goes off the payroll at this time; so if someone did remain, the individual would be working off the clock. This highlights a major problem in many organizations: policies and rules are designed to give top priority to cost containment and not to customer satisfaction.

Lack of Associate Motivation. Closely linked to inflexible rules is a lack of motivation on the part of the associates. There are a number of reasons for this. One of the most common is that the associates have not been well trained, so they do not know how to respond appropriately to customer needs. For example, because many of them are poor listeners, they tolerate negative comments from customers but do not address them. The associates believe that if they let the customer vent his or her frustration or anger, the person will feel better and the problem will be resolved. They fail to realize that their most important objective should be to resolve the matter to the customer's satisfaction; this typically means taking some direct action. A second, and related, pitfall is that associates do not know how to solve problems creatively. They have not learned how to generate solutions that will delight the customer. Effectively run organizations sidestep such problems by developing programs that teach their associates what to do and how to do it.

> At the Ritz-Carlton, for example, every new hire attends a specially designed orientation program about the company's philosophy and operations. Customer service is a key focus of attention. As a result, when a guest asks for directions to a particular place in the hotel, employees stop whatever they are doing and personally escort the individual there. Employees are also trained to remember the names of guests, so they can address them directly when they pass them in the hallway or are approached by them for assistance. In addition, employees are trained in teamwork and problem solving, so they can work together to identify ways of further improving customer services, such as reducing cycle time in the restaurant and at the front desk, and decreasing the time needed to bring a guest's car from the garage to the front door. The result is a five-star status for the hotel chain.[5]

Another pitfall occurs when the associates are powerless to make changes because they have no authority and no financial resources. For example, Sandra Sanchez, the night manager, may feel that Margaret Beadle and her family should be given a free breakfast in the morning. However, if Sandra is not empowered to make this decision, there is no opportunity for the hotel to recover and win back Margaret's loyalty. This problem can be addressed in a number of ways. One of the most common is to allocate to each associate a sum of money that can be used for helping improve customer service.

> At the Ritz-Carlton hotel chain, employees are authorized to spend up to $2,000 to handle a problem. This amount is usually more than sufficient for such common solutions as mailing a shirt to a guest who accidentally left it in his or her room and then checked out, or bringing a guest with a cold a pot of herbal tea and some aspirin.[6]

Find Out What Customers Want

The most effective way to meet the quality challenge is to determine what customers want—and then give it to them. This can be done in a number of ways. One is by getting feedback regarding buyer preferences and then using this information to tailor the service delivery. For example, what do restaurant guests want? Research shows that there are gender preferences. Before continuing, take the quiz in Box 10.1 and see how well you are able to identify what male and female diners prefer.

Identify Your Customers

From the quiz in Box 10.1, it is obvious that customers can fall into different groupings; the way to cater to one group may be different from that of another. And in the restaurant business, there are other customer groups besides men and women. Today, many eating establishments are catering to a third consumer group: children. At the Fairmont Hotel in San Jose, California, for example, local schoolchildren have helped design the new kids' menu, which features such creations as a "Mega Byte" cinnamon roll and a "Spaghetti Arena" topped with "hockey puck meatballs."[7] At Rockwell's, a three-unit chain in Westchester County, New York, there is free, on-site baby-sitting service from 5 P.M. to 9 P.M. Monday through Wednesday. The restaurant ropes off a section of the dining room, loads the area with toys and games, and supervises the children while their families eat in the main dining room. At The Italian Oven in Latrobe, Pennsylvania, the restaurant gives out pasta-necklace kits, education games, and butcher-paper tablecloths that are ripe for coloring, in addition to free baby food. And Fuddruckers, the nationally known hamburger chain, has a "Kids Eat Free" policy, which offers a free children's meal for every adult meal purchased from 4 P.M. to 10 P.M. Monday through Thursday. There are a number of reasons why restaurants are targeting this group, including the fact that a National Restaurant Association/Gallup poll reveals that children have a substantial influence on where the family dines. Quite clearly, restaurants regard children as an important customer group.

There is one other major customer group, however, that also merits attention—associates. The individuals who work in the organization are internal customers who cannot be ignored in the service equation. How can each associate identify his or her internal customers? It is really quite simple. All the associate has to do is answer the question: Who receives or is affected by my work? Everybody in the organization has internal customers who depend on them for output. The servers depend on the cooks to provide the food, and on the busboys to clean the tables and get them ready for the next group of guests. The reservations clerks depend on the housekeeping associates to clean the rooms and get them ready for the guests. By following the flow of

Box 10.1
Catering to the Customer

Some businesses are organized to appeal to specific customer groups. For example, department stores have men's, women's, and children's departments, and displays, decor, and offerings are designed to target these market niches. In the hospitality industry, this is often more difficult to do. Restaurants are a good example. When a person comes to an eating establishment, he or she orders from the same menu as all other diners. There are no "his" or "hers" offerings, although there may be a children's menu. At the same time, men and women have distinct food preferences and an understanding of these gender differences can help eating establishments better cater to their customers. Here are a dozen brief descriptions of male and female diners. Six of these statements describe male patrons; the other six describe female diners. Place an *M* next to those that you feel are more descriptive of men and a *W* next to those that you think best describe women.

_____ 1. Confirmed meat lovers.

_____ 2. Highly concerned with nutrition.

_____ 3. Confirmed fruit lovers.

_____ 4. Regard taste as more important than nutrition.

_____ 5. Apt to eat out less often, and when they do, they are value-conscious.

_____ 6. Less likely to snack, so they eat more at a sitting.

_____ 7. Enjoy eating foods they first encountered as children.

_____ 8. More adventurous in their food choices.

_____ 9. Tend to snack and have a sweet tooth.

_____ 10. More likely to want entrées than desserts.

_____ 11. Are likely to eat smaller portions.

_____ 12. More frequent restaurant patrons.

Check your answers with the key at the end of the chapter.

this logic, it becomes evident that everyone in the organization depends on one or more people to help them carry out their job. If this is done well, internal efficiency increases and customer service is high. If there is a breakdown, internal efficiency declines and there is customer dissatisfaction. This is why many organizations today are now focusing increased attention on training and motivating their associates. They believe that if the staff do their jobs, customers will like the service and return year after year. This is why, when selecting associates, many major hotels begin by looking for people with the right attitude; this helps create an initial and effective first impression.

Create a Good First Impression

The president of the world-renowned Broadmoor Resort in Colorado Springs recently commented, "We select people on attitude first, experience second. I'd rather run short-staffed with the right people."[8] Simply put, a good first impression is critical in the hospitality business, because it sets the stage for everything that follows. Moreover, first impressions are typically made *within 30 seconds* of the time that the customer and the associate meet. If everything goes well at this stage, customers are likely to have a positive attitude and look forward to an enjoyable experience. If, however, things do not go well, even a minor problem may be the basis for the customer deciding not to come back again. Red Lobster has carefully analyzed the best way to make a good initial impression and insists that its people follow these three pointers:

1. Greet guests as quickly as possible, (*hello, good evening, etc.*). No one, especially not a hungry person, likes to be ignored. Don't allow guests to remain unattended for more than one minute.

2. Posture and the way you carry yourself are what guests notice first. Good posture communicates a message of self-confidence.

3. The tone of your voice sends a very powerful message to guests. The tone of your greeting should be warm and your message welcoming.[9]

These guidelines are designed to make guests feel that they are important and that the server is happy and eager to help them enjoy their visit to the restaurant.

Address the Five Dimensions of Service

In providing outstanding service, there are five dimensions that warrant consideration: personal reliability, tangibles, responsiveness, assurance, and empathy.[10] Figure 10.2 illustrates these ideas.

Personal Reliability. Personal reliability is the ability to provide dependable and accurate service. Quite often, this can be explained with the statement, "no excuses."[11] Reliability means that the organization does what it is supposed to do, it does it right, and it does it right the first time. Keeping this idea in mind, consider the following situation:

> Richard Kilbourne is a middle manager in a well-known international company. Last week, a group of senior-level managers from headquarters came to town to discuss the current operations and future plans of Richard's subsidiary. The group met for three days in a con-

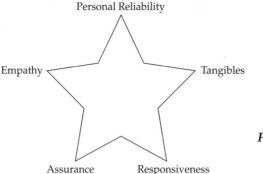

Figure 10.2 *The Five Star Dimensions of Service*

ference room at a nearby hotel. Richard's job was to present a five-minute videotape showing the jet-mold process that was now being used to make engine parts for the North American market and to present a ten-minute financial forecast showing sales growth over the next three years. The hotel's meeting planner had met with Richard and noted that Richard would need a VCR and monitor for the videotape and an overhead projector and screen for presenting the financial forecast material. However, when Richard arrived fifteen minutes before his presentation, there was no equipment in the room. Realizing that he had very little time, Richard quickly located the meeting planner and learned that there had been an error in allocating the equipment and that all of it was in use. "There's nothing we can do," he told Richard, "except make copies of your materials and hand them out to the participants." Feeling that this was the best alternative, Richard agreed and used these handouts to support his talk and to answer questions. After the presentation, his boss told him, "You did a very good job. However, it would have been more physically attractive and effective if you had shown the film and used an overhead to present your color transparencies. I thought we agreed that this is what you were going to do."

What went wrong? The meeting planner failed to follow up properly and correct the problem. Even if all the equipment were in use, the individual should have had a backup plan, either to immediately rent whatever was needed or to find out how long Richard needed the equipment and see who could have shared it with him. Perhaps one of the other meeting groups could have spared their VCR and overhead projector for 30 minutes. The individual was not personally reliable.

Tangibles. *Tangibles* are the physical appearances of the facilities, equipment, associates, and communication materials. Richard's boss noted that the presentation would have been more effective had he used the VCR and overhead color transparencies. Undoubtedly this method would have been more appealing and would have done a better job of driving home the points that Richard wanted to make. Because the meeting planner failed to get the equipment to the room, Richard's presentation lacked the tangibles that could have improved his overall performance. The managers at the meeting may not have realized how much better it would have been if the equipment had been there, but Richard's boss (who undoubtedly reviewed the presentation with him and had seen the video and transparencies) was able to tell the difference.

Responsiveness. Responsiveness is the willingness to help customers and to provide prompt service. In this case, the meeting planner did neither; the individual was totally unresponsive. The person told Richard, "There is nothing we can do . . . ." What the individual meant was that there was nothing he intended to do. There apparently was no backup plan for this type of eventuality and the planner did not intend to improvise on the spot. Simply put, the person was unresponsive.

Assurance. Assurance is the knowledge and courtesy of associates and their ability to convey trust and confidence. If the meeting planner had wanted to provide assurance, he would have had a backup plan and conveyed this line of action in positive and decisive terms. For example, if he had already determined that there was no way in which the necessary equipment could be provided, he should have told Richard, "Give me your materials and come with me to the photocopying center. We'll get them color-copied and either stapled or paper-clipped and be back here within five minutes." The individual would then have called the photocopying center on his cellular phone, told them he was coming over immediately and that he needed priority assistance. This effort would not have solved all of Richard's problems, nor would it have ensured that all five dimensions of service were being met. However, it would have gone a long way toward providing Richard with the assurance he should have received from the hotel.

Empathy. Empathy is the ability to provide caring, individualized attention to a customer. In this case, the planner provided no empathy at all. The only thing he did was recommend that the material be photocopied, so that Richard would have something in the hands of the participants that could be used as a basis for explanation and discussion. The planner seemed oblivious to the problem that confronted Richard. However, based on his boss's comments after the presentation, it is apparent that the situation was a serious one—and if the planner had done his job properly, he would have been aware of this and gone out of his way to help protect Richard's credibility. Additionally, the individual had written down these equipment needs, so if other groups already had all of the available equipment, this individual apparently had not done his job correctly. He should have found out what the demands were for that day, realized that there would not be sufficient equipment to handle all of these requests, and taken steps to acquire what was needed.[12]

These five dimensions of service can be used in analyzing and responding to the needs of all customers. For example, consider hotel customers. What are the basic things that they want? Research shows that guests have four primary demands. First, they want a clean room in which they can feel comfortable and certain that all hygiene steps have been taken. Second, they want the room to be secure and safe so that when they go out for the day or turn in for the evening they do not need to be concerned that someone will break in. Third, they want to be treated like a guest and not an unwelcome intruder who has dropped by at the last minute and is bothering their host. Fourth, they want promises to be kept; if they arrive at 4 P.M. with a confirmed reservation, they do not want to learn that their assigned room has not yet been made up. Here is how these four demands match up with the five dimensions of service:

Expectation	Service Dimensions				
	Reliability	Tangibles	Responsiveness	Assurance	Empathy
Clean room	X	X			
Secure room	X	X			
Treated like a guest			X	X	X
Promises kept			X	X	X

Other Useful Tips

How much service is sufficient? The answer depends on the situation. People who travel a great deal and/or eat out often are knowledgeable regarding the type and degree of service that is available. As a result, they are often able to get better service because they know when to speak up and what to request. Those who travel less often or eat out infrequently typically have lower expectations because they have less experience regarding what is available. In either event, however, everyone has a service-level expectation and it is up to the hospitality organization to reach at least the lowest point of this level. This idea can be explained in terms of a *zone of tolerance*, which is the level of service which a customer expects. This is illustrated in Figure 10.3 and shows that service should be at least adequate. Anything below this level is unacceptable. Conversely, if the organization can provide a degree of service that is above the desired level, this will result in customer delight and typically ensures that the person will return again and again.

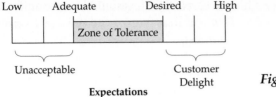

Low   Adequate   Desired   High

Zone of Tolerance

Unacceptable

Customer
Delight

Expectations

Figure 10.3 *Degrees of Service-
Level Expectations*

There are a variety of ways that hospitality organizations can ensure that their service is never unacceptable and often falls into the "customer delight" range. The following are ten of the most useful.

1. Make things simple for the customer by limiting the number of options from which the person is asked to choose. If a guest is checking into a hotel, it is all right to ask if he or she would like a smoking or nonsmoking room and if a queen-size bed is acceptable. However, if there are some rooms with minibars and others without, some with a sauna and others without, and so on, this is going to become too confusing. The guest wants a room, not a quiz. Similarly, if a restaurant offers specials that are not described in the menu, these should be limited to four or five or the customer will not be able to remember everything. Simply put: Do not confuse the customer.

2. Make it easy for guests to find their way around the facility. Good signage will let them get places on their own without having to continually ask for directions. In hotels, maps and signs can help guests find their rooms and locate service areas such as restaurants, clubs, health and fitness centers, and the pool. These also make it easy for guests to find the concierge, get change for a $20 bill, and check out of the hotel.[13]

3. When serving guests, have an established sequence so that everything is done right and in the proper order. For example, at Red Lobster, eight steps are taught to all servers:

   a. Approach the guests with a warm greeting within one minute of their being seated.

   b. Get and deliver a beverage/appetizer order.

   c. Describe the fresh fish available and featured entrées, get the entrée order, and remember to ask all guests if they would like to add shrimp to their salads.

   d. Precheck the order by guest number and deliver salads, bread, and bread plates.

   e. Pre-bus the salad plates and deliver the entrées, being sure to name each item as it is being served; then check with the guests shortly thereafter to ensure that they are satisfied with their meal.

    f. Silently, check back for additional sauces, refills, etc., periodically.

    g. Return with the dessert tray and make the presentation; suggest coffee and/or after-dinner drinks.

    h. Present the check, collect payment, and sincerely thank the guests and ask them to return.[14]

4. Make it easy for guests to interact with associates. One way is to have those who come in contact with the customers wear name tags, so that the guest feels comfortable calling them by name. Additionally, if the guest gives his or her name (as in the case of a person checking into a hotel), encourage associates to remember the person's name and use it when saying hello.

5. When speaking to customers, put them at ease and convey the message, "You are not bothering me at all. I am happy to be of assistance." This can be done by smiling, remaining calm, listening carefully, and either thanking them for coming by or saying, "It was my pleasure."

6. If guests have to be kept waiting, be candid in determining how long it will be before they are seated or their room is ready. Additionally, give them an opportunity to pass their time leisurely. If there is a 50-minute wait for a table, send out a plate of hors d'oeuvres or some snacks for the guests to munch on. This helps them pass the time.

7. Train associates to sell. For example, if a customer says, "I'll have some potato skins," teach associates to reply, "Would you like to try guacamole or spiced chicken with that?" After guests have finished their dinner, servers should not ask, "Would you like some dessert?" Instead, train them to be more aggressive and direct by saying something such as, "Now we're ready for the best part of the meal—our great desserts." Then they can describe each of them and encourage the guests to place their order.

8. Teach associates to anticipate guest needs. There are a number of ways that this can be done. For example, good servers always fill a half-empty glass without ever being asked. They also know how to "schmooze" with customers by smiling, maintaining eye contact, listening carefully to what is being said, and keeping their responses short. They interact in a friendly way, are careful to include children in the conversation, and continuously remain alert to pick up cues and identify concerns before they become problems. For example, if a group has been waiting for a while and the food has not yet arrived, a good server does not make a negative comment about how long it is taking, but says, "Let me check on your meal; I'll be right back."

9. Teach servers to improve by practicing their delivery and their technique. For example, if the restaurant serves wine, have servers practice opening wine bottles daily, either by opening them for the bartender or by using

Why do customers return to a restaurant or hotel? The answer is: Because the establishment gives them the goods and services they are seeking. The following twelve factors can play a role in getting people to return. Some of these are very important, while others are of limited value. Carefully read over the list and decide whether each of these factors is in the top half (more important) or the bottom half (less important) of the group. Place an *M* next to the six that are more important and an *L* next to the six that are less important. Answers are provided at the end of the chapter.

_____ 1. unique menu items

_____ 2. fresh food

_____ 3. wide menu variety

_____ 4. prompt service

_____ 5. cleanliness

_____ 6. convenient location

_____ 7. being greeted by name

_____ 8. relaxed atmosphere

_____ 9. no lines or waiting

_____ 10. high food quality

_____ 11. comfortable seating

_____ 12. easily able to accommodate kids

"dummy" bottles that wine vendors can supply. One of the major reasons many restaurants do not serve more wine is that the servers are afraid that they will have to open the bottle in front of customers—and they do not know how to do it well.

10. Be aware of what customers want and focus on providing it. For example, recent research reveals that the main thing that customers are looking for at restaurants is a good dining experience; status and prestige are far down their list of considerations. People go out to enjoy themselves and they want to have a positive experience. In every area of hospitality there are a host of important reasons that explain what customers want. By identifying these reasons, an organization can attract and retain the business of these people. The quiz in Box 10.2 provides insights regarding this statement.

Handle Complaints Effectively

In the previous section, the focus of attention was directed to providing customers the type of service they want. However, even the best organizations are going to find themselves facing complaints from customers who feel that they are not being treated fairly. In dealing with these situations, it is important to know how to diffuse them and then turn them into positive experiences for all involved.

Understanding the Ramifications

People complain because the service they have received is below their zone of tolerance (see Figure 10.3). There are many reasons for this. For example, some common pet peeves that are registered by disgruntled hotel guests include unclean rooms, uncomfortable beds, inoperable climate controls, thin walls, and inadequate housekeeping.[15]

What makes these complaints particularly troublesome is that if they are not resolved to the satisfaction of the guest, there can be serious ramifications. In particular, the individual is likely to tell others of the poor service. In one survey conducted among guests at nine hotels in a 21-hotel chain, a total of 479 respondents gave the following answers:[16]

I would be likely to tell others outside my family about the complaint, regardless of how it was resolved.	62%
The number of people I would tell (average response) would be:	12
I would be likely to tell others when my complaint was not satisfied.	73%
I would be likely to tell others not to use the hotel, regardless of how the complaint was resolved.	43%
The number of people I would urge not to use the hotel (average response) would be:	8
If the complaint were not resolved, I would be likely to tell others.	71%

On the other hand, there are also positive ramifications if things are done well. Research shows that those customers who have had problems that have been satisfactorily resolved tend to be the most loyal customers of all. Moreover, five out of six people who complain will continue doing business with the organization even if the problem is not resolved to their satisfaction, if they perceive the person who took the complaint to be friendly, enthusiastic, nondefensive, and committed to the relationship. These are interesting findings and show that efforts to resolve customer problems (even if unsuccessful) are important. However, even if the problem is resolved, the customer is *not always* happy and may sometimes stop doing business with the enterprise. Steve Shapiro and Philip Wexler explain it this way:

- Three out of six customers who complain and have their problem resolved will stop doing business with you in spite of the fact that they "got what they wanted," *if they perceive the person taking the complaint as cold, unfriendly, defensive, and uncommitted to the relationship. In other words, if the person doesn't care.*[17]

Taking the Proper Action

There are a number of things that can be done to ensure that complaints are handled properly. One of the most important is to learn what they are. This can be difficult, as most complaints go unreported—the customer simply stops coming back. So the organization must develop easy-to-use methods that allow for feedback and, most important, it must then take the proper action to correct any problems. At the same time, the enterprise would like to know where it is doing well, so that it can continue to emphasize these strengths. Figures 10.4 and 10.5 provide examples of comment cards from two nationally known organizations.

Once problems have been identified, the next step is to address them. This can be done in a number of ways. In the case of dissatisfied or difficult customers, six steps are particularly helpful.

First, listen to what the customer is saying. This means allowing the individual to complete what he or she is communicating. Research shows that quite often irate customers have a tendency to overstate their case. However, if the associate suddenly jumps in and begins correcting the customer, this merely serves to make things worse. Now the client believes that the organization does not want to correct things, and the associate's behavior is clear evidence of this. Another important reason for allowing the customer to talk is that this communicates the message, "I am listening to you and am doing my best to understand what it is that has made you angry."

Second, as the individual is explaining the situation, maintain eye contact with the person and, if appropriate, take notes. Also, give the individual positive feedback by nodding your head or saying, "I see," or "Right." However, be careful not to give the impression of agreeing with the individual's point of view; when all the facts are evaluated, it may turn out that the customer's explanation is not completely correct, and it will be necessary to backtrack and erase that erroneous impression—something that is bound to upset the individual.

Third, after the customer has finished speaking, ask any questions that will further clarify the situation. If there are some things that were not understood, ask for them to be reexplained. If the person made any comments that seemed to be exaggerative, ask the individual to restate them. For example, the person may have said, "We've been waiting for a table for over two

Guest Room Services — EXCELLENT | GOOD | FAIR | POOR
- Accuracy of your Reservation
- Quality of Check-In
- Doorman/Valet greeting upon arrival
- Baggage Services
- Clean and Fresh Guest Room (upon check-in)
- Clean and Fresh Guest Room (throughout stay)
- Condition and Appearance of your Bedroom
- Condition and Appearance of the Bathroom
- Ample Lighting (Bedroom and Bathroom)
- Working Condition of TV/Bathroom and Facilities
- Wake-up Calls and Telephone Services
- Professionalism and Courtesy of Staff

Room Service
- Menu Selection and Variety
- Accuracy of your order
- Timeliness of delivery
- Quality of Food and Beverages
- Professionalism and Courtesy of Staff

Restaurant and Lounge Services

Arthur's 27
- Menu Selection and Variety
- Quality of Food and Beverages
- Atmosphere/Decor/Cleanliness
- Professionalism and Courtesy of Staff

Outback
- Menu Selection and Variety
- Quality of Food and Beverages
- Atmosphere/Decor/Cleanliness
- Professionalism and Courtesy of Staff

Watercress
- Menu Selection and Variety
- Quality of Food and Beverages
- Atmosphere/Decor/Cleanliness
- Professionalism and Courtesy of Staff

Laughing Kookaburra
- Atmosphere/Decor/Cleanliness
- Quality of Food and Beverages
- Quality of Entertainment
- Professionalism and Courtesy of Staff

Restaurant and Lounge Services Cont. — EXCELLENT | GOOD | FAIR | POOR

Pool and Snack Bar
- Quality of Food (Snack Bar)
- Quality of Beverages (Pool Bar)
- Professionalism and Courtesy of Staff

Courtyard
- Quality of Food and Beverages
- Professionalism and Courtesy of Staff

Other Facilities and Services
- Parking/Entrance/Exterior Lighting
- Banquet Functions
- Meeting Facilities
- Business Center
- Hotel Security
- Condition of Public Restrooms
- Recreational Facilities and Services
- Hotel Transportation

Overall Evaluation
- Overall how would you rate the Buena Vista Palace

If in the area again, would you return to the Buena Vista Palace YES ☐ NO ☐

Would you recommend the Buena Vista Palace to a friend ☐ ☐

Please Tell Us More

Did any particular employee(s) make your stay especially enjoyable?
_____
_____
_____

Is there anything else you'd like to tell us?
_____
_____
_____

Figure 10.4 Guest Comment Card: Buena Vista Palace, Walt Disney World Village
Courtesy Walt Disney World.

301

MIAMI

GRAND BAY HOTEL®

COCONUT GROVE

Thank you for visiting the Grand Bay Hotel. Our entire staff is committed to providing each of our guests with excellent service and comfort and we trust your stay with us is most enjoyable.

We would welcome your comments and opinions regarding our services and facilities. Your impressions will assist us in maintaining the high standards our discriminating guests expect.

Please take a moment to complete this card. You may leave it with the concierge or mail it at your convenience.

All of us at the Grand Bay Hotel thank you.

(Optional)

PLEASE PROVIDE THE FOLLOWING INFORMATION:

Please print:

Arrival Date: ______/ ______/ ______ Room # ________

Name ________________________________

Preferred Mailing Address ________________________

City________________ State ________ Zip ________

Telephone (   ) ________________________

This information is strictly confidential and for evaluation response purposes only.

GUEST EVALUATION

	Excellent	Good	Fair	Poor
Reception				
Greeting upon arrival	o	o	o	o
Check-in experience	o	o	o	o
Reservation information	o	o	o	o
Luggage handling	o	o	o	o
Parking facilities	o	o	o	o
Message and wake up call services	o	o	o	o
Guest Rooms				
Quality of guest room	o	o	o	o
Quality of bathroom	o	o	o	o
The Grand Cafe				
Service and ambiance	o	o	o	o
Food selection and quality	o	o	o	o
Overall restaurant experience	o	o	o	o
Room Service				
Friendly and knowledgeable order-taker	o	o	o	o
Menu selection and food quality	o	o	o	o
Delivery and clearing of order	o	o	o	o
Ciga Lounge				
Service	o	o	o	o
Atmosphere	o	o	o	o
Check-Out				
Accuracy of bill	o	o	o	o
Offer for Express check-out	o	o	o	o
Overall check-out procedure	o	o	o	o
Friendliness of Guest Service Agent	o	o	o	o
How would you rate the hotel?	o	o	o	o

Would you return to the hotel on your next visit to the area? o YES o NO

Is there anything in particular you liked or disliked about the hotel?

____

____

Are there any employees who deserve special recognition for providing outstanding service?

____

____

How did you hear about the hotel: Travel Agent o Newspaper Ad o Company o Personal Referral o

Other: ________________

Figure 10.5 *Guest Comment Card*

Courtesy Grand Bay Hotel.

hours." However, the restaurant may have opened for business only 75 minutes ago. An effective way of revisiting this area would be to say, "Tell me again what time you gave your name to the reservations clerk to enter in the book."

Fourth, paraphrase the customer's comments so that there is agreement regarding the issue. In the process, state the problem clearly and concisely. This lets the customer know that he or she has been able to convey the desired message.

Fifth, apologize for the inconvenience and acknowledge that you are sorry their experience has been unsatisfactory. In the process, be careful not to blame anyone else; if it is unclear who created the problem, do not accept personal responsibility. Use a neutral apology, such as, "I am sorry that this has happened. We pride ourselves on excellent service and like to do everything possible to correct any problems that arise and keep our customers happy."

Sixth, work to resolve the customer's problem by making suggestions and getting the individual to accept one of them, or allow the person to offer an alternative that is acceptable to the organization. If this process gets bogged down, it may be necessary to have a higher-level associate get involved. However, research shows that 90 percent of the time, customer problems can be resolved by the customer and the associate who initially works with this individual to make things right. In carrying out this last step, two useful strategies are important: (1) never get emotionally involved—always remain calm and objective; and (2) solve the problem with a "win-win" solution, in which both sides arrive at an acceptable solution.

These six steps can be particularly helpful in gaining and keeping customer goodwill. However, they are greatly influenced by the amount of empowerment delegated to the associates. When associates have the authority and resources to resolve problems, customer service is often maintained at a very high level. When they lack the authority to make and implement suggestions that are acceptable to the customer, service suffers and the enterprise loses business. More will be said about this in Chapter 11.

SUMMARY

1. Well-run hospitality organizations meet the quality challenge in a number of ways. One is by creating the right philosophy, so that all associates understand the organization's service goal and service strategy. A second is by being aware of the cost of providing poor service, keeping in mind that a disgruntled customer typically tells ten others about his or her poor experience.

2. There are a number of ways to deal with pitfalls to outstanding service. One is by addressing inflexible policies and rules. A second is by motivating the associates through well-designed orientation and training programs.

3. The most effective way to meet the quality challenge is to determine what customers want—and then give it to them. This can be done in a number of ways. One is by getting feedback regarding customer preferences and using this information to tailor the service delivery. A second is by learning how to create a good first impression with the customer. A third is by

carefully addressing the five dimensions of service: personal reliability, tangibles, responsiveness, assurance, and empathy.

4. In handling complaints effectively, hospitality associates should take a number of steps. These include listening carefully, maintaining eye contact, asking questions, paraphrasing the customer's comments, apologizing for any inconvenience, and working to resolve the problem in a way that is acceptable to all parties involved.

KEY TERMS

personal reliability
tangibles
responsiveness

assurance
empathy
zone of tolerance

REVIEW AND APPLICATION QUESTIONS

1. Of what practical value is the formulation of a customer service goal statement or a customer service strategy? How does this help the organization improve the quality of its operations?

2. The Chandling Hotel estimates that poor service results in the loss of approximately 25 of its loyal customers every year. The head of financial operations has estimated that each of these customers spends approximately $1,600 annually at the hotel. Based on this information, approximately how much revenue does the Chandling lose every year because of poor customer service? Show your calculations. (Hint: Use Table 10.1 in your calculations.)

3. One of the rules of total quality management is the "85:15 rule," which holds that 85 percent of all the mistakes made in dealing with customers are a result of incorrect or outmoded rules and policies and 15 percent of the mistakes are a result of errors by associates. How does this rule provide useful advice to hospitality organizations? Based on this rule, what action would you suggest for managers of restaurants and hotels? Be specific in your answer.

4. Why is it critically important that a server make a good impression on guests within 30 seconds of the time the server reaches the table? What is the benefit of doing this?

5. Carlinda Ruiz is a customer service representative for a major hotel. Last week she received a call from a group of executives who were meeting in the large conference room. Carlinda had handled the party's booking and

Part IV   Understanding Customers

was the main contact point for any requests or problems. The executive told her that lunch was scheduled for noon, but no food had yet been served. Carlinda looked at her watch, which showed 12:27 P.M. and told the executive, "I'll check into it and be up within ten minutes." In solving this problem, how could Carlinda use the five dimensions of service: personal reliability, tangibles, responsiveness, assurance, and empathy?

6. When a customer lodges a complaint regarding the quality of service, how should an associate handle the situation? Discuss the six steps that can be of most value in successfully resolving this matter.

SELF-FEEDBACK EXERCISE: WHAT TYPE OF SERVICE DO YOU PROVIDE?

The following ten statements are designed to help you identify the type of customer-driven service you provide to customers, as well as to offer insights regarding how you believe a hospitality organization should function. Circle your answer to each of these statements and then follow the instructions in the scoring key.

1. Of these choices, a hospitality organization's first priority should be to:
   a. control costs
   b. get things done on time
   c. ensure the quality of its products/services
   d. understand and meet customer needs
   e. maintain high associate morale

2. When a customer complains, the organization should be set up to:
   a. use this information as a basis for improvement
   b. encourage customers to feel free to register complaints
   c. tolerate this type of behavior from customers
   d. ignore this feedback from customers
   e. discourage this feedback from customers

3. The objective of a hospitality organization should be that of:
   a. being the lowest-cost producer
   b. being the highest-value provider
   c. staying up with the competition
   d. continually finding out how to improve customer service
   e. finding markets and niches where there are no competitors

4. When it comes to repeat customer business, a hospitality organization's objective should be:

   a. 80–100% repeat business

   b. 60–79% repeat business

   c. 40–59% repeat business

   d. 0–39% repeat business

   e. to discourage repeat business and continually get all new customers

5. What percentage of a hospitality organization's associates should be rewarded based on customer-linked measures?

   a. none

   b. less than 20 percent

   c. 21–40%

   d. 41–60%

   e. 61+%

6. How often do you personally meet with your internal customers?

   a. once a week

   b. twice a week

   c. three times a week

   d. once every other week

   e. monthly

7. How often do (or would) you personally meet with your external customers?

   a. once a week

   b. twice a week

   c. three times a week

   d. once every other week

   e. monthly

8. How well do (or would) you understand how customers are using the product or service you are providing?

   a. extremely well

   b. very well

   c. fairly well

   d. I am a little knowledgeable

   e. I have no understanding

9. When it comes to meeting customer expectations, which of the following best describes your philosophy?

  a. I try to meet minimal expectations

  b. I do the best I can

  c. I try to make the customer happy

  d. I often go the extra mile

  e. I work to delight the customer

10. When it comes to dealing with customer problems, which of the following best describes your philosophy?

  a. I enforce company rules

  b. I enforce company rules but try to help the customer as well

  c. I try to work out a solution that is best for both the customer and the organization

  d. I support the customer but try to enforce the rules where possible

  e. I support the customer and ignore company rules

Scoring: Circle your answer for each of the ten responses. Then add up the number of points you received in each of the two categories: customer-driven (#1 to #5) and customer-contact (#6 to #10).

Customer-Driven Score

	a.	b.	c.	d.	e.	
1.	1	2	3	5	4	
2.	5	4	3	2	1	
3.	2	3	1	5	4	
4.	5	4	3	2	1	
5.	1	2	3	4	5	
Total	___	___	___	___	___	= ___

Customer-Contact Score

	a.	b.	c.	d.	e.	
6.	3	4	5	2	1	
7.	3	4	5	2	1	
8.	5	4	3	2	1	
9.	1	2	3	4	5	
10.	1	2	5	4	3	
Total	___	___	___	___	___	= ___

Now transfer your two totals to the following customer service grid and place an X in the quadrant where the two scores intersect.

Customer Service Grid

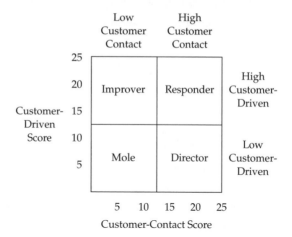

Interpretation: Based on your scores, you fit into one of four customer-driven styles. Here are the four descriptions:

Improver. An improver is interested in providing better customer service, but does not come into direct contact with the customer on a regular basis. This individual gathers customer-related information and works to make customer-driven decisions. He or she highly values service excellence and is interested in identifying new and better ways of determining and providing what customers need.

Responder. A responder has a high degree of customer contact and a strong desire to address customer needs. This individual listens carefully to what people say, and does his or her best to build relationships and offer goods and services that exceed customer expectations. At the same time, a responder is supportive of the organization and tries to fashion solutions to customer-related problems that provide a "win-win" result for both groups.

Mole. A mole has little customer contact and little interest in responding to customer needs. The individual buries himself or herself in work-related activities that have nothing to do with customer satisfaction—and the individual is happy to engage in this type of work.

Director. A director has a great deal of customer contact, but does not listen to what he or she hears. Instead, the person prefers to tell the customer what the organization wants him or her to do. A director often focuses on enforcing rules, even if they conflict with customer needs. If there is a conflict between rules and customer requests, the rules are always given priority.

What type of service provider are you? Is this style getting the results you want? If so, continue doing what you are doing. If not, look for ways of improving your customer-driven and/or customer contact scores.

CASE 10.1: IT'S JUST BUSINESS

Every month the Women Presidents Club (WPC) of a large midwestern city meets for dinner. There are currently 47 members and the number is growing at the rate of 10 per year. The objective of the members is to network among themselves and to share useful ideas. A typical evening begins with drinks and hors d'oeuvres at 6 P.M., followed by dinner and a short talk by an invited guest. There is then a brief formal business meeting, with adjournment around 9 P.M. This gives everyone an opportunity to stay around and talk to each other for an hour, discussing new business developments, sharing ideas, and making contacts.

The WPC has been meeting at the Royal Mountain Restaurant for the past fifteen months. However, the meeting last week was a disaster. The room was not set up on time; there was only one bartender, so it took almost ten minutes to get a drink; the food was served late and it was cold; and the microphone at the head table did not work. Before adjourning for the evening, the group voted to move its monthly meeting to another restaurant. This was not the first time service had been poor, although it was worse at this meeting than ever before. Last month the president of the WPC had called the restaurant owner and told her, "We spend an average of $35 per person at these monthly get-togethers and the service is just terrible. If things don't get markedly better, we're going to move to another restaurant." The president was assured that everything would be taken care of to the satisfaction of the group.

After the most recent fiasco, the reservations committee of the WPC met and visited with representatives from three prominent restaurants. They then reported back to their group and a few days later signed a contract with one of the restaurants for a one-year period. The prices are the same as those at the Royal Mountain, but the assigned room is more spacious and the restaurant has guaranteed in writing that if service is not satisfactory the group will be given a 50 percent discount on that evening's bill.

Yesterday the owner of the Royal Mountain called the president of the WPC and asked if there was anything that could be done to get the group to return. "I know that we didn't do a very good job in serving your group and we would like an opportunity to rectify our mistakes. I would be willing to cut our current price by 35 percent and, if you are dissatisfied with the service at any of your meetings, I will not charge for that evening." The president thanked the individual, but explained that a new contract had already been signed with another establishment. "We're not blaming anyone," she told the owner, "but we think it's time we moved on to another location. All of the members have different business contacts, and it's not right that we always meet in the same place. Don't take it personally. It's just business."

1. How much revenue did the Royal Mountain Restaurant lose when the WPC took its business elsewhere? Show your calculations.

2. What could have been done to prevent this from happening? Offer three suggestions.

3. In what way were the five dimensions of service neglected by the Royal Mountain? In each case, give an example.

CASE 10.2: THEY'RE GOING ELSEWHERE

When Mark Davidson checked into his complimentary suite, there was a basket of fruit and a note from the hotel manager welcoming him and his convention to the hotel complex. Mark is the president of a large group of medical doctors who meet annually to present research papers and familiarize themselves with the latest developments in the field. Approximately 1,400 doctors and their families are attending this year's meeting, and the number has been growing by 15 percent annually for over five years.

One of the events at the convention is the "President's Reception," to which the current president invites members of the group's board of governors as well as those who have played an active role in helping with the current year's program. This dinner is always provided, complimentary, by the hotel. So when Mark received a bill for the meal, he put it aside and gave it to his local arrangements chairperson, Carole Stewart. She, in turn, called the meeting planner and learned that the dinner had not been comped by the hotel. Apparently, there had been a misunderstanding somewhere, but the individual promised to get back to Carole within the hour. When the associate called back, he had a copy of the contract that the medical association had signed with the hotel. There was no promise of a complimentary dinner anywhere in the agreement.

This news surprised Mark, since this was the first time in the history of the organization that the dinner had not been comped. The last time the association stayed at this hotel complex, it had been written into the contract, and it was Mark's understanding that the current agreement called for the same conditions as the previous one. Apparently someone forgot to write it in and no one caught the oversight. The bill for the dinner was $4,410 and, in Mark's opinion, not a great deal of money given that the association had rented a total of 3,450 rooms at an average price of $110 per night, in addition to all of the food and other purchases the members made during their stay at the complex. However, this was not the view of the meeting planner, and when Mark discussed the matter with him, he said, "I'm sorry, but my hands are tied by the written contract."

In a last effort to correct the situation, Mark and two of his board members met with the hotel manager. The individual was extremely friendly, but firm in that the hotel would not make changes in the agreed-upon terms. "Our prices are all based on what we will be billing. We gave you rooms at $110 that typically go for $165. If we had known that we would have to assume the cost of the dinner, we would have quoted a higher rate on the rooms." Mark let the man finish speaking. "Well, we're not going to start a war over this, but I think we both know that there was an oversight in the contract and I had hoped that we could work it out. Thanks for talking to us."

Each year after the convention, the board of governors meets and picks a location for its meeting five years down the road. In the past the group has had five hotels and has rotated its business between them. So wherever it had just gone would be the site five years from now. However, by a unanimous vote the board decided to choose another hotel and has begun the process of soliciting bids from seven of them.

1. Using the zone-of-tolerance concept (Figure 10.3), how can you explain the board's decision?

2. Which of the five dimensions of service did the meeting planner and the hotel manager fail to consider when discussing the matter of the president's dinner? Explain.

3. How should the hotel manager have handled this situation? Offer three recommendations for action.

ANSWERS TO BOX 10.1: "CATERING TO THE CUSTOMER"

1. M	4. M	7. M	10. M
2. W	5. W	8. W	11. W
3. W	6. M	9. W	12. M

ANSWERS TO BOX 10.2: "WHY CUSTOMERS RETURN"

Here is the importance of the twelve items, along with the order of each.[18]

L	1.	unique menu items (11)
M	2.	fresh food (tied for 2)
L	3.	wide menu variety (7)
M	4.	prompt service (4)
M	5.	cleanliness (1)
L	6.	convenient location (9)
L	7.	being greeted by name (12)

M	8.	relaxed atmosphere (6)
L	9.	no lines or waiting (8)
M	10.	high food quality (tied for 2)
M	11.	comfortable seating (5)
L	12.	easily able to accommodate kids (11)

ENDNOTES

1. Chris Baum, "The Six Basic Features Any Business Hotel Must Have," *Hotels,* November 1993, pp. 52–56.
2. See, for example, Frederick F. Reichheld and W. Earl Sasser, Jr., "Zero Defections: Quality Comes to Services," *Harvard Business Review,* September–October 1990, pp. 105–111.
3. These ideas can be found in *Red Lobster Server Workbook* (GMRI Training Department, September 1994), pp. 3–4.
4. For more on this approach, see Joan Koob Cannie and Donald Caplin, *Keeping Customers for Life* (New York: AMACOM, 1991), p. 17.
5. Richard M. Hodgetts, *Blueprints for Continuous Improvement* (New York: American Management Association, 1993), p. 86.
6. Ibid., p. 90.
7. Bill McDowell, "Child-Friendly Restaurants Aren't Kidding Around," *Restaurant and Institutions,* September 1, 1994, p. 112.
8. Craig Wilson, "Star Treatment is the Norm at the Broadmoor," *USA Today,* February 3, 1995, p. 9D.
9. *Red Lobster Server Workbook,* p. 20.
10. A. Parasuraman, Leonard L. Berry, and Valarie A. Zeithami, "Understanding Customer Expectations of Service," *Sloan Management Review,* Spring 1991, pp. 39–48.
11. For more on this topic, see James M. Bleech and David G. Mutchler, *Let's Get Results, Not Excuses* (Hollywood, Fla.: Lifetime Books, 1995).
12. For additional insights, see Denney G. Rutherford and W. Terry Umbreit, "Improving Interactions between Meeting Planners and Hotel Employees," *Cornell Hotel and Restaurant Association Quarterly,* February 1993, pp. 68–80.
13. Also see Andrew Lockwood and Peter Jones, "Creating Positive Service Encounters," *Cornell Hotel and Restaurant Association Quarterly,* February 1989, pp. 44–50.
14. *Red Lobster Server Workbook,* pp. 9–10.
15. Reported in Grace Wagner and Edward Watkins, "Pet Peeves," *Lodging Hospitality,* December 1994, p. 117.
16. Robert C. Lewis and Susan V. Morris, "The Positive Side of Guest Complaints," *Cornell Hotel and Restaurant Association Quarterly,* August 1987, p. 14.
17. Steve Shapiro and Phil Wexler, *The Art of Professional Serving* (San Diego, Calif.: Resource Publishing Group, 1990), p. 76.
18. These data can be found in Bellamy Gail, "Guess Who's Coming to Dinner, and Why," *Restaurant Hospitality,* October 1994, p. 109.

CHAPTER ELEVEN

Understanding the International Customer

LEARNING OBJECTIVES

As national economies continue to grow, an increasing number of firms in the hospitality industry are looking at the world as one giant marketplace for their goods and services. In particular, many of these companies are finding that there are markets everywhere that would welcome their services. The overriding objective of this chapter is to examine human relations in an international context with primary emphasis on the customer. When you have finished studying all of the material in this chapter, you will be able to:

1. Define the term *culture* and describe four of the characteristics that are common to all cultures.

2. Discuss some of the general categories that can be helpful in gaining insight into culture, including knowledge about organizational loyalty, decision making, and the development of relationships.

3. Identify and describe the five cultural dimensions that help differentiate cultures—power distance, individualism, masculinity, uncertainty avoidance, and time orientation—and then discuss how this information can be useful in identifying similarities and differences in national cultures.

4. Examine human relations concepts as they apply to providing hospitality-related services in specific countries, including China, India, and France.

The Nature of Culture

Culture is the acquired knowledge that people use to interpret experience and to generate social behavior. This knowledge forms values, creates attitudes, and influences behavior. To a large extent, culture dictates the way people are expected to behave, and it both guides and influences personal and group interactions. For these reasons, understanding culture is critical to an understanding of international human resources.

In particular, it is important to remember that what is an accepted custom or belief in one country can have no value for another. For example, in early December a hotel manager in Omaha, Nebraska, might have the front of the hotel decorated with a Christmas-related theme, and might wish the clientele "Merry Christmas" on December 25. If this same manager were running a hotel in Spain, the individual would realize that Christmas is celebrated on January 6, the feast of the Magi (the wise men who came to the stable). If this person were running a hotel in Kuwait City, there would be no Christmas celebration, except perhaps for those guests whom the manager knew to be Christians. Simply put, holidays in one country often have no meaning or relevance in other countries; individuals doing business internationally need to be familiar with the culture of the nations where they are operating. Additionally, it is important to remember that culture has a number of characteristics that help explain why there is so much difference between peoples.

Characteristics of Culture

There are a number of different characteristics of culture. Most scholars agree on at least four: learned, shared, transgenerational, and symbolic. Each merits consideration.

Learned. Culture is learned. It is not inherited or biologically based. It is acquired through interaction and experience. The culture of people in one country may be markedly different from those in another—and this can create problems. For example, people in the Americas are taught to read from left to right, but in many Asian countries, including China and Saudi Arabia, people read from right to left. This learned behavior can greatly influence such business activities as advertising and promotion, as a U.S. hotel chain recently learned. The company put up a billboard with three pictures on it. The one on the left showed a weary traveler carrying his bag, the one in the center showed the individual checking into the hotel, and the one on the right showed the person relaxed, smiling, and satisfied. This ad was extremely effective in both the Americas and Europe, but it flopped in Asia because viewers read it "in reverse" and concluded that a contented person checked into the company's hotel and emerged tired and carrying the bag. Obviously this was not a pleasant experience for the traveler; to Asians, the sign indicated that service at this hotel was extremely poor. The hotel soon learned of its mistake and quickly reversed the first and last pictures.

Shared. Culture is shared. It is not unique or specific to single individuals. Everyone in the culture uses these common behaviors and activities. For example, in Japan people are expected to come to work on time and to stay until their work shift is complete. This is in sharp contrast to the United States, where many people pride themselves on getting to work a little late or leaving a little early—and still getting all of their work done. In Japan many people would not understand this behavior. William Ouchi, an expert on Japanese management, explains this idea with the following anecdote:

> A student of mine from Japan told me the story of his good friend who worked at . . . a major bank and had been kept exceptionally late at work for a period of months in order to complete a major project. When the project was complete, the section chief sent the staff home early every day for a week. After two days of coming home in the afternoon, the young man was confronted by his mother, with whom he lived. "Please," she asked him, "go to a bar, go play *pachinko,* but don't come home early. The neighbors are stopping me on the sidewalk to ask whether you are having troubles at work, and it is embarrassing to have to explain to everyone."[1]

Transgenerational. Culture is passed on from one generation to another. In this way, people know what is expected of them and how they should behave in specific situations. This does not mean that all of the people in a particular culture will act uniformly, but it does mean that there is a great deal of uniformity and there are clear, discernible patterns of behavior. A knowledge of these behaviors helps outsiders gain a fundamental understanding of how to interact in the host country. A good example is provided by customs and manners, which often differ greatly from one country to another.

> For example, in Arab countries, it is considered bad manners to attempt to shake hands with a person of higher authority unless this individual makes the first gesture to do so. In Latin countries, it is acceptable to show up late for a party, whereas in England and France, promptness is valued. In many western countries, it is acceptable to talk business when golfing since this is often the underlying reason for the golf match, but in Japan business is never discussed over golf. In the United States it is acceptable for a boss to give a secretary roses to express appreciation for helping to close a big deal; in Germany and in many Latin countries, such action would be seen as a sign of romantic attachment and therefore inappropriate.[2]

Symbolic. Culture consists of more than just words and behaviors. There are also nonverbal, implied meanings that are conveyed by the way people walk, stand, and gesture. These nonverbal communications are often misunderstood (or not understood at all) by outsiders. For example, when Richard Hodgetts, Jane Gibson, and Charles Blackwell conducted research among international groups, they found that nonverbal communication messages clearly understood by Americans were often misunderstood (or had no meaning) among Asians, and vice versa.[3] This led them to conclude that the greater the geographic distance between two cultures, the more likely it is that the nonverbal forms of communication are different. Other researchers echo these feelings, as seen by these examples offered by Michael Czinkota and his associates:

> Individuals vary in the amount of space they want separating them from others. Arabs and Latin Americans like to stand close to people they are talking with. If an American, who may not be comfortable at such close range, backs away from an Arab, this might incorrectly be taken as a negative reaction. Also, Westerners are often taken aback by the more physical nature of affection between Slavs—for example, being kissed squarely on the lips by a business partner, regardless of sex.
>
> International body language must be included in the nonverbal language of international business. For example, an American manager may, after successful completion of negotiations, impulsively give a finger-and-thumb OK sign. In Southern France, the manager will have indicated that the sale is worthless, and in Japan that a little bribe has been asked for; the gesture is grossly insulting to Brazilians.[4]

Cultural Diversity

Because cultures are diverse, it can be extremely difficult to avoid making mistakes. However, there are some general categories that can be helpful in gaining insight into cultures and learning to minimize these errors. The following sections examine three of these.

Organizational Loyalty. In some countries organizational loyalty is extremely important. People identify with their company and it is a source of pride for them. For example, when the Japanese are asked what they do for a living, they answer, "I work for [name of company]." This is in sharp contrast to most Americans, who will say something such as, "I'm an engineer." The Japanese identify with their company and are part of a group. Americans identify with themselves and are proud of what they have personally accomplished. So when communicating with the Japanese, it is important to speak highly of their company and the fine products and services that it produces. This, in turn, makes the Japanese feel good because they are being praised *indirectly*, and this is far more important than being singled out for praise. In contrast, when communicating with the American engineer, it is important to single out something the individual does well and seek to *directly* praise the individual.

Decision Making. In some societies, individuals are encouraged to make decisions on their own. This willingness to assume personal responsibility and get things done quickly and efficiently is important. This is particularly true in cultures such as the United States, Great Britain, Australia, and other Anglo countries. When dealing with these customers, an effective strategy is to present the facts and then wait for the other party to make the decision. A company that is interested in having a quarterly meeting at a major hotel on Miami Beach might send a manager to talk to three or four of the hotel managers and choose the one that best meets the company's needs. The individual might then return to the home office, present the recommendation, and have it approved at once. In contrast, some cultures such as those of China and Japan are characterized by group decision making, which takes quite a bit of time. In this case, no matter how many managers the company sent to talk to the hotel people on Miami Beach, no decision will be made for quite a while. The individuals will simply gather information and report back to the home office. Then, after extended discussion by the home office, one of the hotels will be given the business. In the first case, a hotel manager might manage to close a deal on the spot by throwing in a few sweeteners such as free breakfast or half price for the meeting room. However, this tactic would have no value with Japanese or Chinese businesspeople because they are not empowered to commit the company to a decision.

Developing Relationships. In some cultures, people do business based heavily on price and opportunity. For example, many Americans will purchase something because they feel it is a good buy. An American company will put out a request for bids to supply the company with food service for the next year. The proposals will then be evaluated and the company will choose one. The decision almost always is based on what the firm feels it is getting for its money. This is in sharp contrast to other countries such as Japan, where personal relationships are extremely important and no supplier would get a contract without the company first meeting these individuals, talking to them, finding out about the price and quality of their service, and perhaps having them cater a small dinner for the company to show what they are capable of doing. In the process, the managers would develop a relationship with the food firm and draw conclusions regarding their reliability and integrity. Box 11.1 gives a real-life example of how Japanese firms go about learning as much as possible about their suppliers before deciding to enter into a business arrangement with them.

Box 11.1
What Was the Question?

A Japanese hotel decided to replace all of the kitchen appliances in its facilities with more modern and efficient units. The company invited four major appliance manufacturers to examine the hotel's current facilities and then make a formal proposal regarding how they would change these facilities. Each company reconfigured the kitchen area and drew up plans showing the types of equipment it would install and blueprints illustrating where each unit would be placed in the kitchen and why. Each then was given one hour to come to the company and make a presentation to the committee that was charged with choosing the finalist. This was then followed by questions from the committee members.

Aware of the large amount of money involved in the project, each manufacturer put together a well-formulated presentation that included multicolored slides showing the proposed new facilities as well as the benefits of buying this equipment. Each presentation was extremely professional and was timed to end at exactly 60 minutes. It was difficult to determine which proposal was best because the presentations were so well done and covered just about everything. However, at the end of the hour, when the person who was leading the manufacturer's presentation said, "Thank you for listening to us. Are there any questions we can answer for you?" the head of the selection committee asked each group the same question. This question was designed to be insightful and to help cut through the glitter of the presentation and find out if this company was the one from whom the firm wanted to buy. Can you think of what question the Japanese manager asked? Read the answer at the end of the chapter and compare it to the one you believed the manager had asked.

As you can see, the question the manager asked was designed to cut through the presentation and find out what the firm was going to be getting for its money. It was also designed to answer the question: Are these the type of people with whom we would feel comfortable working?

Cultural Dimensions

The preceding discussion provides some insights regarding how international customers tend to size up those who are selling them goods and services, as well as some of the ways that these customers like to be treated.[5] However, before you conclude that every international customer is totally different from every other, we want to look at the cultural dimensions that can be useful in helping group customers into somewhat uniform categories. Of course, we do not mean to imply that all French customers are the same or that if you are effective in dealing with the first couple of Germans with whom you have business, you should deal with all other Germans the same way. On the other hand, there are some general cultural patterns that can provide you with important human relations insights to various nations. One of the most significant research studies in this area was conducted by Geert Hofstede, who initially found four cultural dimensions: (1) power distance, (2) individualism, (3) masculinity, and (4) uncertainty avoidance.[6] More recently, Hofstede and his colleagues have uncovered a fifth dimension: time orientation. The following sections examine the first four of these and then address the last one.

Power Distance

Power distance is the extent to which less powerful members of institutions and organizations accept the fact that power is distributed unequally. In countries with high power distance, people learn to obey the orders of their superiors without asking questions. Those in authority can wield their power, and those who are subordinate respond to these directives as a matter of procedure. In countries with low power distance, those in power do not act officious. They often request (rather than demand) compliance, and they share their authority through the use of decentralization. Table 11.1 provides a list of the countries and regions of the world in Hofstede's research and Figure 11.1 shows the importance of power distance in each of these countries. A close review of the figure reveals that the United States is a low-power-distance society (see the southwest quadrant), as are many countries in western Europe (including Germany), while many Latin and Asian countries (including Japan) are high-power-distance societies.

An analysis of the power distance dimension provides a number of human relations implications for hospitality management. These include:

1. In high-power-distance societies, customers expect those providing them goods and services to know the answers to their problems or at least pretend they know them. In contrast, in low-power-distance societies, customers expect to be included in the decision-making process, have information shared with them, and be given some options regarding how things are to be done.

2. In high-power-distance societies, there is an aura of formality. Hotel associates, for example, wear uniforms and address guests in a respectful way. In low-power-distance societies, there is a fairly large degree of informality. For example, associates will be helpful to guests but are also likely to talk to them as equals and work to establish a bond of familiarity.

3. In high-power-distance societies, there are strict rules and regulations that dictate how things are to be done. For example, if coffee is to be served at

Table 11.1 Countries and Regions Used in Hofstede's Research

ARA	Arab countries (Egypt, Lebanon, Libya, Kuwait, Iraq, Saudi Arabia, U.A.E.)	JAM	Jamaica
		JPN	Japan
		KOR	South Korea
ARG	Argentina	MAL	Malaysia
AUL	Australia	MEX	Mexico
AUT	Austria	NET	Netherlands
BEL	Belgium	NOR	Norway
BRA	Brazil	NZL	New Zealand
CAN	Canada	PAK	Pakistan
CHL	Chile	PAN	Panama
COL	Colombia	PER	Peru
COS	Costa Rica	OHI	Philippines
DEN	Denmark	POR	Portugal
EAF	East Africa (Kenya, Ethiopia, Zambia)	SAF	South Africa
		SAL	Salvador
EQA	Equador	SIN	Singapore
FIN	Finland	SPA	Spain
FRA	France	SWE	Sweden
GBR	Great Britain	SWI	Switzerland
GER	Germany	TAI	Taiwan
GRE	Greece	THA	Thailand
GUA	Guatemala	TUR	Turkey
HOK	Hong Kong	URU	Uruguay
IDO	Indonesia	USA	United States
IND	India	VEN	Venezuela
IRA	Iran	WAF	West Africa (Nigeria, Ghana, Sierra Leone)
IRE	Ireland		
ISR	Israel	YUG	Yugoslavia
ITA	Italy		

Source: Adapted from Geert Hofstede, *Cultures and Organizations: Software of the Mind* (London: McGraw-Hill U.K., Ltd., 1991), p. 55.

9 A.M., it arrives at precisely this time. In a low-power-distance society, associates may deliver the coffee at 9:05 A.M. and this is considered acceptable behavior.

Individualism/Collectivism

Individualism is the tendency of people to look after themselves and their immediate family only. This is in contrast to *collectivism*, which is the tendency of people to belong to groups or collectives and to look after each other in

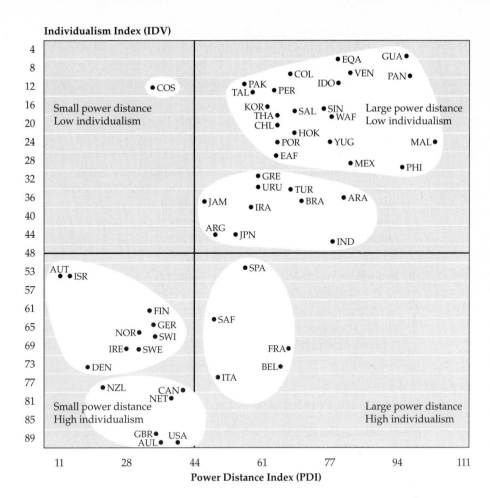

Individualism Index (IDV)

Small power distance
Low individualism

Large power distance
Low individualism

Small power distance
High individualism

Large power distance
High individualism

Power Distance Index (PDI)

Figure 11.1 *A Power-Distance and Individualism Plot*

Source: Adapted from Geert Hofstede, *Cultures and Organizations: Software of the Mind* (London: McGraw-Hill U.K., Ltd., 1991), p. 54.

exchange for loyalty. As seen in Figure 11.1, the United States is very high in individualism (southwest quadrant), as are a host of western European nations. Conversely, Japan (northeast quadrant) and many other Asian countries, as well as Latin nations, are high-collectivism societies. In fact, Hofstede found that countries with high individualism are more likely to have low power distance.

Individualism/collectivism provides a number of human relations implications for hospitality management. These include the following:

1. In high-individualism societies, people often expect services to be designed to meet their personal needs. For example, an American tourist

at a hotel in New York City may ask for a map showing a walking tour of lower Manhattan. Armed with this information, the individual will pick and choose those spots he or she wants to see. Conversely, a Chinese tourist will often travel in a group and will look for services that will meet the needs of all the members.

2. In high-individualism nations, people like the choices to be theirs to make. So the American will take the one-person walking tour because it provides flexibility and freedom of action. Anything the person wants to learn will be obtained from the map and related information provided by the concierge, information provided at the respective sites, or by talking to other tourists and learning more about the particular landmark. In contrast, individuals from high-collectivism countries will typically opt for a formal tour designed to ensure that everyone sees and hears what is going on and that everyone is treated equally.

3. In high-individualism societies, tasks take precedence over relationships. So the American would enjoy the walking tour because it allows him or her to see 25 different sites within a three-hour period. In high-collectivism societies, relationships take precedence over tasks and the Chinese tourists on the tour bus would enjoy the opportunity to talk and socialize with each other and share the tourism experience.

Masculinity/Femininity

Masculinity is the degree to which the dominant values of a society are success, money, and material things. In contrast, *femininity* is the degree to which the dominant values of a society are caring for others and the quality of life. The contrast is perhaps best explained in terms of "things versus people." Figure 11.2 shows the relative ranking of the countries in Hofstede's research on the basis of this cultural dimension.

Masculinity/femininity provides a number of human relations implications for hospitality management. These include the following:

1. When purchasing goods and services, individuals from high-masculinity countries often buy on the basis of price, and place high importance on getting the best possible bargain. Conversely, individuals from high-femininity nations place greater importance on the pleasure that will be obtained from the purchase.

2. Individuals from high-masculinity nations place great importance on owning things that impress others; they are willing to pay a premium price for a sports car or one that carries a great deal of prestige. People from high-femininity nations are more interested in a product's reliability and the pleasure they will get from using the purchase; when buying a car they are more likely to opt for general quality than high prestige.

Uncertainty Avoidance Index (IDV)

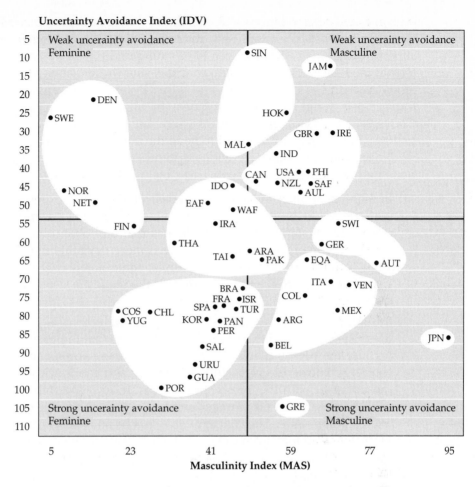

Figure 11.2 *A Masculinity/Femininity and Uncertainty Avoidance Plot*

Source: Adapted from Geert Hofstede, *Cultures and Organizations: Software of the Mind* (London: McGraw-Hill U.K., Ltd., 1991), p. 54.

3. People from high-masculinity societies enjoy challenges and are likely to opt for such sports as tennis or white-water rafting. They like to pit themselves against someone or something and try to succeed. This is in contrast to high-femininity societies, where people enjoy sports that require teamwork and cooperation. In these countries soccer is quite popular; so is golf—when played for social, not competitive, purposes.

Uncertainty Avoidance

Uncertainty avoidance is the extent to which people feel threatened by ambiguous situations and have created beliefs and institutions that try to avoid these outcomes. As seen in Figure 11.2, the United States is characterized by weak uncertainty avoidance (northeast quadrant) while the two other economic superpowers, Japan and Germany, have strong uncertainty avoidance. A close look at the table shows that Anglo countries and those that have been closely affiliated with the United States and Great Britain (for example, Singapore, India, Hong Kong, and the Philippines) are all in the top half of the figure. Conversely, the Germanic countries (Germany, Switzerland, Austria), Asian nations, and Latin countries tend to be in the bottom half of the figure.

Uncertainty avoidance provides a number of human relations implications for hospitality management. These include the following:

1. In high-uncertainty-avoidance societies, a large number of rules and regulations govern how things are to be done. When a guest complains about a service, the staff know the guidelines that are to be followed. In low-uncertainty-avoidance countries, there is more flexibility in solving problems. In the United States, for example, some hotels will ask the guest, "What would you like to see us do?" If the request is considered reasonable, it is granted.

2. In high-uncertainty-avoidance societies, strong emphasis is given to the use of specialists and experts. This helps ensure that things are done right, because the person doing them is highly trained. For example, the hotel concierge knows the nightclubs in the city and can quickly recommend those that fit with the guests' preferences. In low-uncertainty-avoidance countries, there is a far stronger emphasis given to the use of generalists and common sense. The concierge may not be an expert on all of the best nightclubs and may even call over the bell captain for assistance.

3. In a high-uncertainty-avoidance society, people believe that there is often one best way to do things. In a low-uncertainty-avoidance society, people believe there are a number of ways of doing things and, depending on the situation, any one of them could be best. So if a person in a high-uncertainty-avoidance nation did not feel that his or her meal was properly cooked, he or she would expect the server to return it to the kitchen and see that the necessary steps were taken. In a low-uncertainty-avoidance society, the guest would elaborate on what is wrong with the meal and offer suggestions regarding how to correct the problem.

Time Orientation

In recent years, Hofstede and other researchers have found that there is a fifth cultural dimension: time orientation. *Time orientation* is the way in which people view and use time. Some countries have very short time orientations. People there want things done immediately. On the other hand, some countries have very long time orientations. People in these nations have patience

Table 11.2 Cultural Value Dimension Scores for Ten Selected Countries

Country	Power Distance	Individualism	Masculinity	Uncertainty Avoidance	Time Orientation
United States	40	91	62	46	29
Germany	35	67	66	65	31
Japan	54	46	95	92	80
France	68	71	43	86	30˚
Netherlands	38	80	14	53	44
Hong Kong	68	25	57	29	96
Indonesia	78	14	46	48	25˚
West Africa	77	20	46	54	16
Russia	95˚	50˚	40˚	90˚	10˚
China	80˚	20˚	50*	60˚	118*
Range	35–95	14–91	14–95	29–90	10–118*

˚Estimated.

Source: Geert Hofstede, "Cultural Constraints in Management Theories," *Academy of Management Executives,* February 1993, p. 91.

and are prepared to wait for things. In general terms, Westerners tend to have short time orientations, while Asians tend to have long time orientations. This is illustrated in Table 11.2, where scores for ten nations on all five dimensions are provided. Notice that China, Hong Kong, and Japan have long-term time orientations, while the United States, France, and Germany have short-term time orientations.

Time orientation provides a number of human relations implications for hospitality management. These include the following:

1. In long-term time-orientation societies, individuals plan for the long run. Customers often place orders well in advance, such as booking cruises and airline reservations. And in selling these services, the focus is more heavily on the future ("Here is a wonderful cruise you might consider for next year") as opposed to the short run ("We are offering a special cruise to Alaska next month and still have a few available cabins"). On the other hand, in short-term time-orientation societies, such as the United States, many people would jump at the latter offer—if the price were right.

2. Customs and tradition are important in long-term time-orientation societies. Birthdays, anniversaries, and similar occasions are always celebrated with enthusiasm. Customers do not skimp on preparing for these occasions, for they regard them as important life events; when marketing to these individuals, it is important to keep these things in mind. Conversely, in countries such as the United States, where tradition is often of less

importance, hospitality services are commonly marketed on the basis of short-run need satisfaction, and "new" services are often in great demand. For example, many young college graduates would rather receive a seven-day boat cruise in the Caribbean than a party at which all of their relatives gathered to congratulate the graduate, take pictures, and celebrate the person's success.

3. Individuals with a long-term time orientation also tend to be thrifty. Asian-Americans, for example, have the highest savings rate of any ethnic group in the United States; the Japanese have a national savings rate of approximately 14 percent, far in excess of the 3 percent average for Americans. When making purchases, individuals with a long-term time orientation look for value both today and tomorrow. This is why they tend to purchase things that support their tradition or that last. On the other hand, many Americans and others with short-term time orientations are more interested in living for the moment—for example, by spending an evening at a rock concert.

Pulling It All Together

It can be difficult to fully understand international customers because country clusters differ so greatly. An analysis of Figures 11.1 and 11.2 would leave the average person confused and unable to answer the question: Overall, how similar or different is the United States compared to Germany and Japan? Fortunately, researchers have been able to synthesize the findings and provide a relative comparison of similar and dissimilar cultures. An illustration is provided in Figure 11.3. Notice that the Anglo countries tend to cluster, so in meeting the needs of customers in these countries, there can be similar human resources approaches. However, opposite the Anglo culture is the Arab culture. The way business is done there is often quite different from that in the U.S. market. So hospitality organizations must learn to adapt to different cultures and realize that what works well in one geographic locale may be of little value in another. For this reason, we now turn our attention to doing business in specific worldwide locales and examine some of the "dos and don'ts" of effective international human resources.

Doing Business in Selected Countries

There are many countries of the world where human resources practices are different from those in the United States. The following examines three selected countries: China, India, and France. Another that we have been mentioning throughout the chapter is Japan. Additional insights regarding how to do business there are provided in Box 11.2.

Figure 11.3 *A Synthesis of Country Clusters*

Source: Simcha Ronen and Oded Shenkar, "Clustering Countries on Attitudinal Dimensions: A Review and Synthesis," *Academy of Management Journal,* September 1985, p. 449.

China

The People's Republic of China (PRC or China, for short) has long had a tradition of isolation. However, in recent years China has become the focal point of investor attention. There are a number of reasons that make China attractive to outsiders. One is that the country has a population in excess of 1.2 billion. A second is that the country's gross domestic product (GDP) has recently been recalculated and is now estimated to be in the range of $1,000 per capita.[7] This is far greater than earlier estimates and indicates that the purchasing power of the average Chinese consumer is substantial. Moreover, the economy is growing at a faster rate than any other in Asia. During the 1980s, for example, China averaged real GDP growth of 10 percent, which was higher than that of South Korea, Hong Kong, Singapore, Taiwan, or any of the other rapidly industrializing nations in that area of the world.

On the other hand, doing business in China can be a long, grueling process. The PRC is famous for buying only what it needs and for hammering out a hard bargain in the process. For those who know what they are doing,

Box 11.2
Human Resources Update: Doing Business in Japan

Outsiders conducting business in Japan should know and understand a number of customs. Here are ten of the most useful.

1. Always try to arrange for a formal introduction to any person or company with whom you want to do business. These introductions should come from someone whose position is at least as high as that of the person whom you want to meet or from someone who has done a favor for this person. Unlike in the United States, you cannot simply pick up the phone and get through to a person with whom you have not done business.

2. If you know that the other person does not speak English or would personally feel more comfortable having a bilingual individual present, bring along an interpreter. This is a perfectly acceptable practice. However, be sure that your interpreter is not also a lawyer; this would indicate a lack of trust in the other person and you may find yourself unable to generate any business interest from this individual.

3. Work to achieve a thorough personalization of all business relationships. The Japanese trust those with whom they socialize and come to know more than they do those who simply are looking to do business. Accept after-hours invitations. However, remember that a night of socializing will not necessarily lead to your host signing a contract with you the next day.

4. Do not deliver bad news in front of others. If possible, have your second-in-command handle this chore. Also, never cause other people to lose face by putting them in a position of having to admit failure or say they do not know something that they should know.

5. Concern for tradition is important and may outweigh any profit considerations. The fact that your company can offer better hotel accommodations for the price than anyone else does not mean that the Japanese company will book your hotel. If the firm has been staying with a competitor for the last five years, they will probably go there again because they have a relationship with that hotel and it is becoming part of the company's tradition to stay there. Don't take this rejection personally, but do work to help create a new tradition—staying at your hotel!

6. The Japanese tend to make group decisions, so any presentation to a Japanese potential customer is likely to be met with the equivalent of, "We'll get back to you." Then, after the group has had time to discuss the matter, a decision will be made.

7. Remember that the Japanese communicate in a less direct way than Americans. For example, they do not say no in public; they simply don't say yes. It is up to you to realize that their failure to use the positive case is a negative response. Additionally, they make wide use of implied meanings, so you have to remain

Box 11.2   Continued

alert to what they are saying and what they actually mean.

8. The Japanese are logical people, but they do not always respond positively to a logical argument. Oftentimes emotional considerations are more important than facts.

9. When you meet people for the first time, you should exchange business cards with them. The card should be conveyed by using both hands and the card should contain the informa-

tion in both English and Japanese. Additionally, their card should be treated with respect and never bent or written on in their presence.

10. When you dine with the Japanese, the interaction and ritual is often more important than the actual consumption of food. Also, refrain from talking business, unless your host broaches the matter. Dining is typically a social and not a business function.

Source: Some of this material can be found in Philip R. Harris and Robert T. Moran, *Managing Cultural Differences,* 4th ed. (Houston: Gulf Publishing, 1996), pp. 268–276.

however, China can be a very important customer. Effective human resources practices are sometimes the key to success.

Human Resources Practices. There are a number of things that outsiders need to know about doing business in China. One is that the Chinese tend to be punctual, so it is important to arrive on time for all meetings. During these meetings, like the Japanese, the Chinese may ask many questions and nod their assent at answers. However, this nodding typically means that they understand, or it is a sign of politeness; it seldom means that they like what they are hearing and want to enter into a contract. In fact, it often takes a long time before the Chinese agree to move forward on a deal, so patience is an important characteristic to cultivate.

It is also important to be a good listener. This sometimes means having to hear the same story many times about the great progress that has been made by the PRC over the past decade. The Chinese are proud of their recent accomplishments and like to share them with outsiders.

China is a collective society. People pride themselves on being members of a group; it is important never to single out a Chinese and praise him or her for a particular quality such as intelligence or kindness, because this may well embarrass the individual in the face of his or her peers. The Chinese are also less animated than Westerners and they avoid open displays of affection. Unlike Latins, who often embrace each other when they meet, or Americans, who commonly slap each other on the arm or back, the Chinese are more reserved and retiring. They do not display the same type of boisterous behavior that is common among many other people. Other guidelines that are of value in doing business with the Chinese include the following:

1. The Chinese place a great deal of emphasis on trust and mutual connections, and they are true to their word.

2. Business meetings typically start with pleasantries such as tea and general conversation about the guest's trip to the country, local accommodations, and family. Additionally, the host often has been briefed on the visitor's background, resulting in many guests being surprised that their hosts already know so much about them.

3. When a meeting is ready to begin, the Chinese host will give the appropriate indication. Similarly, when the meeting is over, the host will indicate that it is time for the guest to leave.

4. Once the Chinese decide who and what is best, they tend to stick to these decisions; they may be slow in formulating a plan of action, but once they get started, they make fairly good progress.

5. In negotiations, reciprocity is important. The Chinese are willing to give concessions, but they expect some in return. As negotiations start to come to a close, it is common for the Chinese to slow up. This usually results in the other party trying to keep things moving by giving even more concessions.

6. Since negotiations can sometimes involve a loss of face, the Chinese usually negotiate through intermediaries. This allows them to convey their ideas without fear of embarrassment.[8]

India

India has long had a love-hate relationship with multinational businesses, and this has proven to be a major stumbling block in attracting capital. However, over the last five years there has been a dramatic turnaround in government policy.[9] As a result, between 1991 and 1995 foreign direct investment rose from $100 million to over $1 billion and a number of large multinational companies began flocking into the country. India is now closing deals worth $5 billion for eight privately financed power plants and has approved projects for Coca-Cola, Daimler Benz, Ford Motor, General Electric, Kellogg, and Wrigley, among others. Much of this has been a result of the government's willingness to reduce the bureaucratic red tape that accompanies the necessary approvals to move forward with investments. Today India is also opening power and telecommunications projects to foreign multinational enterprises, speeding approval of manufacturing investments by outsiders, reducing important barriers, and allowing the private sector to compete with national monopolies in railroads and postal services. At the same time, however, many old barriers still remain in place. For example, labor laws make it extremely difficult to lay off workers, and many businesses must have local partners because the operation cannot be 100 percent foreign-owned.

Human Resources Practices. When doing business in India, it is important to remember that businesspeople there are very familiar with American customs. They speak English, shake hands upon meeting other businesspeople, and typically dress in Western business attire. However, a number of cultural differences influence the way business is done. For example, most Indians do not drink alcoholic beverages, and many are vegetarians; the menu is often different from that in the United States. Additionally, when a guest is invited to a businessperson's home, the individual is always asked to have more food. This is done to ensure that the person does not go away hungry. Once the person has had enough to eat, however, it is acceptable to politely refuse more food. Other useful human resources guidelines that are of value when doing business in India include the following:

1. It is important to be on time for meetings.
2. Personal questions should not be asked unless the other individual is a friend or close associate.
3. Titles are important, so people who are doctors or professors should always be addressed this way.
4. Public displays of affection are considered inappropriate, so one should refrain from backslapping or touching others.
5. Beckoning is done with the palm turned down, while pointing is often done with the chin.
6. When eating or accepting things, the right hand should be used since the left hand is considered unclean.
7. The *namaste* greeting (pressing one's palms together in front of the chest) can also be used to convey other messages such as to signal that one has had enough food.
8. Bargaining for goods and services is common, in contrast to Western traditions, where bargaining might be considered rude or abrasive.[10]

France

Many Americans believe that it is more difficult to get along with the French than with other Europeans. This is undoubtedly a reflection of the French culture, which is markedly different from that of the United States. One of these differences is that in the United States, people can rise rapidly through the economic and social ranks based on hard work and economic success, but in France a successful person might, at best, climb one or two rungs of the social ladder. Additionally, the French are very status conscious and like to provide signs of this status, such as a knowledge of literature and the arts; a well-designed, tastefully decorated house; and a high level of education.

The French also tend to be friendly, humorous, and sardonic in contrast to the Americans. They tend to admire or are fascinated with people who disagree with them, in contrast to Americans who are more attracted to those who agree with them. Additionally, the French often determine a person's trustworthiness based on their firsthand evaluation of the individual's character, in contrast to Americans, who tend to evaluate a person's trustworthiness on the basis of past achievements and other people's evaluation of the individual. The French are also accustomed to conflict and, during negotiations, accept the fact that some positions are irreconcilable and must be accepted as such. Americans, on the other hand, believe that conflicts can be resolved and that if both parties make an extra effort and have a spirit of compromise, there will be no irreconcilable differences. There are also differences regarding the view of work. The French admire the Americans for their industriousness and devotion to work, but they believe that quality of life is more important. As a result, they attach a great deal of importance to leisure time, and are often unwilling to sacrifice the enjoyment of life for a dedication to work. These observations help explain why doing business with the French can be challenging for Americans. On the other hand, there are many opportunities for successful dialogue and deal making.

Human Resources Practices. In addition to the preceding, other useful human resources practices that are of value when doing business in France include the following:

1. It is extremely important to be on time for meetings and social occasions. There is no such thing as being "fashionably late."

2. When shaking hands with a French person, a quick shake with some pressure in the grip should be used. However, a firm, pumping handshake, so common in the United States, is considered uncultured. Also, when shaking hands with a woman, it is good manners to wait until she first offers her hand and then respond, rather than holding out one's hand and waiting for her to follow suit.

3. During a meal, it is acceptable to engage in pleasant conversation, but personal questions and the subject of money should never be raised.

4. Great importance is placed on neatness and taste; visiting businesspeople should try very hard to be cultured and sophisticated.

5. Decision making in French companies tends to be much more centralized than that in U.S. firms; the more important the decision, the more likely that it will have to be acted on by a member of senior-level management—regardless of the fact that current negotiations may not include a member from this hierarchical level. And the hierarchy in French firms is often far

less flexible than in U.S. companies, so the pace of activity is much slower and bureaucratic in nature.

6. The French place great pride in the quality of their work and they are extremely productive during the workday. However, they frown on working overtime and have the longest vacations in the world (between four and five weeks a year). Unlike the Americans, they carefully divide their work and personal life and try not to let one interfere with the other.

SUMMARY

1. Culture is the acquired knowledge that people use to interpret experience and to generate social behavior. This knowledge forms values, creates attitudes, and influences behavior. It also helps dictate the way that people are expected to behave.

2. There are a number of different characteristics of culture. Four were discussed in this chapter: learned, shared, transgenerational, and symbolic. Culture is acquired through interaction and experience. It is shared by all of the people in the country or cultural subgroup. It is passed on from one generation to another. It is symbolic in that it consists of more than just words and behaviors; nonverbal and implied meanings are also included.

3. Because cultures are diverse, it can be extremely difficult to avoid making mistakes. However, some general knowledge can be helpful in gaining insights to cultures and learning to minimize these errors. Examples include knowledge about organizational loyalty, decision making, and the way people go about developing relationships in the culture.

4. There are five cultural dimensions that help differentiate cultures. One is power distance, which is the extent to which less powerful members of institutions and organizations accept the fact that power is distributed unequally. A second is individualism, which is the tendency of people to look after themselves and their immediate family only. This is in contrast to collectivism, which is the tendency of people to belong to groups or collectives and to look after each other in exchange for loyalty. A third is masculinity, which is the degree to which the dominant values of a society are success, money, and material things. In contrast, femininity is the degree to which the dominant values of a society are caring for others and the quality of life. The contrast is perhaps best explained in terms of "things versus people." A fourth is uncertainty avoidance, which is the extent to which people feel threatened by ambiguous situations and have created beliefs and institutions that try to avoid these outcomes. The fifth is time, which is characterized by long-term and short-term time orientations.

5. Cultural dimensions make a nation unique. However, there are often a great many similarities in the dimensions of various nations, allowing them to be clustered based on similarities. Researchers have found six general cultural clusters, and nations within each of these six tend to be similar to each other. An example is the Anglo cluster, which consists of countries such as the United States, Great Britain, Canada, Australia, and New Zealand.

6. In many countries of the world, human resources practices are different from those in the United States. China, India, and France are good examples in illustrating that human resources practices are not universal. What works well in one country may have little or no value in another. The specific culture of the nation must be studied so that the needs of the customers there can be directly addressed.

KEY TERMS

culture
power distance
individualism
collectivism

masculinity
femininity
uncertainty avoidance
time orientation

REVIEW AND APPLICATION QUESTIONS

1. What is meant by the term *culture* and what are four characteristics that are common to all cultures? Be complete in your answer.

2. An American hotel chain is considering a business arrangement with a Japanese firm in which the Japanese will put up the financing to build a large hotel and shopping complex and the American firm will manage the operation. In what way will cultural diversity be an issue for the American firm? In your answer, include a discussion of organizational loyalty, decision making, and the developing of relationships.

3. What are the five cultural dimensions? Briefly define and describe each.

4. An American firm is thinking about buying a hotel in Cancun, Mexico. The company currently operates a very successful hotel in San Francisco and believes this expansion would be an excellent way to go international while still focusing heavily on the customer it knows best—the American guest. The company estimates that 50 percent of its business will come from Americans vacationing in Cancun. The remainder will be Europeans (30 percent), South Americans (10 percent) and Mexicans (10 percent). In what way will power distance and uncertainty avoidance be

important issues to consider when addressing the needs of this client base? Use examples to support your answer.

5. A British airline would like to negotiate landing rights with the government of China. The airline is convinced that air travel in China will become increasingly popular throughout the next two decades, and the firm would like to get in on the ground floor. In what way will an understanding of the following cultural dimensions be of importance to the airline representatives who are negotiating with the Chinese: individualism, masculinity, and time orientation? In each case, give an example to support your answer.

6. A Japanese company with restaurants throughout Japan has decided to expand into the European market. The company would like to set up units in France and the Netherlands and, if things go well, expand into other European countries. Using Table 11.2 as your point of reference, describe how cultural dimensions will prove to be a major challenge for this company. Be sure to include in your answer a comparison of the similarities and differences of the cultural dimensions in both countries.

7. The company you are working for has decided to try to secure an agreement with the Chinese government that will allow the firm to build and operate a sports complex in a suburb of Beijing. The company is in the process of lining up Chinese partners and hopes to begin negotiations with the government within six months. What are four human resources suggestions you would give to your company that could increase its ability to deal effectively in this cultural environment?

8. Henry Gallagher, a personal friend of yours, has been approached by a group of Indian businesspeople who are interested in hiring him to run a major hotel in Agra, the site of the Taj Mahal. Many tourists come to Agra every year and, based on Henry's success in running a large hotel in Los Angeles for the last six years, these businesspeople believe he has the requisite skills to do an outstanding job for them. Henry has asked you for some information regarding the human resources challenges he will face if he takes this new job. What are four things you would tell Henry that could be useful to him in understanding the challenges he faces in this multicultural market?

9. You have an offer to go to France to work for a world-famous restaurant. You have never been to Europe and are apprehensive about the cultural problems you may face in France. Based on your reading of this chapter, what are four things you would be sure to do (or not do) in order to impress your employer and show this company that you are indeed able to work well in another culture?

Read each of the following 20 statements and, using your best judgment, decide whether each is true or false and circle your choice. The answers and a scoring key are provided at the end of the exercise.

T F **1.** French managers are likely to be on time for a meeting—and they will expect you to be also.

T F **2.** People in most countries see Americans as very energetic, industrious, and interested in getting as much done in as short a time as possible.

T F **3.** Among Dutch employees, low importance is assigned to socializing on the job.

T F **4.** Money is a bigger motivator for British employees than it is for Japanese employees.

T F **5.** A person's position in the hierarchy is far more important in India than it is in Australia.

T F **6.** In Japan, managers rely very heavily on intuition as opposed to gathering facts.

T F **7.** Italian managers are much more likely than German managers to bypass the hierarchical chain and go right to the person with whom they want to speak.

T F **8.** Dutch employees are well known for their willingness to be friendly and cooperative.

T F **9.** If someone is a little late for a meeting with a manager in Latin America, this is usually not a major problem, since the other individual is also often late.

T F **10.** In Mexico, the amount of money a person makes is much more important than it is for Americans in the United States.

T F **11.** Americans tend to like people who agree with them, while French people are more likely to be interested in people who disagree with them.

T F **12.** In Germany, guests usually remain seated when the host enters the room and stand only when they are directly approached by the individual.

T F **13.** In Latin America, people shake hands when they meet, but they do not shake hands when they part company.

T F **14.** Like the Japanese, the Filipinos rarely say no.

T F **15.** In India, a stranger would not be expected to help a woman out of a car, boat, and so on, as her husband might resent it.

T F **16.** In India, backslapping is a sign of affection.

T F **17.** In negotiations, the Chinese are much more interested in short-term benefits than long-run benefits.

T F **18.** Calling cards are very necessary in Korea and should be used by foreign or Western businesspeople at all times.

T F **19.** The Japanese tend to like pressure on deadlines or delivery dates and perform better when such pressure is placed on them.

T F **20.** One of the best times for an American to talk business with a Japanese client is when the individual is golfing at the client's golf course.

Answers

1. True	6. False	11. True	16. False
2. True	7. True	12. False	17. False
3. False	8. False	13. False	18. True
4. False	9. True	14. True	19. False
5. True	10. False	15. True	20. False

Scoring Key: 18–20 You know a great deal about international behavior in the work place.

15–17 You have a good understanding of international work behavior.

12–14 You have an average understanding of how people around the world behave at work.

< 12 Your understanding of international workplace behavior could be improved with more study.

Source: Richard M. Hodgetts and Fred Luthans, *International Management*, 3rd ed. (New York: McGraw-Hill, 1997); Emily Slate, "Tips for Negotiations in Germany and France," *HR Focus*, July 1994, p. 18; and Philip R. Harris and Robert T. Moran, *Managing Cultural Differences*, 4th ed. (Houston: Gulf Publishing, 1996).

CASE 11.1: IT COULD BE A GOLD MINE

Contreras Ltd. is a travel agency in southern Florida that specializes in putting together special tour packages. The owner, Emilio Contreras, and his staff typically identify a series of different types of tours that would be appealing to particular groups and then market them to these target audiences. A few months ago the agency, working closely with travel agents in Russia, put together a two-week tour of southern Florida for 50 Russians. "The key to our success," Emilio recently told the local newspaper reporter who interviewed him, "is that we look for untapped international markets, identify the needs of a customer group there, and then work to attract the requisite number of people to make the tour financially successful for us. No one realizes that there are many Russians with a great deal of money who would like to come and visit the United States and spend time relaxing, fishing, swimming, and seeing the sights. Southern Florida is an ideal spot, and we have been so successful with this first tour that we are now planning to repeat it twice a year."

While the Russian tourists were in southern Florida, Emilio put them at a world-famous hotel on Miami Beach and let them spend the first couple of days on the beach getting a tan and enjoying the water. He then bused them down to Key Largo for a day of fishing. In the days to follow, the group went on a tour of some of the world-famous sites in the region, including a trip to Everglades National Park, a visit to the giant Metro Zoo, and a tour of the Vizcaya (a large Italian Renaissance palace located on Biscayne Bay) before going on to Orlando and spending three days at Disney World. The group spent the last four days of the trip back on Miami Beach, where they had the opportunity to shop, relax, and dine at some of the area's finest restaurants on the beach as well as in Coral Gables and Ft. Lauderdale. The tour was a great success, and all of the Russian tourists agreed that it was the best vacation they had ever had.

In fact, Emilio believes that his fourteen-day package would be attractive to many different target groups around the world. As a result, he is currently working with a group of travel agents in Japan to see if they can help him put together a group of 40 people. "I think I have stumbled onto a winning formula that knows no cultural boundaries. This package is appealing to everyone regardless of where they live or how old they are. Older people like the beach and the opportunity to go home with a tan. Younger adults love the fishing. Kids are crazy about the trip to Disney. In short, there's something here for everyone. Now all I have to do is go out and market it. This could be a gold mine!"

1. How do the cultural dimensions in Japan differ from those in the United States? (Use Table 11.2 to help you answer this question.)

2. Based on your answer to the preceding question, are there any issues that Emilio needs to keep in mind in his effort to attract Japanese customers? Explain.

3. When interacting with his Japanese clients, what are some useful human resources principles that can be of value to him? Describe three of them.

CASE 11.2: THEY'RE GOING TO THINK ABOUT IT

The Open Arms Hotel is a very popular lodge located in Vermont. The hotel does a thriving business during the ski season as well as during the summer, when many people are seeking a somewhat remote facility that will allow them to get away from the bustle of the metropolitan area. The lodge also is a favorite among business firms looking for a place to conduct a strategic planning retreat or some related activity that is best handled off-site.

A few years ago a German businessman spent a skiing weekend at the Open Arms and was very impressed with both the facilities and the service. He came back the next year with his wife and most recently with his entire family. On each occasion he was extremely pleased and went away convinced that such a hotel could be very successful in Germany.

Last week the man, Hans Schmitz, returned to the hotel to talk to the owners, Julie and Tim Flanders. Hans and a group of his friends in Germany do a great deal of business investing and they have located a hotel in a ski region that is for sale. "The owners want to retire," Hans explained to Julie and Tim, "and are willing to sell at a reasonable price. Unfortunately, they never did a very good job of catering to their market, the way you do. If my partners and I were to buy this hotel and get you to come over and run it, we are convinced it would be a profitable venture for all of us. Of course, you still have your hotel here in Vermont, but if you came for three months during your slowest season of the year and got everything organized, then you could commute between the two facilities on a bimonthly basis. I know that this strategy would work—and you would just love Germany. The people are wonderful and your style of managing things would attract them in droves."

Julie and Tim have promised Hans that they will think about his proposal. However, they are somewhat concerned that German customers are quite different from Americans and that they will not be able to live up to Hans's expectations.

1. How do the cultural dimensions of Germany differ from those of the United States?

2. Based on your answer to the preceding question, what types of challenges would you see in Julie and Tim accepting Hans's offer?

3. Based on your knowledge of international human resources, what are three suggestions you would make to Julie and Tim that could help them deal effectively with German customers?

ANSWER TO BOX 11.1: "WHAT WAS THE QUESTION?"

The manager asked the individual, "Can you do it again?" When the individual asked, "Which part?" the manager said, "The entire presentation." In this way, the committee was able to listen a second time to what the company was offering and get a clearer idea of the value that would be received. Additionally, the second presentation was shorter and more direct because the presenters omitted information that was not critical to the presentation but had been used as filler. When the group finished its presentation, the manager asked for a third run-through. This procedure was followed with each presentation group. Then, after deliberating for a few days on which group offered the most value and appeared to be the best one with whom to work, the committee made its decision. The winning manufacturing team later said that this was the most challenging presentation it had ever made because the Japanese forced them to strip away the glossy presentation and get down to the critical essentials.

ENDNOTES

1. William Ouchi, *Theory Z: How American Business Can Meet the Japanese Challenge* (Reading, Mass.: Addison-Wesley, 1981), p. 27.
2. Alan M. Rugman and Richard M. Hodgetts, *International Business* (New York: McGraw-Hill, 1995), p. 130.
3. Richard M. Hodgetts, Jane W. Gibson, and Charles W. Blackwell, "Cultural Variations in Nonverbal Communication," *55th Annual Business Communication Proceedings,* San Antonio, November 8–10, 1990, pp. 211–229.
4. Michael R. Czinkota, Pietra Rivoli, and Ilkka A. Ronkainen, *International Business* (Chicago: Dryden Press, 1989), p. 236.
5. Also see Chuck Y. Gee, "It's a Fine Line," *Lodging,* November 1994, pp. 80–84.
6. Geert Hofstede, *Culture's Consequences: International Differences in Work-Related Values* (Beverly Hills, Calif.: Sage Publications, 1980); Geert Hofstede, *Cultures and Organizations: Software of the Mind* (London: McGraw-Hill U.K., Ltd., 1991), pp. 251–252; and Geert Hofstede, "Cultural Constraints in Management Theories," *Academy of Management Executive,* February 1993, pp. 81–94.
7. Rugman and Hodgetts, *International Business,* p. 550.
8. For more on this topic, see Philip R. Harris and Robert T. Moran, *Managing Cultural Differences,* 4th ed. (Houston: Gulf Publishing, 1996).
9. Sharon Moshavi et al., "India Shakes Off Its Shackles," *Business Week,* January 30, 1995, pp. 48–49; and Rahul Jacob, "India Gets Moving," *Fortune,* September 5, 1994, pp. 100–104.
10. Harris and Moran, *Managing Cultural Differences,* p. 263.

CHAPTER TWELVE

Developing Outstanding Service

LEARNING OBJECTIVES

In the last two chapters, customer needs and desires, including those of international clients, were examined. This information helps firms pinpoint customer groups or market niches. The primary focus of this chapter is to study how hospitality organizations fill these market niches through the use of outstanding service. In addition to examining the laws of service, attention will be given to how companies create the right service strategy and then stay on track. When you have finished studying all of the material in this chapter, you will be able to:

1. Define the term *service* and discuss the three laws of service.
2. Explain the five fundamentals that are used to create the right service strategy and how associates can help in this process.
3. Relate how hospitality organizations focus their strategy and then go about niching their market with value-added services and unconditional service guarantees.
4. Describe how these organizations ensure that they are staying on track through the use of feedback and effective recovery strategies.

The Nature of Service

Service is anything of value, other than physical goods, that one person or organization provides in exchange for something.[1] Service is critical to the success of every hospitality organization because it often helps distinguish between those enterprises that customers perceive as outstanding and those that are judged to be less than this. There are a number of ways that businesses try to develop what is popularly called "knock-your-socks-off service".[2] One is by clearly understanding the laws of service and communicating this to everyone in the company. Another is by carefully analyzing the ABCs of service. The following sections examine both of these areas.

Laws of Service

There are many ways to provide high-quality service. All are influenced by the three laws of service that help guide these efforts and provide an umbrella for the service strategy.

First Law of Service. The *first law of service* is expressed in the statement: **Satisfaction equals perception minus expectation.** The degree to which customers are satisfied is determined by the amount of service they receive (perception) minus the amount they believe they should get (expectation). This law is illustrated by many hospitality organizations that focus their service strategy on creating customer delight. They not only end up giving the client good service—they end up giving the person more than he or she expects. In turn, this creates a positive experience for the client and increases the likelihood that the individual will return in the future. Moreover, the generation of high customer satisfaction does not have to take a great deal of time or effort. It can be a result of simply doing things better than expected—or somewhat differently.

> My wife and I stopped by a restaurant for breakfast before starting our day . . . . Up walks Frances Russell . . . the creator of an exceptional service experience. She was polite, friendly, and efficient. You could tell she took a great deal of pride in her work, and I began to see that the service would be good. But the unexpected came when she prepared to pour my coffee.
>
> Normally, if 90 percent of your coffee in a standard restaurant lands in your cup, you're doing well. But before serving my coffee, she asked if I was right-handed or left-handed. . . . When I answered that I was left-handed, she proceeded to reposition everything on the table to be more convenient to a southpaw, including setting the coffee cup to my left and moving everything else aside.

Before that time, I was quite accustomed to moving the cup and other items myself. In fact, I was so accustomed to it that before this experience, I never even realized I was doing it! But now, Frances Russell has spoiled me for life.[3]

Second Law of Service. The *second law of service* is: **First impressions are the most important.** Typically, this impression is created when a guest first comes in contact with an associate. For example, an individual who has just driven up to the front of a five-star hotel will encounter a valet who will park the car and a bellperson who will bring the guest's luggage into the hotel. These associates must be cheerful and efficient if the hotel is to create a good first impression. In other cases, a first impression may involve a series of events. For example, an international traveler who is flying on British Airways for the first time will typically evaluate the entire flight as a first impression. So in ensuring that this is a positive experience, the airline has developed a series of strategies. The chairman of the airline recently described some of them in this way:

> When we found that many long-haul travelers felt poorly when they arrived at their destinations, we began our Well-Being in the Air program to help passengers combat fatigue and improve their circulation. It consists of healthful meal choices and a video demonstrating exercises that customers can perform in their seats. That's relatively small. But we also designed a whole new service—our Sleeper Service—for First Class customers flying long routes. They can eat a real dinner in the lounge before boarding and change into "sleeper suits" (pajamas) on the plane. Upon arriving in Britain, they can use our arrival lounges, which are a major innovation. They're places where our First Class and Club World customers can get their messages left overnight while they were in the air; have breakfast; read a newspaper; shower; get a manicure, haircut, or shave; have clothes pressed; and then catch a taxi or subway or train into town.[4]

Third Law of Service. The *third law of service* is expressed in the statement: **A service-oriented attitude alone will not assure good service.** An organization also has to have an infrastructure that can promote and deliver service.[5] This can be accomplished in a number of ways, including implementing training programs and carefully monitoring feedback so as to ensure that high service standards are maintained.

> The Ritz-Carlton hotel chain trains all its associates—from those on the front desk to those in maintenance and housekeeping—how to converse with customers and how to handle complaints immediately.

In addition, it provides each associate with a "guest preference pad" for writing down every preference gleaned from conversations with and observations of customers. Every day, the company enters these preferences into a chainwide database that now contains profiles of nearly a half million patrons. Employees at any of the 28 Ritz-Carlton hotels worldwide can gain access to these profiles through a . . . travel-reservation system.[6]

The Behavioral ABCs of Service

Closely linked to the third law of service, which relies heavily on informational feedback (how well service is being delivered) is *motivational feedback*, which encourages associates to continue certain types of behaviors and terminate others. These basic ideas were discussed earlier in Chapter 9, where positive reinforcement was examined in terms of individual motivation. They are also useful in ensuring high levels of service. The application of motivation feedback rests on the behavioral ABCs of service: antecedents, behaviors, and consequences.

An *antecedent* is something that happens before a behavior occurs. The antecedent is the trigger or stimulus for the behavior and often takes the form of a cue or hint. For example, the hotel manager tells the desk clerk, "When Mr. Robert Robinson checks in, be sure to put him in Penthouse 4. He is a very important guest of the hotel."

A *behavior* is a response to an antecedent. These can take a wide variety of forms including greeting a customer, addressing a complaint or, in the preceding example, taking special care of a guest. In Mr. Robinson's case, the desk clerk may have already checked to ensure that the penthouse is ready for occupancy, there are extra towels in the bathroom, and a complimentary fruit basket has been delivered to the room.

A *consequence* is the outcome of a behavior. If Mr. Robinson is impressed with the service and conveys this feeling to the hotel manager, the desk clerk is likely to be praised by the manager and will repeat this performance in the future. Of course, there are other consequences that could result, but regardless of what they are, it is this outcome which dictates future behavior. Table 12.1 provides an illustrative example of the linkage between antecedents, behaviors, consequences, and future outcomes.

In ensuring the highest level of continued service, organizations must use the right form of reinforcement. As two experts in outstanding service put it, "To sustain the behavior that produces Knock Your Socks Off Service, you should reinforce positive behavior and minimize the amount of attention paid to poor behavior."[7] This approach is particularly important in helping create the right service strategy.

Table 12.1 Antecedent-Behavior-Consequence-Future Outcomes

Antecedent	Behavior	Consequence	Future Outcome
An associate is encouraged to keep an up-to-date and accurate record of customer complaints and the ways in which they were resolved.	The associate, who has only an average number of complaints, carefully and completely records all of the desired information.	Supervisor ignores the associate	Associate eventually stops recording complaints unless specifically reminded. Corrective actions and recovery are ignored or carried out improperly.
An associate is encouraged to keep an up-to-date and accurate record of customer complaints and the ways in which they were resolved.	The associate, who has only an average number of complaints, carefully and completely records all of the desired information.	Supervisor bawls out the associate for complaints.	Associate becomes "creative" in defining what is and is not a "real" complaint.
An associate is encouraged to keep an up-to-date and accurate record of customer complaints and the ways in which they were resolved.	The associate, who has only an average number of complaints, carefully and completely records all of the desired information.	Supervisor compliments the associate on the detail in the reports and notes reductions in types of complaints and quality of recovery.	Associate continues to record information accurately and works to reduce the causes of complaints and improve the quality of recovery.
An associate is encouraged to keep an up-to-date and accurate record of customer complaints and the ways in which they were resolved.	The associate, who has a higher-than-average number of complaints, carefully and completely records all of the desired information.	Supervisor compliments associate on the detail in the report and makes suggestions for reducing complaints.	Associate continues to report accurately and seeks ways of reducing complaints.

Source: Excerpted by permission of the publisher, from *Sustaining Knock Your Socks Off Service* by Thomas K. Connellan, et al. © 1993 Performance Research Associates Inc. Published by AMACOM, a division of American Management Association. All rights reserved.

Creating the Right Service Strategy

In developing outstanding service, hospitality organizations need to create the right service strategy. In addition to addressing the five dimensions of service, which were discussed in Chapter 10, this involves consideration of two other areas: (1) focusing the strategy and (2) niching the market. The following sections examine each.

Focusing the Strategy

The focus of every well-conceived service strategy is directed toward giving customers what they want. Services that are provided by one type of hospitality organization may have little value for another because of each company's focus. For example, consider quick-service and full-service restaurants. A quick-service establishment will emphasize the speed of service. As a result, it will offer efficiency of delivery, drive-through facilities, and takeout. In contrast, a full-service restaurant will emphasize selection and will put a strong emphasis on the presentation and quality of the food.[8] When comparing these two types of restaurants, there are many similarities. Each will offer tasty food, have competent servers, and be prepared to correct any mistakes that occur. On the other hand, the two establishments have different target markets, as seen by the price and ambiance that are offered.

When focusing its strategy, a service-driven firm will try to develop a competitive advantage by stressing certain areas. Examples include customer treatment, speed, price, variety, and the use of unique skills. Table 12.2 shows how different companies use these factors in creating a market niche for themselves. Notice that each of the selected companies in the table employs a different mix of the five factors. So while some of them are in the same industry, they employ different strategies in order to better differentiate themselves.[9] This approach is true not only for large firms, but for small ones as well.

> Kimco Hotel and Restaurant Management Company is a small, privately held chain of hotels on the West Coast specializing in what William Kimpton (founder and CEO) calls "affordable elegance." Mr. Kimpton purchases older buildings in various cities and converts them into European-style hotels that are comfortable, not glitzy, and contain few amenities—except charm.
>
> To make his establishments a notch above the bed and breakfasts but not quite full-fledged hotels, Mr. Kimpton also decided to add dinners when clients indicated they wanted the kind of atmosphere he provided for breakfasts to accompany their evening meals. This combination of charm, affordability, understated elegance, and good food appeals to a somewhat upscale business traveler and the leisure market.[10]

Table 12.2 How Selected Companies Focus Operations for Competitive Advantage in the Marketplace

Company	Treatment	Speed	Price	Variety	Unique Skills
Disneyland	X				X
McDonald's Corporation		X	X		
Domino's Pizza		X[a]	X		
Marriott Corporation	X				
Club Med Resorts	X[b]		X		
American Airlines		X[c]		X	
Singapore Airlines	X				
Southwest Airlines			X[d]		

[a] First to use the automated pizza maker, where an attendant puts in a raw pie on one side and takes out a cooked pie on the other.

[b] All-inclusive, low-cost resorts where staff known as Gentils Organisateurs (GOs) co-produce a fun vacation with the guests, Gentils Members (GMs).

[c] SABRE reservation system makes it easy for travel agents to book seats and for the company to instantaneously change prices to counter competitors' rates.

[d] No-frills service (*i.e.,* no computerized reservation system, no assigned seating, and no meals) allows lowest prices in the industry.

Source: Adapted from R. B. Chase and W. E. Youngdahl, "Service By Design," *Design Management Journal,* Winter 1992, p. 11.

Niching the Market

A *market niche* is a target group to which a business wants to sell its goods and services. One way of cultivating a market niche is by offering outstanding service to members of this niche. In the preceding example, the Kimco Hotel and Restaurant Management Company has carefully targeted its niche and is focusing on providing these guests the goods and services they want. The key to such success is being able to identify guest needs. An example is provided in Box 12.1. Before continuing, take the quiz and see how well you can identify what Japanese and American guests prefer in hotel facilities.[11]

There are a number of ways in which hospitality organizations try to improve the service being offered to their customers. One way is to focus on value-added services. Another, and complementary, approach is that of employing an unconditional service guarantee. The following sections examine these approaches.

Value-Added Services. *Value-added services* are perceived by customers as increasing the benefits they are receiving.[12] These benefits can take a number

Every year, U.S. hotels are finding themselves having to compete vigorously for business. While most of their customers are Americans, a growing number now come from overseas. As a result, the Sheraton is now targeting international travelers by developing strategies for attracting their business. One of these groups is Japanese guests. How do they differ from American guests? In answering this question, rank the importance that is assigned by each group to the six factors below. (Hint: There is very little similarity in the rankings.)

Japanese	American
_____ a. health and function facilities	_____ a. health and function facilities
_____ b. price	_____ b. price
_____ c. location	_____ c. location
_____ d. room condition	_____ d. room condition
_____ e. personal service/associate attitude	_____ e personal service/associate attitude
_____	
_____ f. security	_____ f. security

When you have finished ranking both lists, compare your answers to those in the key at the end of the chapter. Based on the results, what conclusions can you draw about how the Sheraton attracts Japanese travelers? How does this strategy differ from that used with American guests?

of different forms. In the case of a hotel, they can include faster check-in and check-out service, a complimentary newspaper every morning, and free use of the health club. In the case of a restaurant, they could include a special menu for children, price discounts for seniors, and a guarantee that every meal will be served within fifteen minutes of the time the server takes the order. The important thing to remember about value-added services is that *not* everything the organization does will add value. For example, a man who does not work out will assign no value to the free use of the health club; and a 35-year-old woman will derive no value from price discounts for seniors. This is why it is so important for hospitality organizations to get feedback from their customers (see Chapter 10) and learn what is important to them. Fortunately, many organizations have done just this, and the result is that they have managed to capture and hold select market niches. One way is to teach associates how to provide sensational service.

Providing Sensational Service. Sensational service can be achieved in a variety of ways. One way is learn how to greet and deal with guests. At The Mansion restaurant on Turtle Creek in Dallas, for example, associates are taught to follow four basic guidelines:

- Always use guests' last names and refer to them as Mr., Mrs., Ms., or Dr.
- Acknowledge each guest with a warm greeting.
- Make eye contact with each guest.
- Smile generously.[13]

A second way to provide sensational service is to give something for nothing. For example, while they are waiting for their food, diners at La Montagne in Memphis can borrow books from the restaurant's lending library and read them while they wait. At C. A. Muer restaurants in Michigan, guests waiting for a table are served lemonade in the spring and summer and hot cider in the fall and winter. Box 12.2 provides additional insights regarding how some restaurants provide sensational service to guests waiting for a table.

A third way to provide sensational service is to establish service rituals. For example, at the Ritz-Carlton hotels, associates are encouraged to remember guests' names and to greet them by name (and title), such as, "Good morning, Dr. Anderson."

These behaviors all add value to the service and help create and sustain a market niche. Closely linked to this concept of value-added service is the unconditional service guarantee, which has become increasingly popular in recent years.

Unconditional Service Guarantees. An *unconditional service guarantee* is a promise that if things do not go as intended, the organization will correct the situation to the satisfaction of the customer. These guarantees have five characteristics.[14]

First, the guarantee is nonnegotiable. For example, if a hotel promises that the room will be acceptable to the customer, there is no negotiation with the individual regarding a discount on the price of the lodging. If the customer is not satisfied, he or she gets a refund—period!

Second, the guarantee is easy to understand and communicate. A restaurant with a posted guarantee of "10-Minute Lunch Service or It's Free" leaves no doubt in the customer's mind regarding what is being promised. The sign is direct and clear.

Third, the guarantee is meaningful to the customer because it emphasizes something that the person values. If time is important, then rapid delivery is emphasized. If price is important, then the organization will promise to "meet or beat" any advertised price. Additionally, the guarantee has to be financially meaningful. If a hotel guest is not pleased with the accommodations, it is

Box 12.2
Effectively Handling Waiting Lines In Restaurants

Sometimes waiting lines are inevitable. This is particularly true in popular restaurants. Despite this inconvenience, however, a number of steps can be taken to minimize the inconvenience and keep the customer's goodwill. Five of the most useful are the following:

1. *Keep the customer occupied while waiting.* One of the simplest ways is to send out a plate of hors d'oeuvres for guests to nibble on. Another is to have a television in the waiting area and tune it to a sporting event; most of these events can be followed visually, so the volume can be turned off and those who do not want to watch can do other things without being distracted.

2. *Minimize anxiety by letting entering guests know the waiting time.* This allows them to decide whether they want to stay or go elsewhere. If they decide to stay, it also helps them remain calm because they know the extent of the wait. Of course, if there is going to be a further delay, this must be communicated to everyone. Otherwise, when the initial waiting time has expired, diners are going to

start coming up and asking for their tables.

3. *Let customers know why they are waiting.* If a large party showed up an hour ago and has taken six tables, perhaps they will be done in another 30 minutes and it is worth waiting. On the other hand, if most people were seated less than fifteen minutes ago, the wait may be extensive and the customer can then decide to leave.

4. *Make waiting equitable.* When people come in, note their names and give service on a "first in, first out" basis. Unless the service is unique and guests are willing to wait for an extended period of time, do not convey the message that there are regular customers who are automatically moved to the front of the line.

5. *Keep people waiting in a group.* This makes the wait more bearable because everyone feels that they are suffering together. And when one of the group is seated, this heartens the rest, who feel they cannot be far behind.

unlikely that the individual will feel that a complimentary breakfast is of any value. The guest probably does not want to stay at the hotel any longer than necessary because of the bad experience. On the other hand, if the hotel offers to tear up the room bill the individual might feel that this indeed was meaningful.

Fourth, the guarantee is easy to invoke. The customer does not have to talk to three people, fill out two forms, and fully justify the reasons for the dissatisfaction. The guarantee is invoked by simply calling to the company's attention the fact that the service was unacceptable.

Fifth, it is easy to collect on the guarantee. If the room is not comfortable, the cashier will refund the person's money or tear up the bill.

In recent years, a growing number of hospitality organizations have been offering unconditional guarantees. At Hampton Inn, for example, guests are guaranteed a clean, comfortable room and prompt, courteous service. If they do not receive this, they get a free night's stay. The same is true for Howard Johnson, Sleep Inn, and others.[15] Additionally, research shows that these guarantees are paying off. Feedback from customers who invoked their guarantee at Hampton Inn has led management to realize that 99 percent of these guests would stay with the hotel chain again because of the attitude of the hotel staff when they requested or received compensation under the guarantee.[16]

Staying on Track

One of the primary ways that organizations ensure that they are continuing to deliver outstanding service is through evaluation of customer feedback. As noted in Chapter 10, this typically comes in the form of surveys, although it is also common to find interviews being conducted and customer panels being formed for the purpose of obtaining feedback. In all of these cases, the customers are asked to evaluate the service. Then the organization will determine if any changes are needed and, if so, how these are to be implemented. Research shows that there are ten areas in which feedback is generally sought. In some cases, a couple of these may have great importance to the organization, while a few others may not be relevant.

1. *Reliability.* Is the service consistent and dependable?
2. *Responsiveness.* Do associates provide the service in a timely way?
3. *Competence.* Do associates have the necessary skills and knowledge to provide the service correctly?
4. *Access.* Is the service easy to receive because it is being widely provided and available most (if not all) of the time?
5. *Courtesy.* Are associates polite, respectful, considerate, and friendly?
6. *Communication.* Do associates communicate clearly with customers, and do they listen carefully to what customers are telling them?
7. *Credibility.* Do customers view the organization as being trustworthy, believable, and honest?
8. *Security.* Does the customer feel free from the fear of danger or risk of being hurt in any way?

9. *Understanding.* Do associates make the necessary effort to understand customers' needs?

10. *Tangibles.* Does the organization offer physical evidence of its services as seen by the presence of associates and facilities?[17]

The answers to these questions help the organization determine whether its service program is on track. If changes are needed, they occur in three ways. One is by examining the current system to see how internal changes can bring about improvements—for example, by reducing serving time in the restaurant. A second is by incorporating new offerings into the service strategy, such as delivering a newspaper to every guest room by 6 A.M., and providing a complimentary dessert to every guest who has to wait more than 20 minutes for a table. A third way is by continuing to offer training and development to associates, so that they are better able to respond to the ever-growing need to improve service. Of course, despite all of these efforts, sometimes errors will occur. When this happens, associates must know how to recover quickly.

Service Recovery

There are a number of things that associates can do to correct situations that have gone awry. Some of these solutions are a result of on-the-job experiences that have taught associates how to act. Many of them, however, are a result of effective training programs that have pinpointed typical problems and taught the participants how to deal with them. This training provides associates not only with solutions, but with the confidence needed to implement them, and it reduces the risk of compounding the problem by improvising an improper response. Quite often organizations begin this training process as soon as the associate joins the company.

> Sonesta Hotels uses games as part of its orientation program for new employees. Trainees are divided into two teams, each of which in turn receives a description of a problem and is asked to come up with a solution. The opposing team has five possible answers to compare the response with. Points are awarded depending on how well the responses fit the general criteria of keen observation, responsiveness, care and concern, and compensation for true loss.[18]

Use Apologies Effectively. One of the most important ways to begin service recovery is with an apology. It is important to remember that if a customer perceives a slight or mistake, an apology is in order. In fact, many service-driven organizations insist that their associates apologize even if the customer is unaware of the mistake.

Mike Bates of the Widman Popcorn Company was enjoying lunch with a friend at a Red Lobster restaurant. According to Mike, the service was friendly and fast and the food right on target. Imagine his surprise when the manager approached the table and explained that, because it took eleven minutes, rather than the promised ten, the entire meal would be on the house. Now guess who is one of Red Lobster's most loyal customers! And all for the price of lunch.[19]

Make Amends Greater than the Mistake. When an error occurs, the associate needs to do something to offset the mistake. In the preceding example, Mike Bates did not know that he had waited eleven minutes for the food, and he certainly was not upset with the service. So the free lunch was more than he expected. On the other hand, if he had known he had waited eleven minutes and was entitled to a free lunch, he might have been less delighted. And if he had known he had waited eleven minutes and had to insist on being given the free lunch, he might have been disappointed with the service even though he received the desired outcome. So in making amends that are greater than the mistake, associates must keep in mind that the customer's perception of the situation is critical. As an example, compare the following two situations and decide which organization provided the best service recovery.

Situation 1

A businessperson who had checked into a hotel found that the magnetic door lock was not working. He returned to the front desk, where the manager suggested that he wait in the lounge while the lock was repaired. While in the lounge he was offered free drinks. After two hours had passed and the door was still not repaired, he went on to dinner in the restaurant with another member of his management team. When the manager came by to ask him if the complimentary drinks were sufficient compensation for the inconvenience, the businessperson said no and proposed that the manager also include complimentary dinners for him and his associate. The manager suggested that they split the difference, commenting, "How about for one?"[20]

Situation 2

A group of vacationers who were on a Club Med trip from New York to Cancun, Mexico found that their flight was six hours late leaving, made two unexpected stops, and circled for 30 minutes before landing in Cancun. The trip took ten hours more than planned, ran out of food and drinks, and arrived at 2 A.M. The landing was so rough that oxygen masks and luggage dropped from the overhead, and a lawyer on board had already begun collecting names and addresses for a class-action lawsuit. The general manager of the Cancun resort got advance word of the flight and took half his staff to the airport, where they laid out a table of snacks and drinks and set up a stereo system to play lively music. As the guests filed through the gate, they received personal greetings, help with their bags, a sympathetic ear, and a chauffeured ride to the resort. Waiting for them there was a lavish banquet, complete with mariachi band and champagne. In addition, the staff rallied other guests to wait up and greet the newcomers, and the partying continued until sunrise.[21]

Obviously the guests in situation 2 felt much better about their treatment than did the individual in situation 1. The tour group felt that the Club Med people did more than was expected. After all, it was not the latter's fault that the plane was delayed. On the other hand, the hotel manager is responsible for ensuring that hotel guests have an enjoyable stay. The lock on the door should have been fixed promptly, or some action taken to ensure that the guest did not have to sit in the lounge for two hours. The manager should not have negotiated on such a minor request as two free dinners, given the inconvenience that was caused for the customer.

Have a System for Resolving Problems. If every problem requires a unique solution, it will take an inordinate amount of time to resolve mistakes. An organization should have a series of well-communicated steps for handling problems. For example, if the waiting time for a table is more than fifteen minutes, the cook will send out a plate of hors d'oeuvres for the waiting guests to nibble on. If a customer's car battery needs to be charged, a call will be placed to the local service station (whose telephone number is available on a master list) by the concierge. If a guest feels ill, one of the three doctors who is on call for the hotel will be asked to come by immediately. These procedures are useful in dealing with problems, because they reduce the situation to a matter of implementing preplanned steps. They are also useful in dealing with one-of-a-kind situations.

> The Four Seasons hotel in Washington was once asked by the State Department to make room for a foreign dignitary. Already booked to capacity, the Four Seasons had to tell four other customers with reservations that they could not be accommodated. However, the hotel immediately found rooms for them at another first-class hotel, while assuring them they would remain registered at the Four Seasons (so that any messages they received would be taken and sent to the other hotel). When rooms became available, the customers were driven back to the Four Seasons by limousine. The Four Seasons also paid for their rooms at the other hotel.[22]

Use Empowerment. *Empowerment* is the authority to make decisions without having to check them with anyone else. While a great deal more will be said about this topic in the next chapter, it is important to remember that when associates are empowered, they are able to solve problems on the spot.[23] As a result, they can adjust their behaviors to fit the situation. Here is an example of a discussion between a guest who is checking out and the associate who is handling the bill.

Guest: There are some charges on my bill that are not mine.

Associate: Okay. Which ones are they?

Guest: Well, first, these two long-distance phone calls are not mine. And the charge for the minibar does not belong to me. Also, my restaurant bill last night was $32.27 including the tip, not $47.86. I think these were all misposted.

Associate: I'm sorry for these errors. Let me make the corrections and get you a revised bill immediately. Would you like to leave your charges on the credit card you gave us when you checked in?

Guest: Yes.

Associate: Fine. I'll be back in just a minute with the new bill.

The associate is empowered to make changes in the bill when errors are pointed out by guests. This facilitates the time needed to provide the service and helps maintain the goodwill of the customer. It also makes associates feel that they have authority in their work areas, and is thus a useful motivation tool. Additionally, empowerment helps associates avoid what are called the ten deadly sins of customer service. (See Table 12.3.)

SUMMARY

1. Service is anything of value, other than physical goods, that one person or organization provides in exchange for something. The three laws of service help guide these efforts and provide an umbrella for every service strategy. The first law of service holds that satisfaction equals perception minus expectation. The second law is that first impressions are the most important. The third law of service is that a service-oriented attitude alone will not assure good service. An organization also has to have an infrastructure that can promote and deliver service.

2. Closely linked to the third law of service is motivational feedback, which encourages associates to continue certain types of behaviors and terminate others. The application of motivation feedback rests on the behavioral ABCs of service: antecedents, behaviors, and consequences. An

Table 12.3 How Empowerment Helps Associates Deal with the Ten Deadly Sins of Customer Service

The Sin of Saying or Conveying the Message:	The Use of Empowerment to Overcome This and to Convey the Message:
I don't know the answer.	I do know the answer and I'm going to use this knowledge to help you.
I don't care about your problem.	I do care about your problem and I'm going to do something about it.
I can't be bothered with your problem.	I can be bothered with your problem and I have the authority to resolve it.
I don't like you.	I do like you and I'm going to show it by helping you deal with this problem.
I know everything there is to know about how to handle this situation.	I don't know everything there is to know about how to handle this situation, but I am going to work with you to straighten out the matter.
You don't know anything.	Your question is a good one, and I'm happy to answer it.
We don't want your kind of customer around here.	We do want your kind of customer and I'm going to prove it by solving your problem.
Don't come back again.	I want you to come back again. I'm going to do what what it takes to solve your problem.
I'm right and you're wrong.	You are not wrong, you are right. And I'm going to prove this to you by solving this problem to your satisfaction.
Hurry up and wait.	I respect your time and I'm going to handle your problem immediately.

Source: Excerpted by permission of the publisher, from *Delivering Knock Your Socks Off Service* by Ronald E. Zemke. © 1991 Performance Research Associates, Inc. Published by AMACOM, a division of American Management Association. All rights reserved.

antecedent is something that happens before a behavior occurs. A behavior is a response to an antecedent. A consequence is the outcome of a behavior. Future outcomes are determined by reinforcement of positive behavior.

3. When focusing its strategy, a service-driven firm will try to develop a competitive advantage by stressing certain areas. Examples include customer treatment, speed, price, variety, and the use of unique skills.

4. A market niche is a target group to which a business wants to sell its goods and services. One way of cultivating a market niche is by offering outstanding service to members of this niche. Hospitality organizations try to do this in a number of ways. One way is to focus on value-added services. Another, and complementary, approach is to employ a satisfaction guarantee.

5. One of the primary ways that organizations ensure that they are continuing to deliver outstanding service is through evaluation of customer feedback. Research shows that there are ten areas in which feedback is generally sought: reliability, responsiveness, competence, access, courtesy, communication, credibility, security, understanding, and tangibles.

6. Sometimes things will go wrong and a service recovery strategy will be needed. Associates can do this in a number of ways. One is to begin with an apology. A second is to make amends that are greater than the mistake. A third is to have a system for resolving problems. A fourth is to empower the associates.

KEY TERMS

service	behavior
first law of service	consequences
second law of service	market niche
third law of service	value-added services
motivational feedback	unconditional service guarantee
antecedent	empowerment

REVIEW AND APPLICATION QUESTIONS

1. Of the three laws of service, which one is most important to a hospitality organization? Defend your answer.

2. You have been asked to explain to a group of new hospitality associates how an understanding of the behavioral ABCs of service can be of value in creating and sustaining motivational feedback. What would you tell them? Be complete in your answer.

3. Charles Wade, a personal friend of yours, is in the process of opening a new hotel. Charles would like to create a service strategy that will help

him develop a market niche. What would you recommend to Charles to help him accomplish this objective? Offer two practical suggestions.

4. Rhonda Marzelli spent the evening in a hotel that is well known for its advertising slogan, "If you're not satisfied, your stay is on us." Rhonda found the accommodations to be extremely poor and has told the manager that she wants to invoke the service guarantee. The manager expressed his disappointment and has offered to give her a 40 percent refund on the room. If you were the manager's boss, what would you do and why? Explain.

5. Dave Lionel and his family waited almost two hours to get a table at a restaurant. It turned out that the maitre d' had mistakenly failed to call Dave's name, and it was not until Dave came and asked that the maitre d' discovered his mistake. The individual immediately admitted his oversight and Dave and his family were seated within five minutes. What would you suggest that the restaurant do to recover from this mistake? Be complete in your answer.

SELF-FEEDBACK EXERCISE: WHAT TYPES OF SERVICE BEHAVIORS ARE IMPORTANT TO YOU?

There are many types of service behaviors that are important to customers. The following are five clusters of these behaviors. Read the three statements in Cluster 1 and rank each statement from 3 (most important to you) down to 1 (least important to you). Remember that this is a forced ranking, so you cannot give equal scores to all three statements. When you are done, go on to the next cluster. When you have finished all five clusters, enter all of your answers on the scoring sheet and read the interpretation of your responses.

Cluster 1

_____ 1. When something goes wrong, I like to get an explanation of what happened.

_____ 2. When something goes wrong, I want to be able to talk to someone in authority.

_____ 3. When something goes wrong, I want to be treated as a person and not as an account number.

Cluster 2

_____ 1. When I call about a problem, I do not want to be put on hold without first being asked.

_____ **2.** When I have a problem, I want to be told what number I can call to start getting some action.

_____ **3.** If the problem I am facing cannot be solved, I want to be given some alternatives to consider.

Cluster 3

_____ **1.** When I call about a problem, I want to be able to speak to someone on the first call who has the authority to solve my problem.

_____ **2.** I want to feel that the company that is getting my business really appreciates it.

_____ **3.** If I called about a problem and now it has been resolved, I want to know about this promptly.

Cluster 4

_____ **1.** I want to know how long it will take to solve a problem I have.

_____ **2.** I want to be told about ways that I can prevent this problem in the future.

_____ **3.** I want to receive an apology when an error is made.

Cluster 5

_____ **1.** I like to be given ideas about how I can cut the costs of using this service in the future.

_____ **2.** I like to be addressed by name and not Mr./Mrs./Miss.

_____ **3.** If my problem cannot be resolved immediately, I want to be given progress reports on how things are going.

Scoring: Transfer your answers to the following scoring key by matching the cluster and number. For example: 1-1 means cluster 1, answer 1; 3-3 means cluster 3, answer 3.

Column A	Column B	Column C
1-1 _____	1-2 _____	1-3 _____
2-2 _____	2-3 _____	2-1 _____
3-3 _____	3-1 _____	3-2 _____
4-1 _____	4-2 _____	4-3 _____
5-3 _____	5-1 _____	5-2 _____
Total _____	_____	_____

Interpretation: Keep in mind that the higher the total, the more important that column is to you. Column A measures the importance that you assign to information. You want to know what is going on and value this service highly. Column B measures the importance of results. You want problems to be straightened out as soon as possible. Column C measures the importance you assign to respect. You want to be treated well.

If one of your column totals is more than five points higher than any other, you place strong importance on this service. If any of the column totals are within five points of each other, you assign similar importance to these behaviors.

CASE 12.1: IF IT'S LATE, IT'S FREE

Dorothy Aldridge and her husband, Phil, worked in a restaurant near the financial district for almost fifteen years. Dorothy waited tables and handled the cash register, while Phil worked in the kitchen. Three years ago the Aldridges decided to quit their jobs and open a food delivery service. Their reasoning was fairly straightforward: Most of the bankers, stockbrokers, and other financial personnel who came into the restaurant for lunch were always in a hurry to eat and leave. They could not afford to be away from the office for more than 30 minutes. In fact, many of them were on their portable telephones the entire time they were in the restaurant. Dorothy and Phil began to believe that if they could offer these customers an appealing lunch that was delivered to their office, they could build a very profitable business.

Before quitting their jobs, the Aldridges began to talk to potential clients and found that there was a strong demand for on-site food service. So they opened a small diner that focused primarily on delivery. The operating procedures are quite simple. People who want to order food must place their orders before 10 A.M. This allows the people in Phil's kitchen to cook and box the food before 11 A.M. At exactly this time, the delivery service begins. Dorothy has six delivery people and each is given orders for customers who are located near each other. As a result, each of these associates is able to deliver to five different locales and be back at the restaurant within an hour. Between 11 A.M. and 1 P.M. the group can collectively drop off food at 60 different offices. A typical delivery will have orders for six to eight people.

There are three other food delivery companies that work the financial district, but none is willing to match the Aldridges' customer service guarantee, which holds, "If we don't get the food to you within ten minutes of the promised delivery time quoted when the order is placed, it's free." To date no order has been delivered late. As a result, the restaurant is gaining a reputation for good food and reliable service, and more and more customers are beginning to place orders. "If this keeps up," Phil noted last week, "we're going to have to expand the business or end up giving a lot of customers a free lunch." Dorothy agreed, but also noted that this was a problem that did not particularly trouble her.

1. How have Dorothy and Phil created a market niche for their business? What does this niche look like? Describe the customer base.

2. What types of value-added services does the restaurant offer its clientele? Identify and describe two of them.

3. How do the Aldridges use their policy of delivering the food within ten minutes of the promised time to help increase customer satisfaction and build goodwill in their market niche? Explain.

CASE 12.2: NO ROOM IN THE INN

When Frederico Fernandez finally got to his hotel, he was exhausted. He had left Madrid 30 hours earlier; because of bad weather, his plane had been diverted to Heathrow, where it waited for six hours. Finally, the weather cleared and the plane took off for Kennedy International. However, a snowstorm hit the city and the pilot landed in Boston. After a twelve-hour delay, Frederico went on to New York where, because of the fourteen-inch snowfall, it took him another four hours to get a taxi and reach his hotel.

Tired and somewhat upset over his long journey, Frederico entered the lobby of his five-star hotel and gave his name to the reservations manager. The women excused herself for a minute and, upon returning, told Frederico, "I'm terribly sorry, Mr. Fernandez. We do have your reservation but because of the tremendous snowstorm we had here yesterday, a number of guests have not yet checked out, so your room is not ready. Have you had lunch?" Frederico said that he had not and the manager suggested that he go into the restaurant and order whatever he would like. "Please be our guest and I will get back to you very shortly," she told him.

As soon as Frederico entered the restaurant, the manager called together her work group and began reviewing the room availability situation. The hotel had a total of 475 rooms and all of these were filled the night of the storm. That morning, 142 guests were scheduled to check out, and there were an equal number due to check in. As of 3 P.M. only 96 of these guests had checked out, and more than a dozen had called to ask if they could extend their stay because of the weather. One couple was scheduled to fly to Chicago but their airline had canceled the flight because of the weather conditions in the city. Three other parties found that the meetings they had scheduled in mid-Manhattan had been delayed for a day and they needed to remain another night in the city.

After they had reviewed all of the available information, the manager and her staff concluded that the hotel was going to have at least 20 people with reservations who could not be accommodated. "We're not going to turn away our current guests, given the difficulties they are already facing," she told the group. "What we need to do is to decide how we are going to deal with those guests who are scheduled to check in today. Obviously there is no room for them here, but we are going to have to do something for them." For the next 30 minutes the staff put together a plan of action. When they were finished, the manager thanked them for their assistance. She then went into the restaurant where Frederico was just finishing his lunch. "How was the food?" she asked. He said the lunch had been quite good. "I'm glad to hear it," she told him. "We pride ourselves on providing the best service in the city, and I hope that by the time you check out you will agree with me." She then began to talk to Frederico about her proposed plan of action for dealing with his problem.

1. Should the manager apologize for the fact that the hotel does not have a room for Frederico? Why or why not?

2. What should the manager do to make amends for this problem? Offer a suggested course of action.

3. How did the use of empowerment fit into your answer to the preceding question? What does this relate about the value of empowerment in providing outstanding service? Explain.

ANSWERS TO BOX 12.1: "GIVING PEOPLE WHAT THEY WANT"

The answers for the two groups are as follows:

Japanese	American
a. 6	a. 6
b. 3	b. 5
c. 2	c. 4
d. 5	d. 1
e. 1	e. 3
f. 4	f. 2

These rankings show that the Japanese traveler values personal service and good associate attitude very highly, while the American guest is most interested in the room's condition (cleanliness, comfort, and amenities). Additionally, location and price are the second and third most important items on the Japanese traveler's list, but these are ranked fourth and fifth respectively by the American guest. The conclusion to be drawn from these data is that it is often necessary for hospitality organizations to employ a variety of different service strategies because their target market may have more than one niche. In the case of the Sheraton, for example, Japanese travelers are different from American travelers, so the factors in the product/service package have to be prioritized differently.

ENDNOTES

1. Donald M. Davidoff, *Contact: Customer Service in the Hospitality and Tourism Industry* (Upper Saddle River, N.J.: Prentice-Hall Career and Technology, 1994), p. 257.
2. See, for example, Thomas K. Connellan and Ron Zemke, *Sustaining Knock Your Socks Off Service* (New York: AMACOM, 1993).
3. Hal F. Rosenbluth and Diane McFerrin Peters, *The Customer Comes Second* (New York: Morrow, 1992), pp. 120–121.
4. Steven E. Prokesch, "Competing on Customer Service: An Interview with British Airways' Sir Colin Marshall," *Harvard Business Review,* November–December 1995, pp. 104–105.
5. Carol A. King, "Service-Oriented Quality Control," *Cornell Hotel and Restaurant Association Quarterly,* November 1984, pp. 92–98.
6. B. Joseph Pine II, Don Peppers, and Martha Rogers, "Do You Want to Keep Your Customers Forever?" *Harvard Business Review,* March–April 1995, p. 112.
7. Connellan and Zemke, *Knock Your Socks Off Service,* p. 111.
8. "R&I '95 Industry Forecast: Segment Trends," *Restaurant & Institutions,* January 1, 1995, p. 50.
9. Robert C. Lewis and Michael Nightingale, "Targeting Service to Your Customer," *Cornell Hotel and Restaurant Association Quarterly,* August 1991, pp. 18–27.
10. Benjamin Schneider and David E. Bowen, *Winning the Service Game* (Boston: Harvard Business School Press, 1995), pp. 43–44.
11. The information in this quiz can be found in Carol Sage, "Extending Service: Sheraton Woos the Japanese Traveler," as in Germaine Shames and Gerald Clover, eds., *World Class Service,* (Yarmouth, Maine: Intercultural Press, 1989), p. 147.
12. Also see Craig Cina, "Creating an Effective Customer Satisfaction Program," *Journal of Services Marketing,* Winter 1989, pp. 5–13.
13. Sharon Vega, "Sensational Service," *Restaurant Hospitality,* July 1994, p. 64.
14. Christopher W. L. Hart, "The Power of Unconditional Service Guarantees," *Harvard Business Review,* July–August 1988, pp. 54–62.
15. Grace Wagner, "Satisfaction Guaranteed," *Lodging Hospitality,* June 1994, pp. 46–47.
16. Chip R. Bell, *Customers as Partners* (San Francisco: Berrett-Koehler Publishers, 1994), p. 38.
17. A. Parasuraman, V. Z. Zeithami, and L. L. Berry, "A Conceptual Model of Service Quality and Its Implications for Future Research," *Journal of Marketing,* Fall 1985, p. 47.

18. Christopher W. L. Hart, James L. Heskett, and W. Earl Sasser, "The Profitable Art of Service Recovery," *Harvard Business Review,* July–August 1990, p. 154.
19. T. Scott Gross, *Positively Outrageous Service* (New York: Master Media Ltd.), p. 94.
20. Adapted from Wagner, "Satisfaction Guaranteed," p. 47.
21. Hart, Heskett, and Sasser, "Service Recovery," pp. 148–149.
22. Hart, "Unconditional Service Guarantees," pp. 59–60.
23. Also see Geoff Pye, "Customer Service—A Model for Improvement," *International Journal of Hospitality Management,* March 1994, p. 3.

CHAPTER THIRTEEN

Maintaining Total Quality Service

LEARNING OBJECTIVES

Developing outstanding service, as seen in the previous chapter, can be a difficult task. However, most organizations find that maintaining outstanding quality is even more challenging. This is because of the tendency to slip back to the old way of doing things. The overriding objective of this chapter is to examine how hospitality organizations go about sustaining their total quality service emphasis. In addition to examining the total quality service concept, consideration will be given to service quality tools and techniques that can be used to ensure the highest possible service levels, the various forms of empowerment that can be employed in resolving quality-related issues, qualitative and quantitative ways of obtaining feedback on performance, and flexible approaches for recognizing and rewarding associate performance. When you have finished studying all of the material in this chapter, you will be able to:

1. Define the term *total quality service* and discuss three major factors that influence this service: paradigms, associates, and costs.
2. Describe some of the most common and useful service quality tools and techniques, including cost analysis, cause-and-effect diagrams, flow-charting, and cross-training.
3. Compare and contrast structured and flexible empowerment and note the value of each.
4. Describe some of the ways that hospitality organizations obtain feedback on results.
5. Identify the six tests for effective rewards and some of the most common types of recognition programs that are used by hospitality organizations.

The Total Quality Service Concept

Total quality service (TQS) is the implementation of a strategy that meets and/or exceeds customer service expectations. Achieving TQS status requires consideration of three areas: changing paradigms, the associate factor, and the cost factor.[1] The following sections examine each of these.

Changing Paradigms

A *paradigm* is a mental frame of reference that dominates the way people think and act.[2] Paradigms help people make sense of the world around them; quite often these paradigms are a result of their day-to-day experiences. For example, American diners are accustomed to having a salad before their main course. They do not eat salad after the main meal. Americans are also taught to switch hands when they eat. For example, in formal dining they will cut the piece of meat on their plate with their right hand, put down the knife, switch the fork into their right hand, and then eat the piece of meat. This is an American paradigm; not everyone follows the same dining procedures as Americans do.

The preceding paradigms continue to exist. However, there are many examples of paradigms that are changing. Service is a good example. Until just a few years ago, customers were accustomed to receiving mediocre service. More recently, however, the service paradigm has changed. Now customers are in the driver's seat; if they do not receive the level of service they want, they will look elsewhere—and quite often they will find that there is another organization that will provide the desired level of service. The main reason why this paradigm has changed is that organizations are now finding that TQS pays off. It generates new business and helps organizations grow and prosper. As a result, hospitality organizations are finding that they must accept the newly emerging TQS paradigm—or else!

Service is not the only changing paradigm in hospitality organizations. Other examples include the way that associates are treated by management, the rewards that are offered, and the way that the enterprise is structured. Table 13.1 provides a series of examples related to changing paradigms in the hospitality industry. As a result of these changes, many organizations are now developing TQS programs that can help them maintain their competitiveness. One of the critical factors addressed in the process is the role and importance of associates.

The Associate Factor

Quality service is greatly influenced by associate motivation and commitment. When this is lacking, clients immediately realize that the organization is incapable of providing high-quality service. How can firms ensure that their

Table 13.1 Paradigm Shifts in the Hospitality Industry

Paradigm Dimension	Old Hospitality Paradigm	New Hospitality Paradigm
Basic mission of companies	Selling goods and services	Delivering superior value to the customer
Profit principle followed by companies	Efficient use of assets in order to generate a profit	Effective addressing of customer needs results in profits
Customers	Viewed as expendable and replaceable	Viewed as assets that must be maintained and nurtured
Associates	Obey orders and operate within strict rules and procedures	Highly empowered individuals who can make decisions and solve customer problems on the spot
Nature of work	Carrying out of assigned tasks	Ensuring quality results every time
Measurement of work performance	Evidence of task completion such as work output	Evidence of customer approval such as survey/questionnaire feedback
Rewards	Objective and material, such as bonuses and financial incentives	Both objective and subjective, such as financial rewards, praise, and recognition
Supervisors	Taskmasters who determine what is to be done	Leaders who are motivators, mentors, enablers, and supporters
Organization	Structure and systems designed to ensure that the work gets done	Structure and systems designed to serve the client's needs
Executives	Preside over the organization and give general direction	Act as inspirational leaders, enablers, and supporters

Source: Adapted from Karl Albrecht, *The Only Thing That Matters* (New York: HarperCollins, 1992), p. 40. Copyright © 1992 by Karl Albrecht. Reprinted by permission of HarperCollins Publishers, Inc.

associates are living up to customer expectations? One way is by hiring the best people. Recent research reveals that associates who provide the highest quality of service tend to have a strong need for achievement (see Chapter 8) and a desire to do a good job.[3] Thus there are screening criteria that can help a firm choose the best job candidates.

In addition, the company must retain these individuals because the cost of associate turnover can be extremely high. As noted in Chapter 6, Marriott International annually loses approximately 60 percent of its front-line staffers in its flagship Marriott Hotels, Resorts, and Suites divisions and estimates that it costs as much as $1,100 to recruit and train each replacement.[4] Moreover, when there is a great deal of turnover it disrupts the ability of the enterprise to deliver consistent high-quality service at a competitive price, because such turnover destroys the organization's momentum.[5] What can organizations do to prevent these problems? Two experts in the field have recommended the following dozen steps for retaining valued associates:

1. Develop associate profiles and then hire and train "right."
2. Offer psychological and monetary compensation.
3. Inform people of pertinent information and respect their right to know.
4. Ask for help and advice of your staff and keep them involved.
5. Earn the respect of the associates.
6. Foster teamwork and reward those who are able to work well with others.
7. Do not hold associates responsible for things that are not under their control.
8. Create moments for associates to feel good about their contributions.
9. Develop a sense of involvement and responsibility in the associates.
10. Keep criticism constructive.
11. Listen to associate complaints; adjust and correct accordingly.
12. Emphasize skill development rather than rules, and foster personal talent.[6]

In addition to these guidelines, TQS organizations empower their people to make decisions in their areas of operation[7] and provide career guidance for them.[8] They adhere to the credo of the Marriott Corporation: "If you take care of your associates, your associates will take care of the customers, and profits will take care of themselves."[9] This is particularly important, given that many people in the workforce at large do not believe that their organizations have the infrastructure or management capability to develop and maintain a motivated workforce. Box 13.1 illustrates this idea by reporting the percentage of the workforce that feels organizations are not addressing critical workplace issues. A close look at these data reveals a number of factors that need to be addressed in order to prevent erosion of associate commitment to the enterprise, a key element in the delivery of TQS.

The Cost Factor

A third major area that merits attention in total quality service is the cost factor. If hotels, restaurants, and other hospitality organizations begin increasing the quality of their service, will their costs not skyrocket? This is a question that had long plagued managers, and until recently the most common answer

Box 13.1
Commitment Erosion Index

How committed are associates to the organization? Do they believe that the firm is hiring the best people, paying a fair wage to associates, and giving them an opportunity to be heard? These types of questions were recently asked of workers, in an effort to determine both the importance of workplace issues and how well management is responding to these issues. In evaluating the responses, two indexes were used. The first was a "broad commitment erosion index," which measured the percentage of survey respondents who rated the issue as either "very important" or "extremely important" *and* the company's performance as "fair" or "poor." The other was a "stringent commitment erosion index," which reported the percentage of only those survey respondents who rated this issue as "extremely important" *and* the company's performance as "fair" or "poor." The following results were obtained for each commitment erosion index (CEI).

Workplace Issue	Broad CEI	Stringent CEI
Having a system to select the most qualified employees for promotion	34	15
Earning a fair wage, considering one's duties and responsibilities	29	14
Having a supervisor with good "people management" skills	27	14
Having policies that are applied fairly to all employees	29	12
Feeling job security	24	10
Having an opportunity to be heard by management above the boss	22	9
Having opportunities to fully use personal skills and abilities	20	9
Being able to understand the organization's vision and goals	16	6
Having constructive conversations with the supervisor about personal performance	14	5
Having a job that does not interfere with personal life off the job	12	4

These results show that organizations need to address a number of workplace issues. In particular, workers at large feel that promotions, wages, and job security need to be improved. They also feel that more attention needs to be given to supervisors with good people skills, the uniform application of organizational policies, and greater upward communication in the hierarchy. To the extent that these issues are not addressed, enterprises are likely to see a continued erosion of their workforce's commitment.

Source: Reported in Russell A. Bell and Lewis C. Winters, "Using Marketing Tools to Improve Employee Relations," *Cornell Hotel and Restaurant Association Quarterly,* December 1993, p. 42.

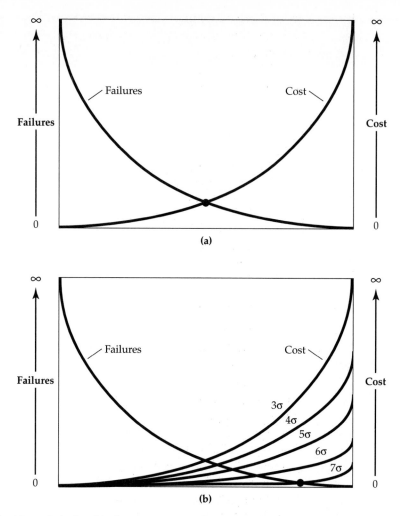

Figure 13.1 *Relationship between Cost and Quality: (a) Old Assumption; (b) New Findings*

was, "Provide sufficient quality but do not go overboard." The logic of this statement was that quality will pay for itself—but only up to a certain point. After this, increases in quality cost far more than what they generate in revenue. This idea is illustrated in Figure 13.1(a), which shows that as the number of failures or mistakes declines, the cost of the improved service increases. Because of this trade-off between cost and quality, service levels will be restricted to the point where the two curves intersect.

In recent years the logic of Figure 13.1(a) has been challenged and proven wrong. Research now shows that as the number of failures or mistakes declines, so does the cost of providing these services. This is illustrated in Figure 13.1(b), where five cost curves are presented. A close look at the figure reveals that as the failure rate declines, so does the cost of service. The cost curves are labeled 3 sigma, 4 sigma, 5 sigma, 6 sigma, and 7 sigma. Sigma is a mathematical calculation of errors or mistakes per million tries. They are the following:

3 sigma	66,810 errors per million
4 sigma	6,210 errors per million
5 sigma	233 errors per million
6 sigma	3.4 errors per million
7 sigma	virtually no errors per million

Figure 13.1(b) shows that if a hospitality organization can eliminate service mistakes, it will greatly reduce its current costs. Why is this so? This question is best answered by looking at the three costs of delivering customer service and examining the impact of doing it right the first time.

1. Performance cost—the basic cost of doing it one time, assuming it happens perfectly, without errors or problems.
2. Failure cost—the additional cost of having to correct or redo things including the cost of making amends to the customer.
3. Prevention and detection cost—the cost of safeguards and processes that exist for the sole purpose of minimizing failure costs, including inspection, double-checking, special accuracy procedures, and extra processes that act as safeguards for proper performance.[10]

When these costs are eliminated, quality can often be delivered for a small percentage of what it previously cost. This statement reinforces what is called the *quality axiom:* Doing things well usually costs less than doing them poorly.[11] A corollary statement often repeated by quality experts is: "You seldom improve quality by cutting costs, but you can often cut costs by improving quality."

Additionally, it is important to remember that higher quality service can command a higher price.[12] There are often customers who are willing to pay more for this service. Of course, not everyone wants highest quality service if the price is going to be higher, but there is a market for it. As seen in the previous chapter, these niches will pay a premium price for premium service. The important thing to remember is that no matter what service is being offered, a TQS program provides people *more* than they expect to receive—and this is the key to total quality!

How can a hospitality organization improve its service and reduce costs? One way is by training associates to use service quality tools. Another is by employing techniques such as cross-training.

Useful Service Quality Tools and Techniques

Every hospitality organization would like to improve service, but quite often management does not know how to go about doing so. Fortunately, there are a host of useful service quality tools that can be taught to associates to help them both identify and deal with quality issues. The following sections examine some of these.

Cost Analysis

One of the simplest, most direct ways of improving quality is to examine costs and identify areas where money is being wasted or could be spent more profitably. Sometimes the analysis reveals that the organization is paying too much for its purchases; by shopping around these expenses can be reduced. In other cases the analysis reveals that the firm needs to upgrade its purchases and buy higher-quality input. For example, consider a restaurant that has changed the lettuce in its salads and now uses a less-expensive lettuce. Here are the costs associated with this new "low-cost" strategy:

Lettuce purchases for salads:	$30,000/year (a savings of $9,000 over the premium-grade produce that used to be purchased)
Salads made:	120,000 per year
Yield of usable lettuce:	75 percent
Cost per salad:	$0.25
Salads rejected by food servers:	6,000 per year
Salads rejected by customers:	3,000 per year
Average cost of placating guests:	$.75 per upset customer

The question the restaurant has to answer is: Does the $9,000 savings offset the cost of salads that are rejected by the food servers and the customers, as well as the cost of placating the guests? The only way to answer the question is by making a comparison of the cost of serving premium-grade lettuce and the cost of serving a lower-quality offering. In examining the comparison figures, remember that each salad that is rejected costs the restaurant 25 cents. Also keep in mind that there are four types of costs that must be examined: (1) prevention costs, which are the expenses associated with buying the higher-quality lettuce and training associates in how to create the salad; (2) assurance costs, which are the expenses associated with inspecting the produce; (3) internal failure costs, which are a result of throwing out some of the product because of waste or failure to meet minimal standards of acceptance; and (4) external failure costs, which are a result of customer dissatisfaction. Table 13.2 provides the annual cost analysis. Carefully read and study the material in the table before continuing.

Table 13.2 Annual Cost Analysis Comparison of the Low-Cost Strategy and the Alternative Strategy

Cost Category	Item	"Low-cost" Strategy	Alternative Strategy
Prevention costs	Lettuce price premium	$ 0	$ 9,000
	Employee training	0	200
Assurance costs	Receiving inspection	0	100
	Chef's inspection	1,800	900
Internal failure costs	Lost lettuce	7,500	500
	Server rejections	1,500	100
External failure costs	Customer rejections	750	100
	Placating guests	2,250	100
	Total cost of quality	$13,800	$11,000

Source: Adapted from D. Daryl Wyckoff, "New Tools for Achieving Service Quality," *Cornell Hotel and Restaurant Association Quarterly,* November 1984, p. 86.

Notice from the data in the table that the cost of the premium lettuce is *less* than that of the low-cost substitute. The main reasons for this differential are accounted for by the cost of the lettuce that must be discarded, the need for the chef to conduct a detailed inspection, rejections by both customers and servers, and the cost of placating the guests.

The conclusion from this analysis is obvious: The restaurant should return to its old strategy of purchasing higher-quality lettuce. This will save the firm $2,800 annually ($13,800 minus $11,000) and will result in greater satisfaction from both the servers and customers, who will now reject far fewer salads.

Cause-and-Effect Diagrams

Another valuable quality tool is the *cause-and-effect diagram,* which can be used to pinpoint the reasons for quality problems and develop action plans for resolving them. A good example of where this tool can be used is for addressing common time-wasters such as unproductive meetings. Many hospitality organizations find that they spend far too much time in meetings. How can these meetings be made more productive? Using a cause-and-effect diagram, this question can be answered by following four simple steps.

1. A group of individuals who have attended meetings and seen how unproductive they can be are called together and asked to identify the reasons that these meetings are not more productive. As the group members call out their reasons, one of them writes down what is being said. During the process, members are encouraged to be creative and build on the comments of the others.

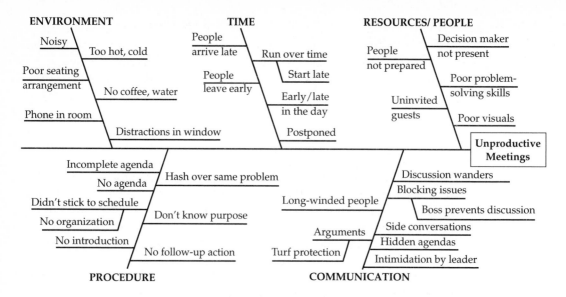

ENVIRONMENT

Noisy
Too hot, cold
Poor seating arrangement
No coffee, water
Phone in room
Distractions in window

TIME

People arrive late
Run over time
People leave early
Start late
Early/late in the day
Postponed

RESOURCES/ PEOPLE

People not prepared
Decision maker not present
Poor problem-solving skills
Uninvited guests
Poor visuals

Unproductive Meetings

Incomplete agenda
No agenda
Hash over same problem
Didn't stick to schedule
No organization
Don't know purpose
No introduction
No follow-up action

Long-winded people
Arguments
Turf protection

Discussion wanders
Blocking issues
Boss prevents discussion
Side conversations
Hidden agendas
Intimidation by leader

PROCEDURE

COMMUNICATION

Figure 13.2 *A Cause-and-Effect Diagram for Dealing with Unproductive Meetings*
Source: Richard M. Hodgetts, *TQM in Small and Medium-Size Organizations* (New York: AMACOM, 1996), p. 109.

2. After the group has exhausted all of the possible reasons for these unproductive meetings, the responses are categorized into groups such as poor meeting procedures, lack of communication during the meeting, and a poor physical environment for getting things done.

3. The group now enters its reasons on a cause-and-effect diagram. This is done by first drawing a horizontal line across the page on which the diagram will be constructed, and at the right end of the line writing the major problem (unproductive meetings) and boxing it in. Then, for each of the major categories that have been identified, the group will enter the reasons associated with it. Figure 13.2 provides an example. Notice in the figure that the group identified five major categories: environment, time, resources/people, procedure, and communication. Then the causes associated with each of these reasons are identified and placed below the respective reason.

4. The group then analyzes the diagram and decides which one of the major categories is most likely to be causing the problem. They then formulate a plan of action for addressing this cause and begin making the necessary changes. When they are finished, they then identify the next major reason for unproductive meetings and begin attacking this cause.

Cause-and-effect diagrams are extremely useful in helping hospitality organizations deal with service problems. There are three reasons for this: (1)

the focus is placed on identifying causes that are directly related to the problem under analysis; (2) the associates who will be responsible for solving the problem are the ones who are involved in the analysis process; and (3) the result is an action plan designed to bring about effective action. Because the cause-and-effect diagram is so action-oriented, it continues to remain one of the most popular TQS tools.

Flow-Charting

A *flow chart* is a pictorial representation of the steps in a process or job. The objective of flow-charting is to examine all of the steps involved in carrying out a task, and then see if some of these steps can be eliminated or shortened. Because it is so simple to do, flow-charting is a commonly used TQS tool.

In constructing a flow chart, it is typical to begin by having those who do the work draw the flow chart with all of its steps. Then the chart is examined by others who are familiar with the job to see if any steps have been left out. Finally, attention is focused on how long it currently takes to carry out each step and how these times can be reduced or eliminated. Sometimes the jobs of associates in a host of different departments will be integrated into the flow chart for the purpose of examining how the overall time total can be reduced. Figure 13.3 provides an example.

As seen in the figure, the flow chart details the steps involved in a customer ordering and paying for room service. The hotel associates get involved in the process when the customer calls and asks to be connected with the kitchen; their involvement ends when the customer gets and pays the bill. After examining this flow chart, how can the hotel reduce or eliminate the steps carried out by the associates? One way is by allowing the customer to call the kitchen directly and place the order. This eliminates the need to go through the switchboard and saves time for both the customer and the hotel. A second way is by teaching kitchen associates how to take customer orders quickly and accurately, as well as how to cook the food and prepare the tray. Additionally, the bell-service function might be improved by finding faster ways to get the food to the customer's room. The time for the accounting function could be reduced by designing a bill that can be electronically scanned into the computer. Finally, the front desk could reduce time by printing the customer's bill and slipping it under the guest's door the night before check-out. In this way, the customer can review the charges and, if everything is correct, simply keep the bill as a receipt. Of course, if any of the charges are incorrect, the guest can then go to the front desk and have the bill revised. Otherwise, the person can check out at his or her leisure.

The preceding paragraph details a number of changes already being used by total quality service hotels that have flow-charted the room service and check-out functions. As a result, they are now able to provide high-quality service more quickly than ever.

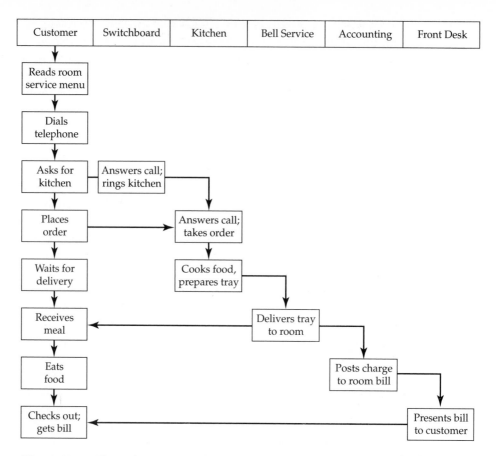

Customer	Switchboard	Kitchen	Bell Service	Accounting	Front Desk

Figure 13.3 *Flow-Charting Room Service with a Customer/Departmental Blueprint*

Source: Karl Albrecht, *The Only Thing That Matters* (New York: HarperCollins, 1992), p. 223.
Copyright © 1992 by Karl Albrecht. Reprinted by permission of HarperCollins Publishers, Inc.

Cross-Training

Another common approach to improving quality is to break down the walls between the various departments that provide service and get everyone to work as a team. A good example is the servers and the cooks at a restaurant. Quite often each believes that they are working very hard while the other is not doing enough. Here, for example, are comments made by a server and a cook. Notice the contrasting differences.

Server

The cooks always have a fit when we have special orders and holds. They yell, "Why can't you just sell the food the way we make it?" Like it's something personal. They don't understand or don't care that people have allergies, special diets, or just special tastes that they expect a good restaurant to accommodate. If customers aren't satisfied, they'll find another restaurant that doesn't have a problem preparing dishes to fit their taste.[13]

Cook

I don't mind filling special orders if a request comes from a customer. What drives me crazy is when servers lead a customer into making a special request—say for lobster tail, which is not on the menu, but that we have in case someone wants it. Not only is it not a profitable item to serve, but I have to stop what I'm doing to prepare it.[14]

How can these attitudes be changed and the two groups learn to work with each other? Some restaurants do this with cross-training. For example, they will require servers to help prepare the meals so that they better understand the problems and challenges faced by the cooks. Similarly, they will have the cooks spend a few days waiting tables. In this way, each gets to appreciate what the other does. A good example is provided by a kitchen supervisor at a Marriott hotel who was continually complaining about the banquet servers. Commenting on the experience, he noted:

My boss got so fed up with me that he made me put on a tux and get out on the floor. It was the most eye-opening experience of my professional career. Those guys work hard—my feet were killing me, I had to make split-second decisions, and I had to face customers' reactions face to face. It was tough.[15]

Cross-training gives associates empathy for their co-workers. They begin to realize that the other associates are working just as hard as they are. Some restaurants take this idea a step further and develop group incentive plans that encourage the associates to work together. For example, they will form a team consisting of a bartender, host, cook, and server. The team's goal will be to sell the most chef's specials. When this happens, a camaraderie develops between departments. More important, associates in different parts of the restaurant encourage each other and interact with customers in order to sell more. Ultimately, the common goal brings them together and results in better service and higher profits.

Empowerment

As noted in the previous chapter, *empowerment* is the authority to make decisions without having to check them with anyone else.[16] In practice, there are two types of empowerment: structured and flexible. *Structured empowerment* allows associates to make decisions as long as they remain within specified and detailed limits. The quiz in Box 13.2 helps illustrate the options that are

Box 13.2
Using Structured Empowerment

Under a structured-empowerment situation, associates are authorized to take action, but their options are limited. The following six situations each have specific actions that should be taken by the front-desk clerk, according to a major national hotel. Carefully read each situation and see if you can determine the action that the individual is authorized to take by the hotel.

Guest Complaint or Problem	Actions that the Front-Desk Clerk Is Authorized to Take
a. During check-out, a guest announces that he or she had a room-related problem, *e.g.,* no hot water, bad television reception, the room was too noisy.	_____ 1. Make an adjustment in the room rate
b. During check-out a guest complains that the service in the dining room was extremely poor.	_____ 2. Offer an upgrade for the next visit, or adjust the current bill by as much as $100.
c. During check-out a guest complains that mail or messages were not delivered to him or her.	_____ 3. Make the adjustment on the guest's bill.
d. A guest points out that the rate being charged is higher than the rate that was quoted at check-in.	_____ 4. Adjust the guest's bill by $100.
e. A guest complains about a rude or insensitive associate.	_____ 5. Refer the problem to the assistant manager.
f. A guest insists that he or she did not incur any minibar charges.	_____ 6. Adjust the guest's bill by $50.

When you have finished, check your answers with those of the hotel at the end of the chapter.

available to associates operating under this form of empowerment. *Flexible empowerment* provides associates with greater latitude and allows them to improvise on-the-spot decisions. This form of empowerment, while not as widely used as structured empowerment, is gaining in popularity in hospitality organizations.

The empowerment process always begins with a commitment from top management. Senior-level managers have to be willing to allow associates at all levels to make decisions that affect their own area of operations. This support for empowerment must then be accepted by middle-level managers, because it is this group that feels the effect most heavily. After all, when lower-level associates are empowered, they typically receive authority that used to be held by their boss. On the other hand, there are a number of benefits to empowerment for middle-level managers including the following: (1) they have more time to devote to other tasks; (2) their associates learn to accept responsibility and thus become more effective in their jobs; (3) a cadre of potential middle-management talent is nurtured; and (4) guest satisfaction often increases, and this enhances the manager's status in the organization.

In moving the empowerment program to the front line, a series of steps are commonly taken. The first is to have a meeting of the front-line people and the senior-level managers in order to discuss the need for improving guest services and the role that can be played by empowerment. At this time, it is common to explain the type of associate empowerment that will be implemented—structured or flexible—and to ensure the associates that they will not be reprimanded or punished for making decisions they believe are in the best interests of the guest and the organization.

The next step is to train the associates in the necessary empowerment tools and techniques.[17] These extend from learning how to take control of situations using cost analysis, cause-and-effect diagrams, and flow charts.

The final step is to monitor the results, ensure that middle-level managers are supporting the effort, and use feedback to take corrective action. Some of the ways in which this is done include: (1) determining whether there is an increase in the number of positive guest comment cards; (2) finding out whether there has been a reduction in the number of times a manager has been summoned to resolve a guest problem; (3) determining whether associates are able to attend to guest needs more quickly and more personally; (4) finding out whether the overall level of interest and job satisfaction among the associates has increased since the empowerment program has been introduced; (5) determining whether management's level of trust and respect for the associates has improved; and (6) finding out whether associates are suggesting new and better ways to improve guest service and satisfaction.

Feedback on Results

The preceding section examined ways of measuring the effect of empowerment. However, hospitality organizations do not limit their attention solely to this issue. They also want to know how well they are doing in all areas. This feedback can be measured in two ways: anecdotally and quantitatively.

Anecdotal and Quantitative Feedback

Anecdotal feedback consist of verbal comments or stories that describe performance, for example, when a hotel manager says, "Roberta Contana, who was a guest last week, told me that our service is better than that of any hotel she has ever stayed in." *Quantitative feedback* consists of objective measures of performance. An example is an increase of 15 percent in the number of guest survey responses that report "service is excellent." Here are some examples of quantitative feedback related to the introduction of empowerment at select hotels:

- Front-office clerks at one hotel were empowered to adjust guests' bills in any amount in response to disputes over charges. The hotel recorded *fewer* adjustments, while receiving many positive guest comments about service at the front desk.

- To make guests happy and to compensate for nonworking equipment, members of a hotel's engineering staff were given the power to make adjustments on the spot, including comping the room. Guest comments have been positive, even though no rooms have yet been comped—and engineers' morale has improved.

- Housekeepers were empowered to notify the front desk to change the status of completed rooms to "ready for occupancy" without prior inspection by a housekeeping manager. The results were that guests were able to occupy their rooms more quickly and room-inspection scores improved.[19]

Another way that organizations measure results is by examining costs and determining if they are being effectively controlled. In the earlier case of the hotel that switched to a less-expensive lettuce, the cost analysis revealed that the organization was losing money as a result of the decision. So the company went back to using premium lettuce.

A third way in which feedback is measured is by analyzing the results of customer comment cards. In this way the organization is able to determine such things as whether the customer was treated courteously, the room was clean, and the service in the restaurant was prompt. Table 13.3 provides an example of such results as compiled by a large national hotel that wishes to remain anonymous. A fourth way in which feedback is measured is through *benchmarking,* which is a process of comparing in-house job performance with that of other organizations in order to determine how well the enterprise is doing. For example, if a hotel were to benchmark its check-in time with that of competitive hotels in the local area, it could determine how well it compares and learn whether it needs to make any changes in the way this process is conducted. There are a number of ways that benchmarking can be carried out. One is by sharing information with competitive organizations. This is something that many enterprises are willing to do because it helps them identify areas for improvement. Another way to benchmark is to focus on the

Table 13.3 Feedback Results at a Major Hotel (Partial Results)

	Always	Sometimes	Mostly No	Not At All
Facilities & Services				
Did our conference room meet your expectations?	88%	12%		
Did the quality of the food and beverage served meet with your approval?	83	17		
Did our Reservations and Front Desk departments meet your expectations?	88	12		
Was your bill prepared according to instructions, including a summary, and presented in a timely manner?	83	17		
Staff				
Was our Sales/Catering staff responsive and accurate with requests for information?	89	11		
During the event, was the hotel management and staff available when needed?	83	17		
Were all your requests responded to swiftly and to your satisfaction?	88	12		
Did our staff anticipate your needs throughout your stay?	82	18		
Overall Satisfaction				
Would you consider our hotel for a future meeting venue?	95	5		
Would you recommend us to others looking for a meeting site?	89	11		

process, which, in this case, is check-in time; and to look at banks, fast-food restaurants, and other organizations that have developed procedures for rapid service. Based on the results, the hotel can then make any needed changes in its own process.

Comparative Analysis

Closely linked with the gathering of quantitative data is comparative analysis from one period to the next. The value of this activity is that it helps companies examine trends and determine whether things are getting better or becoming worse. There are two complementary ways in which this is done. First, organizations will look at feedback such as customer response cards from last month and a year ago last month and examine the trends. Second, they will carefully review all written comments on these survey forms to see if these provide any additional insights. Table 13.4 provides some examples of the first type of response as provided by a well-known regional hotel chain. Look over the table and examine the responses that were received last month and 13 months ago. What conclusions can you draw?

A close review of the table shows that the hotel chain's service is improving. In most cases, the associates are providing service that is the same as or better than before. On the other hand, there is some disturbing feedback. When asked to rate the overall hotel service and facilities, the number of "excellent" responses declined to 75 percent from the previous 80 percent; and when asked to rate the overall attitude of the staff, the percentage of "excellent" comments declined to 81 percent from the previous 94 percent. The good news is that the number of "fair" and "poor" comments also declined, but it appears that the associates are achieving this feat at the expense of excellent performance. So management will want to examine these responses and develop an action plan for moving more of the responses from "good" to "excellent."

In conjunction with the preceding actions, management will review the written comments that accompany these quantitative evaluations in order to determine if there are any suggestions that can be used to further improve performance. For example, in the case of overall performance, here are five of the negative comments:

> Too expensive for the level of service and quality. Also, why were people on nonsmoking floors allowed to smoke?
>
> Simply not worth the price. Lots of small items let the hotel down, *e.g.*, our room was not cleaned until 3 P.M.
>
> Service at the restaurant was substandard.
>
> People at the Tennis Shop were never there.
>
> There should be cable channels in all rooms.

These responses will be used in conjunction with the quantitative comments to determine how service quality can be improved. After the changes are made, additional feedback will be obtained in order to determine how effective the changes have been and whether any additional changes are now needed.

Rewarding Performance

In order to maintain a TQS strategy, it is necessary to keep the associates highly motivated. This is where performance rewards enter the picture. When developing a recognition-and-reward system, hospitality organizations need to keep two things in mind. First, the system must pass certain effectiveness

Table 13.4 Customer Survey Data from a Major Regional Hotel:
A Comparative Analysis of Results

Question	Last Month Yes	No	13 Months Ago Yes	No
Was your reservation handled promptly and courteously?	100%	0%	97%	3%
Was the valet courteous and efficient?	100	0	100	0
Was the bellperson courteous and informative?	96	4	97	3
Was your check-in handled promptly and courteously?	98	2	96	4
Did you find your room clean and comfortable?	99	1	96	4
Did you have sufficient supplies of towels, soap, hangers, etc.?	100	0	98	2
Were your messages delivered promptly?	100	0	97	3
Were the pool and beach facilities clean?	100	0	100	0
Was the food in the restaurant prepared to your satisfaction?	100	0	92	8
Was the order taker for your room service courteous and efficient?	98	2	98	2
Was the food from room service prepared to your satisfaction?	98	2	96	4
Was room service prompt and friendly?	95	5	92	8

	Last Month Exc.	Good	Fair	Poor	13 Months Ago Exc.	Good	Fair	Poor
How would you rate the overall service and facilities?	75%	19%	4%	2%	80%	13%	7%	0%
How would you rate the overall attitude of the staff?	81	16	3	0	94	13	3	0

	Last Month Yes	No	13 Months Ago Yes	No
When convenient, would you stay with us again?	93%	7%	90%	10%

tests. Second, the system must be developed so that it addresses the unique needs of the associates. The following sections examine both.

Tests for Effective Rewards

Motivation researchers have long noted that organizations give people financial rewards mainly for showing up. They do not reward them for outstanding performance. As a result, many associates do the minimum amount of work because there is no benefit for doing more. In correcting this problem, it is important to note that there are six tests for effective rewards, and every motivation program must meet them.

1. *Availability.* Rewards have to be available and they have to be given in large enough amounts that associates feel they are motivational. For example, a hotel that offers $1 for each good idea submitted may find that few associates are motivated to submit suggestions. However, if the organization also promises a reward of 5 percent of all cost savings generated as a result of the idea, this may increase the number of submissions.

2. *Flexibility.* The system must be able to give rewards to individuals whenever they do a good job and not be limited to quarterly or annual recognition programs. In this way, the manager who wants to single out an individual for doing a good job can do so at any time.

3. *Performance contingency.* Rewards have to be closely tied to performance: the greater the performance the higher the reward.

4. *Visibility.* Rewards must be seen and their value should be understood. Associates must know who is being rewarded and they must understand why these individuals have been given this recognition.

5. *Timeliness.* Rewards should be given immediately after the performance. This helps associates establish a link between what they do and the reward that is given for this performance.

6. *Durability.* Rewards should last for a while. If they do not, it becomes necessary to reward associates again for a job well done; this repetition ends up costing the organization money.

When all rewards are financial, it is often difficult to sustain associate motivation. This is why nonfinancial benefits are so important. As David Bowen and Benjamin Schneider have noted:

> The message is that pay is severely limited as a reward. That doesn't mean you should stop giving it . . . . But you should also consider what *other rewards* can be used and how they might score even higher when subjected to the . . . tests of effectiveness. Furthermore, those other rewards tap into more than the need for security; they also help satisfy the need for esteem, in particular.[20]

Table 13.5   T.G.I. Friday's Inc. Recognition Pin Program

Level I	Level II	Level III
Technical Skills	Leadership	Guest Service/ Building Sales/Optimizing Profit
Certification Pins:	A-Team Pin	Division Store of the Quarter
Baker	City Pin	Pin (Circle of Excellence)
Barback	City Trainer	Idea Pin (Lightbulb)
Bartender	Guest Obsession	$750 Pin
Broiler (Friday's)	Most Valuable Player Pin	$1000 Pin
Busser	Top Five Pin	
Cashier	Top Ten Pin	Star Program:
Delivery	Field Trainer Pin	Five-Diamond Presidential
Dishwasher	In-Store Trainer Pin	Gold Star
Door	New Store Opening Pin	Gold Star with Logo
Expediter		Silver Star with Logo
Fry		Bronze Star with Logo
Grill/Assembler (Dalts)		WOW Pin
Nacho (Dalts)		
Plate/Nacho (Friday's)		
Saute		
Steward		
Waiter/Waitress		
Window		
Master Bartender Pin		
Sanitation Pin (Nifi)		

Source: T.G.I. Friday's Inc.

Types of Rewards

Organizations give a wide variety of rewards to their associates in order to promote and sustain motivation. T.G.I. Friday's, for example, gives recognition pins for technical skills, for leadership, and for providing guest services, increased sales, and profit. Table 13.5 describes the pins that are awarded at each level. The company also gives service awards for 5, 10, 15, and 20 years of continuous service. Other common examples of rewards include plaques, special luncheons, certificates, days off, a picture in the company newspaper, tickets to special events, special parking spaces, and cash. And in some cases, associates can recognize their peers for outstanding accomplishments. For example, the Hotel Phillips in Bartlesville, Oklahoma, has an "extra effort awareness" program, which allows associates to recognize other associates who have performed above and beyond the call of duty.[21]

Each of these programs can be extremely motivational. However, in order to sustain the motivation, programs must be continually revised or new ones developed. Examples of new programs include:

1. Create a "Best Accomplishments of the Year" booklet and include everyone's picture, name, and statement of their best achievement.
2. Create group awards to recognize the outstanding teamwork of associates.
3. Write a "letter of praise" to associates to recognize their specific contributions and accomplishments, and send a copy to your boss or higher-level managers as well as to the human resources department.
4. Send associates to special seminars, workshops, or meetings outside the organization that cover topics in which they are especially interested.
5. Ask your boss or CEO to send a letter of acknowledgment or thanks to individuals or groups making significant contributions.
6. Introduce your peers and management to individuals and groups that have been making significant contributions, thereby acknowledging their work.
7. Create symbols of a team's work or effort (T-shirts or coffee cups with a motto or logo, and the like).
8. Develop a "behind-the-scenes" award specifically for those whose actions are not usually in the limelight; and make sure such awards *are* in the limelight.
9. Recognize (and thank) people who recognize others. Make it clear that making everyone a hero is an important principle in your department.
10. Take out an advertisement in an appropriate publication thanking your associates.[22]

The important thing to remember about these awards is that they often have a limited life. However, by continually modifying or changing the reward-and-recognition system, it is possible to sustain motivation for TQS. As a result, service continues to improve and the organization is able to maintain its market niche in the face of ever-increasing competition because customers are not just satisfied with the service they are receiving—they are delighted with it!

SUMMARY

1. Total quality service (TQS) is the implementation of a strategy that meets and/or exceeds customer service expectations. Achieving TQS status requires consideration of three areas: changing paradigms, the associate factor, and the cost factor. Paradigms require organizations to change the

way they do business, or lose out to competitors who are willing and able to do this. Today the service paradigm is changing and the customer is becoming more powerful than ever. As a result, organizations are now developing TQS programs that help them maintain their competitiveness. Associates are critical to this process and many enterprises have now accepted the credo, "If you take care of your associates, your associates will take care of the customers, and profits will take care of themselves." The third major consideration in TQS is the cost factor. Hospitality organizations are now coming to realize that by eliminating service mistakes, they can greatly reduce costs.

2. In teaching associates to increase quality, organizations rely on a host of tools and techniques. One is cost analysis, which involves examining expenses in order to determine where money is being wasted or could be spent more profitably. Another quality tool is the cause-and-effect diagram, which can be used to pinpoint the reasons for service problems and develop action plans for resolving them. A third is the flow chart, which is a pictorial representation of a process or job that is used to examine all of the steps involved in carrying out the work, and then to see if some of these steps can be eliminated or shortened. Another common approach is the cross-training of associates.

3. Empowerment is the authority to make decisions without having to check them with anyone else. In practice, there are two types of empowerment. Structured empowerment allows associates to make decisions as long as they remain within specified and detailed limits. Flexible empowerment provides associates with greater latitude and allows them to improvise on-the-spot decisions. The empowerment process always begins with a commitment from top management followed by acceptance by middle-level managers. Finally, the process is moved to the front line through a carefully designed strategy that involves commitment, training, and monitoring of results.

4. TQS feedback can be measured in two ways: anecdotally and quantitatively. Anecdotal feedback consist of verbal comments or stories. Quantitative feedback consists of objective measures such as increases in positive survey responses. These forms of feedback are used to help organizations control costs as well as evaluate customer feedback, including using comparative analyses to examine trends and determine whether things are getting better or becoming worse.

5. In order to maintain a TQS strategy, it is necessary to keep associates highly motivated. In developing a recognition-and-reward system, hospitality organizations need to keep two things in mind. First, the system must be available, flexible, contingency-based, visible, timely, and durable. Second, in order to sustain the motivation, programs must be continually revised or new ones developed.

KEY TERMS

total quality service
paradigm
quality axiom
cause-and-effect diagram
flow chart
empowerment

structured empowerment
flexible empowerment
anecdotal feedback
quantitative feedback
benchmarking

REVIEW AND APPLICATION QUESTIONS

1. In what way has there been a paradigm shift in the hospitality industry and what impact has this had on the way in which organizations in the industry now deliver services?

2. The Stanmuller Hotel would like to improve the quality of its service. It intends to begin its efforts with a thorough cost analysis of operations. In what way could this strategy help improve overall quality? Offer an example.

3. How could a restaurant use a cause-and-effect diagram to reduce the amount of time needed to serve food? What would this diagram look like after it has been completed? Would it also be possible to develop a plan of action based on the diagram? Explain.

4. The Grandview Hotel is thinking about empowering its associates in order to increase the quality of service. However, it has not decided whether to use structured or flexible empowerment. What would be a major advantage to the use of each? Which of the two types of empowerment would you recommend? Why?

5. Jerry Honsworth's restaurant used to be very popular, but in recent months business has dropped off sharply. Jerry finds this hard to believe, given that over the years so many of his customers have told him how much they enjoy eating there. What is wrong with Jerry's data collection method? How can he get more accurate information? Explain.

SELF-FEEDBACK EXERCISE: WHAT DO YOU KNOW ABOUT TOTAL QUALITY SERVICE?

The following 20 statements are designed to provide you with feedback regarding your approach to and beliefs about total quality service (TQS). Read each statement and then indicate whether you believe it is true (T) or false (F) by circling the answer. The scoring key and accompanying explanations are provided at the end of the exercise.

T F **1.** When an organization creates a TQS system, it should first obtain support from the lower-level associates.

T F **2.** Empowerment is a key area of consideration in the development of a TQS organization.

T F **3.** A TQS approach works well for a large hospitality organization, but it has little, if any, value for a small one.

T F **4.** Many hospitality organizations are now finding that TQS is no longer a luxury; it is a cost of doing business.

T F **5.** Most hospitality associates who support a TQS system do so primarily because of the potential increases in their own salaries.

T F **6.** For many organizations, TQS involves a paradigm shift and they have to be prepared to address these new changes.

T F **7.** Research shows that the easiest way to improve quality is by cutting the number of people in the organization.

T F **8.** When a company loses a customer, it should try to overlook this loss and quickly replace the individual with another customer.

T F **9.** Organizations should monitor their service quality by collecting not just anecdotal evidence but quantitative evidence that shows how well they are doing.

T F **10.** People throughout the organization should be taught how to use total quality tools, so they can measure and improve performance in their own area of operations.

T F **11.** Listening is a critical skill that must be developed by all associates if TQS is to become a reality.

T F **12.** When someone does something very important, he or she should receive positive feedback and praise, but if the activity is a minor one, it should be ignored because there is not enough time in the day to praise everyone for everything they do exceptionally well.

T F **13.** All units should have clear measures for tracking quality performance and they should use these measures in determining how service can be improved.

T F **14.** Most customers are so demanding that hospitality organizations now make far more use of structured empowerment than ever before.

T F **15.** The focus of an effective TQS program should be on preventing problems, rather than fixing them as soon as they are uncovered.

T F **16.** One of the reasons why costs go down as quality goes up is that associates do not waste time correcting mistakes.

T F **17.** A well-run TQS organization will increase the quality of service by getting the various departments to compete with each other, because internal competition and in-fighting helps drive quality up and costs down.

T F **18.** Effective TQS organizations put the customer first, even if this means that the associates are treated poorly.

T F **19.** One reason why cause-and-effect diagrams are so popular among TQS organizations is that this tool helps the team members develop an action plan for dealing with the problem under analysis.

T F **20.** Cross-training is popular with managers but not with lower-level associates because the latter believe it is nothing more than a way to get them to do more work.

Scoring: Check your answers with the key below. Where you missed an answer, carefully read the explanation. Then total the number you had right and give yourself 1 point for each.

1. False. The first place to start is with the upper-level associates, whose support is going to be critical to the entire total quality effort.
2. True. Empowerment allows everyone to participate in the total quality effort.
3. False. A TQS approach works for all organizations, both large and small.
4. True. Organizations are finding that today it is "total quality—or else."
5. False. They support it primarily because it helps them do a better job and makes them feel that they are making an important contribution through their own efforts, skills, and abilities.
6. True. It often involves a paradigm shift.
7. False. Cutting people is often a short-term solution only. The most effective ways are those that increase service and generate customer satisfaction.
8. False. The company should be more interested in retaining its current customers than in replacing them with new ones.
9. True. Quantitative data are very helpful in providing objective feedback on performance.
10. True. Everyone should be involved in the process.
11. True. Listening is critical to TQS.
12. False. Everyone should receive positive feedback and praise regardless of how minor the activity was.
13. True. This is a critical step in providing TQS.

14. True. This is helping hospitality organizations respond quickly and effectively to customer demands.
15. True. Prevention is more important than correction because it keeps the focus on quality while helping reduce costs.
16. True. Costs and quality tend to be inversely related.
17. False. A well-run TQS organization will increase the quality by getting the various departments to cooperate with each other.
18. False. Effective TQS organizations believe that if you treat your associates well, they will treat the customer well and everyone will profit.
19. True. These diagrams are action oriented and very helpful in addressing quality problems.
20. False. Cross-training is popular with lower-level associates because it helps them better understand and appreciate what other associates are doing and builds a feeling of teamwork in the process.

Score	Interpretation
16–20	Your approach to total quality service is excellent and shows a sound understanding of how and why the system is so important.
12–15	You have a fairly good understanding of TQS but need to review the answers you missed in order to better understand the total quality process.
11 or less	You need to carefully review the material in this chapter and the answers that you missed. When you have done so, take the assessment quiz again and note your progress.

CASE 13.1: DETERMINED TO MAINTAIN A TOTAL QUALITY FOCUS

The Prenticell Hotel is located in a popular resort area in the southwestern part of the United States. When the hotel was first built, there were only three competitors in the area and the Prenticell was the best of the group. The hotel had more rooms, a larger banquet area, two outstanding restaurants, a giant pool, and a championship golf course. Since then, seven more hotels have been built and most of them now offer strong competition to the Prenticell.

In an effort to determine how it can maintain its current market, the hotel has begun developing a TQS strategy. One of the first places it turned for feedback was customer surveys. The company does not have competitive data, so it is impossible to say how the other hotels are being rated by their own clients. However, the Prenticell does keep monthly customer survey records so it can measure response trends. Last week the TQS committee decided to focus attention on the two restaurants and see if there were any areas where improvements were needed. The trend data for the last year for both units is the following:

	This Month				One Year Ago			
Restaurant 1	*Exc.*	*Good*	*Fair*	*Poor*	*Exc.*	*Good*	*Fair*	*Poor*
How would you rate the quality of the food?	75%	15%	5%	5%	85%	12%	3%	0%
How well did the chef do in preparing the food to your satisfaction?	88	12	0	0	86	14	0	0
How would you rate the promptness of the service?	50	20	20	10	65	22	13	0
How would you rate the friendliness of the associates?	95	5	0	0	92	7	1	0

	This Month				One Year Ago			
Restaurant 2	*Exc.*	*Good*	*Fair*	*Poor*	*Exc.*	*Good*	*Fair*	*Poor*
How would you rate the quality of the food?	71%	14%	8%	7%	82%	10%	8%	0%
How well did the chef do in preparing the food to your satisfaction?	91	9	0	0	86	12	2	0
How would you rate the promptness of the service?	45	25	20	10	75	10	15	0
How would you rate the friendliness of the associates?	92	8	0	0	88	11	1	0

The TQS team has data that go back further than twelve months, but they believe recent trends are more important than any others. Additionally, they believe that the most important thing they can glean from this information is emerging problems that need to be addressed as soon as possible. The chairperson of the committee expressed her feelings this way: "If we can get on top of things right now, we can ensure that our two restaurants are the best in this geographic region and that's going to help us maintain a total quality focus."

1. If you were helping the chairperson identify areas for improvement in the restaurant operations, in which area would you focus attention first?

2. How would it be possible to use a cause-and-effect diagram to address the problem you identified in the preceding question? Explain.

3. In addition to a cause-and-effect diagram, what other TQS tool would you employ? Why?

CASE 13.2: MOVING THEM THROUGH IN RECORD TIME

Yesterday was a very busy one for Nan Wilson, who works at the front desk of a popular midwestern hotel. The hotel caters to businesspeople who are looking for competitive rates and a location close to the downtown business district. These guests typically leave the hotel by 7:30 A.M. so that they can be in the business district before 8 A.M. As a result, beginning at 6:15 A.M. and for the next 90 minutes, there is a rush of activity in the hotel. Each day approximately 40 percent of the guests check out, but this usually does not present a problem for the cashier because many of them use express check-out. Around 2 A.M. every day, those guests who are checking out have a copy of their bill slipped under their door. They can review the bill and, if everything is correct, keep it as a receipt and leave at their leisure. Since the hotel has an imprint of their credit card, they do not need to come to the front desk.

Yesterday was Nan's day as cashier. Typically she will have four or five people in line at any one time and it will take approximately three minutes to address each one's problems or concerns. However, yesterday the line had fourteen people at 7:25 A.M. and all of them had to be in the business district by 8 A.M. In almost every case the guest had a concern or complaint to register. The four most common ones were the following: (1) some of the minibar charges were not accurate; (2) service in the dining room was extremely poor; (3) the rate on the bill was higher than the one that had been quoted at check-in; and (4) messages that were critical to business operations had not been promptly delivered to guest rooms.

In each case, Nan was able to resolve the problem quickly. In particular, since a number of the guests raised the same issue, it often took less than a minute to resolve each. Here is a typical scenario:

Guest: These four minibar charges are not mine. Otherwise, everything else on the bill is correct.

Nan: I'm sorry about that. I'll take these four charges off the bill, and later today I will send you a revised statement in the mail. Is there anything else I can do for you?

Guest: No, that's it. Thank you very much.

Later in the day the hotel manager came by to see Nan and congratulate her on the efficient handling of the check-out line. "You really moved them through in record time," he noted. "I don't think anyone stood in line for more than fifteen minutes. I was very impressed." Nan thanked him for his comments and noted, "Since I'm empowered to make whatever changes I deem proper, it's easy to correct bills and accommodate customers. All I have to know is the problem and I can take it from there."

1. What type of empowerment does Nan have: structured or flexible? Defend your answer.

2. How would you recommend that Nan handle each of the four guest complaints that were listed in the case?

3. How might the manager reward Nan for her outstanding performance? Suggest and explain three things he might do.

ANSWERS TO BOX 13.2: "USING STRUCTURED EMPOWERMENT"

1.	d	3.	f	5.	e
2.	a	4.	c	6.	b

ENDNOTES

1. Also see Joanne C. Plichta, "Total Quality Management in the Quick Service Restaurant Industry," *Food Technology,* September 1994, pp. 152–154.
2. Karl Albrecht, *The Only Thing That Matters* (New York: Harper Business, 1993), p. 45.
3. Glenn F. Ross, "Service Quality Ideals among Hospitality Industry Employees," *Tourism Management,* August, 1994, pp. 273–280.
4. Ronald Henkoff, "Finding, Training, and Keeping the Best Service Workers," *Fortune,* October 3, 1994, p. 114.
5. Ibid.
6. Chase L. LeBlanc and Kristine E. Mills, "Retaining Employees: Make Them Feel Indispensable," *Nation's Restaurant News,* April 18, 1994, p. 30.
7. See Larry Armstrong and William C. Symonds, "Beyond 'May I Help You?'" *Business Week,* Special Quality Issue, 1991, p. 100.
8. Cristine Antolik, "Empowering Employees," *Hotel and Motel Management,* September 6, 1993, pp. 20–21.
9. Adapted from Michael Hartnett,, "Marriott Addresses Quality Service by Taking Care of Its Employees," *Discount Store News,* May 3, 1993, p. 105.
10. Albrecht, *The Only Thing That Matters,* pp. 171–172.
11. Ibid., p. 173.
12. Barbara Whitaker Shimko, "Breaking the Rules for Better Service," *Cornell Hotel and Restaurant Association Quarterly,* August 1994, pp. 19–20.

13. Beth Lorenzini and Brad A. Johnson, "Restaurant Wars," *Restaurant & Industry,* May 1, 1995, pp. 148–149.
14. Ibid., p. 150.
15. Ibid., p. 154.
16. Also see Rick Van Warner, "Make Store-Level Employees a Part of the Decision Process," *National Restaurant News,* January 16, 1995, p. 21.
17. Also see Timothy W. Firnstahl, "My Employees Are My Service Guarantee," *Harvard Business Review,* July–August 1989, pp. 7–8.
18. For more on this topic, see Phil Alfus, "Empowering Your Employees Gets the Best Results," *Restaurant Hospitality,* May 1994, p. 24.
19. Lawrence E. Sternberg, "Empowerment: Trust vs. Control," *Cornell Hotel and Restaurant Association Quarterly,* February 1992, pp. 70–71.
20. Benjamin Schneider and David E. Bowen, *Winning the Service Game* (Boston: Harvard Business School Press, 1995), p. 156.
21. Denise Morgan, "Power to the Employees!" *Lodging,* February 1992, p. 44.
22. Adapted from Chip R. Bell and Ron Zemke, *Managing Knock Your Socks Off Service* (New York: AMACOM, 1992), pp. 171–172.

PART FIVE

Horizons

What does the future hold for the field of human resource management—and where do you fit in this picture? These are the two main questions answered in this part of the book.

Chapter 14 examines future human resource management challenges. One of these is the challenge of diversity, which is being brought about by the changing nature of the workforce in the industry. An analysis of the composition of today's workers shows that there are far greater percentages of women and other minorities than there were in the past. The days of the White male workforce are behind us. Today's workforce is highly diverse and includes younger (18 to 25 years of age) and older (65 years of age and above) workers; larger percentages of African-Americans, Asian-Americans, and Hispanic-Americans; and individuals with varying degrees of education (some very poorly educated and others highly educated). The hospitality manager's job is becoming more challenging because the individual is having to deal with an increasingly diverse work group. In this chapter, you will learn some of the ways in which this can be done. Attention is also focused on ethics and discrimination issues and the ways in which they create challenges for the industry. Consideration is also given to dealing with associates with disabilities, as well as to examining your place in the industry and the personal cost that such a career can exact.

Chapter 15 continues this focus on you by examining ways of developing an effective career plan. First, the topic of personality, addressed in Chapter 2, is revisited and attention is given to identifying and describing successful personality traits in the hospitality industry. At this point you are given the opportunity to examine your own personality and job-related behaviors and to profile yourself. Then consideration is given to writing an effective résumé. In addition to setting forth useful rules, examples of both a cover letter and the design and format of the résumé itself are provided. The next part of the chapter provides guidelines and tips for effective interviewing, including how to prepare for the meeting and how to conduct yourself during the interview. The last part of the chapter offers useful guidelines for managing your career.

When you have finished reading the material in this part of the book, you will know some of the major challenges that will be confronting the industry during the next decade and how firms are trying to deal with these issues. You will also know how to write a résumé and interview for a job, as well as be aware of ways in which you can effectively manage your own career.

CHAPTER FOURTEEN

Future Challenges

LEARNING OBJECTIVES

The hospitality industry faces a variety of human resources challenges. Many of these have been identified and examined in this book, and ways of dealing with them have been discussed. The purpose of this chapter is to look at some of the future challenges that will confront industry management and review the current practices and future strategies that will have to be implemented in order to address these challenges effectively. Particular attention will be given to diversity, ethics, discrimination, associates with disabilities, and the personal costs that hospitality jobs exact from associates. When you have finished studying all of the material in this chapter, you will be able to:

1. Explain some of the reasons for the increasingly diverse workforce in the industry and ways in which hospitality organizations can manage this diversity.

2. Define the terms *ethics* and *sexual harassment* and discuss some of the steps that companies are going to have to take in dealing with these two challenges.

3. Describe the general nature of the Americans with Disabilities Act and explain how organizations are meeting this challenge in terms of redesigning physical layouts and developing training programs.

4. Give some examples of the types of personal demands that hospitality organizations make on associates and why this area will continue to be a challenge for these businesses.

Dealing with Diversity

Over the last two decades, the U.S. workforce has become exceedingly diverse; this trend will continue well into the future. In terms of race, for example, Hispanic-Americans, Asian-Americans, and African-Americans are now entering the workplace in increasing numbers; their respective percentages are going to increase over the next decade. The U.S. Bureau of Labor Statistics recently offered the projections in Table 14.1, which show that the percentage of White males in the labor force over the next decade will continue to decline, while that of women and other minorities will keep rising.

Reasons for Diversity

One of the major reasons for the emergence of diversity as a future challenge for the hospitality industry is that of changing demographics. Older workers, women, minorities, and those with more education are now entering the industry in record numbers.[1]

A second reason is the changes in legislation designed to protect people in the workplace. Although the Civil Rights Act of 1964 prohibited discrimination in employment, the full effects of that landmark legislation, and other laws that have subsequently been enacted, are only now beginning to be felt in the workplace. Examples include the following:

Age Discrimination Act of 1978. This law at first increased the mandatory retirement age from 65 to 70, and was later amended to eliminate an upper age limit altogether.

Pregnancy Discrimination Act of 1978. This law gives full equal opportunity protection to pregnant employees.

Americans with Disabilities Act of 1990. This law prohibits discrimination against essentially qualified individuals who are challenged by a disability and requires organizations to reasonably accommodate them.

Civil Rights Act of 1991. This law refined the 1964 act and reinstated burden of proof to eliminate discrimination and ensure equal opportunity in employment.

Family and Medical Leave Act of 1993. This law allows employees to take up to twelve weeks of unpaid leave for family or medical reasons each year.

These laws, and the threat of legal action, have put teeth into the diversity challenge. Individuals who find themselves excluded from organizations or managerial positions can now bring lawsuits to overcome discrimination barriers and ensure equal opportunities for themselves.

A third reason for the emergence of the diversity challenge is that hospitality organizations are beginning to realize that diversity can help them meet competitive pressures. A willingness to recruit associates regardless of their

Table 14.1 Percentage of the Overall Workforce

Category	1980	1993	2005 (projected)
White males	51	47	44
White females	36	38	39
African-Americans	10	11	12
Hispanic-Americans	6	8	11
Asian-Americans and Others	NA*	NA*	4

*NA—Not available.

Source: U.S. Bureau of Labor Statistics, 1995.

race, color, gender, or national origin is going to increase the pool of talented individuals from which a hospitality organization obtains its associates. In turn, this is going to increase the skills, abilities, and talents of the enterprise and make it more competitive.

To more fully understand the nature and scope of diversity, it is useful to examine some of its specific characteristics. When hospitality firms do this, they are then in a better position to set forth a plan of action for managing diversity.

Characteristics of Diversity

There are a number of specific, objective characteristics of diversity. The most widely recognized deal with age, gender, ethnicity, and education.

Age. The U.S. workforce is getting progressively older; this trend is going to continue into the next century. The percentage of employees under the age of 35 is declining, while the percentage in the 35-to-54 age group is increasing. One reason for this change is that the baby-boom generation following World War II is accounting for the increasing number of workers in their forties, and the declining birth rate among the post-baby-boom generation is accounting for the declining percentage of workers in their teens and twenties. A second contributing factor is that people are now living longer, more productive work lives and they are choosing to spend this time at work, something that is now possible thanks to the Age Discrimination Act of 1978.

This development is resulting in a number of changes by hospitality organizations. One is teaching their managers to deal effectively with both older and younger associates, both of whom often have markedly different values—and yet both groups must be taught to work as a team.

Gender. Women have been entering the workforce in record numbers over the last four decades. By 1975 they accounted for approximately 40 percent of the total; by 1994 they constituted around 46 percent of the working population; by 2005 they will make up around 48 percent of the workforce; and they will eventually become a majority of the labor population.[2]

Managing women effectively will be a challenge for hospitality managers, especially at the middle and upper levels of the hierarchy, where women are not well represented. These organizations will have to address issues such as equal pay and promotion opportunities. The latest statistics show that women continue to be paid less than men, and while they account for the majority of the hospitality industry workforce, they hold only a small percentage of senior-level posts. One reason is the so-called *glass ceiling effect*, a term that refers to women being prevented from receiving promotions into top-management jobs. These diversity-related issues of pay and promotion will continue to challenge the industry as it enters the 21st century.

Ethnicity. The term *ethnicity* refers to the ethnic composition of a group or organization. As noted in Figure 14.1, census data show that between 1995 and 2050, Hispanic-Americans are projected to pass African-Americans as the nation's largest minority. During this same period, the percentage of Asian-Americans in the United States will almost triple, the percentage of Hispanic-Americans will more than double, and the number of African-Americans will see an increase of approximately 20 percent. At the same time, the percentage of White men and women will decline by almost one-third. The challenge for management will be to deal with these ethnicity changes, especially in terms of policies and practices concerning pay and promotions. Like women, minorities on the average are paid less and are less well represented in the upper-management ranks.

Education. The educational level of the American workforce has been rising. The proportion of 18- to 24-year-olds enrolled in college, which hovered around 30 percent in the 1980s, has jumped up to the 40 percent level today. At the same time, the number of people with little or no formal education is also increasing. This has led some analysts to note that while the top third of our nation's young people are the best educated in the world, the bottom third are at Third World standards.[3] In fact, a survey of 3,600 young people (ages 21 to 25) by the Educational Testing Service found that less than one-third were able to determine the tip and correct change for a two-item restaurant bill, and less than 25 percent could interpret a complicated business schedule.[4]

These data help identify one of the major challenges that hospitality organizations will face over the next decade. In dealing with them, there are a number of steps that businesses can take, including developing training programs, introducing technology, and providing associates with reward-and-recognition systems that will help tap their full innovative potential.[5] Some of the ways in which this can be done were examined earlier in the book.

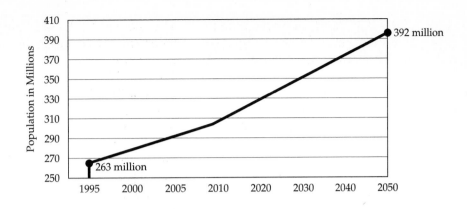

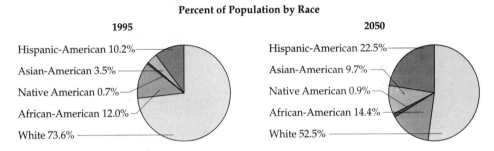

Figure 14.1 *Overall U.S. Population Growth and Racial Composition*
Source: U.S. Census Bureau report, 1993.

Managing Diversity

There are a number of steps that hospitality organizations will have to take to manage diversity effectively.[6] From an organizational standpoint, one is to value diversity (see Box 14.1). Others include careful training, testing, and mentoring.

Training. One of the biggest challenges in managing a diverse workforce is that of understanding and dealing with personal biases. Sometimes managers are ineffective in managing minorities or older associates because they do not know how to address people who are different from themselves. So they treat these associates as they would treat themselves. This process of "doing what comes naturally" is often ineffective because it does not focus on the real differences between the manager and the associates. For example, a young manager may appreciate the fact that his boss always acts in a formal, authoritative way when talking to him. However, an older associate who is working for this young manager may not appreciate this style of leadership. The associate

Box 14.1
A Dozen Useful Ways to Value Diversity

There are a variety of ways to value diversity and take advantage of the talents and skills of a multicultural hospitality workforce. The following are twelve of the most useful.

1. Get a commitment from top management to fully support the diversity effort.

2. Include a declaration about diversity in the company's values or vision statement.

3. Give diversity training to managers, especially those at the senior level, so that they better understand what it is like to be a minority and how to effectively communicate and interact with a diverse workforce.

4. Assign managers as mentors to associates of a different gender, ethnic group, or age group, so that these managers learn how to work effectively with diverse work groups.

5. Create a recognition system designed to encourage managers to set diversity goals, and then reward them for their successes.

6. Form pairs or teams of people who are different in terms of race, gender, and age, and coach them in ways to work collaboratively.

7. Subscribe to one or more newsletters on diversity and circulate them to all associates.

8. Ask associates, "How do you feel you are treated here? What can the organization do to help you achieve your goals?" and then act on the responses.

9. Celebrate the differences among cultures by encouraging associates to share their cultural diversity and stress the fact that the organization welcomes these differences.

10. Increase the supply of diverse associates by systematically recruiting and hiring women, older workers, individuals with disabilities, and individuals from widely differing cultures.

11. Involve people who are not part of the organization's dominant culture in succession planning and promotion sessions, especially when women and other minorities are part of the candidate pool.

12. Get continual feedback on diversity efforts and use this information to correct problems and continue progress.

Sources: Julie O'Mara, "How to Value Diversity," as found in Katie Smith and John Soeder, "Solving the Diversity Puzzle," *Restaurant Hospitality,* March 1994, p. 58; and Faye Rice, "How to Make Diversity Pay," *Fortune,* August 8, 1994, pp. 80–84.

may feel that the young manager is too stuffy and bureaucratic. In helping organizational managers deal with a diverse workforce, training can play an important role. In particular, training can help managers learn to better understand their work groups.

One currently popular approach to training is to help participants identify and address perceived differences among diverse groups. This is done by putting all of the trainees into groups based on their ethnic origin. Then each group is asked to describe the others and to listen to the ways its own group is described. The purpose of the exercise is to offer insights into the way one ethnic group is perceived by another ethnic group. Each group is also asked to openly relate the difficulties it has in working with other ethnic groups and to identify the reasons for these problems. At the end of this type of training, both managers and associates often report that they have a much better understanding of their personal biases and ways that they can improve their interaction with members of other ethnic groups.

Another popular training approach is the use of diversity board games, which require the participants to answer questions related to areas such as gender, race, cultural differences, age issues, sexual orientation, and disabilities. On the basis of the response, players are able to advance on the board or are forced to back up.[7] For example, participants may be asked to focus on cultural issues by answering the following question:

> In Hispanic-American families, which one of the following values is probably the most important:
>
> a. achievement
> b. money
> c. being on time
> d. respect for elders

The correct answer is "d." As participants play the game, they gain a better understanding of the values and beliefs of other cultures.

In most cases, diversity-related games are supplements to other forms of training. For example, they are often employed as icebreakers to get the diversity training session started or to maintain participant interest. They also serve as a link to other areas, such as improved testing, by helping managers gain a better understanding of the legal issues involved in employment practices. For example, one diversity game asks the players to respond to this situation:

> Two White workers and one African-American worker were charged with theft of company property. The White employees were discharged, but the African-American employee was retained because of concerns about racial-discrimination lawsuits. The employer's action was:
>
> a. Illegal. The law prohibits racial discrimination.
> b. Legal. The law protects only minorities.
> c. Legal. This case involved theft.

The correct answer is "a"; by teaching participants this type of information, organizations reduce the probability that their managers will involve the enterprise in a lawsuit and increase the likelihood that all associates will be treated fairly.

Testing. Another ongoing challenge for hospitality organizations will be the use of nonbiased tests for selection and evaluation. This is a problem that confronts most enterprises, but because of the large workforce diversity in restaurants, hotels, and other hospitality firms, it is of particular importance to this industry. Research reveals that most tests traditionally used in selection and evaluation are neither suited nor valid for a diverse workforce.[8] Fortunately, there are a number of ways to deal with this challenge.

> One way to make tests more valid for diverse employees is to use job-specific tests rather than general aptitude or knowledge tests. For example, a company hiring word processing personnel may give applicants a timed test designed to measure their speed and accuracy. The applicant's age, gender, or ethnic background are not screening criteria. This approach differs sharply from using traditional tests that commonly measure general knowledge or intelligence. . . . People from different cultures . . . often did [poorly] on traditional tests because [the tests] were culturally biased toward individuals who had been raised in a white, middle-class neighborhood. Older applicants and those who are functionally illiterate may also do poorly on such culturally biased tests. Job-specific tests help prevent diversity bias by focusing on the work to be done.[9]

Besides being culturally unbiased, tests used in effectively managing diversity should be able to identify whether the applicant has the necessary skills for doing the job. The preceding word-processing example is a good illustration; the test measures specific skills required for the work, not subjective personal characteristics. In some cases, carefully conducted interviews or role playing can be used to identify whether the person has the necessary skills. For example, a person applying for a customer service job at a hotel would need to understand the relevant language of customers and to be able to communicate well. The job would also require someone who can listen carefully, maintain his or her personal composure, and solve problems quickly and efficiently. Carefully constructed and conducted interviews can be useful in helping identify whether the applicant speaks well, can communicate ideas, and has the necessary personal style for dealing effectively with job challenges. Role-playing exercises can also be useful in identifying the applicant's ability to focus on problems and solve them to the satisfaction of the customer. Additionally, the applicant can be given a case or exercise in a group setting to assess interpersonal skills. These types of multiple measures are useful in ensuring valid assessment. Here is an example of how one hospitality organization helps screen managers by using job-related interviews that focus on work performance:

Judith: Robert, you've told me a great deal about your experience and your strengths. Now I'd like to focus on areas where you feel you need to improve further. Can you give me an example of a situation where you analyzed things incorrectly and tell me what you learned from this experience?

Robert: Well, about six months ago I was responsible for supervising operations in the main lobby. Around 10 P.M. an elderly lady and her husband arrived. Their plane was late getting in and they had not guaranteed their reservation. We were totally booked. Realizing the problem, I called housekeeping and learned that there was one room that had been undergoing minor remodeling and could be cleaned and made ready for occupancy within 30 minutes. I explained the situation to the guests and they were quite pleased. Unfortunately, in my haste I made a mistake and learned about it the next morning after the couple had checked out. The hotel manager called me into his office and told me that the woman had been irate. Her husband's health was quite fragile; they always sleep in a no-smoking room. The one I had assigned to them was on a smoking floor. I learned an important lesson from this. I should have asked the lady if she had any special requirements and then tried to accommodate these. In my haste, I failed to remember that elderly guests often have special needs.

This particular interview process of getting the applicant to focus on weaknesses or mistakes is useful in screening candidates because it helps pinpoint sensitivity to job-related problems and the ability to identify and learn from mistakes. It also helps organizations meet the challenge of nonbiased employment screening.

Mentoring. A *mentor* is a trusted counselor, coach, or advisor who provides guidance and assistance. In recent years an increasing number of hospitality organizations, such as Radisson Hotels International, have begun assigning mentors to women and other minorities.[10] The purpose of the mentor program is to help support members of a diverse group in their jobs, socialize them in the cultural values of the organization, and improve their chances for development and advancement.[11] There are a number of specific benefits that mentors offer, including:

1. Providing instruction in specific skills and knowledge critical to successful job performance.
2. Helping to understand the unwritten rules of the organization and how to avoid saying or doing the wrong things.

3. Answering questions and providing important insights.
4. Offering emotional support.
5. Serving as a role model.
6. Creating an environment in which mistakes can be made without losing self-confidence.[12]

In some cases mentoring is an informal process. A senior-level manager will identify someone who appears to be promotable and can benefit from careful guidance and encouragement and either take the person under his or her wing or assign the individual to another manager for mentoring assistance. Increasingly, however, formal mentoring programs are becoming more common. In many cases, these programs have five steps. First, top-management support is secured for the program. Second, individuals who are to be mentors and protegés are carefully chosen. Third, both groups are given orientation; the mentors are taught how to conduct themselves and the protegés are given guidance on the types of questions and issues that they should raise with their mentors so that they can gain the greatest value from the experience. Fourth, throughout the mentoring period, which usually lasts one year or less, mentors and protegés meet individually and together with the support staff of the program to see how well things are going. Fifth and finally, at the end of the mentoring cycle, overall impressions and recommendations are solicited from both mentors and protegés regarding how the process can be improved in the future. This information is then used in helping the next round of mentors do a more effective job.

While mentoring is only now gaining a foothold in the hospitality industry, it offers a great deal of promise in helping organizations manage diversity. It also helps protect associates against discrimination.

Addressing Ethics and Discrimination Issues

Ethics and discrimination are closely linked concepts, and both are going to be important in the effective management of human resources over the next decade. Researchers have found that there is a strong correlation between quality service and sound ethics.[13] At the same time, ethics helps ensure that associates are not discriminated against in the workplace.

Ethics on the Job

Ethics is a set of moral principles and values that are used to answer questions of right and wrong.[14] While some hospitality organizations have their own code of ethics, all subscribe to the industry code that is presented in Box 14.2. In addition, many enterprises try to institute the concept of ethics by asking

Box 14.2
Code of Ethics: Hospitality Service and Tourism Industry

1. We acknowledge ethics and morality as inseparable elements of doing business, and will test every decision against the highest standards of honesty, legality, fairness, impunity, and conscience.

2. We will conduct ourselves personally and collectively at all times so as to bring credit to the service and tourism industry at large.

3. We will concentrate our time, energy, and resources on the improvement of our own products and services, and we will not denigrate our competition in the pursuit of our own success.

4. We will treat all guests equally regardless of race, religion, nationality, creed, or sex.

5. We will deliver all standards of services and products with total consistency to every guest.

6. We will provide a totally safe and sanitary environment at all times for every guest and every associate.

7. We will strive constantly, in words, actions, and deeds, to develop and maintain the highest level of trust, honesty, and understanding among guests, clients, associates, employers, and the public at large.

8. We will provide every associate at every level all of the knowledge, training, equipment and motivation required to perform his or her tasks according to our published standards.

9. We will guarantee that every associate at every level will have the same opportunity to perform and advance, and will be evaluated against the same standard as all other associates engaged in the same or similar tasks.

10. We will actively and consciously work to protect and preserve our natural environment and natural resources in all that we do.

11. We will seek a fair and honest profit—no more, no less.

their associates to consider the following seven key questions, which are useful in ensuring that a decision is ethical:

1. Is it legal?
2. Does it hurt anyone?
3. Is it fair?
4. Am I being honest?
5. Can I live with myself?
6. Would I publicize my decision?
7. What if everyone did it?

How important is ethics to hospitality managers and how supportive are they of the belief that ethical conduct is vital to the effective operation of the business? Research reveals that ethics is regarded as very important; organizations now try very hard to get all of their associates to fully understand "proper behavior." While this may seem fairly easy to accomplish, in the hospitality industry many situations arise that present associates with conflicts of interest. On the one hand, they want to do what is best for the guest. On the other hand, they feel a loyalty to the organization and want to help the enterprise succeed. Sometimes it is difficult to balance these two concerns. Additionally, there is the ever-present temptation to cut corners or do things that "do not hurt anyone else," but should not be done unless the organization agrees that it is acceptable. In examining this statement in more depth, take the quiz in Box 14.3 and decide whether the person should or should not carry out the act. When you are finished, read the explanation in the next paragraph.

In each of these three cases, hospitality managers agree that the associate should not take the anticipated action. Sheila should not let the man into the room, because it is not his room and she does not know if he has permission from the guest to come in. Bill should not take the blouse unless he first tells Clara and she gives him her okay. The reservations clerk should tell the guest that the pool is under repair and will not be available during the weekend that the family is there.[15]

What can hospitality organizations do to ensure that their ethical standards remain high? One is to make everyone aware of these standards. A second is to continue reinforcing them through both words and actions. Management must continually point out the importance of high standards and set a good example for everyone else by personally living up to these standards. They must also recognize outstanding ethical behavior, such as associates who turn in gifts given to them by suppliers, and be prepared to discipline and dismiss those who violate the organization's ethical code.[16]

Discrimination

Discrimination in the hospitality industry takes a number of different forms. One, mentioned earlier in the chapter, is the glass ceiling effect.[17] Another is nonintentional discrimination, which is a result of subconscious perceptions that affect decisions. As one specialist in hotel operations has stated, "Very few people now sit down and say, 'Oh, I don't want a woman in this job.' [But] there's still a lot of reaction on image and presentation. I think sometimes that emphasis may get in the way of making the decision based purely on qualification."[18] For example, one major hotel recently admitted that it had assigned an all-White staff to wait on the visiting Indian prime minister, apologized to the two associates who were affected by the decision, reimbursed them for lost

Box 14.3
Test Your Ethics

Here are three ethical situations. Read each carefully and decide whether or not you would recommend that the associate take the proposed action. When you are finished, return to the text and read the discussion and analysis of each situation.

Situation 1

A man rushes out of the room that Sheila from housekeeping is going to clean next. The man joins another guest at the end of the hall, who says, "Hurry up, John. We're going to be late." About ten minutes later, as Sheila is cleaning the room, she hears a frantic knock on the door. The man who was with John in the hall is standing there. He says, "Can I please come in and pick up Mr. Davis's notes? He needs them for his presentation." Should Sheila let him in?

Situation 2

Bill is in charge of Lost and Found. Three months ago, an expensive silk blouse was turned in by Clara, a room attendant. To date, no one has claimed it. The hotel's policy is that any item unclaimed after 90 days is given to the associate who turned it in. Bill is sure that Clara has forgotten the matter and believes that the blouse would make an excellent addition to his wife's wardrobe. Should Bill take the blouse home?

Situation 3

A man makes a telephone call to a hotel to obtain reservations for his family. They will be staying for three days beginning next Friday. At the end of the conversation, he asks the reservations clerk, "You do have a pool, don't you?" Indeed the hotel does have a pool, but it is under repair and will not be ready for three weeks. Should the reservations associate tell the man, "Yes, we do have a pool"?

tips, and pledged to contribute $75,000 to an education effort on state antidiscrimination laws, to increase representation in management ranks, to hold weekly group discussion with its minority associates, and to hire an outside consultant to give associates diversity training.[19] While the hotel management may not have consciously discriminated against these two associates, the company's action was indeed discriminatory. Other common forms of discrimination relate to sexual harassment, salary and promotion.[20]

Sexual Harassment. Sexual harassment is the use of unwelcome sexual advances, requests for sexual favors, or the use of other verbal or physical conduct of a sexual nature.[21] There are two common types of sexual harassment. One is called *quid pro quo*, which is Latin for "something for something." An example of *quid pro quo* harassment is when an associate's raise or promotion is dependent on the individual doing something such as submitting to the sexual demands of the boss. The other form of sexual harassment is the creation of a *hostile environment,* such as subjecting an associate to emotional and psychological stress. An example is the case of a woman who was required to wear a sexually provocative uniform that resulted in lewd comments and innuendoes by customers. When the woman refused to wear the uniform any longer, she was fired. The court ruled that the employer was responsible for sexually harassing behavior because of the hostile environment that had been created.[22]

Sexual harassment is illegal, but it continues as seen by the number of sexual harassment cases filed with the Equal Employment Opportunities Commission. In 1990, over 6,000 cases were lodged; the number has steadily increased each year;[23] in 1994, over 14,000 cases were filed. Moreover, recent research reveals that sexual harassment is a growing issue of concern in the hospitality industry as seen by the fact that both women *and* men in the industry report that they have been sexually harassed—and such harassment appears to be greater in the industry than in business at large. Table 14.2 shows comparative data that support this statement.

When people are sexually harassed they have legal recourse, but many times they hesitate to speak out. Some of the most common reasons include fears regarding losing one's job, being rejected by co-workers, being called overly sensitive or unstable, feeling embarrassed, and/or not being believed. On the other hand, many people do speak out and are not hesitant to pursue legal action. Six ex-employees of a southern Florida Holiday Inn recently filed suit against the parent company for unspecified damages.[24] Their complaint charges that the management of the hotel where they worked allowed guests to make sexual advances toward the associates and did not take steps to prevent or curtail such behavior. If the company loses the lawsuit, it could find itself facing a heavy penalty because recent court decisions and new legislation have given associates more legal rights and have removed many of the limits on the awards that juries can make in sexual harassment cases.[25] A good example is provided in the case of *Dias v. Sky Chefs, Inc.* The plaintiff, a female white-collar associate, worked under the supervision of the general manager of a supplier of meals to airlines. In her lawsuit, she testified that she was subjected to ongoing sexual harassment by the general manager. When she complained to her immediate supervisor, the general manager changed her work location, interfered with her receipt of benefits, and had her followed. Ultimately, she was discharged at the recommendation of the general manager. The jury awarded her $125,000 in general damages and $500,000 in punitive damages. On appeal, the company argued that it was not responsible for the actions of its general manager. The reviewing court rejected the appeal.[26] The lesson is clear: Businesses are responsible for the sexual-harassment actions of their associates. If they did not know about such actions, they should have known! This is why many hospitality organizations are now

Table 14.2   Reported Sexual Harassment

	Hotel Industry Study	Industry-at-large Study
Women		
Insulting sexual comments	40.4%	19.8%
Complimentary sexual looks or gestures	32.6	16.2
Insulting sexual looks or gestures	28.1	15.4
Nonsexual touching	16.9	3.6
Sexual touching	28.1	24.2
Expected socialization outside of work with job consequences	6.7	10.9
Expected sexual activity with job consequences	6.7	7.6
Men		
Insulting sexual comments	17.8%	12.1%
Complimentary sexual looks or gestures	13.3	8.1
Insulting sexual looks or gestures	13.3	9.6
Nonsexual touching	6.6	3.5
Sexual touching	8.9	12.3
Expected socialization outside of work with job consequences	0	7.4
Expected sexual activity with job consequences	0	3.2

Reported in Martha E. Eller, "Sexual Harassment: Prevention, Not Protection," *Cornell Hotel and Restaurant Association Quarterly*, February 1990, p. 85.

developing formal programs for combating such harassment and ensuring that all problems are promptly and thoroughly investigated and resolved.[27] Many of these programs are designed around the following five steps:

1. *Start with a strong sexual-harassment policy.* Use plain language, be direct, and let everyone know that the company opposes sexual harassment in any form.

2. *Educate the managers.* Train these individuals to look for signs of sexual harassment in associate interactions and to react sensitively to all complaints, as well as to carefully document all evidence, which can be used in the case of a lawsuit.

3. *Conduct a prompt investigation.* Once a complaint is lodged, act swiftly to gather the necessary information, and ensure witnesses that no retaliatory measures will be taken against them if they provide information.

4. *Make the discipline fit the deed.* Take whatever action is fair—verbal warning, written warning, suspension, transfer, probation, demotion, immediate termination—and provide counseling for the victim and the harasser, if they are going to remain with the organization.

Table 14.3 In What Context Does Sex Discrimination Occur Most Frequently?

	Women		Men	
	n*	%	n*	%
Promotion	135	40	40	16
Salary	128	38	62	25
Selection	73	22	67	27
Responsibility	1	0	52	21
Other	0	0	30	12

*The number n refers to those respondents who reported in what areas they believed sex discrimination occurred. The number does not include respondents who believed no discrimination occurs in any of these areas.

Source: Robert H. Woods and Raphael R. Kavanaugh, "Gender Discrimination and Sexual Harassment as Experienced by Hospitality-Industry Managers," *Cornell Hotel and Restaurant Association Quarterly*, February 1994, p. 19.

5. *Monitor the situation.* Ensure that the in-house complaint procedure continues working properly, that there is no retribution against complainants, and, if the harasser remains with the company, that he or she continues to act properly.[28]

Salary and Promotion Issues. Two other areas where discrimination is a challenge for hospitality organizations are salary and promotions. A recent nationwide survey conducted among 613 hospitality managers revealed that women, in particular, believe that they are discriminated against on the basis of gender. Their responses are reported in Table 14.3 and reveal that salary and promotion head the list. Even more disturbing is the fact that both men and women in the survey had approximately equal salaries by the end of their first year of managerial experience. However, by the fifth year the average annual salary gap had grown by around $10,000. These findings are reported in Figure 14.2.

Why are women not being accorded the same opportunities as men? One current study conducted among 287 female hospitality managers found that two of the biggest perceived roadblocks were the "old-boy network" and the lack of female mentors. Well over half the women rated these two reasons as very significant factors that blocked their career development. Another roadblock was the lack of female role models. At the same time, the female managers reported that sexual harassment was not a problem for them. They rated this issue of far less importance than others, such as lack of equity in pay and the belief that they had to work much harder than their male counterparts in

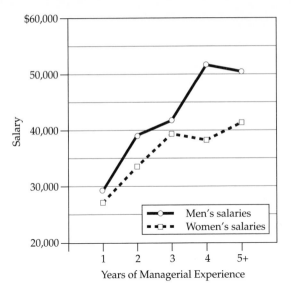

Figure 14.2 *Men's and Women's Salaries Compared*

Source: Robert H. Woods and Raphael R. Kavanaugh, "Gender Discrimination and Sexual Harassment as Experienced by Hospitality-Industry Managers," *Cornell Hotel and Restaurant Association Quarterly,* February 1994, p. 19.

* *n* = 613: 260 men, 353 women.

order to succeed.[29] These findings point out the need for top managers to both groom and promote women into the upper levels of the hierarchy. Given that two-thirds of the more than 8 million people in the hospitality workforce are women, but less than 5 percent are presidents or chief executive officers (CEOs),[30] this suggestion is not unfounded. What can CEOs do to expedite this process? A female executive vice-president of a major hotel chain has suggested the following advice for chief executives:

1. When you are in a position to bring people along—whether it's in hiring, promoting, or granting awards—make sure you ask the important question: Have women who qualify for the position or the recognition been considered?

2. Identify women who have already shown promise. Meet with each to discuss her career path: where she would like to go and what help she needs to achieve her goals.

3. Establish a mentor program.

4. Consider whether women with leadership potential on staff can be assigned a special, high-profile project that allows them to demonstrate their skills and gives you the opportunity to observe their ability.[31]

Promotion of women into the upper ranks of management will continue to be a challenge for many hospitality organizations. These four suggestions can be useful in helping management meet this challenge.

Dealing with Employees with Disabilities

Another current human resources challenge facing hospitality organizations is that of dealing effectively with associates who have disabilities. A *person with a disability* is someone who: (1) has a physical or mental impairment that substantially limits one or more major life activities, (2) has a record of such impairment, or (3) is regarded as currently having an impairment.[32] Common examples include associates who are physically disabled, obese, emotionally disabled, or who have AIDS (Acquired Immune Deficiency Syndrome).[33] Many of the rights of associates and obligations of employers are spelled out in the Americans with Disabilities Act.

Americans with Disabilities Act

The *Americans with Disabilities Act* (ADA) requires employers to make reasonable accommodations for disabled associates and prohibits discrimination against disabled associates. The ADA covers all employers with fifteen or more employees and imposes certain legal obligations on employers, including the following:

1. An employer cannot deny a job to a disabled individual if the person can perform the essential functions of the job; and if the person is otherwise qualified but unable to perform an essential function, the employer must make a reasonable accommodation unless this would create an undue hardship.

2. Employers do not have to lower existing standards for a job as long as these standards are job related and uniformly applied to all associates and applicants.

3. Employers may not make pre-employment inquiries about a person's disability, but they can ask questions about the person's ability to perform specific job functions and can promise a job offer based on the results of a medical exam.

4. Employers cannot ask applicants questions about their health, disabilities, medical histories, or previous worker's compensation claims.

Employer Responsibilities and Responses

The ADA presents a number of important challenges to hospitality organizations. In the case of an associate with AIDS, for example, the company is prohibited from firing the individual, because the person is protected under the ADA. The firm must accommodate the associate because AIDS is a disability.[34]

Other common responsibilities include changes in the design and layout of the enterprise to accommodate both associates and guests. Examples include wider aisles and lower work counters for associates in wheelchairs, increased light levels for sight-impaired associates, and ramps for guests in wheelchairs. A good example of a responsive organization is provided by the Embassy Suites Resort in Lake Buena Vista, Florida. When the hotel was still under construction, the company received letters urging it to design the layout to accommodate individuals with disabilities. This resulted in the management halting construction and modifying the design.

> The result is a great-looking hotel that is completely accessible, and a staff who can graciously and comfortably communicate with everyone. When patrons enter the restaurant, located in the atrium lobby, they can feel a textural difference in the floor tiles—a technique that allows someone with a visual disability to discern that they are moving from one kind of space into another. Illuminated strips on steps indicate floor level changes. High-contrast color schemes on doors and walls help those with poor sight to detect doorways. These and other design techniques aren't obtrusive or exclusionary; they're part of a whole picture that doesn't look any different to able-bodied guests than any other attractive interior.[35]

Hotel and restaurant organizations are also focusing their efforts on providing assistance to associates with special disabilities. For example, the Chicago Marriott, working with the International Association of Machinists Center for Administering Rehabilitation and Employment Services, has created a partnership to train individuals with disabilities and find them jobs at the Marriott or other local businesses. Working through a program known as the Transitional Employment Program (TEP), the partners help train individuals with mental-function disabilities, physical disabilities, hearing impairments, or learning disabilities. TEP provides the trainees with job skills, job experience, and assistance in securing employment. The training program lasts twelve weeks and is designed to teach the participants a hotel-related job in areas such as housekeeping, convention services, and cafeteria work.

Once the trainees have completed the twelve-week program, many are hired by the Marriott and put through the company's orientation program with other new hires. In addition, if they are unable to do the job because of their disability, changes are made to accommodate them. Sometimes this involves revising the work demands and allowing them to focus on areas where they excel, while delegating the remainder of the job to others. In other cases it involves providing special equipment or resources that allow them to perform well. One individual associated with the Marriott program put it this way: "People have a tendency to look at their limitations. We're not going to put them in an area in which they're going to fail because they can't accomplish a task. But we're going to look at what they can do and work on their capabilities and functional skills and build on that so that they can be as independent as possible."[36]

Understanding the Personal Cost

The hospitality industry is a very demanding one. The long hours and week-end work can put a strain on balancing career and family responsibilities. Both anecdotal comments and industry research show that the personal toll can be quite heavy. The following sections provide specific examples of each type of feedback.

Anecdotal Feedback

Recent research reveals that many people in the hospitality industry have an extended workweek, take minimal (if any) vacations, suffer mental exhaustion, and often have trouble keeping their social relationships on an even keel. What is particularly troubling is that many of these problems do not go away as associates rise in the hierarchy. If anything, they seem to get worse, so that those in senior-level positions are working longer and harder than ever before. Here are three select comments from managers in a variety of different hospitality positions.

> I'm working twelve to fourteen hours a day, six days a week. My goal? Right now, I'd feel balanced working ten to twelve hours a day, five or six days a week. I'm close to achieving it because we've been open eight months . . . . I've done five openings and never during one have I ever achieved any balance. It's usually six months of chaos, at least for me. And that can extend into infinity if you don't make an effort to do something about it.
>
> Female, executive chef

> I'd say for the last ten years, I've been at the grindstone really, really humping . . . . There has always been a driving force behind me to excel. I realized this when I was nine years old, when my parents broke up. It caused this need to prove myself.
>
> So, I wouldn't say there was ever much in the way of balance because I was always pushing myself. It was always school, sports, restaurant work. In some sense that hasn't changed a bit. There's simply a demand in this business for twelve- and fourteen-hour days. It's not an uncommon requirement.
>
> Male, restaurant owner

> I can't tell you how many nights I've been on the verge of walking out of here, coat on and all, when somebody comes in and says, "Hey, Rick, glad we caught you." Then there are those times when I'd like to leave at six o'clock. But I see somebody in the reservation book that I

wanted to say hello to. I believe some customers just expect either my partner or me to be there.

Male, restaurant co-owner

Empirical Research

The preceding anecdotal comments are supported by survey research. One of these studies found that two of the main reasons why managers leave the industry are the work hours and the pressure.[37] Other reasons include dissatisfaction with pay and poor treatment by superiors.

Moreover, recent research reveals that industry managers pay a high personal career cost. A study conducted by Mort Sarabakhsh and his associates compared responses from hotel and restaurant managers with managers in a nonhospitality field with respect to the quality of work life, trait anxiety, self-esteem, and life stressors. Forty-two of the 151 individuals surveyed were managers or assistant managers in food service operations, 41 were hotel managers or assistant managers, and the remaining 68 were Blue Cross/Blue Shield (BC/BS) managers. The purpose of the study was to identify differences between the hospitality managers and their counterparts in an unrelated industry.

A comparison of the demographic profiles of both groups revealed that the only major differences were those related to education, income, and marital status. While only one-third of the hotel and restaurant respondents had graduated from college, over 60 percent of the BC/BS managers had college degrees. Additionally, while almost half of the hotel and restaurant managers made less than $20,000 annually, only 3 percent of the BC/BS managers fell into this category. Finally, while 17 percent of the hospitality managers had been divorced, only 5 percent of the BC/BS managers fell into this category.

The two groups were then surveyed regarding the quality of working life, stress, and other factors related to their jobs. An analysis of the responses revealed the following:

1. A statistical analysis showed that life-stress scores were significantly higher for the hospitality groups. The scores for the latter were in the upper range of the moderate-risk category, while the average for the BC/BS group was in the lower range.

2. The statistical analysis showed significantly higher scores on career interference with social life for both the hotel and restaurant groups compared to the BC/BS group. The hotel group, in particular, was significantly lower than the other two groups in quality of life, and its scores on career interference with a happy marriage were higher than either of the other two groups. These findings were closely tied to the number of hours that these managers were required to work each week and the requirements to work on weekends and holidays.

3. Self-esteem ratings for the hospitality groups were at the norm, while those for the BC/BS group were slightly higher.

4. The hospitality groups reported higher life stress and greater interference of career with social life than did the BC/BS group.[38]

These findings reveal that careers in the hospitality industry are very demanding on personal life. Stress runs high and the job often forces managers to make major adjustments in their style. As one group of researchers put it:

> It is important to recognize that . . . limits exist and to address the problems created by the demanding nature of hospitality management before . . . limits are exceeded and talented managers leave the industry. Both hospitality educators and industry professionals should concern themselves with teaching management techniques that emphasize delegation and staff development, and hospitality firms that want to reduce management turnover should ensure that their managers have the assistance they need.[39]

Ways in which the latter can be achieved have been discussed in this book. Other ways, which are related directly to you and your career, are examined in the next chapter.

SUMMARY

1. The hospitality industry workforce is becoming increasingly diverse in terms of age, gender, ethnicity, and education. In managing this diverse workforce, it will become increasingly important for enterprises to do a number of things. One is to train the management staff regarding how to deal effectively with diverse work groups. A second is to continue working to develop nonbiased tests for selection and evaluation. A third is to create mentor programs that can be used to provide guidance and assistance to women and other minorities, thus ensuring that these individuals are given an equal opportunity to move up in the organization.

2. Ethics is a set of moral principles and values that are used to answer questions of right and wrong. Many organizations have their own code of ethics, and there is an industry code as well. However, this is not enough to ensure that associates act ethically in all situations. Other steps that management needs to take include making everyone aware of ethical standards, setting good personal examples, and recognizing and rewarding outstanding ethical behavior while also disciplining and dismissing those who violate the organization's ethical code.

3. Discrimination in the hospitality industry takes a number of different forms. Typical examples include sexual harassment, low salaries, and lack of promotion for women. In dealing with sexual harassment, businesses need to be firm and fair. Recent lawsuits by associates have shown that failure to protect associates from sexual harassment can have dire financial consequences for a business. In addition, hospitality firms have to work harder to ensure that women and other minorities receive the same salaries and have the same promotion opportunities as those accorded to others.

4. Another current human resources challenge is that of dealing with associates who have disabilities. The Americans with Disabilities Act requires employers to make reasonable accommodations for disabled associates and prohibits discrimination against disabled associates. There are a number of steps that organizations can take, including redesigning physical facilities and providing training for individuals with disabilities.

5. The hospitality industry is a very demanding one, and the personal costs can be great. Both anecdotal and empirical research reveal that hospitality associates tend to perceive a lower quality of work life than their counterparts in other jobs, while also suffering anxiety, lack of self-esteem, and stress. Organizations will have to continue their efforts to help associates deal with these problems.

KEY TERMS

Age Discrimination Act of 1978   ethnicity
Pregnancy Discrimination Act of 1978   mentor
Americans with Disabilities Act of 1990 ethics
Civil Rights Act of 1991   sexual harassment
Family and Medical Leave Act of 1993   hostile environment
glass ceiling effect   person with a disability

REVIEW AND APPLICATION QUESTIONS

1. A new hotel is being built on the south side of a major city, and management will soon be looking to staff the facility. The hotel manager and a few key associates have already been hired, but everyone else is yet to be recruited. The company believes that approximately half of the new staff is likely to have had some hotel experience, but the rest will not and, in many cases, will be individuals who are entering the workforce for the first time. In what way is diversity likely to be a challenge for the new

hotel manager and what are three steps you would recommend the company follow in meeting this challenge?

2. A major hospitality organization has decided to establish a formal mentoring program. What are some of the steps that the organization should take to ensure that its efforts are successful? Identify and describe three.

3. The human resources review committee of a large hotel chain is about to look into three situations that have been called to its attention by managers who have recommended that the associates be dismissed. The three situations are the following:

Sandra Burrows is a housekeeper. When cleaning a guest room recently, she noticed that a guest had left a couple of bottles of liquor and some unopened bags of chips. Apparently there had been a small party in the room the night before and these were some of the leftovers. Sandra took the liquor and chips to her car, intending to take them home with her. However, one of the managers spotted her and asked her to bring the food to the Lost and Found area and log it in. She was brought up on charges of violating company policy and will be dismissed unless the committee intervenes.

Paul Whitefield was taken to lunch by one of the company's vendors. This is in outright violation of the hotel's policy. During the lunch, Paul managed to negotiate a new contract with the vendor that will save the hotel over $20,000 during the next twelve months. While he admits that the vendor paid for the lunch, Paul argues that the savings to the hotel show that he was not doing anything wrong, and the policy's enforcement should be waived in this instance.

Karl Mannheim works at the hotel's five-star restaurant, which recommends that patrons leave a 20 percent tip. These tips are shared with all of the associates including those providing valet parking, which is where Karl works. Because of the large restaurant tip, the establishment has a strict rule regarding valet parking: no tipping. Last week, as a patron was getting into his car, he gave Karl a $20 tip. Karl has argued that he did not ask for the tip and it would have been bad manners to give it back. So he kept the money. The manager of valet services has asked that an example be set by having Karl dismissed.

In each of these cases, what should the committee do? Explain your reasoning.

4. Joyce Pedersen has complained to her boss on three occasions that she is being sexually harassed by one of the associates in her work group. To date, the boss has taken no action, including talking to the associate.

Earlier this week Joyce mentioned the situation to her aunt, a lawyer, who placed a call to the organization's legal counsel yesterday. Joyce received a call from the counsel a few hours ago and is scheduled to meet with the lawyer later in the day. What action do you think the organization's lawyer will take? Be complete in your answer.

5. Susan Carraway is scheduled to graduate from a prestigious school of hospitality at the end of this semester and is looking forward to a career in the industry. What types of demands is the career likely to make on Susan? If you were going to give her some insights regarding what to expect, what would you tell her? Be complete in your answer.

SELF-FEEDBACK EXERCISE: ETHICS AND YOU: HOW DO YOU COMPARE?*

Ethics can be a challenging area for hospitality associates; what one person regards as entirely ethical behavior can be viewed as only marginally ethical by another person and totally unethical by a third. This is particularly true when one considers the types of ethical dilemmas that are faced by industry people. The following are ten scenarios that present you with ethically oriented challenges. Read each of these scenarios and choose one of the three alternatives: ethical, unsure, or not ethical. When you are finished, compare your answers to those of the 400 managers who took this quiz and see how closely your responses compare.

1. A manager has just received a 20 percent raise that brings her annual salary to $100,000. At the same time, the board of directors has refused to increase the hotel's hourly associates' average pay of $6.25 because the hotel is in financial straits. The manager has decided to quietly accept the pay raise.

   _____ Ethical _____ Unsure _____ Not ethical

2. A manager has just approved a new menu that contains several of his favorite high-calorie, high-cholesterol, high-sodium foods. There are no nutritious alternatives on the menu. He reasons that the hotel guests like what is on the menu and that is why they will keep coming back.

   _____ Ethical _____ Unsure _____ Not ethical

---

*The scenarios in this exercise have been drawn and/or adapted from Raymond S. Schmidgall, "Hotel Managers' Responses to Ethical Dilemmas," _FIU Hospitality Review,_ Spring 1992, pp. 16–18; and the comparative responses by the graduating seniors can be found in Matt A. Casado, William E. Miller, and Gary K. Vallen, "Ethical Challenges of the Industry: Are Graduates Prepared?" _FIU Hospitality Review,_ Spring 1994, p. 7.

3. A restaurant has contracted with a local detective agency to place spotters in the bar to keep their eye on the bartenders in order to determine whether they are preparing drinks according to the standard recipe and are properly charging guests for all drinks served.

_____ Ethical   _____ Unsure   _____ Not ethical

4. A hotel manager approaches one of the organization's best maintenance people and offers to pay the individual the same hourly wage he receives at the hotel if the individual will come and do some yard work at the manager's personal residence.

_____ Ethical   _____ Unsure   _____ Not ethical

5. A very influential guest has just shown up at the hotel and wants to schedule a giant surprise birthday party for next month. Unfortunately, the main ballroom was reserved yesterday by another party for that very date. The influential guest suggests that the reservations manager bump the other party and tell them that the salesperson made a major mistake in booking a room that had been previously reserved. The reservations manager agrees to do so.

_____ Ethical   _____ Unsure   _____ Not ethical

6. The owner of a popular restaurant has decided to test a cashier's integrity. The cashier has been with the restaurant for ten years and has a flawless record. The owner slips $50 into the register receipts, and at the end of the day the cashier shows only a $5 overage. Upon questioning, he admits that he pocketed the $45 difference.

_____ Ethical   _____ Unsure   _____ Not ethical

7. The purchasing manager for a hotel buys 20 cases of wine from a new beverage purveyor. A week later, and unknown to the manager, the purveyor delivers a free case of wine to her residence. Since the gift did not influence her decision to buy from the purveyor, the manager keeps the case for personal use.

_____ Ethical   _____ Unsure   _____ Not ethical

8. The controller has advised the accounts payable clerk to continue to add a 1½ percent monthly charge to all overdue accounts of individuals and small businesses, but to discontinue this procedure for the overdue large corporate accounts. The accounts payable clerk agrees to do so.

_____ Ethical   _____ Unsure   _____ Not ethical

9. The manager of a new hotel is experiencing lower-than-expected occupancy rates. In an attempt to generate greater revenue, the individual rec-

ommends that the hotel advertise a 25 percent discount off the "regular" rack rate of $80, despite the fact that no rooms have ever been sold at this rate.

_____ Ethical   _____ Unsure   _____ Not ethical

10. The controller of a large hotel has just reviewed a report that shows that 2 percent of the rooms reserved each day end up being "no-shows." The individual orders the rooms reservationist to overbook rooms up to 2 percent each day, and informs the front-office associates to be prepared to walk a few potential guests due to the new procedures.

_____ Ethical   _____ Unsure   _____ Not ethical

Scoring: The percentage of responses given by the 400 managers to each of these situations is indicated on the following scoring sheet. Enter your answers to the exercise by circling the percentage with which you agreed.

Situation	Ethical	Unsure	Not ethical
1	36%	16%	48%
2	22	9	69
3	87	3	10
4	55	7	38
5	6	5	89
6	62	9	29
7	24	11	65
8	15	7	78
9	70	7	23
10	73	5	22

Interpretation: Look over your answers and identify those situations in which you were not with the majority of managers. Then go back and reread those situations. Why do you think you and they did not agree? What does your answer relate about the difficulty of dealing with ethical challenges? If you knew the following additional fact, would your evaluation of the managers' responses be changed?

Graduating seniors at a nationally known school of hotel and restaurant management ranked the responses in the same order as the managers, *i.e.*, their highest ranking of each situation was the same as the managers, their second highest agreed in all cases, and so did their lowest ranking.

CASE 14.1: HE SAYS IT'S NOTHING TO WORRY ABOUT

For the last two years, Roberta Dominguez has been a cashier at a local hotel. Her performance evaluations had been outstanding until six months ago, when she was rated as deficient by her new supervisor, Chuck Tepper. On her quarterly evaluation, Chuck wrote that she "lacks initiative and drive and is not cooperative in pitching in and helping out when problems arise." After Roberta read the evaluation, she exercised her option to write a response. She said that she felt the main problem was that Chuck went out of his way to make her life difficult by constantly nagging and coming by to socialize, when she did not have time to talk to him. "He takes me away from my work and then complains that things are not done on time," she wrote. Chuck's boss, Phil McKenzie, read her comments and asked about the situation. Chuck told him that Roberta's statements had no validity. "She's just not used to working hard and she's looking for excuses," he told Phil.

Earlier this week Roberta received her latest quarterly review. Chuck rated her as below average and suggested that she be transferred to another department or terminated. After reading the review, Roberta went to meet with Phil and told him, "For the last three months Chuck has been asking me out and I have told him I'm engaged. He has continued to push the matter, while also making my work life miserable. If he doesn't stop, I'm going to file a sexual harassment charge, and I'll get some of the other women in the department to back up my claim. They've seen what's been going on." Phil assured her that he would look into the matter.

Yesterday Phil called Chuck into his office and they discussed Roberta's comments. Chuck denied everything and told Phil, "She's making up the entire story. We have nothing to worry about. It's all just hearsay." After Chuck left, Phil put in a call to his boss and briefly discussed the matter. An hour later the hotel's lawyer was on the phone to Phil. "Tell me exactly what you heard," he said. Phil related both conversations and concluded his comments by noting, "Chuck feels we have nothing to worry about." The lawyer seemed unconvinced. "Look, I want you to interview Roberta again and I want you to follow up and talk to her co-workers and get their version of what is going on down there. Then I want you to come and see me tomorrow morning at 10 A.M. Can you do that?" Phil assured him that he would be there.

1. Is the lawyer's recommended course of action a wise one, or is he overreacting? Explain.

2. If the lawyer concludes that Chuck has been sexually harassing Roberta, what steps should the hotel take? Identify and describe three.

3. If Roberta takes legal action, is the hotel protected from liability, since it took steps to correct the situation the minute it learned of the situation? Why or why not?

CASE 14.2: IT'S ALL IN THE FAMILY

For the last four years, Sandra Stanford has been head of purchasing for a large restaurant chain. Her largest vendor is Quality Foods, Inc., with whom the chain does approximately $9 million of business annually. The Quality Foods representative, Tom Buchowski, is well known to everyone in the restaurant chain because he and his two assistants spend approximately 28 hours a week working with chain associates.

Three months ago, one of Tom's assistants left to take a job with a competitor. Three weeks ago the assistant, Bill Hartwick, came to Quality Foods headquarters to see if he could bid on some business. Sandra was not there, but her boss, Ellen Mardah, was in, and she and Bill visited for almost an hour. Part of their conversation was the following:

Bill: As you know, Ellen, I'm now with a new firm, but I know a lot about your company's needs and I am convinced that my firm could provide you with the same merchandise you are getting from Quality Foods and we could improve the price and delivery schedule.

Ellen: I appreciate that, Bill, but as you know we have had a long relationship with Quality Foods and I know that Sandra feels very comfortable working with them. So, while I'm sure we could throw some business your way, Quality Foods is going to remain our primary vendor.

Bill: I understand, but we'd really like your business and I know that we would be prepared to include you in the arrangement—as well as Sandra, of course.

Ellen: I'm afraid you've lost me. What arrangement are you talking about?

Bill: Well, you know that Tom Buchowski is her brother-in-law and he gives her a rebate of 1 percent of all purchases. Quality Foods sends the check directly to her home. We'd be prepared to keep this arrangement and give you 1 percent as well, depending on certain guaranteed orders, of course.

At this point Ellen was reminded by her secretary that she had a meeting in the boardroom. She excused herself, but promised to get back to Bill in the near future. Later that day, she called Sandra into her office and confronted her with the story. Sandra admitted that it was true, but defended her actions by noting, "The price we pay to Quality Foods is lower than that of any other bidder, so the 1 percent that my brother-in-law gives me comes out of his company's pocket and not ours. As far as I can see, it's a win-win situation for everyone involved." After Sandra left her office, Ellen put in a call to the president of the company and asked if she could drop by and see him as soon as possible. He told her to come over immediately.

1. Did Sandra do anything that was unethical? In your answer, be sure to define the term *ethics.*

2. What is your evaluation of Sandra's comment that "it's a win-win situation for everyone involved."

3. If you were president of the company, what would you do about the situation? Why?

ENDNOTES

1. See Richard Bruns, "Diversity: From Top Management to the Front Line," *Lodging,* November 1994, pp. 72–78.
2. "Women Are Slowly Approaching Majority of the U.S. Labor Force," *The Wall Street Journal,* January 8, 1996, p. B 7B.
3. Fred Luthans, *Organizational Behavior,* 7th ed. (New York: McGraw-Hill, 1995), p. 55.
4. For more on this topic, see Lynn R. Offermann and Marilyn K. Gowing, "Organizations of the Future: Changes and Challenges," *American Psychologist,* February 1990, pp. 95–108.
5. Also see James T. Davidson, "Managing a Culturally Diverse Work Force," *Hotels,* February 1992, p. 23.
6. Robert H. Woods and Michael P. Sciarini, "Diversity Programs in Chain Restaurants," *Cornell Hotel and Restaurant Association Quarterly,* June 1995, pp. 18–23.
7. See Dawn Gunsch, "Games Augment Diversity Training," *Personnel Journal,* June 1993, pp. 76–83.
8. Luthans, *Organizational Behavior,* p. 59.
9. Ibid., pp. 59–60.
10. Cristine Antolik, "Lingering Discrimination Increases Turnover," *Hotel & Motel Management,* September 6, 1993, p. 21.
11. See Belle Rose Ragins and John L. Cotton, "Gender and Willingness to Mentor in Organizations," *Journal of Management,* Spring 1993, pp. 97–111.
12. Richard M. Hodgetts and K. Galen Kroeck, *Personnel and Human Resource Management* (Fort Worth: Dryden Press, 1992), p. 403.
13. George A. Wolfe, "Ethics on the Job," *Hotels,* April 1992, p. 39.
14. Rocco M. Angelo and Andrew N. Vladimir, *Hospitality Today,* 2nd ed. (East Lansing, Mich.: Education Institute of the American Hotel & Motel Association, 1994), p. 425.
15. Ibid.
16. In addition, see Robert H. Woods and Florence Berger, "Teaching Social Responsibility," *Cornell Hotel and Restaurant Association Quarterly,* August 1989, pp. 61–63.

17. Also see Robert H. Woods and Raphael R. Kavanaugh, "Gender Myth and Reality," *Lodging,* July 1994, pp. 58–61.
18. Antolik, "Lingering Discrimination Increases Turnover."
19. John Kifner, "Hotel Admits It Let Only Whites Serve Official," *New York Times,* May 26, 1994, Section A, p. 18.
20. Also see Susana Barciela, "Beyond the Rhetoric," *Miami Herald,* March 27, 1995, Business Monday Section, p. 13.
21. Luthans, *Organizational Behavior,* p. 65.
22. Gary Dessler, *Human Resource Management,* 6th ed. (Upper Saddle River, N.J., Prentice Hall, 1994), p. 35.
23. Kristin Dunlap Godsey, "Battle of the Sexes," *Restaurants & Institutions,* March 1, 1995, p. 135.
24. Manny Garcia, "Ex-Staffers: Inn Condoned Sex Harassment by Guests," *Miami Herald,* February 14, 1995, pp. B1, B3.
25. Arthur J. Hamilton and Peter A. Veglahn, "Sexual Harassment: The Hostile Work Environment," *Cornell Hotel and Restaurant Association Quarterly,* April 1992, pp. 88–92; and Susan Crawford and Michael McClory,"A Brief History of Sexual-Harassment Law," *Training,* August 1994, pp. 46–49.
26. John E. H. Sherry, "Employer Liability for GMs' Sexual Harassment," *Cornell Hotel and Restaurant Association Quarterly,* August 1995, pp. 16–17.
27. For example, see Richard Alaniz, "Handling Sexual Harassment Complaints," *Restaurant Hospitality,* April 1994, p. 46; Rick Van Warner, "Industry's Future Success Rides on Overcoming Racial, Ethnic Barriers," *Nation's Restaurant News,* September 20, 1993, p. 97; and Kathy Seal, "Hotels and Harassment," *Hotel & Motel Management,* November 25, 1991, pp. 1, 30.
28. Jennifer Batty, "How to Combat Sexual Harassment," *Restaurants USA,* January 1993, p. 13.
29. Judi Brownell, "Women Hospitality Managers: Perceptions of Gender-Related Career Challenges," *FIU Hospitality Review,* Fall 1993, pp. 19–31.
30. Ibid., p. 19.
31. Charlotte St. Martin, "Advice for Chief Executives," *Association Management,* June 1994, p. 54.
32. Hodgetts and Kroeck, *Personnel and Human Resource Management,* p. 110.
33. Jose G. Fagot-Diaz, "Employment Discrimination against AIDS Victims: Rights and Remedies Available under the Federal Rehabilitation Act of 1973," *Labor Law Journal,* March 1988, pp. 148–166.
34. Also see Alan Liddle, "Tower to Appeal AIDS Discrimination Suit," *Restaurant News,* December 13, 1993, pp. 3; 61.
35. Regina S. Baraban, "Designing for the ADA," *Restaurant Hospitality,* January 1994, p. 112.
36. Jennifer J. Laabs, "Individuals with Disabilities Augment Marriott's Work Force," *Personnel Journal,* September 1994, p. 52.
37. James M. McFillen, Carl D. Riegel, and Cathy A. Enz, "Why Restaurants Managers Quit (and How to Keep Them)," *Cornell Hotel and Restaurant Association Quarterly,* November 1986, pp. 36–43.

38. Mort Sarabakhsh, David Carson, and Elaine Lindgren, "The Personal Cost of Hospitality Management," *Cornell Hotel and Restaurant Association Quarterly,* May 1989, pp. 75–77.

39. Barbara J. Slusher, Jerald W. Mason, and Edward J. Metzen, "Job Satisfaction and Its Correlates: Do Family and Nonwork Influences Make a Difference?" *The Missouri Agricultural Experiment Station, University of Missouri–Columbia Journal,* Series 9296, 1980.

CHAPTER FIFTEEN

Developing an Effective Career Plan

LEARNING OBJECTIVES

One of the primary reasons for studying human resources is to improve your career opportunities. The overriding objective of this chapter is to examine important steps you can take in developing an effective career plan. In doing this, consideration will first be given to personality traits and success in the hospitality industry. Then attention will be focused on specific steps that can be of practical value to you, including writing an effective résumé, conducting yourself well during job interviews, and implementing useful guidelines for managing your career. When you have finished studying all of the material in this chapter, you will be able to:

1. Identify and describe successful personality traits in the hospitality industry.

2. Compare and contrast successful traits of male and female managers in the hospitality industry.

3. Discuss seven of the most useful steps in creating an effective résumé.

4. Interview effectively.

5. Follow some of the most important guidelines for managing your career.

Personality Revisited

In Chapter 2 we examined some of your personality traits. Those traits are important in answering the question that was posed in that chapter: Who are you? Now we want to reexamine your personality and focus on those traits that are important to your career.

Personality Traits in the Hospitality Industry

In every industry there are personality traits that help dictate success. In the nursing profession, for example, concern for others and the ability to listen well are important. In most businesses, the willingness to work hard, knowledge of operations, and good interpersonal skills are critical. In education, some of the key traits include the ability to communicate well, enthusiasm, and clear goal orientation.

In the hospitality industry there is a similar group of traits that help differentiate successful individuals. In fact, industry practitioners and researchers have suggested that the hospitality industry is unique and requires a particular set of personal competencies. Additionally, there is a wealth of information that suggests that these personality characteristics may even be gender linked.[1]

Research by G. Stone, for example, has found that hospitality managers have different personality traits from those of managers in general. He found that hospitality managers rated higher on calmness, assertiveness or competitiveness, realism, deliberateness, and detail orientation.[2] Similar findings were uncovered by P. Worsfield, who conducted a study of hotel general managers in a major United Kingdom hotel group and found that these managers were more assertive, venturesome, and imaginative than managers generally.[3] He also reported that hospitality managers place high value on interpersonal and group skills. Additionally, these managers reported that traits needed for success included resilience, self-motivation, and intelligence.

Other research both supports and extends these findings. For example, interviews of top performers in the hospitality industry conducted by SRI Gallup, have found commonality of behaviors such as (1) a desire to be liked, (2) a willingness to assume responsibility, (3) a striving for excellence, (4) the ability to focus energy and drive, (5) a desire to achieve, (6) the ability to motivate others, (7) good leadership skills, (8) the ability to organize, (9) a willingness to delegate, and (10) the ability to develop the personal abilities of others.[4]

The Issue of Gender

The preceding personality traits are common to hospitality managers. However, they are not of equal importance to both men and women. Researchers have recently found that there appear to be gender-linked traits, indicating that the personality of a successful male manager in the hospitality industry is often different from that of his female counterpart. These data are of recent origin and appear to be a result of the increasing number of women in management positions. When these positions were dominated by men, researchers found strong similarities between the traits of male and female managers. This was undoubtedly accounted for the by the fact that many of the women who were promoted into management positions as recently as the 1980s had adapted their behavior to emulate traditional male styles. As the number of female managers increased, however, many of them began to develop their own unique approaches to managing. Judy Rosener, for example, has reported that the increase of senior-level female executives has facilitated a feminine management style characterized by a stronger relationship orientation, more information sharing, and greater concern for associate feelings of self-worth.[5] Bernard Bass, an internationally known expert on leadership, agrees and reports that senior-level female managers make greater use of shared decision making, associate empowerment, and transformational leadership than do their male counterparts.[6]

Judi Brownell recently investigated these differences in the hospitality industry. She interviewed both male and female general managers and asked each to identify personality characteristics that they believed contributed most significantly to their career advancement. Drawing on this information, she developed a questionnaire that was completed by 69 women and 144 men. The results of the survey, showing the most commonly cited characteristics, are presented in Table 15.1.

The data reveal that women had a different view from the men as to which personality characteristics are necessary for success in the hospitality industry. The five highest-ranked items for each group were the following:

Women	**Men**
interpersonal skills	fairness, honesty, integrity
determination	hard work
hard work	interpersonal skills
enthusiasm	commitment
positive attitude	determination

While there is similarity between the lists, there are also distinct differences. Also, as seen in Table 15.1, female managers mentioned enthusiasm, determination, interpersonal skills, a sense of humor, and ambitiousness more frequently than did male managers. Conversely, male managers mentioned integrity, commitment, and financial ability more often than did female managers.

The important point to be drawn from these findings is that successful men and women in the hospitality industry have their own lists of personali-

Table 15.1 Career Advancement Characteristics

Characteristic	Overall Percentage	Women (n = 69)	Men (n = 144)
Hard work	27	30	27
Interpersonal skills	33	44	26
Determination	29	44	21
Fairness, honesty, integrity	20	11	32
Industry knowledgeability	15	13	18
Compassion	13	14	14
Flexibility	13	13	14
Listening skills	11	10	14
Positive attitude	14	19	10
Commitment, loyalty	12	4	22
Goal orientation	9	9	11
Ambitiousness, aggressiveness	8	14	4
Enthusiasm	13	26	2
Sense of humor	8	14	2
Financial ability	6	0	12
Organizational skills	6	11	2

Source: Judi Brownell, "Personality and Career Development," *Cornell Hotel and Restaurant Association Quarterly*, April 1994, p. 42.

ty traits. There is no universal list for success. At the same time, however, there are similar groupings of personality traits that are common to all hospitality managers. Box 15.1 provides you an opportunity to profile your own personality in terms of job-related behaviors. Stop at this point, take the test, and then profile yourself.

Your score reveals how you perceive yourself on two personality traits: assertiveness and responsiveness. Individuals with high assertiveness like to take charge of things, work quickly and actively, and use persuasive skills to get things done. Individuals with low assertiveness prefer to hold back, follow rather than lead, and move cautiously and slowly in getting things done.

Individuals with high responsiveness like to work with others, have good interpersonal skills, and are excellent team players. Individuals with low responsiveness like to work alone, are not particularly effective in interacting with group members, and tend to have poor listening skills.

Successful managers in the hospitality industry tend to have high assertiveness and high responsiveness scores. Their profiles show the greatest areas of coverage in the northeast quadrant of the grid in Box 15.1, and the lowest areas of coverage in the southwest quadrant. However, remember that regardless of your score, you can learn to adapt to the needs of the situation. It is all a matter of getting the right experience. One way to begin this process is by focusing your career in the right direction. The initial step in this process is a well-written résumé.

Box 15.1
Your Personality and Job-Related Behaviors

Read the following statements and decide how accurately each describes you. If the statement is totally descriptive of you, put a 5 in the True column and a 0 in the False column. If just the reverse is true, put a 0 in the True column and a 5 in the False column. Otherwise, divide up the 5 points as you deem appropriate.

	True	False
1. I like to be in control.	(a) _____	(b) _____
2. I like close personal relationships.	(a) _____	(b) _____
3. I like to be left alone.	(a) _____	(b) _____
4. I am poor at listening to others.	(a) _____	(b) _____
5. I work quickly.	(a) _____	(b) _____
6. I have poor counseling skills.	(a) _____	(b) _____
7. I have poor persuasive skills.	(a) _____	(b) _____
8. I work better alone than with others.	(a) _____	(b) _____
9. I like to take spontaneous action.	(a) _____	(b) _____
10. I have a high tolerance for the feelings of others.	(a) _____	(b) _____
11. I enjoy jumping from one activity to another.	(a) _____	(b) _____
12. I am a poor team player.	(a) _____	(b) _____
13. I like to follow rather than lead.	(a) _____	(b) _____
14. I like to cooperate rather than compete with others.	(a) _____	(b) _____
15. I am not a highly competitive person.	(a) _____	(b) _____
16. I do not like working in a group.	(a) _____	(b) _____
17. I set goals and get going rather than wait around for routine instructions.	(a) _____	(b) _____
18. I care deeply for other people.	(a) _____	(b) _____
19. I make decisions slowly.	(a) _____	(b) _____
20. I am a people person.	(a) _____	(b) _____

Scoring: Place your answers in the following scoring key. Be sure to match both the number and letter of the question next to the answer.

Box 15.1   Continued

Group 1				Group 2			
1a	_____	1b	_____	2a	_____	2b	_____
3b	_____	3a	_____	4b	_____	4a	_____
5a	_____	5b	_____	6b	_____	6a	_____
7b	_____	7a	_____	8b	_____	8a	_____
9a	_____	9b	_____	10a	_____	10b	_____
11a	_____	11b	_____	12b	_____	12a	_____
13b	_____	13a	_____	14a	_____	14b	_____
15b	_____	15a	_____	16b	_____	16a	_____
17a	_____	17b	_____	18a	_____	18b	_____
19b	_____	19a	_____	20a	_____	20b	_____
Totals (A)	_____	(B)	_____	(C)	_____	(D)	_____
	High		Low		High		Low
		Assertiveness				Responsiveness	

Interpretation: Take your four scores—A, B, C, and D—and use them to plot your personality profile in the following grid. Do this by placing an X for your A score on the vertical line directly below the letter A. Then place an X for your B score on the lower vertical line that extends from the origin downward. Next, place an X for your C score on the horizontal line that extends from the origin to the right; and an X for your D score on the horizontal line that extends from the origin to the left. Then connect all four Xs with four straight lines, forming a somewhat lopsided figure, and then shade in the area within this geometric diagram. This shaded area shows your personality profile in terms of responsiveness and assertiveness. An interpretation of this profile is provided in the text, beginning at the point where you left off.

```
                         High
                      Assertiveness
                         (A)
                          50 |
     Driving              40 |      Expressive
                          30 |
        Low               20 |        High
   Responsiveness         10 |     Responsiveness
        (D) _____|_____ (C)
           50 40 30 20 10   |  10 20 30 40 50
                          10 |
                          20 |
                          30 |
     Analytical           40 |      Friendly
                          50 |
                         (B)
                         Low
                      Assertiveness
```

Writing an Effective Résumé

Regardless of the job you are seeking in the hospitality industry, you need to put together a *résumé,* or summary of your work experience and education. Many hotels, restaurants, and related service organizations will receive hundreds of applications for job openings. You need to create a résumé that catches the reader's attention and encourages the individual to identify you as an applicant who warrants further consideration.

Before looking at the specifics of a résumé, remember that most organizations do not have time to interview every applicant, so they set up an initial screening process designed to reduce the list to those applicants who are most likely to meet their needs. These individuals are then invited for an interview, and only if the company fails to hire the requisite number of applicants will it go back to those who failed to make the first cut and invite some of them. So it is important to know how to write an effective résumé.

Some Useful Rules

There are a number of things that you can do to create an effective résumé. The following are seven of the most important:

1. Keep the length of your résumé to one page. The person doing the screening does not have time to read a 10-page résumé, and it is unlikely this early in your career that you have more than a page of accomplishments that warrant mentioning.

2. Make the résumé user-friendly. Be brief and be direct. After you have written the first draft, go back and review and revise it. Be sure that the finished product is easy to read and does not raise questions that cannot be answered. For example, if you graduated from high school and then went into the military for three years, be sure to include this fact so that the person reading your résumé does not wonder, "What accounted for this three-year gap between graduation and entering college?"

3. When setting forth your qualifications and experiences, begin with the most recent and work your way back. In this way, if the individual is interested only in your last four years of experience, it is not necessary to read to the end of the résumé to get this information.

4. List both your academic and professional qualifications. Unlike résumés from most college students, which are totally academic in nature, in the hospitality industry the employer wants your résumé to show what you have done that can be of practical value to his or her organization. Additionally, list these two areas in order of importance. If your work experience is outstanding, put it ahead of your academic experience, and vice versa.

5. Make yourself look unique. Stress those accomplishments that help you stand out from the crowd. For example, if you have had experience working in a hotel, write out the title and duties that you carried out and point out one or two things that you did that went beyond the usual scope of this job. Remember that many applicants may have had similar experiences. Try describing yours in a way that is different from theirs.

6. Ensure that the layout of the résumé is clean and professional looking. Use bold type, capital letters, italics, and the like to highlight important information. Also, it is often worth the expense to have a professional printer reproduce the material so that each copy looks identical to the original.

7. Decide the presentation structure that will be best for you. In most cases the order should be (1) name, address, and phone number; (2) education; (3) work experiences; (4) activities and skills; and (5) miscellaneous.

Figures 15.1 and 15.2 provide examples of two résumés. A close comparison shows that the first starts off by emphasizing the person's education and academic honors and then moves on to relevant work experience. The second begins with a summary of qualifications and uses the rest of the résumé to support this focus. So there are a number of different approaches that can be used, depending on your experience and job objectives.

The Cover Letter

If you are going to be sending your résumé to a prospective employer, you also need to write a cover letter to accompany the résumé. This letter should clearly explain the reason you are sending the résumé, so that the individual receiving it can match your résumé with the job you are seeking. The following are six useful rules for creating an effective cover letter.

1. Limit the letter to one page.

2. Address the letter to a specific person, not to a title such as "Director of Human Resources." If the person's name is not listed in the employment ad, call the company and get the name.

3. Use a three-paragraph format, following these recommendations:

    Paragraph 1: Introduce yourself and relate why you are writing the letter and the position for which you are applying.

    Paragraph 2: Sell yourself by emphasizing your strengths and tooting your own horn.

    Paragraph 3: Let the prospective employer know when you will be contacting the firm—and then call at this time and set up an interview. (Remember: do not wait for an interview—call and ask for one!)

4. Send a typed, not reproduced, letter that reflects your writing style, not a form letter you found in a résumé book. (Human resources directors get plenty of these form letters, so they are easy to spot.)

	Paul Shervington Jacobs	
123 N Flamingo Ave.	Miami, FL 12345	(305) 555-1234

EDUCATION

FLORIDA INTERNATIONAL UNIVERSITY—N Miami, FL
Bachelor of Science, Hospitality Management, December 1996
100% tuition paid by AOP Scholarship

HONORS

- American Hotel Foundation, Cecil B. Day Hospitality Scholarship, September 1996
- 29th Annual Governors Council/Tourism, Iris D. Larson Hospitality Scholarship, August 1996
- National Restaurant Association, Educational Foundation's Salute to Excellence Student Delegate, May 1996
- *Who's Who Among Students in American Universities and Colleges,* 1996
- Most Distinguished Hospitality Student, 1995
- Dean's List Fall 1995

RELEVANT EXPERIENCE
August 1996–Present

FLORIDA INTERNATIONAL UNIVERSITY
SCHOOL OF HOSPITALITY MANAGEMENT, PLACEMENT—N Miami, FL
Administrative Assistant
- Assist Director in coordinating recruitment for Hospitality graduates
- Network between School of Hospitality Management Placement and Career Services
- Catalog all hospitality industry employment opportunities with computer database
- Facilitate with the campus visits of hospitality companies for recruitment
- Responsible for all areas of hospitality career placement from orientation workshop to recruitment interviews

March 1995–September 1995

DORAL GOLF RESORT & SPA—Miami, FL
Guest Services Agent
- Performed guest check-in/check-out procedures
- Balanced and posted charges to guest accounts
- Assisted guests with areas of the hotel, room tours, and various golf packages

January 1991–March 1995

EXECUTIVE CATERERS NORTH—Boca Raton, FL
Maitre'D (November 1992–March 1995)
- Compiled service staff team tasks and stations
- Organized menu service with Executive Chef for functions (6 courses, up to 300 guests)
- Designed appetizer station displays for cocktail hour/buffets
- Ensured high quality standards of service with staff

HOSPITALITY INTERNSHIP
Fall 1994

WALT DISNEY WORLD CO., YACHT CLUB RESORT—Lake Buena Vista, FL
Front Desk Host
- Performed guest check-in/check-out procedures
- Handled and balanced guest accounts with a $1200 bank
- Communicated any special WDW events to guests
- Cross-trained: Greeter, Concierge, Valet/Bell Services and Front Desk (Fort Wilderness, Beach Club and All-Star Sport Resorts)
- Attended 12-week seminar that outlined WDW Co. mission, philosophy, and history

FLORIDA INTERNATIONAL UNIVERSITY

- Career Services (Peer Advisor) August 1993–August 1996
- School of Hospitality Management (Hospitality Tradeshow Representative) May 1995–September 1996
- Student Government Council (Vice President) November 1995–May 1996
- Campus Activities (Orientation Peer Advisor) Summer 1994/1995

COMPUTER SKILLS

- PMS HOST (Doral Golf Resort & Spa) and PMS HARGAS (Walt Disney World)
- Wordperfect 6.1 and Microsoft Office
- Internet and World Wide Web

Figure 15.1

Source: Florida International University, School of Hospitality Management.

TIM O'DOOLES

10179 Codbell Street
Scranton, Pennsylvania 18702
(708) 325-7406

Summary of Qualifications

Demonstrated leadership, interpersonal training and development skills with team consensus-building abilities. Excellent analytical and organizational skills. Very personable, motivated, conscientious, responsible, self-disciplined and self-directed.

EDUCATION

BACHELOR OF SCIENCE IN HOSPITALITY MANAGEMENT
Florida International University
North Miami, Florida
GPA 3.83

Earned degree in hospitality. Participated in numerous extracurricular activities to practice and improve leadership abilities. Worked to defray college expenses and gain practical work experience.

HONORS
DELTA DELTA PHI - Honor Society 1991–1993
PHI ETA SIGMA - Freshman Honor Society 1990

ACTIVITIES
Pi Beta Phi: Alumni Committee, 1993; Nominating Committee Chairperson, 1992; Standards Board, 1991.

PREVIOUS EMPLOYMENT

Employed in positions that required constant public and client contact and attention to detail; limited margin for errors; ability to work under pressure and tight deadlines.

SALES ASSOCIATE
Doral Country Club
Gainesville, Florida   November 1993–April 1994

FRONT OFFICE ASSISTANT
Hollywood Beach Hotel
Hollywood, Florida   May 1993–September 1993

BARTENDER
Johnny Rockets
Miami, Florida   Summer 1989, 1990

OTHER

COMPUTER LITERATE
Word Perfect, Lotus 1-2-3, Windows and Microsoft Word

Figure 15.2

Source: Florida International University, School of Hospitality Management.

5. Use quality paper that matches that of your résumé.

6. Make certain that your letter has no grammatical or typographical errors—and then sign it.

Effective Interviewing

If your résumé is sufficiently appealing to a potential employer, you will have the opportunity to interview for a job. This is a two-way street. The interviewer will get an opportunity to get to know you better and to learn how well your abilities and talents mesh with the organization's needs. At the same time, you will have the opportunity to size up the firm and decide if this is the type of organization you would like to join.

Small hospitality firms that hire locally typically will conduct one interview per candidate and make up their mind based on the results. Large hospitality organizations, especially those with multiple locations around the country, often use two interviews. The first interview is to reduce the list of candidates by screening out those who are viewed as not suited for the company. Those who make the cut are then interviewed a second time, in order to make the final decision and to decide where to place them in the organization. If you are going to be interviewed just once, your objective is to sufficiently impress the recruiter so that you are offered a job. If you are going into a screening interview, your goal is to survive the round. In either event, there are a number of guidelines that can be of value to you.

Guidelines for Preparing for the Interview

Your primary objective during the interview is to convince the interviewer that you are the person he or she is seeking. One way of doing this is by anticipating the types of questions that will be asked and formulating, if only in general terms, the responses you will give. Box 15.2 provides a list of some of the common questions asked during these interviews. In recent years, many organizations have gotten away from relying solely on descriptive questions and now pose behavioral questions that are designed to give them an opportunity to see how you respond to job-related situations. Interviewers use these behavioral examples as a basis for predicting whether or not the applicant demonstrates skills that are important for a specific job. This approach is based on the belief that the best predictor of future behavior is past behavior. Box 15.3 provides examples of some of the typical behavioral questions that are often asked.

In some cases, you may even feel stumped. For example, some interviewers will ask, "What is your biggest weakness?" Many individuals ponder this for a minute and say, "I don't think I have one." This is an interesting answer,

---

Box 15.2

Questions Typically Asked by Employers during Job Interviews

1. What are your long-range and short-range goals and objectives, when and why did you establish these goals, and how are you preparing yourself to achieve them?

2. What specific goals, other than those related to your occupation, have you established for yourself for the next ten years?

3. What do you see yourself doing five years from now?

4. What are the most important rewards you expect in your business career?

5. Why did you choose the career for which you are preparing?

6. What motivates you to put forth your greatest efforts?

7. What qualifications do you have that make you think you will be successful?

8. In what ways do you think you can make a contribution to our organization?

9. What two or three accomplishments have given you the most satisfaction? Why?

10. What was your most rewarding college experience?

11. What led you to choose your major field of study?

12. Do you have plans for continued study? An advanced degree?

13. What do you know about our organization?

14. What two or three things are most important to you in a job?

15. What criteria are you using to evaluate the organization for which you hope to work?

Source: Florida International University, *Placement Manual,* 1993–1994, p. 15.

---

but the wrong one. The interviewer will not let you get away with sidestepping the challenge; he or she will say, "No, I want you to keep thinking and come up with one." There are two reasons for this strategy. First, it shows the interviewer how well you respond to difficult, stressful questions. Second, it gives the interviewer insights regarding your perceived major weakness, something that can be extremely useful in making an overall evaluation of your application.

Behavior and Appearance

The primary question that the interviewer is going to try to answer is: "How well will this candidate fit into our organization?" Simply put: Do you have what it takes? Will you make a contribution? Can you be a team player? Will you be an asset to the company? In helping the interviewer answer these questions affirmatively, there are a number of things that you should do (or avoid

1. Describe a time in any job that you've held in which you were faced with problems or stresses that tested your coping skills. What did you do?

2. Give an example of a time in which you had to keep from speaking or not finish a task because you did not have enough information to come to a good decision.

3. Give an example of a time in which you had to be relatively quick in coming to a decision.

4. Can you tell me about a job experience in which you had to speak up in order to be sure that other people knew what you thought or felt?

5. Give me an example of a time in which you felt you were able to build motivation in your co-workers or subordinates at work.

6. Give me an example of a specific occasion in which you conformed to a policy with which you did not agree.

7. Give me an example of a time when you had to go above and beyond the call of duty in order to get a job done.

8. What did you do in your last job in order to be effective with your organization and planning? Be specific.

9. Describe the most creative work-related project that you have carried out.

10. Give me an example of a problem that you faced on any job you have had and tell me how you went about solving it.

Source: Florida International University, School of Hospitality Management, *Selling Yourself Student Handbook*, 1994–1995, p. 12.

doing) in order to impress the person. Before continuing, take the quiz in Box 15.4 and see how much you know currently.

Now that you have reviewed the answers to the quiz in Box 15.4, you have a good idea of some of the "dos and don'ts" of effective interviewing. Here are five others:

1. **Be on time for the interview.** The best way to do this is to plan on arriving early. In this way, if there is heavy traffic or bad weather, or if you have trouble finding a parking spot, you still will not be late. Remember that if you are tardy, this can create a poor first impression and may lead the interviewer to believe that you are not very interested in the job or, worse yet, that you are unreliable.

2. **Maintain your composure at all times** and do not let little things upset you. For example, despite the fact that you will arrive early, the interviewer may have two or three people before you and may be running a little late. So you will have to wait your turn. Do not let this get to you. Keep

Box 15.4
Effective Interviewing Behaviors

A number of important behaviors are associated with successful interviewing. Read each of the following, decide whether you believe it is an effective or ineffective behavior, and put an X in the appropriate column. Answers and explanations are provided at the end of the chapter.

	Effective	Ineffective
1. If you are unsure of how to dress for the interview, err on the side of being conservative.	_____	_____
2. When you enter the room, if the interviewer is on the phone, sit down and wait for the individual to finish.	_____	_____
3. Shake hands with the interviewer in a firm, competent manner.	_____	_____
4. When the interviewer tells you his or her name, respond in kind by telling the individual your name.	_____	_____
5. During the interview, do not refer to the interviewer by his or her first name, unless you have been given permission to do so.	_____	_____
6. If you do not understand something the interviewer has explained, ask the person to clarify it.	_____	_____
7. No matter what the interviewer says, do not lose your temper.	_____	_____
8. When you speak, do so in a confident tone.	_____	_____
9. Try to show the interviewer that you know something about his or her organization; this indicates an interest in the firm.	_____	_____
10. If you have any questions about salary, ask them as soon as possible.	_____	_____
11. If you are asked the salary you would like, set a high figure because you can always negotiate down.	_____	_____
12. If the interviewer asks you if you are flexible regarding work location, say no; this indicates that you know your mind and can stick to your guns.	_____	_____
13. If the individual asks you the position you would like to hold ten years from now, tell him or her that you want to be president of the company.	_____	_____
14. If you chew gum, ask the interviewer if it is all right before doing so.	_____	_____

Box 15.4 Continued

15. If you smoke, offer the interviewer a cigarette before lighting up yourself. _____ _____

16. Take notes on everything the interviewer says, so that you have a record of the interview. _____ _____

17. Try to present yourself as aggressive; this typically impresses interviewers. _____ _____

18. Before the interview is over, be sure to ask the individual, "How much are you paying for this position?" _____ _____

19. Be sure to have the interviewer clearly explain the company's benefit and retirement program. _____ _____

20. Before the interview ends, ask the individual when you can expect to hear back from the organization. _____ _____

a positive attitude; when the interviewer apologizes for your having had to wait, treat the delay as something of no consequence.

3. Wear a business suit or similar outfit, unless you know that you are expected to dress casually. For example, in some resort hotels everyone dresses informally, including the hotel manager, so you would not be expected to show up in a conservative business suit. (In fact, if you did, the manager would think that you did not know much about the way the hotel was run.) The important thing is to look well groomed and presentable.

4. Maintain eye contact during the interview and nod every now and then to indicate that you understand what is being said. Also, smile and present a friendly, positive image of someone who can work well with others—and enjoys doing so.

5. If the interviewer asks if you have any questions, do not hesitate to ask some, but be careful about coming across as negative or picky. For example, if you are asked why you did not do well in your public speaking course in college, do not criticize the instructor or talk about the way the course was taught. Instead, focus your attention on the fact that you did not have a great deal of public speaking experience, learned a great deal in the course, and are looking forward to building on what you have learned.

In addition to these tips, it is useful to understand the structure of the interview. Typically, there are three parts: the introduction, the body, and the close. The introduction is the ice-breaking part of the interview. During this time period, the interviewer will set the tone by trying to establish a positive atmosphere and put you at ease. He or she may talk about the local baseball team or how well your university did in a recent tournament. This part of the interview will usually last about five minutes.

The second part of the interview, the body, deals with requests for specific information. The interviewer will typically use a question-and-answer format to evaluate your qualifications and suitability for employment with the organization. The individual will be looking for information about your specific skills, knowledge, abilities, and attitudes. During this time, you should be prepared to discuss your career objectives, academic qualifications, work experience, and personal goals. At the same time, it is important to avoid some subjects, such as salary. Let the recruiter introduce this area. If you are put on the spot with the question, "What salary are you seeking?" you can always sidestep it by saying, "I'm looking for a salary that is commensurate with the demands of the position. What would you think would be the range that the organization has in mind for this job?" Toss the ball back to the interviewer and let him or her field the question. One of the best reasons for this is that it prevents you from making a mistake. In the quiz in Box 15.4, it was noted that you should not ask for too much money because this may lead to your being dropped from consideration. On the other side of the coin, if you ask for too little money, the interviewer may think that you do not think very much of yourself or are desperate for a job. Moreover, if a fair salary is $30,000 and the individual says, "The range is $25,000 to $27,500, depending on qualifications," you can begin thinking of how you can negotiate the salary upward if the job is offered to you.

The last part of the interview, the close, is used to answer any questions that you have. At this time the interviewer will also tell you what will happen from here. For example, the individual may say, "We are looking at four candidates for this position and should be finished with our interviews and evaluations within two weeks. At that point, I will be back in touch with you." Of course, if the interviewer does not relate any information regarding a follow-up, you should ask.

After the interview, you should wait a few days and then write the individual a thank-you letter. (Remember to check the letter for grammar and spelling accuracy.) This type of letter is considered common courtesy and is usually not used to further influence the individual to hire you. Figure 15.3 provides an example of such a thank-you letter.

Guidelines for Managing Your Career

In addition to getting a job, it is important to know how to manage your career. There are some things you need to do to reach your career goals; four of the most common are discussed in the following sections.

```
                                              8147 Biscayne Towers
                                              Apartment 9D
                                              Miami, FL 33139
                                              May 17, 1996

Robert T. Price
Human Resources Department
Surfside Hotel, Inc.
11400 Granville Place
New York, NY 10022

Dear Mr. Price:

I appreciated meeting with you last week and having the opportunity to
interview for a management trainee position at Surfside. As promised, I
am sending along a copy of the report I wrote last semester, "Growth in
the U.S. Hotel Industry: 1995–2001." I hope you find the information to
be interesting and informative.

If you have any questions regarding either my interview or the report,
please do not hesitate to contact me. I would be happy to provide you
any information you need.

I am very interested in pursuing a career with your company, and am
pleased to have been considered for an interview.

I shall look forward to hearing from you.

Sincerely,

Robert S. Goodfellow

Robert S. Goodfellow

Enclosures
```

Figure 15.3   *Sample of a Thank-You Letter Written after a Job Interview*

Be a High Performer

Nothing succeeds like success. Those who do well early in their careers are
more likely to be put on a fast track and are promoted more often than those
who have average or poor performance. So it is important that you take your
early assignments very seriously and that you perform them well. One way of
doing this is to learn exactly what is expected of you and then go the extra
mile.

Phyllis Andreas helps coordinate business meetings at The Caldwell, a major hotel in Dallas. Last week she was responsible for taking care of the Andersen Group, a high-tech manufacturing firm that was making a major presentation to an investment banking group, which was looking into making an investment in the Andersen Group. Just before the meeting began, one of the Andersen Group's senior managers ran into Phyllis's office and told her that they needed a laptop computer. The one that was being sent over from the office had not yet arrived, and the presentation was scheduled to begin in fifteen minutes. Phyllis picked up the phone, called a computer firm that had provided equipment to the hotel in the past, and asked them to deliver a rental unit to the hotel within ten minutes. "I don't care what it costs," she told the listener. "Just drive over here with it and I'll see that you're paid immediately." The manager was impressed and told Phyllis's boss what a great job she had done. Earlier today Phyllis received a letter of praise from her boss, along with a note telling her that a copy of the letter would be placed in her personnel file.

By showing that she is a high performer, Phyllis has gotten a career jump. She is not waiting for things to happen; she is making them happen!

Be Invaluable to Your Boss

Your boss can be an important person in helping you get ahead. One of the best ways of getting this individual to support you is by becoming indispensable to him or her. In particular, whenever something you do will help the boss and you do it well, the boss is likely to remember. There are a number of ways in which you can become a "crucial subordinate"; the two most common types are complementary and supplementary. A *complementary crucial subordinate* is someone who helps his or her boss overcome a personal weakness.

Don Scott must complete a monthly cost control report for all operations in his area. He not only dislikes this job, but finds that when he does it without any help he completes the report incorrectly. For the past five months, Barbara Pickens, one of his assistants, has been filling out the report. She knows exactly what needs to be done and always has the report on Don's desk three days before it is due to central administration. Don admits that he does not know what he would do about the report were it not for Barbara.

Barbara is a complementary crucial subordinate. Without her Don would be unable to get the report done correctly—and he remembers this when he writes Barbara's performance evaluation.

A *supplementary crucial subordinate* is someone who helps a superior in an area where the latter is capable but does not want to expend the necessary time and effort because there are more important things the person would like to do.

> Beverly Davis finds that a great deal of her time must be spent meeting with her senior managers and coordinating operations at the hotel. So when memos need to be written and disseminated, she relies on Jerry Gelber to take care of them. Beverly is capable of doing this, but she now does so only if the memo is extremely important or needs her personal touch. Otherwise, the matter is delegated to Jerry; Beverly merely reviews, and sometimes modifies, memos before they are finalized and sent out.

> Jerry is a supplementary crucial subordinate. He helps free up Barbara for more important duties and, in turn, helps her succeed. As a result, he always gets an excellent performance appraisal from Barbara.

Document Your Accomplishments

Do not be bashful. If you are good, be prepared to prove it. Save memos from people in the organization that relate what a good job you did on a particular project. If you are singled out by the in-house newspaper as an up-and-coming star, save the clipping. This is called a *hero file*; it is important in helping document your progress and success. It is also useful when you apply for another job, whether within the organization or outside, because you have evidence to back up your claim that you are a superior performer.

Another way of documenting your accomplishments is through influence building. If you have a small group reporting to you and there is an opportunity to increase this number, take it. As the number of people working for you increases or the department size grows, so does your power. And remember that when top management is casting around for a person to head a department or take over a unit, they are often most likely to look at those who currently manage large work groups. They feel that it is a small step from managing a group of 20 associates to running a department with 25 people. Additionally, there is a tendency to equate department size with contribution. So if you head a large department, management will believe you are making a much more significant contribution to the organization than someone who is managing a much smaller department.

Network Effectively

Networking is the process of socializing and politicking, both with associates inside the organization and with outside clients. While this activity sounds like a time waster, research shows that those who network often do better than those who simply keep their nose to the grindstone and continue doing their

Table 15.2 Managers and their Activities

| Type of Manager | Percentage of Time Spent on Each Activity | | | |
	Traditional Activities	Routine Communication	Networking	Human Resource Management
Successful	13	28	48	11
Effective	19	44	11	26
In General	32	29	19	20

Source: Fred Luthans, Richard M. Hodgetts, and Stuart A. Rosenkrantz, *Real Managers* (Cambridge, Mass.: Ballinger Publishing, 1988).

work. This was made particularly clear by Fred Luthans and his associates, who conducted the most comprehensive investigation ever run on how managers spend their time.[7] The group examined managers in the workplace and found that these individuals carry out four activities:

1. Routine communication—exchanging information and handling paperwork.

2. Traditional management—planning, decision making, and controlling.

3. Networking—socializing and politicking with associates and interacting with clients.

4. Human resource management—staffing, training, motivating, and disciplining associates.

They then examined how often each of the managers performed these functions and, in the process, concluded that there were three groups of managers. One group was called "successful," because these individuals were promoted more often than any others. A second group was called "effective," because they had extremely satisfied, committed associates and they produced high organizational results. The third group, managers in general, consisted of the rest of the managers. The researchers then looked at how each of these groups were spending their time. The results are reported in Table 15.2. A close look at the table shows that those who were promoted most often (successful managers) spent more of their time networking than doing anything else. Those who had the most satisfied and committed subordinates (effective managers) spent the bulk of their time in routine communication and human resource management. The remainder of the managers (managers in general) divided their time more evenly among all four activities, but tended to spend more time on traditional activities than any other group.

These data point to two important conclusions. First, socializing, getting to know people, and politicking can be very useful to one's career. Second, those who carry out the routine, expected tasks, such as the managers who spent most of their time on traditional management activities, typically do not do very well. Simply put, career success is often a result of taking charge of your life rather than carrying out rote activities and hoping that things will break your way. You cannot wait for lucky breaks; you have to make them happen!

SUMMARY

1. In every industry, there are personality traits that help dictate success. Researchers have found that in the hospitality industry, managers tend to rate high on calmness, assertiveness or competitiveness, realism, deliberateness, and detail orientation. Other common traits include (1) a desire to be liked, (2) a willingness to assume responsibility, (3) a striving for excellence, (4) the ability to focus energy and drive, (5) a desire to achieve, (6) the ability to motivate others, (7) good leadership skills, (8) the ability to organize, (9) a willingness to delegate, and (10) the ability to develop the personal abilities of others.

2. Researchers have also found that there tend to be gender-linked characteristics that differentiate female hospitality managers from their male counterparts. When asked to describe the personality characteristics needed for success, women mention enthusiasm, determination, interpersonal skills, a sense of humor, and ambitiousness more frequently than do men; and men mention integrity, commitment, and financial ability more frequently than do women.

3. When you are seeking employment, it is important to create an effective résumé, that summarizes your work experience, education, and other noteworthy accomplishments. A number of useful rules can help in this process, including the following: (1) limit the length to one page; (2) make the résumé user-friendly; (3) begin by presenting your most recent qualifications and experiences and work back to the past; (4) list both academic and professional qualifications; (5) make yourself look unique; (6) ensure that the layout of the résumé is clean and professional looking; and (7) decide the presentation structure that will be best for you. In addition, when you are sending the résumé in response to an employment ad, a well-written cover letter should accompany it.

4. It is also important to know how to be interviewed. Some useful rules include the following: (1) be on time for the interview; (2) maintain your composure at all times; (3) wear a business suit or similar outfit, unless casual dress is expected; (4) present a friendly, enthusiastic attitude, (5) maintain eye contact and continually give the interviewer positive feedback; and (6) politely ask questions, if you do not understand something.

A few days after the interview, you should send the interviewer a thank-you letter.

5. Another important step is to take control of your career and carefully manage your progress. Some of the most effective ways of doing this include the following: (1) be a high performer; (2) be invaluable to your boss; (3) document your accomplishments; and (4) network effectively.

KEY TERMS

résumé

complementary crucial subordinate

supplementary crucial subordinate

hero file

networking

REVIEW AND APPLICATION QUESTIONS

1. Are there any differences between the personality traits of successful managers in business and successful managers in the hospitality industry?

2. What are some of the most common types of behaviors of top performers in the hospitality industry? Identify and describe four.

3. The following two lists of traits are those for successful male managers and successful female managers in an international hotel chain. Which list is that of the men? The women? What conclusions can you draw from an analytical comparison of the two lists?

interpersonal skills	commitment
positive attitude	fairness
enthusiasm	industry knowledge
hard work	loyalty
sense of humor	honesty

4. Jorge Rodriguez has written a résumé. A brief reading of the résumé reveals the following: (a) the material is 2½ pages long; (b) it is easy to read and understand; (c) both academic and work experience for the last five years have been carefully explained, beginning with the past and concluding with the present; and (d) despite some typos and erasures, the résumé is fairly neat and clean. Based on this information, what advice would you give to Jorge to improve his résumé?

5. Martha Young has just finished writing a cover letter to accompany her résumé. A brief reading of the letter reveals the following: (a) the letter is two pages long; (b) it is addressed to "Director of Human Resources"; (c) in the first paragraph Martha has introduced herself and explained why

she is writing the letter and the position for which she is applying; (d) the letter was typed (not reproduced) on quality paper that matches that of her résumé; and (e) there are no grammatical or typographical errors. Based on this information, are there any suggestions you would give to Martha regarding how she could improve this cover letter?

6. There are three parts to an employee interview: the introduction, the body, and the close. What takes place during each of these phases of the interview? Briefly identify each.

7. Jim O'Grady is currently being interviewed for a job with a major restaurant chain. Jim has had three years of restaurant experience in a number of jobs, including assistant manager. The interviewer has just asked Jim, "Can you think of a time as an assistant manager when you made a decision that turned out wrong? What did you learn from this experience?" What is the purpose of this question? How should Jim handle the question? Would it be all right for him to say, "Actually, I never had a situation like that"? Why or why not?

8. What are some important behaviors that an interviewee should use when being interviewed? Identify and describe three of them.

9. In managing your career, why is it important to document accomplishments? After all, is this nothing more than bragging about yourself?

10. Three middle managers have applied for a job opening at a company's new hotel. Each of the three has been working for the hotel chain for over five years, and all three have had above-average performance evaluations. A close analysis of how each manager spends his or her day reveals the following:

	Traditional Activities	Routine Communication	Networking	Human Resource Management
Manager A	25	28	21	26
Manager B	9	24	49	18
Manager C	10	41	14	35

Based on these data, which manager is likely to get the promotion? Explain your answer.

SELF-FEEDBACK EXERCISE: HOW DO YOU INTERACT WITH OTHERS?

The following 20 statements are designed to measure your approach to interacting with others. Read each carefully and decide how accurately the two choices describe you. If choice "a" is totally descriptive of you, give it 5 points and choice "b" 0 points, and vice versa. Otherwise, divide the 5 points between choices "a" and "b."

	Column 1	Column II
1. I am:		
(a) quiet and reserved		_____
(b) a good socializer	_____	
2. When in a group of people, I typically:		
(a) talk with the group at large	_____	
(b) talk to one person at a time		_____
3. Overall, I tend to have:		
(a) broad friendships with a lot of different people	_____	
(b) deep friendships with just a few people		_____
4. Among my group of friends, I:		
(a) am full of news about everyone	_____	
(b) the last to hear what is going on		_____
5. I am the type of person who:		
(a) talks only to certain people or in certain conditions		_____
(b) talks easily to almost everyone at any time	_____	
6. When I'm in a group, I typically:		
(a) introduce others	_____	
(b) am introduced to others		_____
7. When I meet new people, they can tell I am interested in them:		
(a) after they get to know me		_____
(b) almost immediately	_____	
8. When it comes to displaying my feelings, I typically:		
(a) keep them to myself		_____
(b) share them freely	_____	
9. I tend to be:		
(a) lively	_____	
(b) quiet		_____
10. Compared to the average person, I am:		
(a) more enthusiastic	_____	
(b) less enthusiastic		_____

11. When I am at parties, I:
    (a) sometimes am bored _____
    (b) always have fun _____
12. I am:
    (a) easy to get to know _____
    (b) hard to get to know _____
13. When I am at a party, I like to:
    (a) help get things going _____
    (b) let everyone have fun in their own way _____
14. I am:
    (a) reserved _____
    (b) talkative _____
15. I am:
    (a) a leader _____
    (b) a follower _____
16. I am:
    (a) sociable _____
    (b) aloof _____
17. I prefer to:
    (a) write _____
    (b) talk _____
18. If I had a choice, I would prefer to go:
    (a) to the theater with a small group _____
    (b) to a big party with many people _____
19. When I meet new people, I:
    (a) carry the conversation _____
    (b) wait for them to start the social interaction _____
20. I would feel most comfortable:
    (a) at a big birthday party _____
    (b) at a small dinner party _____

                                    Total _____   _____
                                    Column I   Column II

Scoring: Plot yourself on the following graph by first taking your score in Column I and placing an X on the vertical axis at this value. Then take your score in Column II and place an X on the horizontal axis at this value. Now place a large X on the graph at the point where these two scores intersect. For example, if your scores for the two columns are 75 and 25 respectively, your dot would be located 75 points up the graph and 25 points over from the left axis.

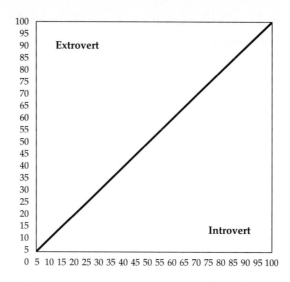

Interpretation: The graph shows whether you see yourself as an extrovert or an introvert. Most people in the hospitality industry view themselves as extroverts, although this is not universally true.

CASE 15.1: BUT ONLY ONE WINNER

Last week Claire Whitney and James Dubno interviewed for a customer service representative job at a large hotel. Claire and James are both in their last semester at a well-known hospitality school; many recruiters come here twice a year to interview new graduates.

The company hopes to hire five customer service representatives, but it never takes more than one from any university. So Claire and James are in a competitive position and each is determined to get the job. Their advisor, Hans Whorklen, coached both of them regarding how to prepare and conduct themselves during the interview. Afterward, he talked to each individually and made notes of what had happened during their respective interviews. Two topics on which he made contrasting notes were company background and salary. In each case, the two candidates had given different responses.

In the case of company background, the interviewer had asked both Claire and James if they knew anything about the history and operations of the hotel. Claire told the individual that she knew a little about the company and proceeded to discuss the hotel's three locations, its client base, and the general image the company has among its customers. James had not done any research on the hotel and told the interviewer, "I'm not really familiar with your hotel but I sure would like to learn more about it."

In the case of salary, the interviewer asked both candidates if they had a particular salary in mind. Claire said, "I'd like $26,000." James said, "I'm flexible on salary. What I'd really like to know more about is the position and what would be expected of me."

In addition to the preceding comments, Hans wrote down a general description of the two candidates. Here is how he sees the two individuals:

Claire	James
outgoing	introverted
friendly	reserved
hardworking	hardworking
enthusiastic	determined
sense of humor	technically proficient

1. Which of the two candidates did the best job of handling the interviewer's question regarding what they knew about the company? Explain.

2. Which of the two candidates did the best job of answering the interviewer's question regarding salary? Explain your answer.

3. Based on Hans's descriptions of the personality traits of the two applicants, which one do you think will get the job? Why?

CASE 15.2: SHE'S READY TO MOVE ON

For the last six years, Teresa Rodriguez has been an assistant manager at a very popular restaurant in Boston. One reason she has stayed so long at this job is that her boss, John Mahoney, has given her substantial salary increases and greater operating authority. However, Teresa believes that it is now time for her to move on and become a restaurant manager. John is going to be staying at his job indefinitely, so the only way that Teresa can achieve her career objective is to move elsewhere.

During her six years as assistant manager, Teresa has acquired a great deal of technical knowledge. She has also honed her interpersonal skills and is able to interact very effectively with both guests and associates. During dining hours, Teresa spends most of her time out in the restaurant, walking around, talking to diners, and keeping an eye out for problems. The minute she sees a server having trouble or an order that is slow in coming out from the kitchen, she moves in and begins working closely with the associates. As a result, service at the restaurant is excellent and a large percentage of the diners eat there regularly.

Her performance has not gone unnoticed by the company. Last year Teresa received an annual commendation that cited her as "Assistant Manager of the Year." She also has a file folder filled with thank-you notes from diners.

In addition, a number of local companies have their annual parties at the restaurant, and Teresa usually works closely with each company's representative, ensuring that the party meets all of the firm's needs. In turn, each of these representatives has sent her a thank-you letter, with a copy to the restaurant's home office.

Teresa believes that her work experience and these letters of support are going to be extremely useful to her as she looks for a manager's job. She also believes that her networking skills with the home-office staff will pay off. The president of the company and the director of human resources have both told her that they would be happy to help her in any way, if she decides that she would like to look elsewhere. At the same time, the HR director has encouraged her: "Consider hanging on. We're going to be opening two more restaurants in Boston in the next three years, and you are certainly going to be at the top of the list to manage whichever one you want." Teresa was pleased to hear this, but still thinks it might be a good idea for her to go out and interview before that time and see what is available. As she put it to a friend, "I think I'd like to get my feet wet in the marketplace, even if I don't jump to another company."

1. What are some personality traits Teresa has that will be of value to her as a manager? Identify and describe three.

2. Will it be of value to Teresa to use the letters and commendation certificate in her job search? Why or why not?

3. Is the fact that Teresa is a good networker likely to be of value to her career aspirations? Explain.

ANSWERS TO BOX 15.4: "EFFECTIVE INTERVIEWING BEHAVIORS"

1. Effective. When in doubt, opt for conservative over casual. You can always shed the tie or take off your jacket, but if you are too casually dressed, there is no way to correct the problem.
2. Ineffective. Wait for the interviewer to ask you to sit down.
3. Effective. This conveys a good, positive image.
4. Effective. Return the greeting and let the individual know how to address you by pronouncing your name or telling the person what you prefer to be called, such as, "My name is Robert Anderson, but everyone calls me Rob."
5. Effective. Do not assume a degree of familiarity unless the interviewer tells you it is acceptable to do so.
6. Effective. If you do not understand something, ask for clarification.
7. Effective. Remain calm at all times.
8. Effective. It is important to convey the impression that you feel comfortable and capable of holding your own during the interview.

9. Effective. Many interviewers are pleasantly surprised when they learn that the other person has taken the time and trouble to learn about their organization.

10. Ineffective. Do not bring up the salary question until the interviewer does. Let this person lead the way when it comes to discussing money.

11. Ineffective. If you set a salary that is extremely high, this may lead the interviewer to conclude that you are outside the company's price range, and may result in your being dropped from further consideration.

12. Ineffective. Many hospitality organizations are looking for people who are willing to relocate; a failure to be flexible on this point can result in your losing a job offer.

13. Ineffective. Pick a job that is higher up in the organization than where you are starting, but do not go overboard. The individual is looking for someone with a desire to achieve, but be careful about coming across as overly aggressive or having unrealistic expectations.

14. Ineffective. Do not chew gum during the interview under any circumstances.

15. Ineffective. Do not smoke during the interview, even if the recruiter tells you it is all right to do so.

16. Ineffective. It is not necessary to write everything down; if you do, you convey the impression that you do not trust the interviewer.

17. Ineffective. If you appear to be overly aggressive, the interviewer is going to wonder whether you are able to interact well with associates and customers.

18. Ineffective. Let the recruiter raise the salary issue; if it is not raised use a tactful approach, such as by asking, "Can you give me an idea of the salary range for this job?"

19. Ineffective. Many recruiters take a dim view of individuals looking for a job who focus attention on benefits and retirement programs, since these are not areas that should be given much attention at this point in time.

20. Effective. You have a right to know when the company will be getting back to you; if this information is not forthcoming, feel free to ask.

ENDNOTES

1. Robin W. Pratt and David L. Whitney, "Attentional and Interpersonal Characteristics of Restaurant General Managers in Comparison with Other Groups of Interest," *Hospitality Research Journal*, Vol. 15, No. 1 (1991), pp. 9–24; and Judy B. Rosener, "Ways Women Lead," *Harvard Business Review*, November–December 1990, pp. 119–125.

2. G. Stone, "Personality and Effective Hospitality Management." Paper presented at the Symposium of the International Association of Hotel Management Schools, Leeds Polytechnic, November 1988.

3. P. Worsfield, "A Personality Profile of the Hotel Manager," *International Journal of Contemporary Hospitality Management*, Vol. 3, No. 1 (1994), pp. 22–25.

4. Judi Brownell, "Personality and Career Development," *Cornell Hotel and Restaurant Association Quarterly*, April 1994, p. 39.

5. Rosener, "Ways Women Lead."
6. Bernard M. Bass, "Debate: Ways Men and Women Lead," *Harvard Business Review*, January–February 1991, pp. 151–152.
7. Fred Luthans, Richard M. Hodgetts, and Stuart A. Rosenkrantz, *Real Managers* (Cambridge, Mass.: Ballinger Publishing, 1988).

Name Index

MacHatton, Michael T., 186
Magao, Dennis H., 186
Marler, Janet H., 259, 279
Marshall, Colin, 363
Marshall, Lincoln, 246
Martin, Christopher L., 186
Martinez, Michelle Neely, 218
Marvin, Bill, 170
Mason, Jerald W., 429
Mausner, Bernard, 245
May, William, 26
McClelland, David C., 223, 245
McClory, Michael, 429
McDowell, Bill, 312
McFillen, James M., 429
McNerney, Donald J.,, 246
Mendel, Werner, 218
Mento, A. M., 245
Metzen, Edward J., 429
Miles, Raymond E., 7
Miller, William E., 423
Mills, Harry N., 48
Mills, Kristine E., 394
Moran, Robert T. 329, 337
Morgan, Denise, 395
Morris, Susan V., 312
Moshavi, Sharon, 340
Mutchler, David G., 312

Nightingale, Michael, 363
Ninemeier, Jack, 198

Offermann, Lynn R., 428
O'Mara, Julie, 404
Osland, Joyce S., 92
Ouchi, William, 340

Parasuraman, A., 312, 363
Pati, Gopal C., 254
Peppers, Don, 363
Peters, Diane McFerrin, 363
Peters, James, 279
Pine II, B. Joseph, 363
Plamandon, William M., 26
Plichta, Joanne C., 394
Powell, Gary N., 25
Pratt, Robin W., 459
Prewitt, Milford, 186
Prokesch, Steven E., 363

Pryor, Mildred G., 48
Pye, Geoff, 364

Ragins, Belle Rose, 428
Ragland, Edward R., 120
Raleigh, Pat, 11
Reichheld, Frederick F., 312
Rice, Faye, 404
Riegel, Carl D., 429
Rivoli, Pietra, 340
Robbins, Stephen P., 245
Robey, Daniel, 141, 154
Rogers, Martha, 363
Romano, Catherine, 25
Romeo, Peter, 245
Ronen, Simcha, 327
Ronkainen, Ilkka A., 340
Rose, Glenn F., 394
Rosenbluth, Hal F., 363
Rosener, Judy B., 459, 460
Rosenkrantz, Stuart A., 450, 460
Rosenmann, R., 120
Rubin, Irwin M., 92
Rugman, Alan M., 340
Rutherford, Denney G., 312

Sadri, Golnaz, 218
Sage, Carol, 363
Sanson, Michael, 25
Sarabakhsh, Mort, 121, 429
Sasser, Jr., W. Earl, 312, 363, 364
Sawin, Linda I., 245
Schmidgall, Raymond S., 423
Schneider, Benjamin, 363, 395
Sciarini, Michael P., 428
Seal, Kathy, 429
Seelhoff, Karen, 218
Seltzer, Joseph, 279
Shames, Germaine, 363
Shapiro, Steve, 299, 312
Shenkar, Oded, 327
Sherry, John E. H., 429
Shideler, Daniel M., 279
Shimko, Barbara Whitaker, 394
Simons, Tony, 227, 229, 246
Slate, Emily, 337
Slusher, Barbara J., 429
Smith, Katie, 404
Smith, Ken, 13

Subject Index

team, 193–194
typical programs, 191–195
Two-factor theory of motivation, 220–222

Uncertainty avoidance, 323–324

Values
   aesthetic, 47

economic, 47
political, 47
profiles, 48, 49
religious
social, 47
theoretical, 47
work-related, 48–49